Historic Bennington

THE
Vermont Story

A HISTORY OF THE PEOPLE OF THE GREEN MOUNTAIN STATE

1749-1949

By EARLE NEWTON

DIRECTOR, VERMONT HISTORICAL SOCIETY

With a Foreword by ALLAN NEVINS *and an Introduction*

by DOROTHY CANFIELD FISHER

THE VERMONT HISTORICAL SOCIETY

MONTPELIER, 1949

TO JO
Who doesn't give a hoot for 1066, 1492—or 1749.

Copyright 1949 *by* EARLE NEWTON

First of a series on
THE AMERICAN STATES
EARLE NEWTON, *General Editor*

PRINTED IN THE UNITED STATES OF AMERICA

BY THE LANE PRESS
Burlington, Vermont

INTRODUCTION

By Dorothy Canfield Fisher

WE HAVE waited a long time for it, but now at last we have it—the story of Vermont which somehow just never could get itself written. Earle Newton's book has a warm welcome from the readers of the Green Mountain state, and, we are thankful to say when you say "Vermont readers," you mean just about everybody here above kindergarten age.

There has been no end to the talk about the need for a full, accurate, modern history of our commonwealth. For years we have all been saying it was absurd that our old state, so dear to us all, should never have had its life-story, completely, down to the present day, and adequately set down, in readable style, in a volume handy to hold.

Why has it taken so long to have such a history written?

There are a good many reasons why. For one thing, to tell the truth, it takes quite a long time in Vermont to get anything done. This often exasperates non-Vermonters. I daresay we do carry our leisurely ways too far, but, on the whole, we are not dissatisfied with such lack of impetuosity. When, for instance, we read newspaper items about states which have somehow let themselves in for spending more money than they have, we think it's not a bad idea to think a situation over before you start doing something about it.

Certainly the delay has not been due to any lack of historical material. Our forefathers from the eighteenth century on, have been, not scholarly exactly, but remarkably literate people. The first settlers were young sons and daughters of stable, reasonably well-to-do, Connecticut, Massachusetts, Rhode Island farmers and merchants. They left all sorts of written records of their doings in diaries, accountbooks (gold mines of accurate economic data for the historical research worker), letters, memoirs and locally written town histories.

In addition to such records in black ink on white paper, there is in Vermont an unusually ample body of oral tradition in the minds of Vermonters. Much of the rich, vivid human color which never gets into the written word, has been preserved in talk here, because in most Vermont towns there are many families directly descended from the pioneers. Vermont is, relatively speaking, not an old state; that is, not old when years are reckoned humanly, in the number of generations. Oral tradition has, in general, not much of what might be called tensile strength. It breaks if stretched too far. In our state, the stretch is not long. The earliest date of settlements here—real settle-ments, permanent homes and towns—is about 1764, after the end of the so-called French and Indian War. Consider what that means in human memories; the Canfields, my own family, are a typical example. My great-grandmother was born in 1786 in our town of Arlington, when the little settlement on the Battenkill was only twenty-odd years out of the unbroken wilderness. Her father was born in New Milford, Connecticut (from which town many Arlington families came). Hence he passed on to his daughter, memories of the very earliest days in Vermont which were, to him, fresh, contemporary. My father was born in 1846, and was brought up by his grandmother who naturally talked to him about memories of her youth and also what her father had told her of earlier days. My father passed on to me these old-time stories and descriptions of daily life which he heard from his grandmother, along with memories of his own mid-nineteenth century youth in Arlington. And I am still alive, my memory fully furnished with talk which comes, with but one change of narrator, from the last third of the 18th century.

Wallace Fahnestock of Dorset generously painted for our school some murals, depicting the departure from New Milford and the arrival here in Arlington, of the very first settlers in 1764. When the time came to have a little ceremony of dedication for these fine paintings, somebody on the program committee remarked that it would be suitable to have the unveiling done by direct descendants of the original settlers, now in the classrooms of our school—if any such could be found. If they could be found! The first casual glance at the list of students showed far more descendants of the original families than we could find a place for on the platform, for that unveiling ceremony.

You can see that is has not been lack of detailed, written and oral records which has delayed until now that writing of a real history of the state, such as Earle Newton has prepared. Materials for such a history lay around in nuggets, on the surface, in every town library, in attics, in family albums, and heaped up and pressed down in ample measure in the carefully kept collections of our State Historical Society. Indeed, it is ironically possible that this plentiful supply of data, especially the oral tradition, may have been one of the factors to delay the writing of the story of Vermont.

In a state where a certain percentage of each generation knows a great deal about local history (and, human nature being what it is, thinks it knows more than it does), there is something formidable about the undertaking of sifting out the data acceptable to modern standards of scholarliness, from picturesque family traditional legends. Vermonters are, on the subject of their history, very articulate, alarmingly quick to leap from their chairs to shout a protest about any statement they consider inaccurate. Ringing in the ears of anybody who tries to set down the ascertained facts of a phase of Vermont life, are exclamations we have all heard and many of us have uttered: "Not at all! He's got that all wrong! The road to East Sunmore ran over Peck Hill and down along Hatcher's Brook, till after 1827. It was the road to Sunmore Center, which . . ."

Well, we will find little to write protesting letters about in Earle Newton's well-balanced, accurate and detailed account of what has been happening in our State since its beginnings to the present. To consider the arduous work involved gives a fellow-writer an admiring shock. Just to riffle over its pages and see how many sides of our history have been covered, and in what ample detail, suggests another explanation for delay in getting such a book written. The mere idea of coping with all those details is enough to deter most writers. Mr. Newton's patient ordering of them provides us with what we have greatly needed, an historical whole into which to fit the local traditions, personal, oral, family, which have come down to us in talk.

And what a relief to have, at last, a history of Vermont to the present day, to hand to newcomers in our state. Naturally, soon after their arrival here, they ask for more information about the region which they have adopted as their own. This request has left us very much at a loss. We are fortunate indeed to have to show them, and to look at ourselves, a book so handsomely presented as this, with its many beautiful colored illustrations, and as many fascinating old photographs of Vermont scenes as they formerly were. Such is the contrast between the old photograph of the long string of yoked oxen hauling Barre granite, and, alongside, the railway freight-train, curving down the valley, a great block of the stone to each flat-car. There are facsimiles of manuscript documents too, among these pictures, old portraits, complete illustrations of our industries, quaint old catalogues, fine colored reproductions of paintings (the one of Main Street Montpelier in 1897 is a beautiful example) and more skillfully taken colored photographs of our Vermont scenery than you could count.

But, although the book is wonderfully rich-looking and attractive through its illustrations, its text is, after all its basic value. It is encyclopaedic in the way it covers our varied Vermont activities. As befits a modern history it has much more to say about our economic development—that is, about the different ways in which Vermonters have made their livings in the last hundred and eighty-odd years—than about battles of which there have been blessedly few in our past. The author sets down the growth of our industries, the quarrying of granite, marble, slate; the weaving of textiles; wood-working and lumbering; he has a chapter amusingly and accurately entitled "The Decline and Revival of Agriculture." He speaks of the scattered and interesting attempts to bring homecrafts to life again. He correctly represents our attitude by his admiring respect for the skilled mechanics, the gifted tool-makers, the high-grade, first-rate industrial brains which flowered into the remarkable industrial centers along the Connecticut River. He tackles with spirit and skill the problem of tracing in a few paragraphs the changes in transportation from ox-teams to air-planes. He gives an able and intelligent interpretation of the way the business of taking care of summer and winter guests has grown from eighteenth century taverns to the tourist cabins and recreational centers of today.

He studies as attentively the way Vermonters give humane and enjoyable values to the lives they work so hard to pay for: the schools, the libraries, the social welfare efforts, religious organizations, politics. He tells about the earlier currents of quixotic idealism, the temperance crusade, the anti-slavery movement; he describes vividly the modern cultural trends, in art, music, literature, painting. And he gives due emphasis to the great Vermont joys of *hunting* and FISHING.

It is a richly spread table to which the Director of the State Historical Society invites the Vermont family and their friends. Mr. Newton has touched on so many sides of our existence, that, humanly speaking, it would be natural to expect him to strike a false note here and there. By "false note" I suppose I mean what people usually do mean by that phrase—a note out of harmony with the complex tradition he is interpreting. My ear did not catch such a dissonance.

And this is an achievement. We detest bragging and boosting. We feel in our hearts that we have, along certain lines especially characteristic of our temperaments, our fair share of what are known as virtues and talents. But any kind of florid talk about these qualities brings out on us the gooseflesh of shamed disapproval. We are brought up on the old adage,

"Praise to the face
Is open disgrace."

All the same, there are no bounds to our affection for and pride in the special variation on the theme of the "American tradition" produced and fostered in our state. We bristle resentfully if the value of this tradition is not recognized. Earle Newton speaks of all this in what we feel is just about the right tone of voice.

DCF

Arlington, Vermont

CONTENTS

PART I, CHAPTER I. *The Face of Vermont*

Its green clad mountains, fertile river valleys, and earth bound resources have determined the development of the Green Mountain State from the days of the pioneer to the era of the railroad, the factory, and the tourist trade.

PART II, *First Century, 1749-1849*

PART III, *Second Century, 1849-1949*

ILLUSTRATIONS IN COLOR

With drawings by ROY F. HEINRICH

VERMONT—and the Other Forty-Seven

By Allan Nevins

FREDERICK JACKSON TURNER predicted in 1893 that the closing of the frontier would probably have two major results: a marked enhancement of regional or sectional loyalties, and a sharp increase of class consciousness and class conflicts. Fortunately for America, neither of these anticipated changes has taken place. The failure of the first to materialize is particularly interesting. Two areas alone, the Pacific Northwest and the Old South, have occasionally shown a heightened interest in regional culture and history; but even this has been slight and transitory.

The principal reasons why Turner in this respect has proved a bad prophet are probably three. For one, communications have grown with such rapidity, breadth, and power—telegraph, telephone, radio, television, railroads, automobiles, airplanes—that they have kept the country closely knit together; have in fact kept it shrinking rapidly. For another, great migrations of population have been constant. The westward movement has been maintained; between the two world wars both white and colored labor flowed from the South into the industrial plants of the Middle West; and the Second World War saw huge transfers of population from New England and the Middle Atlantic States to the Pacific Slope. This churning of the American people naturally operated to reduce sectional consciousness. Finally, the drift to the cities has been steady, and most American cities, wherever the region, are much alike.

At the same time, however, State fealties and State pride have been heightened. If sectional sentiment has not taken deep root, it is partly because State sentiment remains strong. After all, this is a very large nation; too large for most people to love in concrete terms as a unit. Our affections have to have a local habitation, and the State, whether it is as big as Texas or as small as Delaware, is the natural resting point. Every Indianian feels a special throb as he hears an orchestra launch into "On the Banks of the Wabash." Every Kansan knows with Carl Becker that Kansas is a state of mind. Every Kentuckian has somewhere in his inner conscious a picture of Crittenden proudly telling the Spanish officers about to shoot him: "A Kentuckian kneels only to his God." Every Virginian feels that Robert E. Lee was eternally right when he decided that his first loyalty was not to the United States of America, but to the Commonwealth of Virginia.

It is partly the novelists and short-story writers who have nurtured this abiding attachment to the States. Critics may talk of our regional novelists. But Faulkner has always really written of Mississippi, as has Eudora Wety; Willa Cather at her very best wrote not of the Middle West, but of Nebraska; Herbert Quick wrote of Iowa, and William Allen White's novels were Kansas through and through. George W. Cable gave us the Creoles of old Louisiana, and Thomas Nelson Page the people of Virginia, and Charles Egbert Craddock those of Kentucky. It is absurd to speak of Marjorie Kinnan Rawlings and John Peale Bishop as regional writers; the one has written of Florida and the other of West Virginia, a thousand miles apart geographically and culturally. The song-writers, too, have done their part. Of State songs we have an incomparably richer store than of national songs. The feeling may be passionate, as in "Maryland, My Maryland," or sentimental, as in "I Love You, California," or merely hopeful, as in "A Four-Horse Team Will Soon be Seen, Far out in Idaho"; but countless songs enshrine it.

In part, old political and social traditions have built up our state loyalties. The divergence between the Massachusetts and the Virginia tradition was marked when William Bradford and John Smith wrote their respective memoirs, and grew more so as Samuel Sewall and William Byrd penned their respective diaries. Compared with Massachusetts and Virginia, such a State as Tennessee has not much social tradition. But look at war and politics! She has John Sevier and Richard Henderson; she has Andrew Jackson and James K. Polk; she has Andrew Johnson, "Parson" Brownlow, and the fighting war governor Isham G. Harris; and bless her, she has Cordell Hull. Not an Illinois boy but feels faintly superior to his neighbors because Illinois can boast Lincoln, Douglas, and Grant. Sometimes, too, State loyalty owes much to some special institution. It may be a university, like those of North Carolina and Wisconsin. Or it may be a newspaper; for who can measure what the Portland *Oregonian* under Harvey Scott did for State pride in Oregon, or the Louisville *Courier-Journal* under "Marse" Watterson for Kentucky, or the Emporia *Gazette* under William Allen White for Kansas?

Most of all, however, it is history which supplies the basis for State feeling. Of really first-class state histories, unfortunately, we have all too few. If they are judged according to a combination of scholarly and literary standards, we should probably have to assign first place to an author of alien blood and language; for Charles Gayarré's *History of Louisiana* has hardly any peer in the English tongue. At the close of the eighteenth century Jeremy Belknap in his *History of New Hampshire* set a high standard, while a little later William D. Williamson's volumes on Maine possessed solid merit. California has been particularly happy in her historians, from the painstaking and thorough Hubert Howe Bancroft to modern writers like Chapman, Bolton, and Cleland. So has Illinois, where Clarence W. Alvord produced in the five-volume Centennial History a model cooperative work. Such single-volume histories as Reuben Gold Thwaites wrote long ago for Wisconsin and George P. Garrison for Texas, and as Grant Foreman and C. H. Ambler have more recently penned for Oklahoma and West Virginia, have high merit. The political history of New York in D. S. Alexander's four stout volumes is both entertaining and expert, while Edward McCrady's equally bulky history of South Carolina from its founding to the end of the Revolution ranks among the very best writings of the kind. Any State with a good narrative history has an unsurpassable foundation for the best kind of pride: pride in the great achievements of our ancestors, a determination to protect the fruit of their labors, and an ambition to broaden and heighten the structure they built.

The writing of truly good State history—good in the sense exemplified by this admirable volume of Earle Newton's—has become a work for the expert; that is, the expert scholar, and the expert literary craftsman. No longer does a place exist for such writers as Henry Howe, whose *Historical Collections of Ohio*, unsystematic, diffuse, and full of dubious legend (though, it must be admitted, vastly entertaining), were once so popular. No longer can we find much satisfaction in such sketchy, superficial works, however well written, as Thomas Nelson Page's *The Old Dominion: Her Making and Her Manners*, or Nathaniel S. Shaler's resume of Kentucky history. Local history in this country has long been the province of the amateur. Yet the reconstruction of local politics, economic life, manners, and social institutions is in many ways more difficult than the writing of national history; the sources are more meagre, and the changes are more difficult to analyze. The day has now dawned when the thoroughly trained investigator and author, determined to explore the past in a truly scientific spirit and to present its lineaments with human warmth and literary felicity, must take over the field.

Hence the importance of the series of State histories which this volume so delightfully inaugurates. By a marriage of pictorial and literary art with scholarship, they will touch the imagination while they throw light on many a neglected aspect of our record. A true understanding of our national history is impossible without a better knowledge of the State and local record than we have hitherto possessed. Who can fully comprehend Douglas's part in national affairs without some exploration of his impetuous part in the Jacksonian politics of Illinois? Who can measure Thaddeus Stevens's rôle in the Civil War without scrutinizing his previous rôle in Pennsylvania's "Buckshot War"? Some students believe that the basic elements of American democracy are to be found in the Atlantic seaboard communities and in successive waves of influence from the Old World. Some believe, rather, that the special traits of our democracy were born from a union of the pioneer with the wild forest, and were renewed and strengthened every time a new frontier was opened. How can the truth be ascertained without a fuller writing of State history? Our national government may have become Leviathan. But the development of morals, manners, early economic situations, most political institutions, and a great deal of our culture can best be studied against a State background.

It is a happy fact that this series begins with Earle Newton's *Vermont Story*. It was once said that every cultivated man's second country was France; it can certainly be said that every American's second State is Vermont.

The history of this rugged little State has a memorable individuality. In the era of the Anglo-American wars with the French, this wilderness country between the two disputants was left almost untracked. Then, when Canada had been conquered, the district became a tempting pioneer area, and waves of settlement poured in. But New York, Massachusetts, and New Hampshire quarreled over the prize. The pioneers had ideas of their own as to government, and set up for themselves. It took them nearly a generation to establish their independence, and the struggle placed its stamp on the new State. The Vermonters were the first Americans to prohibit slavery and they can boast that no slave was ever held within their limits. They created a sturdy democracy, to which they have tenaciously adhered. They managed their affairs more economically than any sister State. They wrote a glorious record in every American war. They contributed in unsurpassed proportions to the upbuilding of every Western community, and in countless activities, from the founding of the Mormon religion and of the two principal morning dailies of New York to the establishment of a new movement in landscape painting, their sons have furnished leadership.

The greater part of our national heritage is to be found in the record of our States. From the study of that record we can gain a renewal of our most precious possession, faith in the national ideal.   AN

The VERMONT *Story*

PART ONE

THE GEOGRAPHY AND GEOLOGY
Of the Green Mountain State

Its green clad mountains, fertile river valleys, and earth bound resources have determined the development of the Green Mountain State from the days of the pioneer to the era of the railroad, the factory, and the tourist trade . . . .

VERMONT'S first history is her natural history. When Samuel de Champlain first set eyes on the Green Mountains in 1609, from the waters of Lake Champlain, both mount and lake were old far beyond the memory of man. And even at that late date no one had any thought of a future "state" among this green clad wilderness.

Yet it was the shape of her topography which more than anything else was to determine how people were to live, work, move about, and—in more modern times— play in Vermont. As the white man first saw the land, there were no roads spanning the considerable distances, no cities with stocks of the world's goods, no airfields and planes with which to mock at mountain heights. There was only the virgin wilderness of forest-clad mountains, pierced by racing streams and spotted with sky-blue lakes.

It was no coincidence that it was the Green Mountains which first caught the roving eye of the great explorer, Champlain, for this ancient chain has ever been the outstanding geographic fact of both natural and human history in Vermont. Actually, in point of time, these rolling hills watched the rise of the neighboring Appalachians, the distant Rockies, and the far-away Alps and Andes.

It was Mansfield, highest summit, which Champlain saw, towering 4393 feet into the air; but there are five other peaks in excess of 4000 feet, and twenty-one over 3500 feet. This is not high compared to some of the younger mountains mentioned above, or even compared to the barren White Mountains of neighboring New Hampshire. But extending in a long chain from Canada to southern New England, these green peaks stood as both a barrier and a challenge to the first white men to look upon them.

Actually the Green Mountains themselves are only one—though the largest—of a series of ranges which stretch lengthwise of the state. Beginning on the south, the main backbone reaches due north, thrusting peaks into the sky at Mounts Glastenbury, Stratton, Bromley, Killington, Carmel, Breadloaf, Lincoln, Camel's Hump, Mansfield, Belvidere, and far to the north, Jay Peak.

Parallel to the main range are the Taconics, which spill over from Massachusetts into southwestern Vermont. In a series of peaks of which Equinox is the highest (3816 feet), they follow the Green Mountains north, with only a narrow but highly scenic valley between. They peter out about a third of the way up the state in Brandon.

Later on, now to the east, a second series of parallel peaks splits off at Pico—famed today for its ski slopes— and proceeds northward, first as the Braintree and Northfield Mountains, then, leaping the valley of the Winooski, as the Worcester range. Even further to the northeast lie the dome-like Granite Hills, inconspicuous on the landscape, but carrying the important eastern watershed. This separates the rivers flowing into the Atlantic by way of the Connecticut River from those flowing thence via Lake Champlain and the St. Lawrence. This watershed follows the main Green Mountain range to Mt. Cleveland, then hits off to the northeast. The main range to the north, for all its height, is pierced three times by the Winooski, Lamoille, and Missisquoi Rivers, and acts as a watershed only for minor tributaries to these three great streams.

Another group, so low as to hardly register on the map, and sometimes known as the Red Sandrock Hills, extends along the east shore of Lake Champlain. They begin with Snake Mountain, often called Grand View because of the sweep of horizon from its 1271 foot summit rising from an otherwise flat valley landscape. The same formations often crop out even at the Lake's edge as at Red Rocks on the south side of Burlington Bay.

There are other isolated peaks disconnected from the principal ranges, mostly "Monadnocks"—erosion remnants which owe their existence to the fact that they consist of harder rock than their surroundings. One of them in the northeast part of the state is actually called by that name, Mount Monadnock, 3200 feet high, in Lemington. Far to the south, in Windsor, is Mount Ascutney, to the summit of which there today twists a motor road.

The main mountain backbone has, from the beginning, divided the state into two halves. But the early settlers in any event would have faced eastward toward the Connecticut, and westward toward Lake Champlain and the Hudson River, for waterways have historically served as

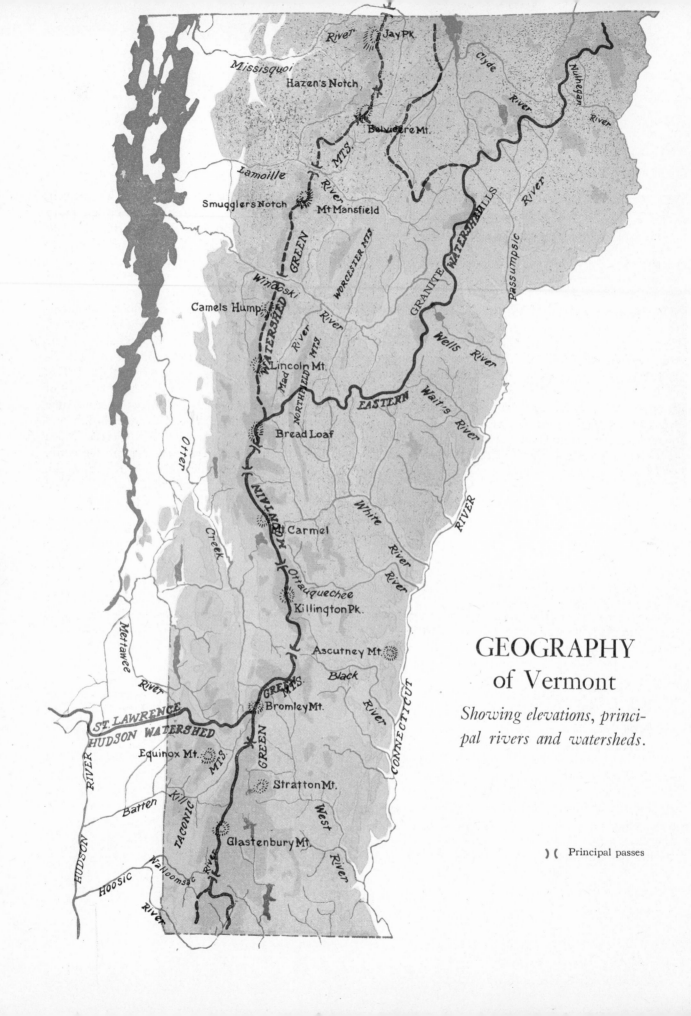

GEOGRAPHY
of Vermont

*Showing elevations, princi-
pal rivers and watersheds.*

)(Principal passes

Samuel de Champlain is believed to have been the first white man to set eyes on Vermont. It was Mount Mansfield that he saw, lying on the horizon in stately majesty. And while now man can effortlessly reach the top by motor car, or power lift, *the mount itself remains unchanged today, as it had remained unchanged for centuries before Champlain. Mansfield is the highest point in the great Green Mountain backbone of Vermont.* (Derick)

the centers of culture and civilization, almost regardless of artificial political boundaries. The early pioneers proceeded up the valley of the Connecticut, settling on *both* sides of the river—which, as a matter of fact, were thought by most to be equally part of New Hampshire. Even after the "New Hampshire Grants," later Vermont, were set apart, these people on the west shore had more in common with New Hampshire men across the river than with their fellow citizens over the mountains. The river served as a highway before roads, and its valley on both sides provided the rich "intervales"—meadows so fertile for pioneer farming.

Across the mountains, Lake Champlain serves as the state's western border for 112 miles, varying in width from a few hundred feet to 9 miles, (419 of its 436 square miles are in the United States, 17 in Canada). Historically, too, it has served as a gateway for settlement, and for the marching and counter-marching of countless armies. For Lake Champlain opens a great valley between the Green Mountains and the neighboring Adirondacks in New York, connecting through the valley of the Hudson River with the great port and metropolis of New York City—even in the early days a political and trading center.

The first settlements in Vermont were from Canada, along the east shore, while other important—and more permanent—colonies were established on the west shore. The Lake served as a highway not only for settlers moving south and for invading armies, but also for trade in lumber and potash northward. It was recognition of the stronger commercial ties of northwestern Vermont to Canada that caused Ethan and Ira Allen, during the Revolution, to favor a permanent union with British Canada rather than with the infant United States.

And, as with the Connecticut, the Champlain Valley provided broad shores stretching back toward the mountains —the greatest single belt of fertile farmland in the state.

The lower third of the western Vermont boundary was an arbitrary political one, resulting from the extension northward of the "20 mile line" (the west boundary of Connecticut and Massachusetts, 20 miles east of the Hudson River). But for a good bit of the way it parallels the Hudson, into which flow the two principal rivers of southwestern Vermont, the Battenkill and the Hoosac—

including the latter's historically important tributary, the Walloomsac.

A glance at the map shows how the topography of the state has thrown it into three principal regions of northern New England and New York: the Champlain Valley—which also includes northeast New York; the Connecticut Valley—which takes in all of western New Hampshire; and the Hudson Valley.

It is also easy to see on the map that, with their principal streams, these very regions in Vermont fall within the main watersheds. In the northwest the Missiquoi, Lamoille, Winooski Rivers and Otter Creek flow into Lake Champlain. Way down to the south, the Poultney and Mettowee Rivers combine with Wood Creek to begin the Lake. (The sources of Wood Creek lie only a stone's throw from the Hudson River, which has its own watershed in Vermont as noted above.) The Lake then, in turn, via the Richelieu River, pours into the St. Lawrence River and Bay, and eventually the blue waters of the Atlantic. The Black, Barton and Clyde Rivers flow north into Lake Memphremagog, only one quarter of whose bulk lies within Vermont and the United States, the rest in Canada. Memphremagog in turn empties into the St. Lawrence, and thereby creates a small watershed of its own, tributary to the main St. Lawrence drainage basin.

The rivers which flow into the mighty Connecticut are smaller than those feeding the Lake, but are generally more rapid. Far to the north the Nulhegan begins the procession, followed by the Passumpsic, Wells, Waits and Ompanpanoosuc Rivers. The northward reaching branches of the White River open up the narrow Williamstown, Brookfield (Northfield) and Granville Gulfs, where also rise important tributaries of the westward flowing Winooski—the graphically named Mad and Dog Rivers and the more commonplace Stevens Branch. (Here again, waters flowing into St. Lawrence Bay via Lake Champlain, and those flowing into Long Island Sound via the Connecticut, rise only a few rods from each other.) It is these three Gulfs which today provide thin channels for the three principal highways running up the center of the state from Rutland to Montpelier-Barre and the North.

South of the White River are the Ottaquechee, Black, Williams, and Saxtons Rivers, and finally the West, or more picturesquely named, Wantatisquet River, which sends tributaries into the southern slopes of the Green Mountains.

Most of these rivers provided the early settlers with fertile valley lands for life-giving crops, as well as with water-power sites for the essential grist and saw mills—the beginnings of industry in the state.

But even more important, the rivers have served as the arteries of transportation before there were roads. And after the building of roads—and, yes, railroads too—their valleys served as the channels for these new pathways of the travel of men. They carved essential gaps through

the formidable range which split the state in half. Early travelers followed rivers from the Connecticut northwest to their headwaters, where they found the sources of other rivers flowing down into the Champlain Valley. The great gaps carved by the Winooski and Lamoille Rivers are still the only passageways which either the railway or main roads can take through the Green Mountain range from Killington and Mendon Peaks—where the road struggles over a high pass—all the way to the Canadian border. South of Killington a low pass lets the railroad and highway through in Mount Holly, but below that two westbound roads must struggle over lofty elevations to reach the narrow valley between the Green Mountains and the Taconics. Even the modern miracles of rail and road play second fiddle to the works of Mother Nature, brought forth millions of years before.

In addition to the larger bodies of water—Champlain and Memphremagog—there are a number of smaller gem-like lakes and ponds, of which Bomoseen in Castleton, Dunmore in Salisbury, St. Catherine in Poultney, and lovely Lake Willoughby far to the north in Westmore, are the most famous. But there are hundreds of other smaller ponds spattered like jewels in the area between the Great Mountains and the Granite Hills, as well as occasionally elsewhere throughout the state. Most of these were left by the melting glacier which once covered all of Vermont, and which had in its southward progress scoured out hollows in the rocks and dammed up stream valleys with its rock waste. But more of that anon.

One should not leave the subject of waters without mentioning the crystal springs which burst from the mountain sides to form sparkling mountain streams and, later, mighty rivers. These are so plentiful as to have furnished, as late as 1900, three-quarters of all the farms in the state with their sole water supply. Many towns and villages obtained their water by combining hillside springs. Many a fortunate city-dweller today still has a lead pipeline to a spring as well as his connection to the municipal reservoir.

Many of these springs, with unusual chemical or mineral content, were thought at one time to have a definite medicinal value. During the nineteenth century a considerable resort business was built up around the springs near Highgate, Clarendon, Brattleboro, and Brunswick. None of these play any considerable part in the recreation business today. But the scenic grandeur of Vermont's mountains and rivers is still her principal attraction for visitors from other states, who have built the tourist business into a venture rivaling in importance both manufacturing and agriculture. Still controlling the latter—and to some extent the former—with wind and rain, soil and sun, Mother Nature has from her bounteous store of emerald-hued beauty, raised up a new industry to challenge both.

NATURAL RESOURCES OF VERMONT

"The time has come," the walrus said, "to talk of
    many things"—

(And if he had been a geologically-minded walrus he
    might have added:)

"Of rocks and folds and overthrusts,
    Of lakes and streams and springs;
    And how the mountains came to rise,
    And what the glacier brings."   FCJ

Alice's walrus, scattering impressive sentiments, would
be no less baffled by the language of geology than the
average person trying to discover how the land was
made, and what lies below its surface today. But without
some knowledge of the earth's gigantic forces, he can
hardly find what he is looking for.

It seems that our geologists divide the vast stretch of
time from "creation" up to the present into a series of
"eras," beginning with what is called the "Pre-Cambrian"
time, some 2 *billion* years ago—as near as they can
figure. This was followed by the "Paleozoic" era, which
began about 500 million years ago. It was during two
periods of this era that most of the important Vermont
rocks were created—the earliest "Cambrian" and the
subsequent "Ordovician" periods. These were followed
by the "Mesozoic" and "Cenozoic" eras. It was during
the most recent period of the latter era—the Pleistocene—

only a million years old—that the shape of modern Vermont was sculptured.

Vermont, like the rest of the earth from time im-
memorial, has been standing in and out of the water,
with its high backbone normally above the water level.
This is but an ancient wrinkle of the earth's surface, like
the Adirondacks and White Mountains which flank it.

Upon these exposed elevations the forces of wind and
water, frost and even the air itself, worked for countless
centuries to wear them down, breaking up the igneous
rocks, and then transporting the resulting sediments—
pebbles, sand, clay—over the nearby shores. Lime-bearing
animals and corals were deposited into limestone layers,
filled today with millions of fossils of a by-gone era.

You would think that with a steady process of this sort,
we would get regular layers of these various deposits.
But this does not take into account the stresses and move-
ments of the earth's crust. For example, it was a sinking
of the earth's surface early in Paleozoic times which
brought the waters of the great St. Lawrence Bay flowing
into the trough connecting what is now the St. Lawrence
and Hudson Valleys. The sea rose up against a higher
land mass, which later became the Green Mountains.
Sand, clay and dolomite muds deposited in these waters
were the origin of the red sandstone and other similar
formations of the Champlain Valley today.

*Our earth is made up of both organic
("living") and inorganic matter. The latter
covers everything that is not organic, including, of course, minerals and rocks. Most rocks
are composed of either a single mineral or a
combination of several: granite, for example,
is composed largely of quartz, feldspar, and
mica.*

*Now the earth's crust is solid rock, which
is mostly buried under a great depth of loose,
"unconsolidated" rock and rotting organic
material, which combine to make soil.*

*Rocks are of three varieties: igneous, sedi-
mentary and metamorphic—all formidable
terms. We can best understand their relation-
ships through the accompanying diagram.
Note at the top of what is known as the "rock
cycle" are the igneous rocks—that is, those
formed as a result of the cooling of what was
once a molten mass. Geologists believe that at
one time the entire earth was such a molten
sphere, and that as a result all rocks were
originally "igneous." Sometimes great masses
of this basic rock are revealed by "erosion"
(the wearing away of the looser surface
covering); these are known as "batholiths."
The great outcropping of granite—probably
the most common igneous rock—are characteristic of this structure.*

*On the one hand (moving to the left on the
diagram) this igneous rock can be altered by*

THE ROCK CYCLE.

*erosion into "unconsolidated" sedimentary or
loose matter—like sand, gravel and clay.
Sediments, in turn, were washed down and
deposited layer upon layer upon the ancient
sea bottoms. Pressure and the action of natural
cementing materials consolidates this loose
matter into familiar rocks which are laid
down in layers, or "strata." Clay, for
example, is compressed into shale; limestone
and dolomite largely result from consolidation of the skeletons of millions of living
organisms.*

*But we can proceed one step further, for
these sedimentary rocks can be made over—
"metamorphosed"—by more pressure, heat,*

*or chemical action, until they are known as
"metamorphic" rock. Our great deposits of
marble, for example, are made-over limestone. Note how the great belt of marble
down the west side of the state flows out of—
and is for some distance paralleled by—a
great strata of limestone which begins way
up at the head of Lake Champlain. In fact,
some of our so-called marble are merely limestone and dolomite which will take a beautiful polish.*

*Likewise, slate is nothing but "meta-
morphosed" shale; the best deposits of which
run along the Vermont-New York border,
with important quarries on both sides. There
is another, less important stratum of
Memphremagog slate in the center of the
state, stretching through Montpelier, Berlin
and Northfield. A third, of little commercial
importance, today follows the Connecticut
River north from Dummerston.*

*But just as igneous rock can be washed
down to sediments, and then consolidated
again into metamorphic rock, it can also be
transformed by pressure directly to this latter
form (follow the arrow to the right, from
the top, now). And it should also be noted
that sometimes either kind of rock can be
eroded back to a loose state, (note the arrow
moving clockwise from the bottom of the
circle and also across its center).*

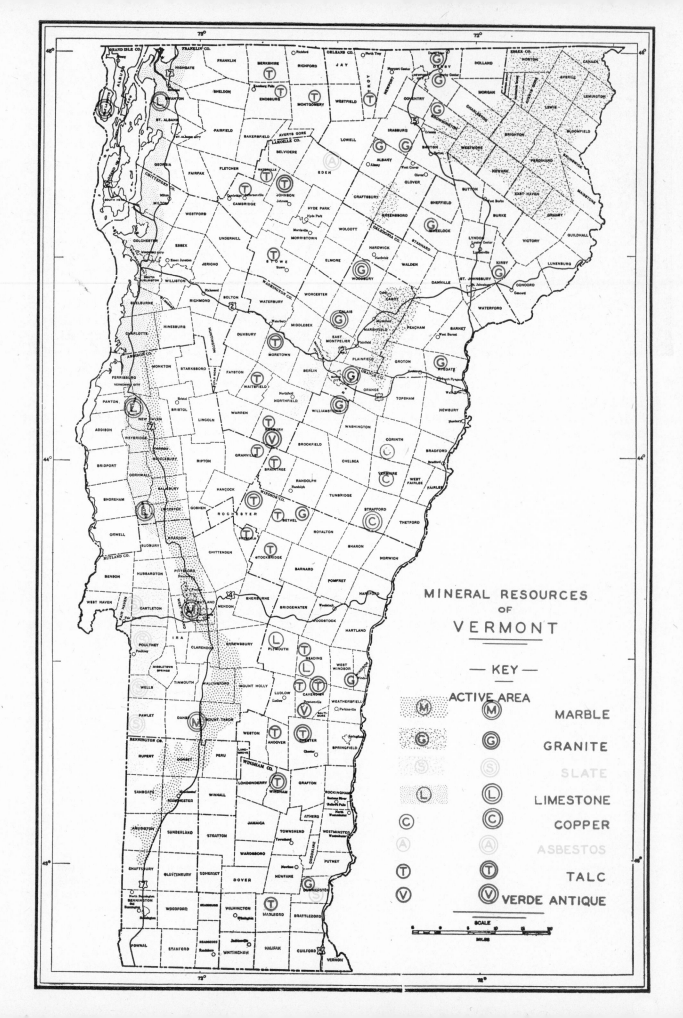

MINERAL RESOURCES
OF
VERMONT

— KEY —

ACTIVE AREA

M	M	MARBLE
G	G	GRANITE
S	S	SLATE
L	L	LIMESTONE
C	C	COPPER
A	A	ASBESTOS
T	T	TALC
V	V	VERDE ANTIQUE

SCALE

MILES

The Rock Point Overthrust near Burlington is one of the outstanding geological phenomena of America. This

Fleming Museum mural is reprinted from The Summer 1947 issue of Vermont Life.

The close of the Ordovician period marks the end of the depositing of sedimentary material, but the beginning of strong disruptive forces in the earth's crust which were to re-make the map of Vermont. The uneasy earth, trying to adjust itself to a shrinking mass, wrinkled again. Strong pressure from the east thrust upward the Taconic Mountains, and in the Champlain Valley produced the unusual "overthrust," which extends from Canada all the way down the east side of the lake in the red sandrock hills. Here the pressure was such as to thrust the older Cambrian layers up over the younger black Ordovician shale. This is, of course, a shift in position, since the newer layer will normally be on top of the older. The overthrust is beautifully exposed at Rock Point, where geologists come from great distances to examine its structure. A mural of the overthrust, accompanied by panels depicting the human history of this region, has been painted at the Fleming Museum in nearby Burlington (see the color illustration above).

There followed a period of great mountain-building, when the peaks of the Green Mountains were raised to great heights, and its rocks subjected to great pressure (and consequent metamorphism). But cracking and crumpling of the earth's surface were not the only forces at work. What was once a nearly tropical climate (as shown by fossil deposits of tropical fruits and nuts) underwent a revolutionary change. As it became colder a great ice sheet began moving down from the north, covering most of Canada and northern United States. That which covered New England had originated in Labrador, and in its southward movement brought many

Labrador rocks with it, crushing and grinding the softer ones, rounding and polishing the harder ones. Mountain tops were shorn off, valleys gouged out, and the soil scraped from its rock base. At its maximum depth, it covered the highest peaks of the Green and White Mountains.

One of the most important products of the glacial period, however, was the soil which overlies almost all the rugged face of Vermont. For Vermont was more fortunate than her eastern neighbor, New Hampshire, who had her White Mountains scraped almost clean. Yet even the high peaks of the Green Mountains are wooded to the top.

The glacier crushed to the earth all living vegetation and left it there to rot amongst the ground-up, loose rocks. A soil of great fertility was thus produced over much of the state, and a new carpet of green spread over the land. Trees, the greatest free-growing natural resource, sprang to great size, and dropping their leaves upon the ground to rot in turn, provided a ground cover of unbelievable fertility, as well as the lumber for the pioneer builder. These great forests were a hindrance to agriculture in that they had to be felled and the stumps up-rooted to prepare fields for the plow. But they were also, when burnt to ash, the source of the first important cash crop— potash. This was exported by the early settlers to Canada and the more settled areas of southern New England.

The rotted leaf cover proved a deceptive fertility for the unscientific frontier farmer, who soon "mined" his soil and moved on westward, leaving in his train a heritage of abandoned farms and declining population. The soils are not very heavy, and with the exception of the fertile river intervales—meadows—are best suited to grass. The abundant summer rainfall, transformed in winter into a snow cover, produces a luxuriant grass cover, well suited to grazing. The determined farmers who did not emigrate recognized the decrees of nature, and turned to livestock—sheep, beef cattle and horses, and finally, in our time, to dairying. Vermont's past and present success in agriculture has hinged upon her ability to turn grass into a saleable product. Today the most profitable product is fluid milk.

In the course of these several paragraphs, we have climbed over numerous complicated words and ideas. But it has all been to the end that the reader may better understand the tremendous influence of natural history on human history—of geography and geology on industry, agriculture, transportation, and indeed, upon recreation.

We have seen how the soils and climate of Vermont have determined the extent and kind of crops which the farmer will raise, and to a great extent, how he will raise them. In addition to grass and agricultural crops, the natural forest cover has today provided the source of not only an expanding wood-working industry, but also Vermont's famed maple products: sap, syrup and sugar.

We have seen how the basic geology of the state has provided her with important mineral resources, upon which are built two of her greatest industries:—marble and granite quarrying and shaping. Slate and limestone, copper and asbestos, Verde antique and talc, are other minerals which are mined extensively within Vermont.

Then, too, basic geography has fixed the routes of travel within and across the state, whether by foot, horse, rail or road. And upon transportation there are dependent many other manufacturing industries.

And last but not least, her marching mountains and placid streams in a verdant landscape have—coupled with the appeal of a substantial way of life—brought to Vermont a great influx of "outsiders"—people touched with the green finger of country living as well as tourists just "passing through." And in these visitors she has found not only a great new industry, but also a new source of population and expansive energy.

This, then, is the story of our natural history, and the prelude to our human history.

Vermont's mountains and green coursed valleys were once thickly clothed with a cloak of timber, the state's first and most available natural resource. Today, while almost all the "first growth" *is gone, through the work of the national and state forestry services a program of conservation endeavors to preserve the new cover for generations to come.*

VERMONT SUGAR BUSH

PAUL SAMPLE spent his childhood years in almost every part of the United States, but married a Vermont girl and settled down at Norwich, while serving as Artist-in-Residence at Dartmouth College across the river. He is a prolific award winner with canvasses in the Metropolitan, Boston, Springfield, Brooklyn and Chicago Museums.

"Sketches for this picture," he says, "were made in the vicinity of my home at Norwich, Vermont. It pictures a typical sugaring scene, and brings together elements from various places and experiences in connection with sugaring. These were recorded in the form of studies and sketches, and the finished painting is thus a summing up or composite of these."

One of the principal natural resources of Vermont is her forest cover. Among these woods, hard and soft, none is more beautiful and at the same time useful than the sugar maple. Milked of its sap as the winter snows melt away, it turns first light, then deep green, casting a sheltering late afternoon shadow on the warm earth. As summer wears into fall, its leaves burst into a riot of reds and oranges that splash the landscape with high color.

For all the romance of the sugar bush, the industry dependent upon it constitutes less than three per cent of the total value of the state's agricultural produce. Yet this three per cent amounts to as much as two million dollars, and up to ten million pounds of sugar.

The nearly five million trees tapped annually constitute only one half the available sugar bush, though probably the more accessible half. However, the maple tree also provides hardwood for the state's woodworking industry. This, as well as the tendency of some short sighted owners to cut their maples for firewood when the price of syrup drops, is beginning the depletion of a basic natural resource.

Second only to the physiography of the state in long run importance is climate, another element in her development which has been under the sole supervision of Mother Nature. Vermont's northerly position dictates a temperate climate, modified locally by the elevation of the landscape. Note on the accompanying maps, how closely maximum average temperature and maximum length of growing season—as well as minimum snowfall—is concentrated along the lower regions of the Champlain and the Connecticut River valleys. Coupled with an excellence of the soil, this fact makes these areas particularly adapted to profitable agriculture. It can hardly be disputed, however, that the general shortness of the growing season has handicapped the Vermont farmer in competing with more southerly areas.

While Vermont is reputedly a cold state—and winter temperatures below zero are frequent—humidity is low. The absence of excess moisture in the air provides an exhilarating atmosphere as contrasted with the damp penetrating cold of the seaboard. This, combined with the heavy snowfall on the mountain slopes (again, see map) has produced the expanding new winter sports industry, which is rapidly turning Vermont into a year-round recreation area, serving the metropolitan East as well as her own residents. A moderate summer climate together with the attractions of her verdant landscape long ago produced an extensive tourist trade in the warmer months.

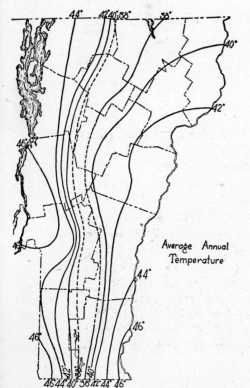

Average Annual Temperature

The lines on this map are drawn through points having approximately the same average annual temperature as indicated at the ends of each line. The general course of such lines for the United States is east and west. The fact that they run north and south on this map shows that altitude is more important than latitude in determining the variations in average temperature in Vermont, and explains why Vermont has good summer resort areas from one end of the state to the other.

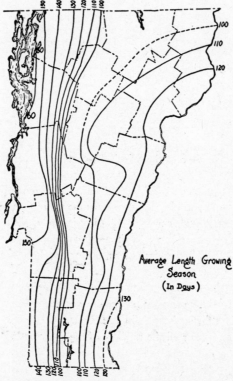

Average Length Growing Season
(In Days)

The lines on this map are drawn through points having approximately the same average number of days between the last killing frost in the spring and the first killing frost in the fall as indicated at the ends of each line.

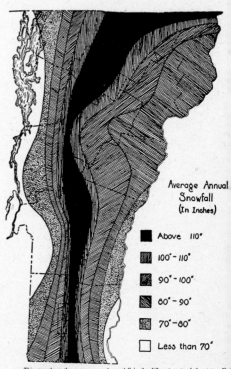

Average Annual Snowfall (In Inches)

- ■ Above 110°
- ▥ 100″–110°
- ▨ 90″–100°
- ▧ 80″–90°
- ▩ 70″–80°
- ☐ Less than 70°

This map shows the average annual snowfall in the different parts of the state. Note that the areas of heavy snowfall, suitable for winter sports, extend the whole length of the state.

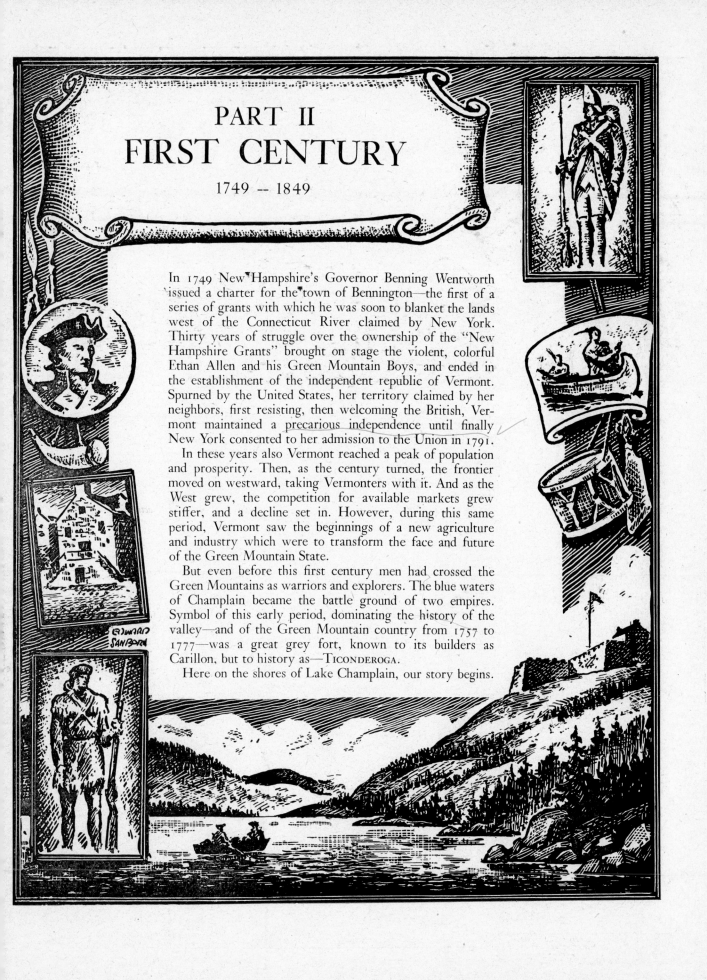

PART II
FIRST CENTURY
1749 -- 1849

In 1749 New Hampshire's Governor Benning Wentworth issued a charter for the town of Bennington—the first of a series of grants with which he was soon to blanket the lands west of the Connecticut River claimed by New York. Thirty years of struggle over the ownership of the "New Hampshire Grants" brought on stage the violent, colorful Ethan Allen and his Green Mountain Boys, and ended in the establishment of the independent republic of Vermont. Spurned by the United States, her territory claimed by her neighbors, first resisting, then welcoming the British, Vermont maintained a precarious independence until finally New York consented to her admission to the Union in 1791.

In these years also Vermont reached a peak of population and prosperity. Then, as the century turned, the frontier moved on westward, taking Vermonters with it. And as the West grew, the competition for available markets grew stiffer, and a decline set in. However, during this same period, Vermont saw the beginnings of a new agriculture and industry which were to transform the face and future of the Green Mountain State.

But even before this first century men had crossed the Green Mountains as warriors and explorers. The blue waters of Champlain became the battle ground of two empires. Symbol of this early period, dominating the history of the valley—and of the Green Mountain country from 1757 to 1777—was a great grey fort, known to its builders as Carillon, but to history as—Ticonderoga.

Here on the shores of Lake Champlain, our story begins.

EDWARD SANBORN

Courtesy *Joseph Dixon Crucible Co.*

LAKE CHAMPLAIN

TO LAKE GEORGE

Map of
TICONDEROGA
Showing the old Fort designed by Vauban
and built by the French beginning 1755

1609
Champlain
claims Ticonderoga
territory for the
King of France

1758
British attack
with gallant
Black Watch
repelled by French

1755–1759
Major R. Rogers'
Colonial Rangers
patrol territory

1775
Ethan Allen
helps to free America
by capturing
Fort Ticonderoga

FORT TICONDEROGA'S massive battlements dominate the narrows of water where Lake George empties into Lake Champlain, controling the "Northern Gateway." *(Kleffel)*

THOMAS JEFFERY'S MAP of 1758 depicts the disastrous British assault by General Abercrombie on "Fort Carillon" in that year. Jeffery Amherst took it in 1759, renamed it Ticonderoga.

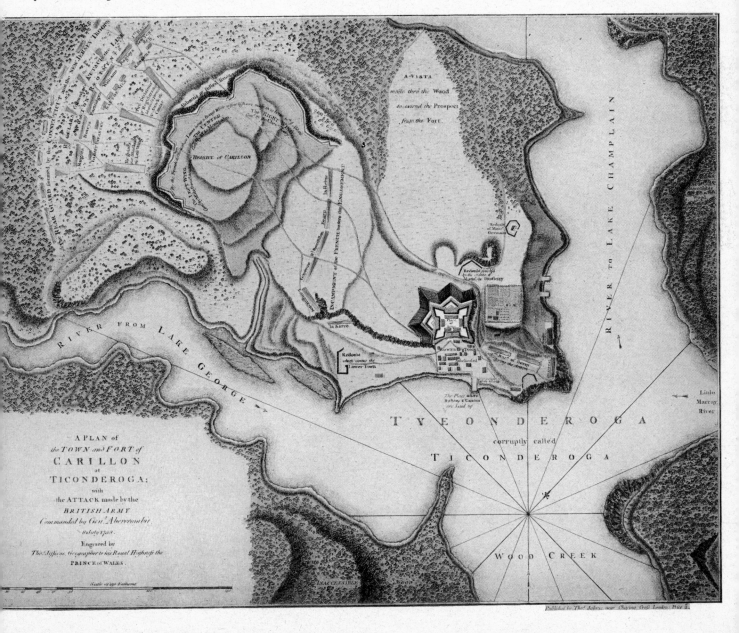

A PLAN of
the TOWN and FORT of
CARILLON
at
TICONDEROGA;
with
the ATTACK made by the
BRITISH ARMY
Commanded by Gen.ʳ Abercrombie,
8 July 1758.
Engraved by
Thoˢ Jefferys, Geographer to his Royal Highneſs the
PRINCE of WALES

II

REDSKINS TO REDCOATS

*The story of the land of which Vermont was a part, from the days
of Indian dominance to the conquest of New France by the British.*

IN the beginning, there was no Vermont. Of course, there were the wandering waters of the great Connecticut in search of the ocean, and the azure expanse of placid Lake Champlain, pouring its waters into the majestic St. Lawrence, also seaward-bound. Between these waterways was a green clad land, studded with towering peaks and sparkling streams, and populated by the bear and the beaver, along with probably a few men with skin of copper hue.

There were then no boundaries, as now, and the Indians of the St. Lawrence and Connecticut River Valleys wandered freely across its well stocked hunting grounds and occasionally camped long enough to plant some corn among the lush meadows of the Great Oxbow at Coos, or near the mouths of Otter Creek or the Winooski River. It is hard to know where Indians lived. The inquisitive shovel of the archaeologist has brought to the surface in many places flints, arrowheads, pottery, and even skeletons of men who inhabited the land, for a while at least, centuries ago. But the northern Indian was ever a wanderer, and his residence in any one spot was usually of short duration. Thus it is hard to say that at any particular spot in Vermont, there lived a certain tribe.

But the pathways of the redman were the blue trails of streams and lakes, and along them—especially Champlain—there were always Indians, coming and going, hunting and fishing, or pursuing a stealthy warpath.

There were two great Indian cities, known as Stadacona and Hochelaga, on the sites of present day Quebec and Montreal, when Jacques Cartier sailed down to St. Lawrence in 1535, in search of the fabled passage to the Indies. At Hochelaga he ascended nearby Mount Royale, from which, looking over the blush of autumn foliage to the south, he may have seen the dim peaks of the Green Mountains.

But Cartier turned back without exploring further south or westward, leaving the blue lake and the green land that edged it to the discovery of another Frenchman who followed in his path some sixty years later. It was Samuel de Champlain who established the foundations of France in the New World. In the long years between, the St. Lawrence was visited only by French and Breton fishermen, who utilized Tadoussac, at the mouth of the Saguenay River, as a trading center.

On the shores of Lake Champlain, probably near Ticonderoga, Samuel de Champlain defended with firearms the Canadian Algonquins against the Iroquois of the Six Nations. He thereby gained for the French the eternal enmity of these powerful Indian tribes, who later allied themselves with the British during the colonial wars of the 18th Century.

COLONIAL VERMONT

The map on the facing page illustrates how the frontier of French Canada, advancing up the St. Lawrence and Champlain valleys, met the British-Yankee frontier, which had pushed up the Connecticut and Hudson Rivers from the earlier settled Atlantic seaboard. During the century of colonial wars, the border line between these two new world empires lay along the watershed dividing the streams emptying into Lake Champlain from those flowing into the Connecticut. Note also on the map how these same streams served as convenient pathways—with brief portages—for invasion back and forth. The most spectacular French invasion was Hertel de Rouville's attack on Deerfield in 1704. Equally well known was British Major Robert Rogers' famous attack on French St. Francis, in 1759. His route from Crown Pt. to Number Four is shown by the dotted line. Principal French outposts were first the Richelieu River forts, and then Crown Point and Ticonderoga. The New Englanders hung on precariously at Fort Dummer and "Number Four."

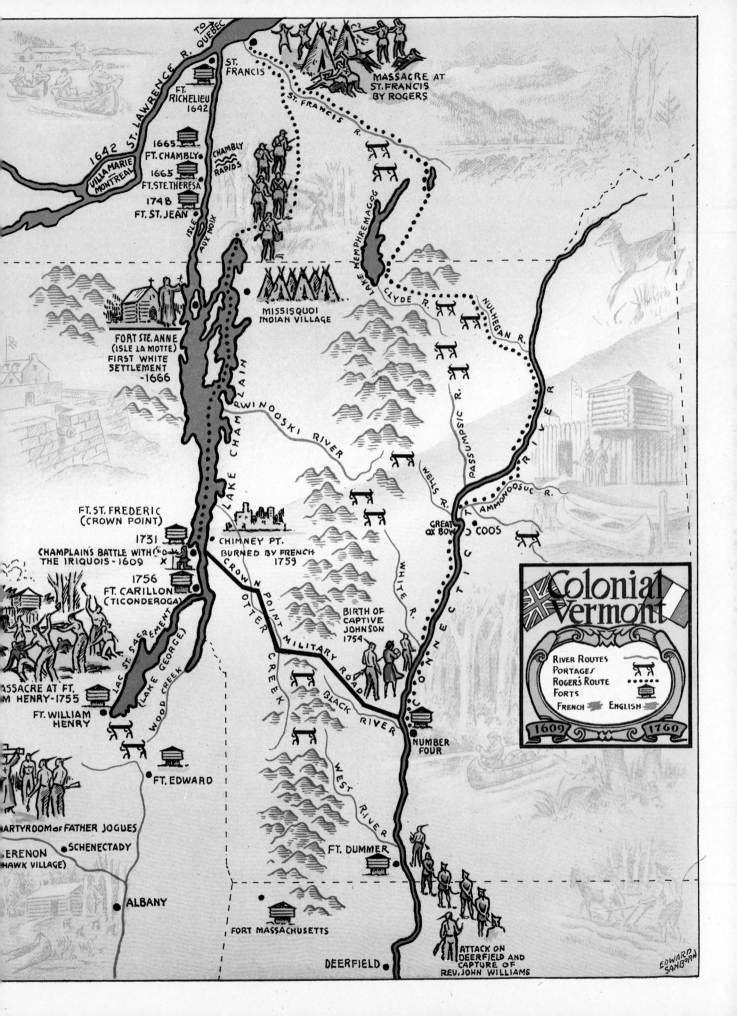

TO QUEBEC

MASSACRE AT ST. FRANCIS BY ROGERS

ST. FRANCIS

FT. RICHELIEU 1642

ST. FRANCIS R.

1665 FT. CHAMBLY

CHAMBLY RAPIDS

1665 FT. STE. THERESA

1748 FT. ST. JEAN

ISLE AUX NOIX

1642 ST. LAWRENCE R.

VILLE MARIE MONTREAL

LAKE MEMPHREMAGOG

CLYDE R.

NULHEGAN R.

FORT STE. ANNE (ISLE LA MOTTE) FIRST WHITE SETTLEMENT -1666

MISSISQUOI INDIAN VILLAGE

WINOOSKI RIVER

PASSUMPSIC R.

WELLS R.

AMMONOOSUC R.

RIVER

FT. ST. FREDERIC (CROWN POINT)

CHIMNEY PT. BURNED BY FRENCH 1759

LAKE CHAMPLAIN

1731

CHAMPLAIN'S BATTLE WITH THE IRIQUOIS -1609

1756 FT. CARILLON (TICONDEROGA)

GREAT OX BOW

COOS

BIRTH OF CAPTIVE JOHNSON 1754

WHITE R.

CONNECTICUT

CROWN POINT MILITARY ROAD

OTTER CREEK

LAC ST. SACREMENT (LAKE GEORGE)

WOOD CREEK

MASSACRE AT FT. WM HENRY -1755

FT. WILLIAM HENRY

BLACK RIVER

NUMBER FOUR

FT. EDWARD

WEST RIVER

MARTYRDOM of FATHER JOGUES

ERENON (MOHAWK VILLAGE)

SCHENECTADY

FT. DUMMER

ALBANY

FORT MASSACHUSETTS

DEERFIELD

ATTACK ON DEERFIELD AND CAPTURE OF REV. JOHN WILLIAMS

Colonial Vermont

River Routes
Portages
Roger's Route
Forts
French   English

1609   1760

EDWARD SANBORN

Courtesy National Life Ins. Co.

Samuel de Champlain, explorer, navigator and historian, founded Quebec in 1608, and the following year laid claim for New France to the lands surrounding the great lake to which he gave his name.

The great historian, Francis Parkman, has painted a reminiscent picture of the arrival of Champlain in 1603: "Like specks on the broad bosom of the waters, two pigmy vessels held their course up the lonely St. Lawrence. They passed abandoned Tadoussac, the channel of Orleans, and the gleaming sheet of Montmorenci [Falls]; they passed the tenantless rock of Quebec, the wide lake of St. Peter and its crowded archipelago, till now the mountain reared before them its round shoulder above the forest plain of Montreal. All was solitude. Hochelaga had vanished; and of the savage population that Cartier had found here 68 years before, no trace remained."

What had happened to the inhabitants of these two greatest cities? Indian legend has it that the Iroquois once dwelt in the lands north of the great river, but were pushed to the southward by advancing Algonquin tribes from the north. Stadacona and Hochelaga were almost certainly Iroquois settlements. Yet in seventy years an enforced shift of population had taken place, and the ground was already being laid for a century and a half of bitter struggle between the tribes of the Iroquois and Algonquin.

In the five years which followed this first voyage, Champlain returned several times to explore the coast of Nova Scotia and New England, and in company with his patron, the Sieur de Monts, to attempt unsuccessfully the settlement of Acadia. On the latter expedition de Monts, a Protestant, had taken both a Catholic priest and a Huegenot minister. The two entered into increasingly

bitter discussion, until the tolerant Champlain wrote in his journal: "I have seen our curé and the minister fall to with their fists on questions of faith—I leave it to you to judge whether it was a pleasant thing to see." By a strange coincidence both died shortly after the expedition struck land, and the relieved sailors buried them in a common grave to see if, in death at least, they might not lie peacefully together.

The incident was an evil portent for the future. Within a generation Jesuit priests were inciting bloody Indian raids against the heretic New Englanders, and Puritan preachers in turn blessed and sometimes accompanied expeditions of revenge against the Canadian settlements. Men combined religious hatred and intolerance with national rivalries to blaze bloodstained trails across the peaceful Green Mountains which lay between them.

In 1608 Champlain returned to the Valley of the St. Lawrence, founding on the rocky heights of Stadacona the citadel of Quebec. The following year he determined to pursue the course of the St. Lawrence further, and if possible, to see with his own eyes the great and beautiful lake which his Indian neighbors had described to him. In the late spring of 1609 he agreed to accompany an Algonquin war party on an expedition against the ancient enemy, now located somewhere to the south of this mighty lake. They paddled up the St. Lawrence until, on the left bank, they came to the mouth of a river of considerable size. Already fear of the terrible Iroquois began to take hold of the redskins, and three quarters of the party turned back. After a difficult passage of the rapids at Chambly, where the explorer sent back all but two of his white companions, the little party burst forth on the

Champlain was born about 1567 at Brouage, France, son of a Naval Captain, and served in the Army and Navy of Henry of Navarre.

placid waters of a great lake, which stretched southward far beyond sight. Let Parkman again draw the picture: Left and right stretched walls of verdure, fresh with the life of June. Encamped on the lake shore, he saw "the vanished sun behind the western mountains, darkly piled in mist and shadow along the sky; near at hand the dead pine, mighty in decay, stretching its ragged arms athwart the burning heaven. . . ."

Then, the next day, as they glided smoothly down the lake, to which Champlain was to give his own name, he saw looming up, now to the east, a chain of green-clad mountains, the highest peak of which (Mansfield) he thought to be capped with snow. During succeeding weeks he wandered along the shores of this primeval wilderness. In this year—when most of the British colonies were yet to be discovered, and while the struggling colony of Jamestown fought for a second breath,—in this year, a Frenchman discovered Vermont.

Eventually, as the Algonquins and their three white companions, proceeded down the lake, they happened upon a large war party of Iroquois. Hurling insults across the water, the redskins made careful arrangements for a battle on the morrow. Champlain and his men had kept carefully out of sight, and when, at daybreak, the opposing forces approached each other in careful formation, the whites were still artfully concealed among surrounding redmen. At a signal the ranks broke apart, and there stood revealed to the astonished Iroquois a strange white god, dressed in shining raiment. He pointed at them a strange stick, from whose end came thunder and lightning. Immediately two chiefs, though clad in arrow-proof cotton and wooden armor, fell dead. The startled warriors released a barrage of arrows, but as thunder belched again from the forest to their side, they broke and ran, pursued by shrieking and delighted Algonquins, who took many prisoners. One of these they tortured mercilessly, until the disgusted Frenchman was granted the "privilege" of putting him out of his misery.

The warriors of the Long House never forgave the French the shame of that day. Yet historians who attribute to Champlain's act the blame for a century and a half of bloody warfare and massacre, conveniently overlook the generations of enmity between Iroquois and Algonquin as well as the age-old rivalries of France and Britain. It was inevitable that the French should ally themselves with the people among whom they had to live, and, in the end, defend them against the raids of their enemy. And already new allies were in the offing for the Long House. As Champlain withdrew from the lake—to which he never returned—a Dutch navigator named Hendrick Hudson sailed up the river which now bears his name—just across a narrow bridge of land from the southern end of Lake Champlain. Across these few miles were later fought the bitter battles of a century of

FATHER ISAAC JOGUES, in the course of his visitations to the Iroquois—who eventually murdered him—discovered the beautiful body of water which he named Lac St. Sacrement (now Lake George). On its shores there now stands a fitting memorial to this humble priest.

conflict between French power from the North, and Dutch and English settlements pressing up from the South.

FATHER JOGUES AND THE MEN IN BLACK

Following the explorers and the trappers—and often even preceding them into the new West of the Great Lakes—came the black-robed missionaries of the Catholic Church, the Jesuits. It has been said of the English settlers of New England that they "fell first upon their knees, and then upon the Indians." Unlike the Puritans who came to save their own souls, the Jesuits came to save the souls of others—the heathen savage. With selfless sacrifice, unswerving devotion to duty, and a violent if sometimes misguided patriotism, these men set out into the wilderness in service of God and Country.

One of the greatest of these was Father Isaac Jogues. In the summer of 1642 he returned from distant missions among the Hurons, accompanied by two lay brothers and a considerable number of Christian Indians. Ambushed by a group of Mohawks, the missionary—fleet of foot as any redskin—escaped, only to return in remorse to join his captive converts in their suffering. And great suffering it was, for the gentle Father ran the gantlet and suffered the abominable tortures of the Iroquois number-

Herman Moll's Map of 1720 (northeast section) emphasizes the extent of early knowledge about both New England and New France, but ignorance of the lands between.

CROWN POINT. *Near its southern end Lake Champlain ...urs through a narrow throat, where a peninsular finger ...ints northward. Some historians believe Champlain fought ...s battle with the Iroquois here; others place it at Ticonderoga. ...ver a hundred years later the French built on one side a fort ...t. Frederic) to command the lake, and on the Vermont side ...very considerable settlement at Chimney Point (center). Crossing ...as as easy for their boats as for modern cars on the great ...rown Point Bridge, which now spans the waters.*

...ARDINAL TASCHEREAU, Canada's first cardinal (lower ...t), silhouetted against the spires of Quebec's Cathedral, ...mbolizes the significant role played by the Catholic Church ...the lands claimed by New France.

...AMUEL DE CHAMPLAIN (lower right) is commemorated ...the rocky heights of the city he founded in 1608—Quebec.

Herman Moll's Map of 1720 (northeast section) emphasizes the extent of early knowledge about both New England and New France, but ignorance of the lands between. Note how out of kilter are Lake Champlain— (French controlled)—and Hudson's River—(British controlled). This is one of the earliest maps to show the forts on the Richelieu River (Sorel, Chambly and Ste. Therese) as well as "Fort La Mothe" (Fort Ste. Anne, on Isle La Motte). Note, too, how easy it would seem to the French (and later the English) to push down Lake Champlain and the Hudson River, thus cutting the American Colonies in half. (Author's Collection)

less times before the party finally reached the Mohawk village of Ossernon. For nearly a year Father Jogues lived as a slave, baptizing captives in their agony and even secretly converting many of his captors, bearing torture and indignities with a never failing humility. It was only when news came that his death was finally decided upon that he suffered himself, a maimed and tattered figure, to be rescued by the Dutch at Fort Orange (later Albany). He was sent by them to Europe and freedom, but returned again to New France and his ultimate martyrdom in 1646. A temporary but uncertain peace had been established between the warring reds, and the indomitable Father went back to Ossernon, to establish there a mission among his enemies. During an absence, however, plague struck the village, which the ignorant redmen blamed on the new God and his earthly disciple. The black-robed priest was again made captive, with his assistant Jean Lalande. His captivity and suffering were briefer this time, for he died from the blow of a war club as he went to plead the cause of his faith with the chief. Lalande was killed the next day, and the skulls mounted on pickets at the village wall. Thus perished a contrite and selfless man of God—a humble hero of stature far greater than the conquerors of martial legend.

It has been hard for history to judge the Jesuits; many in frontier missions mixed religious fervor with patriotism, sending their red Roman converts to prey upon the heretic Englishmen of New England. In bitter anger, the settlers organized an expedition against one of these missions, Norridgewok in Maine, whence had come a series of bloody raids for years past. They slew not only every Indian on whom they could lay hands, but also Father Râle, whom they deeply detested as the torch behind the flame which seared their settlements. Yet anyone reading the quiet autobiographical letter which Râle wrote earlier to his "brother," finds it hard to discover—despite his fervent patriotism—the bloody butcher the New Englanders believed him to be.

THE FORTS AND THE INDIAN WARS

As far back as the middle of the fifteenth century, under the leadership of the great chieftan Hiawatha, the retreating Iroquois tribes had formed themselves into a great confederacy of the "five nations": the Senecas, the Onondagas, the Cayugas, the Oneidas, and—nearest the whites, both French and English—the Mohawks. This league came to be known—and feared—as the "Long House." Gaining strength from their unity, the Iroquois began to strike back at their old enemies, the Algonquins, just as the French began to settle among the latter tribes, in the valley of the St. Lawrence. It was the white man's fate to share the fury of the vengeful invader with his red neighbors, and the settlements along the upper river dwelt in daily fear of the warriors of the Long House, whose canoes might appear stealthily from the mouth of the Richelieu River at any time. It was to block these raids from down Lake Champlain that the French began the construction of a series of forts along the river. Fort Richelieu, built at the river's mouth in 1642, was rebuilt

(Continued on page 24)

On the following page: FORT TICONDEROGA →

in 1665 along with two additional forts—Chambly and Ste. Therese which were raised further on down. In the summer of 1666, the Governor ordered Captain Pierre La Motte to the island which now bears his name, to build there the first outpost on the lake itself—and incidentally to establish the first white settlement in Vermont. Although a large log bastion and a chapel were raised at this Fort St. Anne, its life was short. The French themselves destroyed it within ten years.

In addition to the defence provided by the forts, the Governor determined to carry the Fleur de Lis deep into Iroquois land to awe the enemy into sueing for peace. Several expeditions were only partly successful, and Mohawk retaliation brought the utter destruction of Lachine, only a few miles from Montreal.

By 1689 the French and British nations collided in the beginning of what was to be a century of wars of empire. Into all of these the people of New France and New England were drawn, until finally the colonials themselves continued to fight across ill defined frontiers, even as the mother countries maintained a suspicious peace. During all this period the blue waters of Champlain were stained with pools of red as rampaging Indians from one side or the other proceeded up or down the Lake with stumbling processions of weary captives. The Indians became both a bone of contention and a weapon of warfare between rival empires. Each struggled to divert the allegiance of the other's red allies, and used its own to unloose bitter bloody raids against the frontier settlements. One matched the other in atrocities, though the French excelled in ability to adapt themselves to and actually participate in Indian warfare. Yet it is significant that the first New England newspaper *Public Occurrences*,

was suppressed after one issue, because of its vigorous charges of English mistreatment of the Indians.

Extreme losses by the Iroquois in their struggles during the years 1689–1697 lessened their interest in fighting England's colonial wars for her. Thus, when war broke out again in 1702, the wily French took care to provoke the Long House as little as possible, directing their raids against the New England frontier. Then the great tide of warfare turned across Vermont, for the ancient trails from the St. Lawrence Valley to the rocky lands of New England lay across the Green Mountains.

At this time the tiny settlement of Deerfield marked the northernmost extent of Massachusetts settlement. It was upon this unsuspecting village that a band of painted savages descended in the snows of February 1704. At the end of a night of horror, 47 lay dead, and 120 more began a weary trek into captivity. Among them was the Reverend John Williams—a devoted but exacting minister to his flock—and his wife and son. The good reverend published later a narrative of his painful trip through the Green Mountains north into Canada, in which he was forced to record the murder of his wife before his eyes, as well as the alienation of his son. The latter refused later to return to the land of the white man.

Deerfield was only the first of a series of frontier massacres, and men's spines chilled at the sudden piercing screeches of painted devils as reddened tomahawks rose and fell along the length of a weak and unprotected frontier. The English in turn undertook occasional expeditions of revenge, which normally pursued the retreating Indians across Vermont only to lose them along the shores of the "Great" Lake. One furious raid, directed against the Algonquin settlement of Norridgewok, ended in the

Vermont Historical Society

The weary trek of captives across the Green Mountains to French Canada produced many printed "captivities." One of the most famous of these was Mrs. Johnson's. This lady was delivered of a baby—appropriately called "Captive Johnson"—in the wilderness of Cavendish, Vermont, where now stand two ancient stones marking the site.

JEFFREY, LORD AMHERST *By Thomas Gainsborough*

Hertel de Rouville assembles his party of French and Indians for a raid on unsuspecting Deerfield. (Courtesy National Life Ins. Co.)

massacre of most of its inhabitants as well as its presiding genius, the Jesuit Father Râle.

The New Englanders in desperation began building forts to stop the savage attacks before they reached the settlements. Fort Massachusetts was built near present-day Williamstown, and Fort Dummer, on the west shore of the Connecticut River north of Deerfield, was erected in 1741 on ground which was later to be Vermont. Even more important to the early settlers of the upper Connecticut was Fort Number Four (Charlestown, N. H.), farther up the east shore. It was this fort which Lord Amherst selected for the eastern terminus of his Military road across the Mountains in 1759.

In the meantime, the French themselves endeavored to strengthen their hold upon the lake which was their principal pathway to the enemy. In 1731 they erected at the narrows of Lake Champlain a stockade fort which they named Fort St. Frederic,* to act as a base for raids to the east and south. It quickly became an annoying thorn in the side of the English, and a principal objective of their military policy. Expeditions launched against New France were usually three pronged—the first against Louisbourg in Acadia, the second against Quebec, and the third up Lake Champlain toward Montreal. Throughout the first half of the century the British and their colonial allies had varying degrees of success in the first objective, but never penetrated the St. Lawrence Valley either from its mouth or from Lake Champlain. The latter expeditions, afflicted with disease and desertion, usually stalled in indecision at Albany, or, at best, at the southern end of Lake George.

As the last of the colonial wars began in 1755, how-

* The English, as we shall see, captured and re-named it Crown Point.

ever, the French determined to split the colonies in two by a bold and decisive stroke down the Hudson. Troops under Baron Dieskau proceeded southward from Fort St. Frederick to meet, at the tip of Lake George, the assembled British and colonial forces under the leadership of that amazing and talented friend of the Long House, Sir William Johnson. In the battle which followed, both generals fell wounded, but the French retired with heavy losses, leaving their leader a captive. Johnson was either unable or unwilling to follow, and the vanquished enemy found unchallenged sanctuary again behind the palisades of St. Frederic.

For nearly two years parties of "hair-dressers"—as the scalping savages were known—ravaged the frontier, while a tireless and ruthless scout named Robert Rogers directed lightning raids upon the French posts. Then there appeared on the scene a military leader of unusual talent and surpassing qualities of character. The Marquis de Montcalm took charge of the French forces on Lake Champlain, and in 1757 unleashed a new assault against the English, now barricaded in their own Fort William Henry. Its commander, Lt-Colonel Munro, denied aid by his superior, General Webb—who sat trembling at Fort Edward—surrendered the fort after a gallant defense which brought its walls tumbling under the impact of French cannon. Montcalm's terms were generous, but as the beaten redcoats marched from the fort, the French lost control of their Indian allies. Bursting into the fort they tomahawked the wounded, and then harried the weary column despite French efforts to hold them back. Scores were massacred, and scores more carried off to the torture. The shocked Montcalm was able to force the return of some of these prisoners, but not all.*

The British fortunes of war were rapidly reaching a new low when the kingdom produced its own leader in the great William Pitt. He promptly put General Jeffrey Amherst in command of British colonial forces. This deliberate but competent soldier undertook a successful

* The defense and loss of Ft. William Henry provides the plot of James Fenimore Cooper's famous *Last of the Mohicans.*

Model of Fort St. Frederic, at Crown Point. By A. S. Hopkins

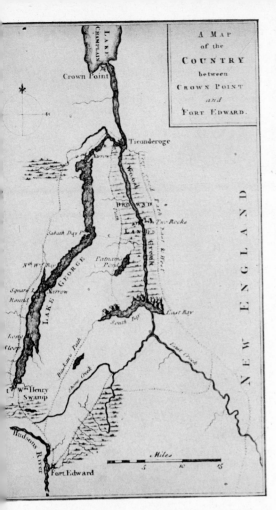

MAPS *contemporary with the French and Indian Wars show in detail the lands involved. On the detail map to the left, note the relationship of Lake Champlain and its French forts to the English controlled Hudson River, with the connecting roads and portages. On the map of New York, (above) the relationship is on a larger scale.*

Note now Fort Dummer, on the Connecticut River, in a land which is labeled "P(art) of New Hampshire." None of this territory is crossed by the roads or trading paths shown in the territory to the west of it. The presence of Fort St. Frederick, in a special inset, indicated its importance to the entire territory covered by this map. (Author's Collection)

campaign against the great fort of Louisbourg, but failed to remove from command the doddering General Abercrombie, in charge now of the forces north of Albany. The English were determined to pursue the old plan of a pincer movement against Quebec, one arm from Louisbourg and the mouth of the St. Lawrence, and the other from Lake Champlain and Montreal.

In 1758 Abercrombie began the movement northward. However, in the years since the defeat of Dieskau, the French had made good use of their time. Montcalm, selecting the strategic point where Lake George empties into Lake Champlain, had erected three years earlier an imposing fort which he named Carillon. Thus, before the British could get at Fort St. Frederic, they had to take the new fort. Undermanned, it looked like an easy conquest for the numerous British and colonials.

English hopes ran high, for second in command to Abercrombie—who was scornfully nicknamed Aunt Nabie-Crombie—was the beloved young Lord Howe,† who was able to claim the devoted allegiance of regular and colonial alike.

Though untrained in frontier fighting, he was willing to learn, and forced the hide-bound regulars to adapt their

† Brother to the Lords Howe who led the British army and navy in the Revolution twenty years later

continental tactics to the New World. But disaster struck the British cause when Howe fell mortally wounded in an ambush, as the opposing forces groped for position before the fort.

Montcalm had furiously slashed the surrounding forest, erecting a formidable "abatis" around the fort itself and leaving the rest of the fallen trees in an almost impenetrable jungle about the neighborhood. There were means of out-flanking the French position, and Montcalm hesitated to attempt to defend it. But the bumbling Abercrombie determined on a frontal attack, and wave upon wave of gallant redcoats dashed themselves against the French cannon, to no avail. Suddenly dismayed at the enormity of his blunder the British General took flight, and his puzzled men, still outnumbering the French even after frightful casualties, followed his flapping coat-tails southward.

Montcalm's position was precarious none the less, and he dared not pursue the English to the south. Indeed, the following year, faced by the careful and deliberate Amherst himself, he ordered the evacuation and destruction first of Fort Carillon, and then of St. Frederic, withdrawing his forces to Isle aux Noix at the northern exit from Lake Champlain. He himself was now in Quebec, where he was to fall victim to the assault of General Wolfe, Am-

Painting by H. A. OGDEN
Courtesy Fort Ticonderoga Museum

MONTCALM CONGRATULATES HIS TROOPS AFTER THE DEFEAT OF THE BRITISH AT TICONDEROGA, 1758.

UNITS OF THE FRENCH ARMY AT TICONDEROGA, 1758.

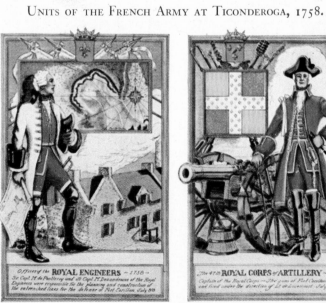

Courtesy Fort Ticonderoga Museum

herst's valiant and youthful deputy, who also perished in the moment of British triumph.

The retiring French regiments were accompanied by a not inconsiderable number of settlers who had settled along the shores of Lake Champlain. They left behind them only a forest of blackened chimneys on the Vermont shore across from razed Fort St. Frederic, and this spot has ever since been known as Chimney Point. There had been other settlements, none large, of varying size and duration. Great seignories—manors in feudal style—had been granted to prominent Frenchmen, many of whom made determined efforts to settle their domain. But all collapsed with the withdrawal of French power from the lakes.

Amherst proceeded to rename and rebuild Carillon as Ticonderoga, and St. Frederic as Crown Point. At the latter spot he abandoned the lake-shore site, and commenced the erection of a massive stone fort back from it. At the same time he ordered the construction of a military road across the Green Mountains to Fort Number Four, on the Connecticut River, which was to become famous as the Crown Point Road.

In the meantime, the General dispatched Robert Rogers and his tough, woods-wise Rangers against the Indian village of St. Francis, whence had gathered most of the remnants of tribes driven from their New England homes by the land-hungry Yankees. Bearing no love for the latter, these Indians became willing instruments of the French policy of frontier raids. Many of the captives dragged across the Green Mountain trails had ended up in St. Francis, along with the scalps of their less fortunate comrades.

It was scores of these dried and reddened hanks of hair that Rogers saw flapping from poles among wildly celebrating redskins, as his Rangers ended a grueling march through the half-drowned lands north of Missiquoi Bay. There was no return for them now, for their boats had been taken by pursuing Frenchmen.

As the last celebrant sank into drunken stupor at dawn, the Rangers descended upon the village, hacking and killing, until virtually the entire population lay massacred at their feet and the waters of the St. Francis River ran scarlet with blood of butchered redmen.

Taking with him a few white captives, Rogers beat a hasty retreat down the river in the direction of Lake Memphremagog, harried by a vengeful pursuit. Food gave out, and many of the hardy Rangers perished by starvation, as well as by the tomahawk. Only a pitiful handful of the original force eventually reached Fort Number Four on the Connecticut River. But this exploit has become legend, and its leader the hero of the rousing historical saga *Northwest Passage* which, in book form and on the screen, has been read and seen by millions.

Amherst moved slowly, but the following year Mon-

treal, the last stronghold of New France, fell to the triumphant British. While peace between the two nations did not come until 1763, the year 1760 marks the end of the French regime in Canada. By the Treaty of Paris all of Canada passed under the English Flag, and New England rejoiced at a permanent end to the bitter warfare with French and Indians.

Moreover, in 1763 that indefinite but blood-soaked border between New France and New England was wiped out, and the land of the Green Mountains passed under the undisputed sway of the Englishman. A new frontier was now open to the surge of restless Yankees, many of whom had crossed this verdant landscape, some as captives, some as soldiers, some as wandering hunters and trappers. Now, one and all, they sought homes in this new and promised land.

Robert Rogers, tireless scout and Indian fighter, drawn by a contemporary. A puzzle to his contemporaries and to historians as well, Rogers was a scourge to French and Indian alike, a trial to his hidebound British superiors, and a hero to his rangers. Yet in 1775 he turned his back on these men and led a Tory regiment against the revolting colonists. (Courtesy Fort Ticonderoga Museum)

TICONDEROGA

A uniformed soldier stands guard over the battlements of Ticonderoga, while within the fort men gamble and women spin. The collections of the Museum boast costumes enough to clothe the actors for a vast pageant of Ticonderoga's history. (Kleffel)

THE PAVILION was the elaborate home built by William Ferris Pell in 1826 on the shores of Lake Champlain, in the very shadow of the ruins of old Fort Ticonderoga. Thirteen years later when his son Archibald was killed in the explosion of a rusty cannon, he lost interest in the restoration and the Pavilion was leased as a hotel. It became a popular stop on the fashionable "Northern Tour." It is today again the home of the Pells.

THE GARDEN OF THE KING (Jardin du Roi) was laid out by French officers in 1756, even as the fort was under construction. Maintained by William Pell, neglected when the Pavilion served as a hotel, it now blooms again as of old, to the delight of thousands of present-day visitors.

(Kleffel)

III

NEW ENGLAND FRONTIER

How the frontier of Northern New England lapped over into the land of the Green Mountains, and how Governor Benning Wentworth laid out the Hampshire Grants.

L ED by black robed priests, hardy explorers, and restless "coureurs du bois,"[1] the French pushed their frontier forward, down the St. Lawrence, through the Great Lakes and into the vast valleys of the Ohio and Mississippi Rivers. They poked an exploratory finger down Lake Champlain, around whose shores they even set off great grants of land. But too many Frenchmen were trappers, rather than farmers, and only a few hopeful settlements ever took root.

It was different with the English. They too were extending a frontier westward, but it was an agricultural frontier. True, they also sought furs from the redman, but it was land—the Indians' land—they wanted most: soil in which to plant crops and establish a home.

These hardy yeomen had barely arrived in the seacoast regions around Boston and Plymouth, before they began to move out into the wilderness. As early as 1635 they pressed their frontier far to the west, into the fertile lands along the Connecticut River at Hartford, Windsor, and Wethersfield, Connecticut. Wasting no time, they began pushing northward up the river, settling, successively, the Massachusetts towns of Springfield, Hadley, Hatfield, Northampton, Deerfield, and finally Squakheag (Northfield) in 1673. But these most advanced towns suffered severely from Indian raids, such as the attack on Deerfield in 1704.

Finally, late in 1724, the General Court of Massachusetts took note of the unhappy plight of its frontier towns and resolved "to build a block-house above Northfield, in the most convenient place on the lands called the Equivalent Lands, and to post in it 40 able men, English and western [friendly] Indians, to be employed in scouting a good distance up Connecticut River, West River, Otter Creek, and sometime eastwardly above Great Monadnock, for the discovery of the enemy coming towards any of the frontier towns . . . ."

The so-called "Equivalent Lands" were one of the results of His Majesty's vagueness in laying out the bounds of his American colonies. When finally the boundary between Connecticut and Massachusetts was settled in 1713, it was discovered that the latter had made many grants of land in what was now declared to be Connecticut. As a compensation, Massachusetts set aside several parcels of land as an "equivalent," which were then sold at auction by Connecticut. One of these was on the west bank of the river above Northfield, and included approximately the present-day towns of Brattleborough, Putney and Dummerston.[2]

It was near the southern boundary of these lands that Lt. Timothy Dwight of Northampton erected the hewn pine walls of Fort Dummer in 1724. Under cover of this protection and despite frequent Indian raids, settlement began to move northward again. By 1738 "Forts" Bridgeman and Sartwell had been erected just south of Dummer, and in 1743 Reverend Hinsdell, Chaplain at Ft. Dummer, built a stockade across the river. These were not really major defense points like Dummer, but fortified "garrison" houses—settlers' homes built strongly to resist the whirlwind of Indian attack. This they did not always do successfully; Fort Bridgeman was burned in 1747 and its inhabitants massacred or carried off captive to Canada.

However, the main fury of "King George's War" from 1744 to 1748 fell upon a new fort, built further up the Connecticut in 1740. This was named "Number 4" for the town[3] in which it was located. In 1747, under the command of the courageous Captain Phineas Stevens, this stout little pioneer stockade held off a major assault on the frontier by several hundred French and Indians, under General Debeline.

For some time, there was reason to believe that both Fort Dummer and Fort Number Four might be abandoned. The former had been built by Massachusetts as one of a chain of large and small forts along its northwestern frontier. But the boundary of his Majesty's colony of Massachusetts was no more definite on the north than it

---

[1] Literally "rovers of the woods": they were hunters and trappers who lived with and like the Indians and had little taste for the "civilization" of Montreal or Quebec.

[2] The sale fell to four Massachusetts men: Lt. Gov. William Dummer, William Brattle of Cambridge, and Anthony Stoddard and John White of Boston. The money from the sale was turned over to the infant Yale College.

[3] In January 1736 Massachusetts had laid out and "numbered" six towns on both sides of the River. On the west side Number 1 later became Westminster and Number 2, Rockingham; on the east side Numbers 1, 2, and 3 became Chesterfield, Westmoreland, Walpole and "Number 4," the most important, was named Charlestown. See the map: "Frontier of Northwestern New England."

FORT DUMMER

FORT DUMMER, *first permanent settlement of the English in what is now Vermont, was begun in 1724 by Lt. Timothy Dwight as a scouting outpost and defense against Canadian Indians. Yellow pine logs were laid one on top of another 180 feet on each side, locking at the angles. The wall of the fort served as the rear wall for shed-like houses inside. Its site, just south of Brattleboro, is now flooded by the waters of Vernon Dam. The drawing to the right is from one made in 1747.*

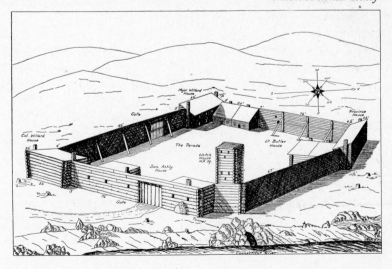

Nov. 29 AD 1564

This is the solemn day I must now die. This is the 90th day since we left the ship. All have perished and on the banks of this river I die too. Farewell; may future posterity know our end. John Graye

VERMONT DISCOVERED BEFORE CHAMPLAIN? This is a copy of a document dug up in a lead tube along the banks of the Missisquoi River in 1853. Extensive researches at the time convinced contemporaries of its authenticity, but the original document has disappeared. It is known that early English sea captains put sailors ashore to explore, and did not always pick them up again. Did a party wander all the way across New England—and Vermont—to the Missisquoi River, in 1564? (Vermont Historical Society)

had been on the south. In 1741 a line was finally run which, to the dismay of Massachusetts, gave its neighbor New Hampshire far more even than she had claimed. The line not only left the newly chartered "Number" towns outside of Massachusetts, but even sliced off the top part of ancient Northfield. Fort Dummer and all the Equivalent Lands were now discovered to be outside their parent colony.

Immediately the Massachusetts Legislature addressed itself to New Hampshire, suggesting that the latter should take over the maintenance of the Fort. Despite the urging of Governor Benning Wentworth and an order from the King himself in 1744, the New Hampshire legislature refused to take action. Fort Dummer was too distant from any Hampshire settlement, they said, and besides, if any protection were needed, it could be given by Fort Number Four.

But Dummer was still protector to the Massachusetts settlements, even though it was now over the boundary line, and the Bay State continued to garrison it out of necessity rather than choice. In fact, despite New Hampshire's reference to Number Four, Massachusetts bore the main responsibility for sustaining that outpost also.

Even before this spell of fighting, the grantees of "Number One" (West) gathered at Taunton, Mass. to prepare for settlement of their lands.[4] The earliest settlers retreated before the threat of bloody tomahawks, but

during the temporary peace, 1748–1754, pioneers began moving again into the lands of the upper Connecticut.

However, in 1754 young George Washington threw down a challenge to the French on the western frontiers of Virginia and Pennsylvania, and with the crushing defeat of Britain's stubborn General Braddock, the colonies settled down to war again in earnest, this time two years before the never ending dynastic struggle re-opened in Europe.

On the northern frontier of New England, colonization of new lands came to a stop. The settlers from Northfield who had rebuilt Westminster (Number One) in 1751, fled to Walpole across the river. Those around the forts in Hinsdale, Brattleborough and Putney, retired behind the stockades and some left, yet in 1755 there were still enough people in Putney, Westminster and Westmoreland to unite in building a considerable fort on the Great Meadows in Putney.

Under the protection of Fort Number Four, settlers hung on in Charlestown, and the pioneers of Dummerston, Springfield, Putney and Westmoreland managed to stay with their lands now as they had during the previous wars. Many settlements were harried by unexpected and bloody raids by the Canadian Indians, and it was not until the fall of Canada in 1760 that the great migration northward really began.

After the definition of the Massachusetts—New Hampshire boundary in 1740, grantees and settlers of the areas to the north began to worry about the title to their lands. Few were actually living on them, but all wished to be confirmed in their ownership. Some succeeded; others did not. In 1752–53 Governor Benning Wentworth issued charters for towns Number 1, 2, 3, and 4 as Chesterfield, Westmoreland, Walpole and Charlestown, and numbers 1 and 2 on the opposite side as Westminster and Rockingham. He also re-chartered the "Equivalent Lands" to most of their previous owners as the towns of Brattleborough, Fulham (Dummerston) and Putney, adding several new proprietors at the same time.

The same year the lands on both sides of the river which had been sliced off Northfield, Mass. by the new boundary, were granted as Hinsdale.[5]

But these were not the first grants of land made by Governor of New Hampshire. In January of 1750[6] he issued a patent to Colonel William Williams, Samuel Robinson and others for the town of Bennington, way across the Green Mountains. And thereby hangs a tale of great complications and much dispute, which runs constantly through the course of our narrative until Vermont's admission to the Union in 1791.

---

[4] The new town was thus first called New Taunton, but when rechartered by New Hampshire in 1752 was named Westminster.

[5] After the New Hampshire Grants became the separate state of Vermont (but not until 1802) the western part of "Hinsdale" was re-named Vernon.

[6] 1749, old style calendar.

INDIAN ATTACKS were a constant threat to the early settlers of the Upper Connecticut. John Kilburn, first settler of Walpole, N. H., in 1755 stood off several hundred from his log cabin, almost single-handed.

GOVERNOR BENNING WENTWORTH AND HIS NEW HAMPSHIRE GRANTS

His excellency, Benning Wentworth, Governor of New Hampshire, was relatively new at his job. The province had only been set off, with its own Governor, in 1741, though his father had served as Lieutenant-Governor for New Hampshire under the Governor of Massachusetts. Benning Wentworth was not an English lord appointed to the job from across the seas, as were most of the royal governors. He was a shrewd Portsmouth business man, who carried his appreciation of the value of smart dealing into the Governor's chair.

Now, the whole interior of New England had been settled under a system whereby the legislature issued grants of land to "proprietors" who wished to go out into the wilderness and make their homes, plowing the land to make farms and erecting their schools and churches. These communities were run by their settler-proprietors in town meeting.

But as New England grew in prosperity and numbers, men of wealth began to look about for a place to invest their savings – their "capital." Opportunities such as now exist were few and far between, and the mother country forbade the establishment of manufacturing in the colonies for fear of competition. Thus investment in land seemed the most available outlet for these growing funds. Groups of men began to apply for charters, though they had no intention of actually settling. Rather they "speculated" that as the settled frontier moved westward, these wild lands would increase in value, producing for them a neat profit. Many did not even wait – having obtained their lands for no cost other than the labor of applying for it plus fees to the officials. They offered their rights in the public market, and sold them to hardy souls who *would* be willing to settle and till the land.

Governor Benning Wentworth, like many another, saw the possibilities in land speculation. He was himself in a particularly favorable position, for like the other governors, he was the King's designated agent for the distribution of crown lands. Of course, the King had emphasized that grants should be made only to people ready to colonize and thus extend his Majesty's dominions. But who would check up on that?

Certainly there were vast, unsettled lands between the capitol at Portsmouth and the Connecticut River. But there were more on the other side of the river. To whom did these belong? To the King, of course. But any distribution of them would be made by the King's agent— the royal governor. And which governor had jurisdiction over the Green Mountains? New Hampshire—or New York?

In 1664 King Charles II had granted all the land between the Delaware River and "Connecticut" (at that time rather vaguely defined) to his brother James, Duke of York (later King) to be known as New York, confirming it in 1674 as extending to the Connecticut *River*. Subsequent to this, Connecticut had succeeded in establishing its western boundary on a line 20 miles east of the Hudson River, and Massachusetts later did the same. But what about the territory north of Massachusetts? Had the King extended New Hampshire to the same 20 mile line when, in 1741, he ran her boundary with Massachusetts until "it meets with our other governments?" It seemed so, since he had ordered New Hampshire to maintain Fort Dummer, which was definitely *west* of the River. Many maps showed New Hampshire stretching westward; others extended New York around the top of Massachusetts all the way to the upper Connecticut. And the authorities in London were so vague about American geography, that few had any idea that there was a conflict in the King's grants and orders.

Wentworth, with his eye on the nice fees and profits which were in prospect, decided to stake a claim to these lands across the River, and in granting Bennington he went all the way to the 20 mile line to do it.[7] During the

---

7 Actually the grant overlapped the line into undisputed New York territory.

HAMPSHIRE GRANTS LANDS were peddled widely by speculators. Many a doubtful title changed hands over a tavern table.

HIS EXCELLENCY, BEN-
NING WENTWORTH,
GOVERNOR OF NEW
HAMPSHIRE (1741-1766),
business man turned politician,
laid out most of the internal
boundaries of Vermont by a
series of land grants in the years
1750-54 and 1760-65. Interested largely for speculative
reasons himself, he often did
not await the usual petitions
from groups desiring land
either for settlement or speculation. He made up his own lists,
conveying land in great grants
upon distinguished friends and
contemporaries who might be of
assistance to his political ambitions. Even the normally dull
sensibilities of the British
authorities were shocked by his
"land-office" business, but he
was permitted to resign in 1766,
and his nephew John Went-
worth, took his place. As his
portrait reveals, Benning was a
pompous, voluminous, gout-
ridden man, blandly crafty, but
perhaps not more so than many
of his contemporaries, to whom
public office was often an invitation to public plunder.

The portrait is a copy of a
lost original, and now hangs in
the State House at Concord,
New Hampshire.

succeeding four years he issued ten new grants[8] – in addition to re-chartering the Massachusetts towns – all *east* of the mountains but still *west* of the River.[9]

However, the Governor was not satisfied with the fees which he got from issuing the grants. He also reserved for himself 500 acres in each town and usually located them in the corner so that the plots in four adjoining towns (they were usually six miles square) would combine to give him one large unit of 2000 acres.[10] He also thoughtfully reserved a plot for the Society for the Propagation of the Gospel in Foreign Parts (a very influential group in England), one for the first settled minister, and one for the Church of England.[11] After 1760 he also reserved one for a school. The Charter stated that every grantee must within five years, plant and cultivate five acres of land for every fifty he received, and continue to do so, or forfeit his share.[12] The Governor must have winked at his faithful Secretary (and brother-in-law), Theodore Atkinson, as he wrote into these grants not only the latter's name, but nearly every Wentworth in the vicinity, assorted other relatives, members of the Council, and other influential persons whose favor would be useful. It was perfectly obvious that none of these worthies intended to turn over a single clod of earth; nor, in fact, did most of the businessmen-speculators who petitioned for the grants. Almost none of the people who appear in the lists attached to these charters ever turned up as settlers in the New Hampshire Grants.

In 1750, when Benning created Bennington, only five years had elapsed since the King had instructed New Hampshire to maintain Fort Dummer as having been brought within its limits. Yet the Governor evidently knew of the great grant to James, Duke of York in 1664 and 1674, and had some doubts about the extent of his jurisdiction. So he took pen in hand and inquired of Governor Clinton of New York as to just what he considered his eastern boundary to be. Clinton, supported by his Council, declared that of course that boundary lay on the Connecticut River as originally granted. And in a second letter, he asserted that Connecticut's extension to the 20 mile line was the result of an agreement between them, confirmed by the King, and that Massachusetts' similar westward reach was quite illegal. (There having been for some time very extensive settlements in that colony west of the Connecticut, one can reasonably

wonder why New York had not resisted, or at least objected to such an invasion of its territory.)

But Wentworth was impatient to be about the business of making grants, and did not wait out the slow mails and the slower processes of government in New York. Shortly after first writing Clinton, he issued the charter for Bennington. Clinton demanded its recall, but Governor Benning refused. He suggested that they submit the matter to the King for decision, and agreed to an exchange of copies of each other's arguments. Wentworth did not send Clinton a copy of his, however, and increased rather than decreased the rate at which he issued new grants, until the war in 1754 ended the speculators' interest in frontier lands for the time being.

The interest aroused in many who had crossed and recrossed the Green Mountains during the French and Indian Wars that ended in 1760, came to a head in the latter year. Governor Wentworth was again besieged by requests for grants. The request for a boundary decision by the King had been lost in the shuffle during the hurly-burly of waging a war. The Governor therefore decided to get on with the profitable business of land grants. He wasted neither time nor energy. In the single year 1761 he issued 60 grants, and rolled up a grand total of 131 townships by the time the King finally decided the dispute in favor of New York in July of 1764.[13] Thus, far in advance of actual settlement, the land which was to become Vermont was well laid out as to its towns and internal boundaries.

Wentworth's activity in the years 1760-1764 had not gone unopposed. The Governors of New York, including the learned Lieutenant (often Acting) Governor Cadwallader Colden, kept up a running fire of protest which struck home in London. Other complaints as to Wentworth's fees, speculations and grants to friends and relatives did not strengthen his position. Furthermore the Governor of New York hinted that it would not be well to strengthen the democratic trend involved in government by town meeting[14] as set up in the Wentworth grants in the face of the increasing restlessness among the colonials generally. At any rate, the King, advised by his Council and the Board of Trade, declared "the western banks of the river Connecticut . . . *to be* the boundary between the said two provinces of New Hampshire and New York." He did not say, however, that this *had been* the boundary since 1664, or even 1674. Lack of a clear statement on that score caused the New Hampshire grantees to contend immediately that this merely

---

8 Halifax (1750); Marlboro, Wilmington (1751); Newfane, Stamford, Townshend, Woodford (1753), and Chester, Thomlinson (Grafton) and Guilford in 1754. *See map, "Northwestern Frontier."*

9 In this same period he granted a number of towns east of the River and indisputably within New Hampshire's bounds.

10 He probably accumulated nearly 100 thousand acres thereby.

11 This, in Congregational New England! There was only one Episcopal Church in all of New Hampshire.

12 The Charters also reserved to the Crown all pine trees suitable for masts for His Majesty's Navy.

13 The decision was not announced in America until 1765.

14 In New York, lands were mostly held by great landlords who rented them to tenants, with no voice in their own government. The native differences of Yankees and Yorkers, plus their attitudes toward government and landholding, unquestionably played a large role in the strife which followed.

The Crown Point Road from "Number 4" to Crown Pt., completed all the way across the Green Mountains in 1760 at the orders of General Amherst, served as the main highway for inland settlement.

meant that the Connecticut was to be the line from *then on*. If so, only political jurisdiction had shifted to New York (no one denied that—not even Benning Wentworth) and actual *land* titles under New Hampshire grants could still be valid.

THE TIDE OF SETTLEMENT

As we have seen, the decisive victories of Generals Amherst and Wolfe ended the threat of French and Indian raids from Canada in 1760. The old tide of settlement which had so often receded before the red terror rushed up the Connecticut Valley again, but now it was reinforced by those who had soldiered back and forth across the mountains during the colonial wars and who had found this green land much to their liking.

As with all migrations of this sort, we like to ask the questions: When? Why? Where? and How?

Geography determined Vermont's role in the colonial period, and set the date for her settlement. Her rugged mountain backbone was cut through several times by free flowing rivers, with only brief "carrying" spots between. (*See maps*.) These linked the French dominated St. Lawrence and Champlain Valleys with the Connecticut River, up which the New England pioneers were pushing. Across this land, therefore, were waged some of the battles of France and England in the new world. And not

until this struggle was ended in 1760 could pioneers hope for tranquility in this dark and bloody ground.

Secondly, the movement of the more settled New England frontier westward began to catch up with its more venturesome scouts, and the older regions to the south and east had become pretty well filled.

Thirdly, of course, the activity of speculators in lands had produced a series of land grants from the Governor of New Hampshire, and the framework for new towns in this appealing land was ready. The salemanship of these very business men had also succeeded in making many a Connecticut man the owner of a few "rights" in the New Hampshire Grants.

There were many motives which impelled men to take advantage of this favorable situation. The same restless spirit and vigorous independence which had carried the Yankees westward, sent them exploring into the Grants. As always, younger sons in large families, unable to inherit their father's estates, sought fortune—and perhaps fame—on the frontier where every man made his own way.

But most important was the Yankee land hunger. The grass on the other side of the fence always looked greener—and usually was, since it hadn't been turned and in time worn out. Too many of southern New England's farms were rock strewn and hilly, in contrast to the lush inter-vales of the upper Connecticut.

In occasional instances, also, men were still seeking religious freedom—freedom from the stranglehold of New England's established Congregational Church and its pious but tyrannical clergy. Those who came to Bennington from Hardwick, Mass. under the leadership of Samuel Robinson were dissenters who had broken off from the regular congregation there. There were other "New Lights" who were not welcome in their home towns, and even a few "agnostics"—doubters—like Ethan Allen, who needed the wide reaches of the wilderness to formulate their challenge to established religion.

Pioneers usually came alone to clear the land and build a rough cabin, then returned to bring their families by rude dugout or ox-sled in spring, or by sledge in winter. Rivers were the principal highways, even when frozen.

Most of the pioneers came from the
[eas]tern parts of Massachusetts and
[nor]thern Connecticut—places which had
[onl]y just begun to slick down the raw
[edg]es of frontier life. But unlike the
[earl]iest settlers who had moved up from
[the] River towns around Northampton,
[mo]st of these newcomers came from fur-
[the]r south. Those who moved on up both
[sid]es of the Connecticut —from the older
[tow]ns east of Hartford, to settle in the
[Equivalent Lands and the "Number"
[tow]ns, were of a fairly conservative turn
[of] mind.[15] Not so those who pushed up the
[Ho]usatonic River from Salisbury and the
[sur]rounding frontier towns in the more
[eas]terly parts of both states. They came
[out] on the other side of the mountains in
[Be]nnington, and spread up the valley of
[the] Battenkill. There were some who
[rea]ched the same valley from New York
[by] the Hoosic River, but many of these
["N]ew Yorkers" were Yankees who had earlier
[spil]led over New England's rather vague
[we]stern border into the valley of the
[Hu]dson. There were some French who
[dri]fted into the Champlain country, and a
[few] Dutch also, but most of these were
[abs]orbed into the dominant English strain.
[O]ver on the upper reaches of the Con-
[nec]ticut, neighbor to the solid New
[Eng]land communities of Newbury and
[Ha]verhill were Ryegate and Barnet. Both
[the]se towns were bought and colonized
[by] organized companies of Scotsmen, who
[cam]e from across the seas in 1774-1775,
[afte]r sending James Whitelaw and
[Ale]xander Harvey as advance agents to
[fin]d them fertile land on which to settle.
[But most of the new settlers were good
[Co]nnecticut people, with a heavy season-
[ing] of Massachusetts men and even an
[occ]asional Rhode Islander or Hampshire-
[ma]n. In the earlier communities along the
[Co]nnecticut a large proportion of the
[po]pulation had come from a single town
[in] Connecticut or Massachusetts.
[H]ere again geography dictated the
[dir]ection of settlement as it proceeded up
[bot]h banks of the Connecticut River and
[stre]tched backward up the West River
[and] the new Crown Point Road. Here the
[fac]tor of common neighborly origin now
[sta]rted to disappear. Inland, drifters from
[the] river towns mixed with newcomers
[fro]m all over New England.
[By 1770 a decade of westward move-
[me]nt had filled in many of Benning
[W]entworth's grants, but often with only
[a] family or two. Those towns off the
[pri]ncipal rivers or roads (and there were
[pre]cious few of these) remained untouched
[un]til after the end of the Revolution.

15 Of 21 Congregational Churches in Ver-
[m]ont of 1780, 19 were on the East side.

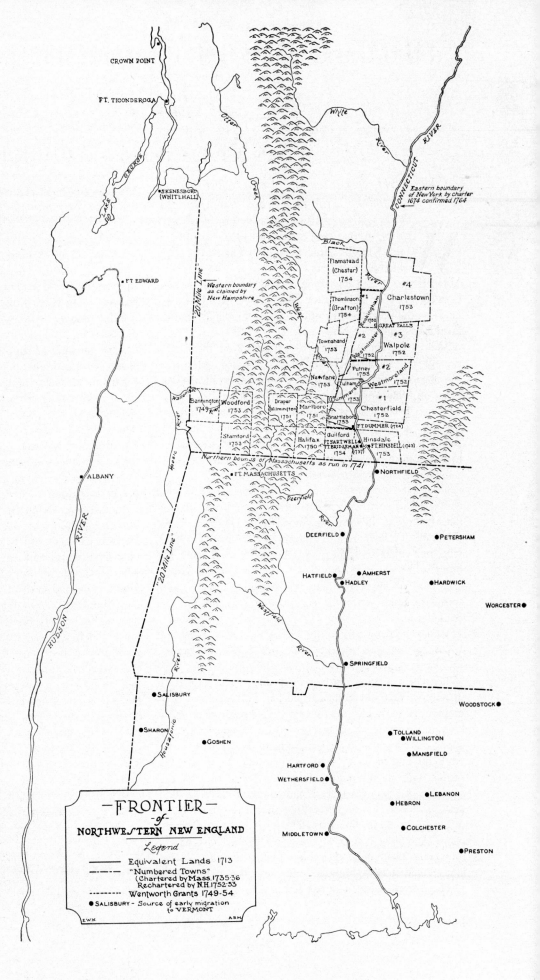

-FRONTIER-
-of-
NORTHWESTERN NEW ENGLAND

Legend

—————— Equivalent Lands 1713

— · — · — "Numbered Towns"
(Chartered by Mass. 1735-36
Recharted by N.H.1752-53

- - - - - Wentworth Grants 1749-54

●SALISBURY - Source of early migration
to VERMONT

IV

YANKEE *versus* YORKER

*How Yankee and Yorker clashed over Benning Wentworth's Hampshire Grants
and how the harassed settlers found a new leader in a man named Ethan Allen.*

WHEN, in the year of our Lord 1764, his Majesty the King declared Benning Wentworths' New Hampshire grants "to be" a part of New York, there opened an action-packed decade of struggle between Yankee and Yorker over these sparsely settled lands on the northwest frontier of New England—and the northeast frontier of New York.

Who were these contending parties? First there were the Yankee speculators who had purchased titles from Wentworth's grantees. But there now appeared a second group in New York, intrigued by the possibilities of new land speculations under grants from that state. The leading spirits of the latter group were James Duane and John Taber Kempe, both influential lawyers and land-holders in aristocratic New York.

Believing the territory hers, this Province had in 1739 made grants in the valley of the Walloomsac River that conflicted in part with Wentworth's later grant of Bennington (1750). In 1765, confirmed in her belief, she made the grant of Princetown to a group of "dummy" grantees, who immediately made over their lands to Duane and others of this group. This lay in the valley of the Batten-kill, and overlapped the Hampshire granted lands of both speculators and settlers in several towns to the north of Bennington.

When the King shifted their lands into New York, and when that state proceeded to make new conflicting grants, the Yankees were undecided whether to resist or not. When Duane came to inspect his lands, he was guided by none other than old Samuel Robinson, first settler of Bennington, who held title to extensive lands under New Hampshire grant. Furthermore, many towns promptly applied for confirming charters from New York.[1] But while the cost of such a confirmation might be small for a settler with his few acres, it became prohibitive for the speculators who held title to thousands of acres of wild land. As we have seen before, they had no more intention of settling on these lands than did their New York counterparts. And they had good reason to believe that unless they could make good their New Hampshire titles, these lands would all be re-granted to the New York speculators.

Their fears were justified. Acting Governor Cadwal-lader Colden was ready to recognize the claims of those who had in good faith actually settled Benning Wentworth's grants. But he was quite unwilling to recognize the validity of New Hampshire titles generally. After all, had not Wentworth himself admitted that in case the King decided in favor of New York, his grants would be "void, of course"?

The unhappy Hampshire speculators, possessed of shaky titles and unwilling to buy New York confirmation for them, decided to appeal to the King. They were aware of the British government's dislike of Wentworth's speculations, but also of its sympathy for actual *settlers*. Therefore they determined to mask their efforts behind the cause of the latter—who actually held very little of the land in question. Samuel Robinson—who was a settler as well as a speculator—was chosen to go to London and present petitions to his Royal Majesty.

In London, Robinson enlisted the support of the influential Society for the Propagation of the Gospel in Foreign Parts, to which, you will recall, shrewd old Benning Wentworth had reserved lots in each of his towns. The result was an order to New York to stop all further granting of land until the King's further "pleasure" was made known. But the King did not follow it up by confirming the validity of the New Hampshire titles,[2] and as more and more pioneers settled under these grants, the problems of managing a fair adjustment of conflicting claims became progressively more difficult. Furthermore, Governor Moore interpreted the King's Order as forbidding even confirmatory grants by New York, so that this avenue of reconciliation was thereby closed.

Of course the Order was a set-back to the New York speculators and an encouragement to the Yankees. Yet the Yorkers determined to make good the titles they already held, and began surveys on the old Walloomsac Patent in 1769. In October, however, at James Breakinridge's farm, the surveying party came upon a grim and de-

---

[1] By November, 1765, 29 towns had asked confirmatory patents; by 1769 there were 69 requests on file; by 1775 there were 92 about equally divided between the east and west side towns.

[2] Poverty-stricken, Robinson died in London in 1767, still attempting to get a decision.

RFH

GIANT WHITE PINES at Windsor and Cornish were most of them eligible for the mark of the "Broad Arrow" reserving them for His Majesty's Navy. Private lumbering was forbidden.

termined group of farmers, who refused to let them continue their work. It was the first group action against New York authority, and an ill omen for the future.

Filled with forboding, the now more numerous settlers of southwestern Vermont framed a petition to the new governor of New Hampshire, John Wentworth, and requested that a second appeal be forwarded to the King. Early next year Breakinridge and young Samuel Robinson got up another petition for the governor to forward. Neither one ever reached His Majesty.

Governor JOHN WENTWORTH was also Surveyor-General of the King's Woods. His suit against Captain William Dean for cutting the King's trees at Windsor started a chain of events which resulted in upheavals and riots on both sides of the Green Mountains.

JOHN WENTWORTH, SURVEYOR GENERAL OF THE KING'S WOODS.

To understand why the west-side settlers addressed themselves to the governor of New Hampshire, who no longer had any jurisdiction over them, we must introduce another Wentworth, Governor John. John took his Uncle Benning's place in 1767 when the latter was permitted to resign to avoid disgrace for his flagrant violations of royal instructions and shady land transactions. We must also make an excursion into the history and sentiments of the east-side communities along the Connecticut River.

As royal governors, both Benning and John had submitted to the King's decision that the land west of the Connecticut was a part of New York. But as unrest increased in these parts, John Wentworth began to believe there might be some hope of upholding the New Hampshire titles, perhaps even of "restoring" the land to that province. While he did not forward the settlers' petitions, he wrote often to the British authorities setting forth in colorful if exaggerated prose the sufferings of the settlers under the tyranny of New York.

Now Wentworth was not only royal governor of New Hampshire, but also "Surveyor General of the King's Woods." As such his responsibility was to prevent any unauthorized cutting, *anywhere* in the colonies, of trees suitable as masts for the royal navy. In January of 1769, in the dead of winter when he would be least expected, Wentworth set out for Windsor to check on a report that one William Dean was cutting the magnificent pines of that town and selling them down the Connecticut for lumber. Arriving unexpectedly he found and seized several logs. Then, fortified with testimony from Benjamin Waite and other prominent citizens of Windsor, he instituted suit against Dean in the New York Admiralty Court.

An engaging man, John Wentworth had made many friends in Windsor, and among them was the influential and energetic Colonel Nathan Stone. As it happened, Stone and others in the Connecticut Valley were becoming increasingly displeased with the operation of New York government in this area.

Now it should be remembered that the familiar system of town government was strictly New England in character, and not recognized by New York. After the King's decision in 1764, New York set up government for the lands east of the mountains by establishing Cumberland County in 1768, with its county seat at isolated and sparsely populated Chester. Early in 1770 Gloucester County was set off to the north, with the county seat at Kingsland (Washington), which had no population at all.[3]

Government under the county system was rather indefinite, and for a long time the settlers went about their business pretty much as they pleased. But it was not long before the county courts began to take action which did not please many of the citizens of the Connecticut Valley. Thus the people of Windsor were highly receptive to Wentworth's whispered suggestion that they organize on the basis of a New England town meeting, just as if they were not really part of New York at all. Wentworth and Stone promptly began to circulate petitions to restore the Grants to New Hampshire.

Hostility to the York government broke out violently the next year—1770—when the courts indicted Nathan Stone and Benjamin and Joseph Wait for manhandling John Grout, the only lawyer in the valley and a confirmed Yorker. Two attempts by the sheriff to arrest these men failed; in the second one he ended up as a captive of his intended victims. Then in June, Stone raised an angry band of about thirty and marched on Chester to prevent the court from convicting the Windsor men. After threatening the judges, they kidnapped poor John Grout—for without the only lawyer, the court could not function. By abuse and by persuasion they tried to get him to leave Chester and settle in Windsor—where they could watch him. Finally, however, Stone winked at his escape. This uprising against New York authority has been called "Stone's Rebellion"; it was only the first of many clashes with the county courts that were to follow.

In the meantime, Wentworth's case against Captain Dean came up for trial in New York. The governor shrewdly decided to make it a test case as regards the validity of the New Hampshire titles, for among the provisions in the original Benning Wentworth grants was one voiding the title to the land if timber reserved for the Royal Navy were cut. If the Court were to confiscate Dean's land for violation of this part of the charter, then necessarily, by implication, the charter *itself* was a valid one. The possibility of a decision of this sort, of course, was an immediate threat to the New York claimants. Although Kempe, as Advocate-General, was forced to prosecute Dean, James Duane—New York's most prominent lawyer—came to his aid. Dean was convicted, for the case was plain, but he was merely fined and jailed. No opinion was given by the court on the matter of his violating the terms of the charter under which he held his land. As you might expect, Wentworth was greatly upset over the miscarriage of his scheme.

Duane and Kempe immediately decided to carry the matter of these conflicting land titles into a court where they could reasonably expect a favorable decision. They instituted suits in the Albany Court to eject several of the west-side settlers who were on land claimed by them and by others under New York charters.

---

[3] Early sessions of the court were held in the wilderness when the justices could not locate the town. All settlements on the west side of the mountain were considered to be a part of Albany County, until 1772, when Charlotte County was established.

ETHAN ALLEN TAKES OVER

The "ejectment suits" threw the New England speculators into consternation. They held troubled meetings in Connecticut to lay plans to contest the suits. At several of these meetings there appeared from nearby Salisbury a hulking and very vocal character who answered to the name of Ethan Allen. Allen was a born speculator, and had an energy and resolution which appealed to the worried proprietors. They immediately packed him off to Portsmouth, New Hampshire, to obtain certified copies of the New Hampshire charters, to enlist the aid of Governor Wentworth, and to hire the distinguished Connecticut lawyer Jared Ingersoll to defend the settlers. For if once the court voided a New Hampshire grant actually *settled*, what chance had they to hold title to *wild* land? After all, even the New Hampshire charters contained a provision providing for the return of the land to the King if it were not settled within a specified time—a provision which was usually ignored.

They might as well have saved their time, for they faced a "packed" court. Lt.-Governor Colden, Attorney-General Duane, the plaintiff's lawyer John Taber Kempe, and even one of the judges, Robert Livingston, all were members of the New York speculators. Of course, the case was decided in favor of the New York claimant, and all New Hampshire titles were thereby deemed to be invalid. "In fine," declared Ethan, "interest, conviction, and grandeur, being all on one side, easily turned the scale against the honest defendants."

"Honest" the settler-defendants themselves were. However, Ethan failed to point out that the real losers were his clients, the Yankee speculators, who held hundreds of acres for every one in the possession of a settler. But his statement marked the real beginning of confusion between the rights of actual settlers and the interest of speculators—a confusion which Ethan intentionally promoted from that time on.

Evidently Governor Wentworth had given Allen considerable encouragement that the New Hampshire titles would be confirmed by the King, perhaps even that the territory would be annexed to New Hampshire, for Ethan immediately began buying up land himself. From then on until his death twenty years later he never ceased to speculate in land.

It seems that Duane and Kempe were also quite impressed with the big man from Connecticut, and after the trials offered him land if he would change sides. Already committed by sentiment as well as his own purchases, he refused. With a grand gesture he informed the puzzled Yorkers that "the gods of the hills are not the gods of the valleys." A rather vague statement indeed, but typical of his grandiloquent style.

Ethan lost no time in repairing to Bennington, where he

JAMES DUANE, *Yorker, aristocrat, land-holder, speculator in Vermont grants, was also one of New York's most prominent Revolutionary leaders and an opponent worthy of Ethan Allen.*

busily set about rousing the settlers against this threat to their homes. As agent for the Yankee speculators he waged an artful campaign to convince the settlers that their lands would be safe *only* if the New Hampshire titles were confirmed. This he promised them if they would firmly resist the Yorkers. This was the one hope of the Yankee proprietors who owned most of the land—to enlist the settlers in opposition to the claims of the rival New York speculators. In the meantime through their English agents, and particularly through Wentworth (whose titled relative, the Marquis of Rockingham had been prime minister and would be again) they hoped that the known sympathy of the British government for *settlers* would cause the King to confirm the New Hampshire grants *as a whole*. The longer he waited, the more settlers there would be. And if the present settlers held off the Yorkers, the new settlers would all be Yankees. This, then, was the strategy they adopted. And it was to Allen's interest to promote it, for he was becoming constantly more involved in speculation in wild lands himself.

In order to carry out such a policy, Ethan needed an organized following, a band of "shock troops" to meet the Yorkers, who had all the forces of "law and order" behind them. He had good allies already on the spot, for his cousins Seth Warner and Remember Baker had al-

Ethan Allen

OF ETHAN ALLEN, Colonel-Commandar
the Green Mountain Boys, we have no pict
record—in fact, not even an adequate descrip
That he was a colorful, violent man, with a l
sense of humor and a vast vocabulary we do kn
But Ethan Allen the man has long been obscure
Ethan Allen the legend.

Over 100 years ago Daniel P. Thompson (
wrote a laudatory two volume historical n
"The Green Mountain Boys," which became a
term best-seller and the nation's favorite
portrait of Ethan. In 1855, at the urging of Tho
son and Henry Stevens, first President of the
Vermont Historical Society, the legislature ap
priated funds to actually erect under him a l
pedestal, which now thrusts the Stephe
Statue high into the sky at Green Mount Ceme
in Burlington (below), where he is buried.

Latter-day historians have tried to reconstruc
man from the dusty, crackling pages of orig
documents, but find it hard to get away from
legend. And no one has yet found a picture of h

Thus any portrait is merely a reconstructio
character, not of known features. The artist,
William Tatseos of Montpelier, completed a
trait once in a conventional manner—and paint
out. It was not the man. It was done again,
laying the paint on with a knife—as Ethan lai
his language—in bright colors reflecting the v
personality of a man who has excited the imag
tion of men for a century and a half.

← DANIEL P. THOMPSON, by Thomas W. W

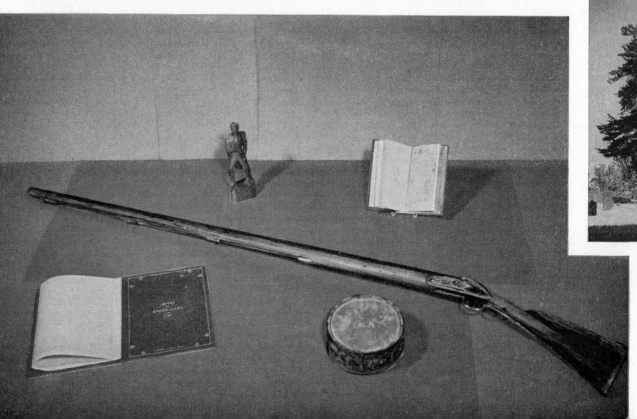

Among memer
of Ethan Allen
the Vermont l
torical Society l
seum are his
and canteen, a le
to his brother L
a copy of his
"Narrative of C
tivity," and
Abrams miniatu
the Kinney statu

CADWALLADER COLDEN, aristocrat, scientist, philosopher, intimate of Ben Franklin, Lieut. (and often Acting) Governor of New York, stayed loyal to his King, as did Governor William Tryon.

Before proceeding to the oft-told tales of the exploits of the Green Mountain Boys, we must turn back a moment to view the situation in New York. Why did the authorities there fail so abjectly in asserting their authority —confirmed by the courts and backed by the law?

Perhaps one answer lies in the lack of any real continuity in policy. Governor Clinton, who waged the war of letters with Benning Wentworth, was succeeded by Sir Henry Moore, who passed from the scene late in 1769. Lt. Governor Cadwallader Colden held the fort until his successor, Lord Dunmore arrived in the autumn of the following year. In the meantime, Colden, as Acting Governor, had resumed the granting—at half fees—of lands not already laid out by Wentworth, as well as some military grants which overlapped the latter. But Dunmore, with a lively appetite for the money involved, refused to accept less than his full fees. To anyone who would pay, he freely issued patents—caring little whether they conflicted with the Wentworth grants or not. Much to his disappointment—for he had worked up a real "land-office" business—he was ordered the next year to exchange offices with Governor William Tryon of North Carolina, who arrived in July of 1771.

Tryon had already smashed the popular uprising of the "Regulators" in that southern state, and could be expected to take positive action against any similar revolt in the New Hampshire Grants. But the trouble was that canny Ethan Allen never gave him excuse enough to obtain the British troops he would have needed to put down the Green Mountain Boys. And the irrepressible "Bennington Mob"—as the Yorkers called them—were not to be over-awed. In fact, in 1773, when a rumor started that Tryon was proceeding with troops against the Grants, the settlers immediately organized, imported some old cannon, and laid an ambush. They were ready to reply to military force with armed opposition, if it became necessary.

It never became necessary. Ethan pursued a cagy policy of threatening death and destruction to all who opposed him, but limited his actual violence to lots of noise and ridicule, some severe whippings, and considerable property damage. As a young man in Salisbury, Connecticut, he had watched the progress of what were known as the Anti-Rent Wars along the New York-Massachusetts boundary. He could not have failed to observe the ineffectiveness of the New York authorities against the rioters. But he also noted that when the latter fell into excesses (several people were actually killed), the Yorkers were able to obtain the aid of royal troops who quickly suppressed the rebellion. Ethan did not propose to fall into the same grievous error.

ready preceded Ethan to the Grants, and he now brought with him several of his brothers as well. But he needed an "incident" to really put the settlers behind him.

This incident occurred in the fall of 1770, as the New York sheriff, accompanied by the Mayor of Albany and a large posse, tried to oust our old friend James Breakenridge. Upon their arrival, they discovered nearly a hundred belligerent looking men awaiting them. The members of the posse quickly melted away in the face of such opposition—thus emphasizing the lack of sympathy the average New Yorker had for his state's efforts to take over the farms of the New Hampshire Grants settlers, on behalf of his own aristocratic overlords. The unfortunate sheriff and the mayor retired in defeat.

Here was an act of blunt resistance backed by a threat of real violence on the part of the settlers. Here, too, was evidence that the Yorkers were actually determined to take over. Thenceforth Ethan had little difficulty in persuading the settlers that they must organize to oppose their "oppressors." Eleven west-side towns each appointed a committee of public defense and raised a military company. And at the head of them all was Ethan Allen as "Colonel-Commandant"—a title which must have given him great satisfaction! Ethan had no trouble in getting his relatives appointed officers under him, and proceeded to take over the defense of the New Hampshire Grants. Here, then, was the beginning of the Green Mountain Boys.

THE GREEN MOUNTAIN BOYS

Who were the Green Mountain Boys? They certainly included all the Allens (though some of the brothers spent most of their time in Connecticut), their two cousins, Remember Baker and Seth Warner, and also Thomas Cochrane and Peleg Sunderland. This was the hard core of a flexible organization, which varied in numbers according to the time and place involved and the differing sympathies of the settlers. There were many substantial farmers who did not approve of Allen's band, and for all their opposition to the Yorkers who had designs on their land, never rode with him. James Breakenridge, despite his tribulations, was one of these. Except in special cases, these moderates and conservatives were in the majority, and the more violent exploits of the Boys were actually the work of a few spectacular performers, supported by some of the more footloose youths. On occasions of direct threat, however, the entire community gathered behind these more riotous "shock troops" to hold their land against York speculators and the governmental authority invoked by the latter.

As is the case with most revolts, opposition increased in violence as time went on. In the summer of 1771 the New York surveyor, William Cockburn, was run out of Socialborough, a New York grant which included parts of Rutland and Pittsford. That same fall several Yorkers endeavored to take possession of military grants in Rupert, where Robert Cochrane had some partly cleared lots. A small handful of the Boys, accompanied by Allen and Baker, helped Cochrane throw them out.

Governor Tryon's response to this double outrage was to place a reward on the head of the rioters, and to warn the Grants settlers that New York's claims would be enforced.

Words were cheap. The New York authorities were unable to lay hands upon any of these outlaws. In high glee, Ethan drew up a counter-proclamation offering a reward for the delivery of Duane or Kempe to Landlord

Fay's Tavern. He then retired to Connecticut for the winter—to wage his own war of words through the pages of the *Connecticut Courant*.

Early in the spring, Justice of the Peace John Munro of Shaftsbury with a posse of a dozen New York sympathisers captured Remember Baker, loaded him on a sled and headed in frantic haste for Albany. But a hard riding group from Bennington overtook the group, rescued the wounded Green Mountain Boy, and laid rough hands on Munro. With exceptional restraint, however, they released him, unharmed.

Another Munro—Sergeant Hugh—was at this time surveying his military grant in Rupert. Again Cochrane mustered a squad to protect his lands, and whipped the offending sergeant out of the Grants.

By this time the New York authorities were well aware that they could not mobilize—at least from citizens sympathetic to their neighbors across the line—strength enough to prevent or punish such outbursts.

Indeed, they could not even protect settlers who occupied land quite peacefully under New York grants. For it was increasingly evident that the Green Mountain Boys were less interested in protecting "settlers" than they were upholding New Hampshire grants, whether settled or held for speculation.

As a matter of fact, the howls of anguish against New York "land jobbers" supposedly turning out "honest settlers" lose some of their force to the reader who recalls how old Sam Robinson tried to drive the Dutch settlers out of Pownal, or how Benning Wentworth ignored the Springfield settlers' petition for a charter and granted the land instead to a group of speculators.[4] Nor did the activities of the Green Mountain Boys among the Otter Creek settlers lend lustre to their role as defenders of the "honest settler."

---

[4] The farmers of the latter town finally obtained recognition of their claims from New York. Both Pownal and Springfield had been settled before Wentworth's grants to the speculator–proprietors of those towns.

IN THE YEARS 1770–1⁊
there was considerable differe⁊
of opinion on the West-side a⁊
what should be done to protect ⁊
interests of settlers on the N⁊
Hampshire Grants. There w⁊
large group of moderates, for ⁊
ample, who wished confirma⁊
of the Wentworth titles, but w⁊
quite satisfied to remain as a ⁊
of New York. Jehiel Hawley⁊
Arlington was the respected lea⁊
of this group, but Dr. Sam⁊
Adams was most vocal.

A second faction, the Gr⁊
Mountain Boys, were compose⁊
the footloose youngsters and l⁊
speculators as well as solid citiz⁊
who had had to fight to prev⁊
Yorkers from taking their la⁊
They had little tolerance for ⁊
cautious counsels of their elde⁊
and one day seized the good Doc⁊
Adams, strapped him to a ch⁊
hoisted him to the Tavern post,⁊
left him there as a butt for lo⁊
wits (LEFT, ABOVE).

They were even less toleran⁊
the third, most conservative gro⁊
who mostly held their lands un⁊
New York titles. Many were pea⁊
ful settlers; others were resid⁊
New York officials. At first th⁊
were warned, then often whipp⁊
out of the Grants by an applicati⁊
of the "beech seal." After pass⁊
of New York's "Bloody Act," ⁊
Boys took more severe measur⁊
The Reverend Benjamin Houg⁊
Justice of the Peace, was seiz⁊
and "tried" for "crimes" agai⁊
people. His judges admitted th⁊
was no fairer magistrate in ⁊
Grants, and that he had ⁊
meddled in the land title co⁊
troversy. But he favored Ne⁊
York, and must receive retribut⁊
therefore, in the form of 2⁊
lashes. He was stripped and ti⁊
and the rope was applied by fo⁊
men working in relays, to assu⁊
sustained effectiveness. Reviv⁊
by a doctor, he was given a "sa⁊
conduct" pass signed by Allen a⁊
Warner and forced to walk his w⁊
to Albany (LEFT, BELOW).

Hough's punishment was ju⁊
about the last act of violence on ⁊
part of the Green Mountain Bo⁊
in their bloodless war against ⁊
York speculators and the gover⁊
mental authority of the State ⁊
New York. Their energies we⁊
soon to be absorbed in a broad⁊
struggle. But during their fi⁊
years of activities they killed ⁊
maimed no one. Was there eve⁊
revolution based less on force, a⁊
more on threats of force?

LAND ON OTTER CREEK

As it happened, the leaders of the Green Mountain Boys had begun to speculate extensively themselves. Ethan, for example, traded constantly, buying and selling. When he went to Portsmouth in 1770 to enlist the help of John Wentworth on behalf of the Yankee speculators, one of the plots of land he bought for himself was old Benning Wentworth's 500 acres in New Haven, at the Falls of Otter Creek. Across the river lay Panton, which had been granted to a group of speculators in Salisbury, Connecticut, Ethan's old hometown. Unwilling to settle themselves, the proprietors in 1765 built a saw mill at the Falls, in the hopes of encouraging others to do so. But Panton was too far beyond the furthest limits of the frontier.

In the same year Colonel John Reid had been voted a New York patent for the land at the Falls. Dispossessing the lone sawmill operator, he held the land until 1769, when he obtained several families from New Jersey to begin settlement. Reid offered to buy the mill from the New Hampshire claimants, but they refused. This lonely frontier community existed peacefully, then, until the summer of 1772.

But before we proceed with the story, let us turn our eyes back toward Bennington as the green of that fateful summer spread over the cleared lands along the banks of the Walloomsac. Late in May the Reverend Jedediah Dewey received a letter from Governor Tryon suggesting that the peaceful citizens of that land lay before him their grievances. He suggested that Dewey, and perhaps Breakenridge and Stephen Fay should come to New York City to talk it over. A meeting from the various towns agreed to send Landlord Fay and his son Dr. Jonas Fay, and provided them with a firm but conciliatory letter signed by Dewey and other leading men of the area, who would, they warned, "closely adhere to the maintaining of our property, with due submissions to your Excellency's jurisdiction." Ethan, somewhat miffed at his exclusion from the discussions, wrote an additional letter on behalf of the leaders of the Green Mountain Boys. The Fays were pleasantly received, and a truce was negotiated which provided that the settlers under grants from either province should remain undisturbed until the King had made a decision on the matter of these troublesome and conflicting titles.

The truce was quite satisfactory to the settlers and was greeted with wild jubilation. The rafters of Landlord Fay's tavern rang far into the night with toasts to the King, to Governor Tryon and to "universal peace and plenty, liberty and property."

It was not so pleasing to the speculators and to the leaders of the Green Mountain boys, however. Despite the peace negotiations, Baker and Warner had set forth in pursuit of Surveyor Cockburn, who was rumored to be working along the Onion River.[5] They caught him, and on the way back, ousted the settlers at Panton. News of the truce reached them at Castleton however, and Cockburn was released. Nevertheless, Tryon considered their actions a violation of the compact, and demanded the reinstatement of the Panton settlers. But the initiative was now in the hands of the Allens, and despite widespread hopes for an enduring truce, the leaders of the Green Mountain Boys refused to curb their activities.

Their reluctance to accept an armistice based on the *existing* situation resulted principally from their hopes for the success of a new land company they had just formed— the Onion River Land Company—under the leadership of Ethan's shrewd younger brother Ira. By hook and by crook—and by means often slightly shady[6]—the company had gained title to most of the choice lands along the lower river, and proposed to build there a little empire of its own. They had disposed of most of their other lands to invest in this grand enterprise, and stood to lose their original investment and future fortune, if the Yorkers got there first.

Thus, late that fall, when Ira and Remember Baker, in course of exploring their lands, came across another New York surveyor, they man-handled him severely and threatened to kill him on the spot if they caught up with him again. They then proceeded to erect a stout fort on the river as a warning to and defense against other Yorkers. This was the last straw for Governor Tryon. Large rewards were posted for the capture of Ira and Remember—which as before, went uncollected. In any event, the truce was at an end.

In June of 1773, Colonel Reid took steps to reestablish his settlement in Panton. A dozen families of eager Scotch immigrants took up residence there. Ethan, after dispossessing the original Jerseyites, had bought land on the Panton side as well, and a couple of families had been settled in the Colonel's houses. Reid in taking re-possession, bought their crops and hay. But news of the new settlement on lands he claimed reached Ethan by the beginning of August. With Warner and Baker he assembled a sizeable force of at least one hundred Green Mountain Boys and descended upon the frightened and puzzled Scotch like an angry whirlwind, burning the houses and destroying the crops. And that was the end of Colonel Reid's attempt to colonize on Otter Creek. Ethan stood in triumphant possession of his lands.

Tryon, of course, was as furious as he was helpless. To a call for troops, he received a humiliating rejection. Civil authority, replied General Haldimand from Boston, should be able to control "a few lawless vagabonds."

---

5 Now known as the Winooski River.

6 Ira's own diary relates gleefully some of the tricks he staged to get possession of choice acres and to dispose of poor ones.

THE "BLOODY ACT"

Most of the unrest and riots during 1773 and 1774 centered in the lands granted by New York along the upper reaches of Otter Creek. Allen had warned the settlers of Durham (Clarendon) that they must purchase New Hampshire titles, though he charitably offered "to mob" the Yankee speculators if they overcharged. In the fall of 1773 with a band of the Boys, he threatened that unless they complied he would return and "reduce every house to ashes and leave every inhabitant a corpse." In November he assembled his full force—about 130 strong —and descended upon Benjamin Spencer, Justice of the Peace. They then held a mock trial, "convicted" him of serving under New York appointment, and set fire to his house, as well as to another.

The Reverend Benjamin Hough held a similar commission as Justice of the Peace in Socialborough, and protested violently to the Governor. The resulting action by the New York Assembly had the character of bitter frustration. It virtually declared an open season on the leaders of the Green Mountain Boys, who promptly labeled it the "Bloody Act." Unless they promptly surrendered, they were to be adjudged convicted, and executed when caught. Assemblies were prohibited, and stiff penalties including death were laid down for riotous behavior.

Perhaps Governor Tryon decided to copy Allen's own tactics, and attempt to accomplish by lurid threats what he could not by either force or conciliation. But this extremely ill-advised Act served only to weld all factions solidly behind the wanted men. A convention of the west-side settlers reaffirmed their loyalty, but also their determination to hold their lands and defend their condemned leaders. Tryon accomplished what the Wentworth proprietors had themselves been unable to realize: a firm alliance between the speculators—reinforced by the new Onion River Land Company—and the settlers themselves. In April of 1774 a convention at Manchester voted that mere acceptance of a commission from the state of New York would constitute the official a public enemy.

Faced with what they felt to be an oppressive government, the west-side settlers were now ready to embark upon resistance to a government they had previously acknowledged. It was no longer a struggle over conflicting land titles—which might be worked out under New York rule. It was direct opposition to the operation of the government their monarch had placed over them. Amidst the storm winds of revolution blowing through the American colonies, it was not such a long step to a declaration against His Royal Majesty, George III, himself.

"MASSACRE" AT WESTMINSTER

Things had been a good deal quieter over in the Connecticut Valley. It was true that many citizens were still having trouble with their New York justices. Times were hard, and there was a rather widespread resistance, on both sides of the River, to the collection of debts by the courts. For example, in 1773 a mob—mostly from New Hampshire—restored to Leonard Spaulding of Putney goods of his which had been seized by the Court. Furthermore, most of the officials were felt to be "outsiders," and were quite cordially disliked.

But there was no struggle over land titles—since New York had made no conflicting grants on that side of the mountains—and there was also much less speculation in wild lands. The movement to annex the Grants to New Hampshire had petered out, and even Governor John Wentworth had deserted the cause. The widely respected Jacob Bayley of Newbury and Nathan Stone of Windsor —leaders of Gloucester and Cumberland counties—had actively favored New Hampshire. They now turned to New York for new charters, and, in 1773, joined with 400 others in a signed expression of satisfaction with New York jurisdiction.

Yet new troubles were brewing. Echoes of the impassioned speeches of Samuel Adams and Patrick Henry resounded up into the distant frontier of the Upper Connecticut. Here, as elsewhere, opinions differed as to how far the colonies should go in resisting British authority,

WESTMINSTER COURT HOUSE, site of the "massacre" is now marked by a bronze plaque. At top of the page is an artist's drawing of the old building.

GRANITE SHAFT marks the grave of martyr William French. But plaque incorrectly attributes struggle to revolutionary fervor.

and the people began to divide into "Whigs" and "Tories," or "loyalists." When, in 1774, the unruly Mr. Spaulding was cast into jail for remarks derogatory to his King, he was promptly released by a mob. And since the officials were representatives of a royal government, resentment against the courts began to get mixed up with the rising tide of revolutionary fervor.

However, when New York's revolutionary "Committee of Correspondence" wrote, early in 1774, to find out how the people of Cumberland felt about colonial resistance to England, the conservative county supervisors tried to suppress the letter. But the Whigs found out about it, and a convention was called for October. The assembled delegates re-affirmed their loyalty to the King, but voted to defend their rights against Parliamentary oppression. And, in order that their motives might not be misunderstood, they agreed to discourage all "riotous and tumultuous mobs." Two more conventions gathered in November and February, and a standing Committee of Correspondence was set up. But they also took time off to complain again about the burden of New York courts.

In March of 1775, just as the Revolution was about to burst into flame, bitter resentment against authority welled up in a single bloody outbreak. Despite an urgent petition that they should not do so, the Cumberland County Court prepared to convene at Westminster to consider a number of actions to collect debts. A determined group of citizens thereupon occupied the new courthouse to prevent the Court from sitting. In the meantime, to protect the Court, the Sheriff recruited a posse from among the Yorkers of Brattleboro, Hinsdale and Guilford to the south. Then he made a furious attempt to dislodge the stubborn occupants of the courthouse, in which several of the latter were badly wounded and two killed, including young William French. The news spread rapidly, and angry citizens poured into Westminster from

both sides of the River. From across the mountains came blustering Robert Cochrane with a force of Green Mountain Boys. The judges, the sheriff, and his posse were themselves clapped into the jail, still stained with the blood of the dead and wounded.

The so-called "Westminster Massacre" has been labeled by over-zealous historians as the first stroke of the Revolution and the unfortunate William French as its martyr. Actually, it was only the last and most bloody of a series of anti-court riots, held at a time when revolutionary fervor was turning friend against neighbor. But it did serve to inflame sentiment against royal government, and for the first time the East-side and the West-side joined hands against New York authority. A convention was quickly called and a committee chosen to draw up a protest. To this committee was appointed Ethan Allen.

But Ethan never served. He had a new project afoot which would shake the foundations of his Majesty's empire in the New World—the capture of strategic Ticonderoga!

MAPS OF THE "GRANTS"

On the pages which follow we reproduce several maps in an attempt to help the reader visualize the progress of settlement and its relationship to the complicated land situation. The descriptive Map of the New Hampshire Grants at the time of the partial census of 1771 (page 52) shows the extent of settlement and its relationship to the river valleys. This is supplemented by actual reproductions of sections of two rare old maps of New York and New England, to illustrate the bewildering extent of land grants and the marked overlapping of the New Hampshire and New York grants on the West side (pages 54–55). They illustrate, too, the lack of accurate knowledge as to survey lines and the true location of towns. In fact, some of the land controversy can be traced to cartographic ignorance. Some of this ignorance resulted, in turn, from constant interruptions to the work of New York surveyors by determined Green Mountain Boys.

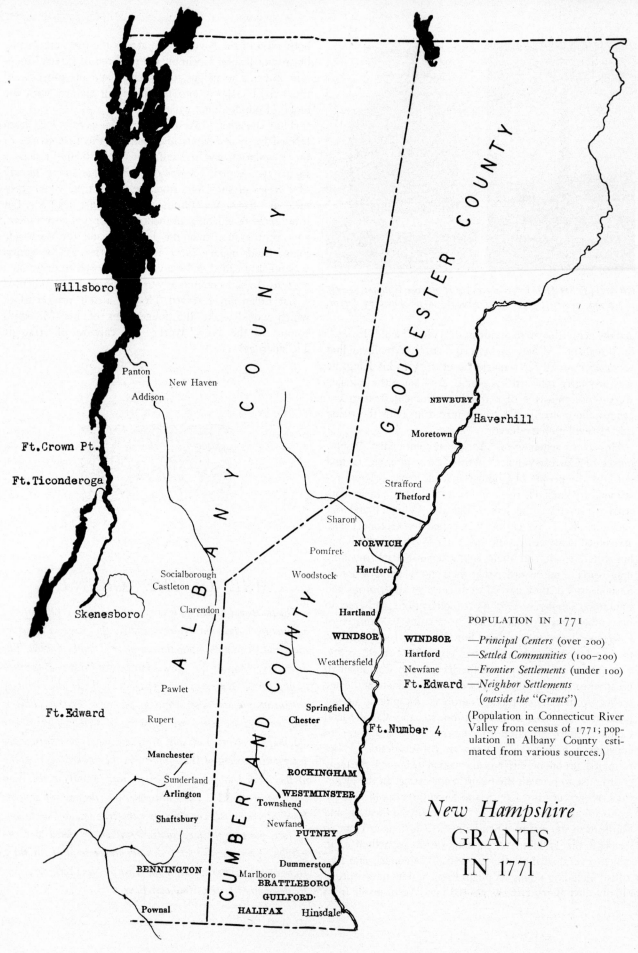

Willsboro

GLOUCESTER COUNTY

ALBANY COUNTY

Panton

New Haven

Addison

NEWBURY

Haverhill

Moretown

Ft.Crown Pt.

Ft.Ticonderoga

Strafford

Thetford

Sharon

NORWICH

Pomfret

Socialborough

Castleton

Woodstock

Hartford

Clarendon

Skenesboro

Hartland

Hartland

WINDSOR

POPULATION IN 1771

WINDSOR   —*Principal Centers* (over 200)

Hartford   —*Settled Communities* (100–200)

Weathersfield

Newfane   —*Frontier Settlements* (under 100)

Ft.Edward —*Neighbor Settlements*

(*outside the "Grants"*)

Pawlet

Ft.Edward

Rupert

Springfield

Chester

Ft.Number 4

(Population in Connecticut River
Valley from census of 1771; population in Albany County estimated from various sources.)

Manchester

Sunderland

Arlington

ROCKINGHAM

WESTMINSTER

Shaftsbury

Townshend

Newfane

PUTNEY

New Hampshire

GRANTS

IN 1771

CUMBERLAND COUNTY

Dummerston

BENNINGTON

Marlboro

BRATTLEBORO

GUILFORD

HALIFAX

Hinsdale

Pownal

Albany

Kodachrome by Earle Newton Courtesy Craftsbury Town Library

COLONEL EBENEZER CRAFTS, FOUNDER OF CRAFTSBURY, WITH HIS
SON SAMUEL C. CRAFTS, LATER GOVERNOR OF VERMONT (1828–31).

In the town library at Craftsbury Common hang two fine and characteristic early portraits, one of the town's founder and his son, the other of his wife and two daughters. The career of this man, Colonel Ebenezer Crafts, is largely representative of the manner in which Vermont towns were organized and settled.

Even the furious land grant activity of New Hampshire's Governor Benning Wentworth in the years before 1765 had not laid out the entire territory which declared its independence as "Vermont" in 1777. Financially embarrassed, the new state began, late in 1779, the issuance of six-mile square grants of land in those areas—particularly the north parts—which had not been set off by Wentworth.

A number of petitions had accumulated by this time. Among those approved in 1780 was one from Sturbridge, Mass. on behalf of one Ebenezer Crafts and fifty-nine others for some land along the famous Hazen Road "in

order for settling a new plantation to be erected into a township." The town of "Minden" was chartered the following year.

But the end of the Revolution brought hardship and strife all over the new republic. Disagreements in Massachusetts burst into the flame of Shays Rebellion, and Ebenezer Crafts, a veteran of Revolutionary service, rode with General Lincoln to suppress it. A new wave of emigration from southern New England began, and Crafts joined it.

During the late war General Jacob Bayley and Colonel Moses Hazen had cut a road northwestward from Newbury through the wilderness toward Canada. Bayley insistently pressed upon his friend and Commander-in-chief, George Washington, the need of an expedition from this northern frontier into British Canada, and the Hazen Road was to carry it. But Washington was unable to spare troops; construction stopped at Hazen's Notch in Montgomery, and the road fell into disuse

beyond Peacham, which had been settled during the war.

It was this road that Ebenezer Crafts reopened in 1788 for eighteen miles from Cabot to his new lands. He cleared ten or twelve acres, built a saw mill and laid out a grist mill—both essential to the pioneer farm. Two families moved in the next Spring, but Crafts did not actually settle with his family and several others until February, 1791. He was clearly to be the leader and patriarch of the new town—the furthest outpost of settlement in the north—and the name was changed in 1790 to Craftsbury in his honor.

But of the sixty who, in 1780, set themselves up as proprietors of a new town on the northern frontier of New England, only eight ever came to Craftsbury, and five of these were the Crafts family. This was not unusual, for even at this late date land was thought to be as much an opportunity for speculation as for settlement.

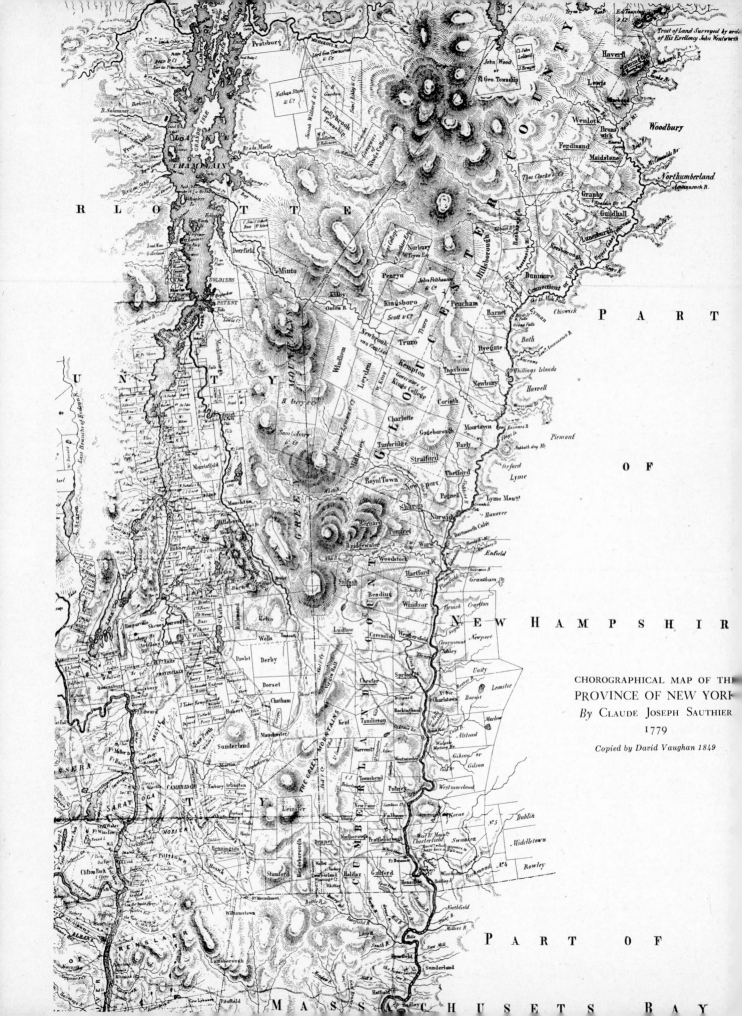

CHOROGRAPHICAL MAP OF THE
PROVINCE OF NEW YORK
By Claude Joseph Sauthier
1779
Copied by David Vaughan 1849

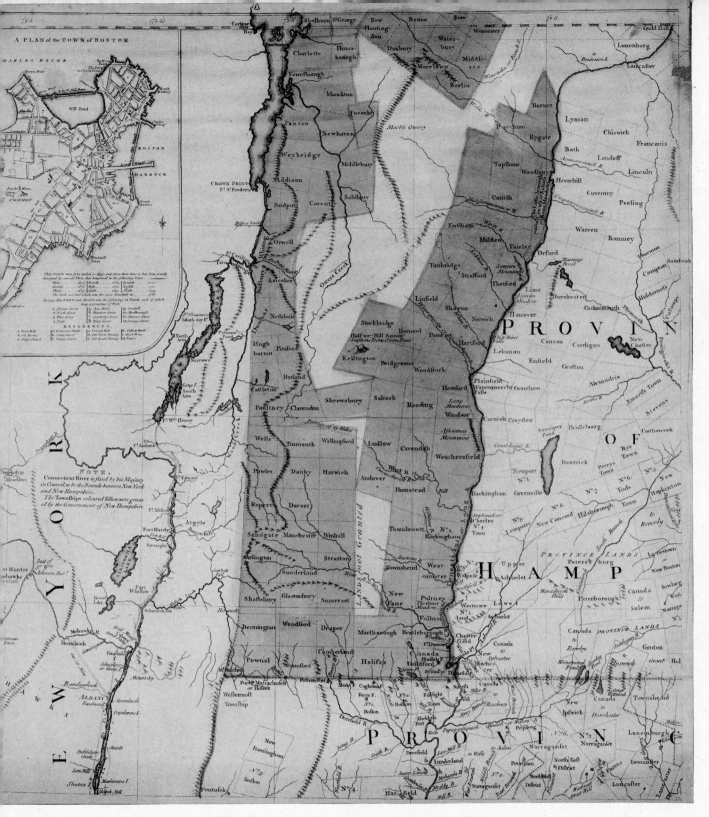

—SAUTHIER'S *1779 MAP OF NEW YORK* included, of course, the eastern counties. *The section shown here (left) is by far the most detailed contemporary map of land grants in this area. It shows the New York grants, as few others do, though it is sometimes in error as to exact location. Note that the Connecticut River towns are shown as granted by Wentworth (underlined on the map); there were few conflicting New York grants on that side of the mountains. In fact, many of these towns received confirming charters from New York. The Gloucester County line shown by Sauthier is the one commonly accepted by historians, but it does not square with the description of its bounds. (Compare with map on page 52.) This map is also important for what it shows of the roads then in existence.*

THOMAS JEFFERY'S *1774 "MAP of the Most Inhabited Part of New England" (above) is strictly from the Yankee viewpoint, and ignores the New York grants. The cartographer adds a note (in the bend of the Hudson River) placing the New Hampshire Grants in New York. But earlier editions had implicitly included this land in New Hampshire. Many other early maps—before 1765—had done the same. Notice inaccuracy in the plotting of upper Lake Champlain and Winooski River towns.* (Author's Collection)

Winter Scene by Derick   CRAFTSBURY COMMON   *Summer Scenes by Earle*

SETTLEMENT CONTINUES

Despite the threat to New Hampshire land titles and the hullabaloo of riotous Green Mountain Boys, settlement proceeded apace all during the period before the outbreak of war. Farms began to spring up on the hillsides back of the more settled river areas, and pioneers pressed further northward up the valleys. Occasionally migrations were carefully organized, such as the one which began in 1763 from Newbury and Haverhill, Massachusetts, to the fertile intervales of the upper Connecticut—the great Oxbow at Coos. Here, under the leadership of Jacob Bayley and John Hazen were founded the twin communities of Newbury, Vermont, and Haverhill, N. H. One of the most remarkable of organized migrations was that of the two Scotch-American companies from Scotland to Ryegate and Barnet in 1774-75.

Growth was rapid after the removal of the French menace, especially in the Connecticut River communities. Guilford, though it boasted no village, became the most densely populated town in the Grants by the time the census of 1771 was taken in Cumberland County. There were then eight towns in the county with more than 200 inhabitants, as against only one each in Gloucester and Albany Counties. (Notice on the map on page 52 the extra heavy population density on the East-side).

The early years of the Revolution, reviving the threat of Indian raids as well as British invasion, not only stemmed the tide of inflowing settlers, but also threw back the line of the frontier to Castleton and Rutland. The scattered log houses to the north were mostly abandoned, and the Onion River Land Company found its land office business brought to an abrupt halt. Thomas Chittenden, who had come to Williston on the Onion River in 1774, retired with his family to Williamstown, Massachusetts, and during the eight years of war made his residence in Arlington and Danby. Ethan and Ira Allen conducted their political maneuvers from Sunderland and Arlington. Lists of delegates to the various conventions often show men from the northern towns, but their actual residence during these years was almost always elsewhere.

But when the defeat of Burgoyne and the subsequent truce with Haldimand brought surcease to the frontier, migration began again. It was now stimulated by vast grants of land made by the new State of Vermont in its northern regions. The names of prominent and influential Americans began to appear on proprietors' lists during the period when Vermont was seeking Congressional favor. And grants were often made in lieu of money payment for services. Ethan and Ira Allen obtained several grants. Seth Warner—most of whose lands had been sold for taxes while he was on military duty—was given a triangle of land up north, known as Warner's Gore. But it was of such poor quality that it remains unorganized and unsettled to this day. Most of the charters, however, were issued to groups of proprietors, some of whom, like Jacob Davis of Montpelier and Calais and Ebenezer Crafts of Craftsbury, actually led a migration to the new lands.

Another prominent factor stimulating migration was the fact that Vermont, as an independent republic, bore none of the burden of continental taxes. In fact, she imposed no taxes of her own, appropriating loyalist property and issuing land grants to cover her political and military expenses. In these years Vermont received a large accession of deserters from the colonial armies, as well as disaffected citizens who found safe haven in a state whose leaders were flirting with the idea of returning to royal allegiance.

By the date of her admission to the union and the first federal census of 1791, Vermont had passed the 85,000 mark, and was just getting up steam. An 80% increase in the next ten years put her over 154,000, but the rate of increase dropped rapidly thereafter.

"COLONIAL" VILLAGES

The veneer applied by modern civilization makes it difficult for us to visualize the early pioneer village as it looked to its 18th Century inhabitant, even where its architecture has survived—as in Old Bennington (right) and Craftsbury (left). Yet, ironically, it has been the wealth of non-native Vermonters which has largely preserved and restored these two communities. It is here that one can still see the grace and charm of the old, combined with the modern comfort of central heating and the beauty of carefully tended gardens.

A MAP of the COUNTRY in which the Army under Lt. GENERAL BURGOYNE acted in the Campaign of 1777, shewing the Marches of the Army & the Places of the principal Actions.

Drawn by Mr. MEDCALFE
&
Engraved by Wm. FADEN.

ETHAN ALLEN CAPTURED AT MONTREAL—SEPT 24, 1775

IRA ALLEN NEGOTIATING AT LOYAL BLOCK HOUSE 1781

BATTLE OF VALCOUR ISLAND—1776

EVACUATION OF FORT TICONDEROGA—JULY 6, 1777

BATTLE OF HUBBARDTON JULY 7, 1777

BATTLE OF BENNINGTON AUGUST 16, 1777

BURGOYNE'S SURRENDER AT SARATOGA—OCT. 17, 1777

BUILDING THE BAYLEY-HAZEN ROAD—1776

GEN. BAYLEY WARNED BY COL. JOHNSTON OF BRITISH SURPRISE ATTEMPT TO CAPTURE HIM—JUNE 15, 1782

FRAMING THE CONSTITUTION WINDSOR—JULY 8, 1777

LEGEND
—— Burgoyne's route
:::::::: Roads in 1777

The route of General John Burgoyne's legions is shown on his own map by the solid line stretching up Lake Champlain, Wood Creek and down the Hudson River to Stillwater. The side expeditions to Hubbardton and Bennington are not marked, but the engagements are shown by tiny crossed swords. Covering as it does almost all of the Grants territory, it is by far the most detailed map of the roads then existent. (From the author's collection.)

London. Published as the Act directs, Feb'y 1st 1780 by Wm. Faden Charing Cross

V

GREEN MOUNTAIN REBELS

How Ethan Allen captured Ticonderoga and then was captured himself; how his friends formed the new state of "Vermont," and threw back the British at Bennington.

ON April 18, 1775 two lights hung high in the belfry of the old North Church, and William Dawes and Paul Revere began their celebrated rides to rouse the inhabitants of every Middlesex village and farm—against the marching British. A spattering of shots at Lexington swelled into volleys at Concord's rude bridge. And while the shots may not have been heard 'round the world', they were heard in the New Hampshire Grants. Many a farmer laid his hoe against the nearest stump and set out for Boston, where an oddly assorted mob of irate colonists were beseiging the redcoats.

But there were men in the Grants who had their own plans for action. As you can imagine, Ethan Allen was ready with a flamboyant proposal. Why not, he said, seize the mighty fortress of Ticonderoga before the British thought to reinforce it?

The idea was not new. At the very beginning of 1775 the Massachusetts patriots sent John Brown of Pittsfield to Canada, to sound out opinion there. He was guided down Lake Champlain by two of the Green Mountain Boys, and late in March wrote secretly back to Sam Adams in Boston that the Grants people had promised to seize the Fort in case of hostilities.

That very month, as the war clouds gathered, worried members of the Onion River Land Co. gathered at Heman Allen's house in Salisbury, Conn. What effect, they asked themselves, would armed conflict have on their promising venture? And what could be done to forestall the inevitable British invasion up the familiar Lake Champlain warpath, which bordered on their lands?

As always, Ticonderoga was the key to this northern gateway; capture of the Fort and a subsequent invasion of Canada might remove the British threat from the northern frontier once and for all. After the meeting broke up Heman hastened to Hartford, to gain aid for such a project from the Connecticut Committee of Correspondence.

Ethan returned to peddle anti-Yorker pamphlets in the Grants,[1] where he learned of the Westminster "massacre." Dashing across the mountains, he offered his talents to the

angry citizens assembled there in a convention of protest. But he had hardly arrived before the news of Lexington and Concord burst upon the delegates. His mind was "electrified," he said later, by this "bloody attempt . . . to enslave America." Jumping on his horse, he rode posthaste to Bennington, where the Green Mountain Boys were already gathering to debate their course. Heman arrived shortly, followed by a group of Massachusetts and Connecticut men with money and instructions from the Hartford Committee. The latter had been galvanized into action by the suggestion of a certain Captain Benedict Arnold, on his way to Boston, that the guns of Ticonderoga would come in mighty handy up there.

In Boston Arnold obtained a commission to enlist men to take the Fort, but when he arrived at Castleton ahead of his troops, the independent Green Mountain Boys refused to serve under anyone but Allen. However, Ethan permitted the furious officer to march beside him at the head of the column, as this most un-military mob straggled toward the shores of the lake. They had very little idea how they were to get across. They'd actually tried to rent boats from the British at Crown Point, which had burned a short while before, but the soldiers there were not to be horn-swoggled. By good fortune, Allen captured a scow heading down from Skenesboro. But only about a third of the two hundred men could get across in the first load.

By this time dawn was approaching, and a return trip was out of the question. Yet Ethan stopped long enough to make an extended, grandiloquent speech to his little band. Then, in a furious rush, they swarmed through the crumbling walls and scared the pitiful, sleepy garrison half out of its wits. Rushing up the stairs to the quarters of the commanding officer—Arnold at his heels—Ethan demanded the fort of a bewildered, pantsless lieutenant, in the name (he said some years afterward) "of the Great Jehovah and the Continental Congress."[2]

Seth Warner took the ruins of Crown Point easily the next day.

---

[1] The expense of which, appropriately enough, was paid by the Land Company.

[2] *Narrative of Colonel Ethan Allen's Captivity,* written after his return, in 1779.

The capture of Ticonderoga was only the first step in the grand plan of the Onion River Land Co., all of whose Board of Directors participated in the exploit. Canada was next. Allen despatched immediate appeals for aid to Boston, Hartford—and yes—even to Yorker Albany.

There was a British sloop-of-war on the Lake, and a garrison at St. Johns. The expedition now acquired a naval aspect, and Ethan hardly knew one end of a boat from the other. Command of a schooner captured at Skenesboro was therefore grudgingly turned over to the haughty Arnold, an old sailor. Arnold raced down the Lake, overpowered the British sloop, and took St. Johns before Allen and his men could catch up in their clumsy boats. Arnold had abandoned St. Johns in the expectation of a powerful British counterattack, but Ethan decided to try to hold it. When the attack came, however, his force fled in confusion back toward the safety of the forts.

GREEN MOUNTAIN BOYS, led by Ethan Allen (above), broke into the officers' quarters of Fort Ticonderoga in the early dawn of May 12, 1775 to demand surrender of this strategic key to the "Northern Gateway." These riotous frontiersmen—to the great disgust of the very military Colonel Arnold—promptly got drunk on the British stores of rum.

CAPTURE OF THE FORTS was announced by Colonel Allen to his Massachusetts and Connecticut backers, to the Continental Congress, and most surprisingly, to the Albany Committee of Correspondence—filled with his old enemies (letter below). But Albany was the nearest source of aid, and on behalf of his "Grand Plan," Ethan was ready to bury the hatchet—at least temporarily.

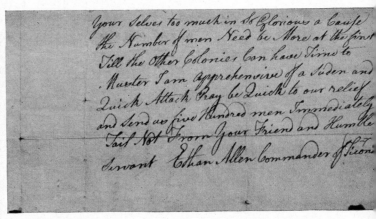

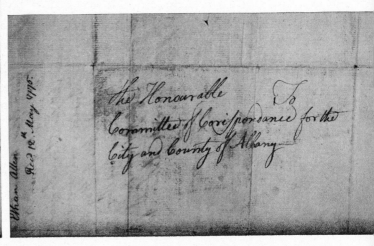

Ethan Allen plots the capture of Ticonderoga at Castleton, May 9, 1775.

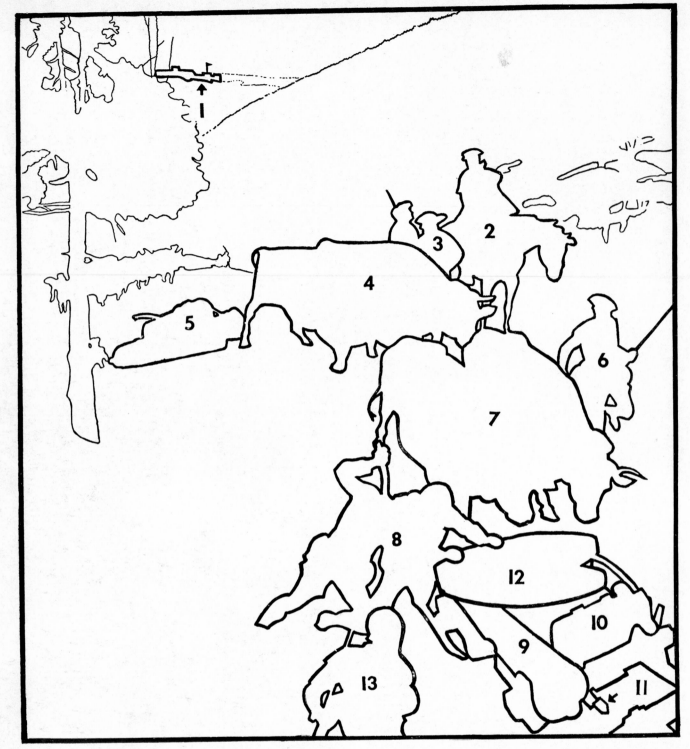

1. FORT TICONDEROGA

2. General Knox (Colonel at that time) in uniform of American artillery.

3. Civilians, farmers who drove their own teams.

4. Team of Holstein oxen. These are short-horned cattle of Dutch origin.

5. Wooden sled carrying 2 British 18 pounders and 2 kegs of flints.

6. American artillery man, private, carrying Tower musket.

7. Team of Devon oxen of British origin.

8. Artillery private (note red artillery facings) and civilian teamster.

9. British 24-pounder.

10. French bronze 13" mortar.

11. Cannon swab.

12. Cannon wheels (wood).

13. Civilian Teamster. The man following sled No. 5 is a soldier. Not all soldiers were fortunate enough those days to have full uniforms. The 2 teams in the background are mixed Devon and Holstein oxen. 2 18-pounders on rear sled.

Fort Ticonderoga's Immortal Guns go to General George Washington ..winter of 1776 ... over hundreds of miles of roadless, trackless, snowclad mountains and valleys, through thick forests, over ice-covered lakes and rivers... on sledges hauled by oxen... in charge of General Knox and his artillerymen in their red-trimmed regimentals, who deliver the guns at Dorchester Heights. There, roaring down at the enemy, they drive him out of Boston Town.

TICONDEROGA

STATUE OF SETH WARNER at the base of the Bennington Monument symbolizes the important role in the Revolution played by this big, quiet and competent man. He ruined himself physically and financially and died in poverty.

The most crushing blow of all came when the townspeople assembled to select a commanding officer for the new regiment. By an overwhelming vote they chose the quiet, capable Seth Warner. Heman Allen was made a captain and Ira first lieutenant. The impetuous Ethan might serve in the ranks, but there was no commission.

Ethan rocked with the punch; his dearest dream was of military glory—in fact, he was the only member of the Company who showed much inclination for the rigors of campaigning. But this severe blow to his pride and his ambitions could not be permitted to interfere with the "grand plan." With General Schuyler's permission he joined—without commission—the forces now gathering for the invasion of Canada. Schuyler made him promise to behave himself, but soon the irrepressible Ethan was cooking up new schemes.

Allen was not the only Green Mountain Boy with a taste for independent action. Remember Baker had served well as a scout. But one day this lean, tough frontiersman stopped a musket ball in a sharp clash with some Indians—to the great annoyance of General Schuyler, who was desperately endeavoring to conciliate the redskins. Ethan swore mightily that he would have revenge, and in the dead of night, in company with one Urieh Cross, he crept stealthily into the Indian camp and removed Baker's head from a pole on which it had been impaled, burying it then with the body which had been left behind by the Indians. And here our story loses one of its principal characters.

But Allen himself was about to undertake an equally rash exploit. Schuyler had sent him down river from Isle-aux-Noix to raise the standard of revolt among the Canadians. But Ethan, impatient with the careful, plodding general, determined to do more. Gathering about him a small group of half-hearted Canadians, he launched a surprise attack on the strategic city of Montreal, having previously arranged with Seth Warner and John Brown for the latter to attack from the south at the same time. But for reasons no one has been able to discover, Brown never carried out his part of the bargain. Allen's motley forces melted away before an attack by the feeble British garrison, and the Green Mountain Boy shortly found himself fleeing pell-mell with equally nimble French and Indians in noisy pursuit. Cornered at last on a stump, Ethan laid about him with his long musket, but finally surrendered to overwhelming force. The picture of the doughty Green Mountain Boy holding off the furious assault is given us—once more—by Urieh Cross, who escaped with three others, as he says, "by putting the best foot forward." Allen was shipped off to England and for nearly three years suffered the indignities and hardships of captivity with admirable and unbroken spirit.

But an even greater blow came from Philadelphia. The Continental Congress—as yet not resolved on independence and an "all-out" war—was more distressed than pleased by Ethan Allen's one-man campaign on the northern frontier. (After all, the Declaration of Independence was still more than a year away.) An invasion of the King's province of Quebec was certainly unthinkable. Cannon and stores, they advised the Albany Committee, should be removed to the south end of Lake George, and held for return to His Majesty when the present "difficulties" should be resolved.

Seizing his ever-active pen, Ethan scribbled off a furious protest to Congress. "Advancing an army into Canada," he wrote "will be agreeable to our friends, and it is bad policy to fear the resentment of an enemy." He then set out for Philadelphia with Seth Warner. By the time he arrived late in June, the temper of Congress in the face of the waxing battle had hardened. The ragged men besieging Boston were adopted as the Continental Army, and a gaunt Virginian named George Washington was selected to lead them. And at the same time careful, patient Phillip Schuyler, an aristocratic New York landowner, was commissioned Major General to lead an attack on Montreal—if the Canadians had no objection!

Thus Allen found a more receptive audience in Philadelphia than he had dared expect. Congress approved his plan for a regiment of Green Mountain Boys. So, surprisingly enough, did the New York Provincial Congress, when this proscribed outlaw appeared before it with a request to serve the cause under New York Commission.

And now, for the moment, a romantic figure has retired back-stage, to prepare, as it were, for a triumphal re-entry.

edict Arnold, brilliant and unpredictable, patriot and traitor.

At the mouth of Otter Creek, Arnold built his tiny fleet for defense of the lakes.

BENEDICT ARNOLD AT VALCOUR

But the war went on without Ethan. The young, competent and likeable General Richard Montgomery took Montreal, with the help of Seth Warner and his regiment. He then pressed on toward the citadel of Quebec, while Benedict Arnold meanwhile led a thousand indomitable frontiersmen through the swamps, mountains and snows of Maine to outflank that city from the north. But the attack went awry. In the confusion the irreplacable Montgomery fell dead, and Arnold retired with a shattered leg. The tattered army, half-starved and ridden with disease, began a disheartening retreat to the sheltering walls of Ticonderoga.

The British pursuit was hampered by the necessity of taking down their ships and reassembling them on Lake Champlain. Efficient General Carleton had foreseen the need, however, and ship builders were ready. By October he began to move down upon the forts. Again the naval defense of the Lake had fallen to Benedict Arnold, who had not been idle that summer. From the virgin forests of Vermont this stubborn, energetic leader had constructed a navy of his own. Laughable it was to trained English seamen, and it was manned by what Arnold himself described as a "wretched, motley crew . . . , few of them ever wet with salt water." Off Valcour Island, in October 1776, the skillful "admiral" maneuvered—and lost—his tiny fleet. But Carleton was so delayed that he postponed his invasion until the following spring, when a new Commander, General John Burgoyne, took over.

*AT VALCOUR ISLAND
Arnold's home-made fleet took a bad beating from a superior British force, but so delayed General Carleton that he postponed his projected invasion until next year.*

Courtesy Fort Ticonderoga Museum

BATTLE'S AFTERMATH: Prisoners' column arrives in Bennington, as depicted in the great mural by Roy Williams for the Bennington Historical Museum.

Captors and captives were exhausted alike from the battle and from the damp heat of that fierce August 16. Stark, Warner and Heman Allen all suffered from heat prostrations. Stark recovered, but Heman died shortly thereafter, and Warner, though he lived to give further service, returned to Bennington at the close of the war a dying man. In the battle Warner lost his brother, and Landlord Stephen Fay his son John. But in all the Yankees lost surprisingly few—about thirty killed and forty wounded, against over two hundred British dead and 750 prisoners.

Parson Allen returned to his ministerial duties in Pittsfield, Mass. In his diary, with true Yankee thrift, he made only the entry: "Expended on my tour to Bennington seven shillings and sixpence."

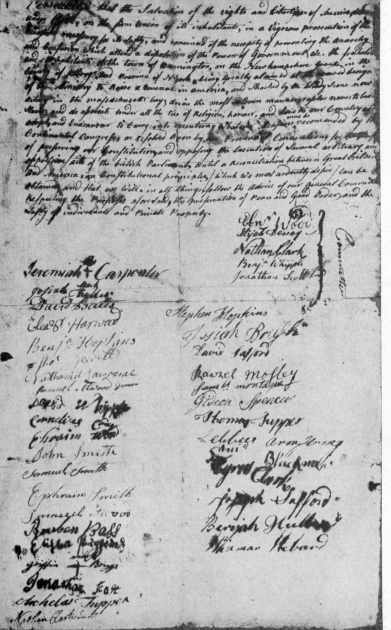

BENNINGTON DECLARATION, once thought unique, is now believed to be one of several signed throughout New York.

REBELS IN THE "GRANTS"

While the frontier waited breathlessly for invasion from the north, men were at work consolidating the political revolution which paralleled—even preceded—the fighting.

We have already seen how the rising revolutionary sentiment in the Connecticut Valley got entangled with the old struggle against New York. Although the frontier generally was isolated from the mainstreams of protest against Parliamentary trade restrictions, there was an increasing number of people on both sides of the mountains who were transferring their enmity against New York's royal government to the King himself. But the first real steps toward revolution came not from the frontier coun-

ties of Albany, Charlotte, Cumberland and Gloucester, but from the merchant groups of New York City and the Hudson Valley, who set up a Committee of Correspondence, and later a Provincial Congress to offset the conservative New York Assembly.[3] When these Yorkers framed a Declaration of Rights in April of 1775, the text was circulated throughout the state for signature by all good patriots. The Bennington copy contains 38 signatures, and it is known to have been approved in several other towns. Many town meetings on both the East and West-sides had given consideration to the issues of British "oppression," and made declarations thereupon. Many of the settlers were thus ready to join Ethan Allen in his attack on Ticonderoga, and Seth Warner in his Continental regiment of Green Mountain Boys.

But there were several whose aims were more expansive, and included dreams of independence.

The Allens' plan for a new state[4] was double-barreled: military and political. When Ethan set forth on the road to military glory, taking Ira, Remember Baker and Seth Warner with him, political affairs were left in the hands of brother Heman—for the organization of public opinion was as important as the military defense of the Onion River sands. Ira soon returned from his brief participation in the Canadian campaign. Now a small group including the Allens and the Fays set about the task of feeling out the people on the subject. Cautiously they issued a call for a convention to see whether the settlers would "consent to associate with New York, or *by themselves* in [the] cause of America."

The forty-nine who gathered hopefully at Cephas Kent's Tavern in Dorset, January 16, 1776, were those already known for their opposition to New York. They came as "representatives" of thirty-two towns, all on the West-side, and many of them uninhabited. Still angrily accusing New York of "land-jobbing," the rebels tempered their revolutionary enthusiasm with a declaration that they would *not* join hands with New York "in such manner as might in the future be detrimental to our private property."

They gathered again in July, and decided to poll the people as to whether the Grants should not be formed into "a separate district." Aware that they were hardly representative of even the least populous half of the Grants, this second convention selected Heman Allen, Jonas Fay and William Marsh as a committee to inveigle the East-side and its influential leaders into their camp.

---

3 Which included the Grant's only representatives—from Cumberland County—Crean Brush and Judge Samuel Wells, both of whom later became loyalists.

4 Ethan had earlier conspired with Major Philip Skene to build all of northern New York, including the Grants, into a new royal province. The Allens believed that Skene was returning with his commission as Governor when he was seized as a loyalist in Philadelphia, in 1775. Ethan had also written Oliver Wolcott even before Ticonderoga proposing independence for the Grants.

Fortunately, events were conspiring to help their plans. The various groups in the Connecticut Valley were beginning to pull together in opposition to New York. The "revolutionaries" over there were divided. The radical wing was led by the religious fanatic Reuben Jones and the boisterous Leonard Spaulding, whose grievances, we have seen, were mostly economic. The conservatives looked to the widely respected Jacob Bayley of Newbury, an ardent patriot, whose inclinations were toward a union with New Hampshire. There were also the Yorkers, mostly in the south part of the county. And there was the large mass of people, as usual, who were waiting to see which way it would be most expedient to jump.

Jones and Spaulding needed no selling; the former was already involved in promoting the "new state" idea. They both showed up at Dorset in September, along with representatives from several from Cumberland County towns. Many of the latter, however, had definitely voted *not* to send a representative, and Gloucester County ignored the entire proceedings. The convention delegates asserted flatly their preference for a new state, and expressed the hope that everyone would get behind the project. They even agreed to ask New York State if it would be all right with her! And to strengthen their bid to the East-siders, they agreed to reassemble over at Westminster, Oct. 30.

When that time rolled around everybody west of the mountains was in an uproar over the defeat at Valcour and the expected invasion, and only six delegates out of seventeen came from across the mountains. The absence of Jonas Fay, customary clerk of these meetings, gave Ira Allen his first chance for a prominent role. He had already been working manfully behind the scenes. After appointing committees and rehearsing their manifestoes, they adjourned until January at the same place. Even fewer came at that time—from only eleven towns in the vicinity and seven from the West-side.

Yet this was the convention which declared independence for a new state, under the name "New Connecticut"— an appropriate recognition of the origin of most of the settlers. The radicals, discouraged in the attempt to draw in the moderates of the Connecticut Valley, decided to take the bit in their teeth, taking heart from the instructions of the Continental Congress to form new governments where there now were none. Still there was little support for a new state struggling to be born. General Jacob Bayley, never present, had hopefully been chosen to various committees—which he pointedly ignored.

But now New York—quite unwittingly—did her arch enemies a very great favor. She completed a constitution for the new State of New York, and in doing so alienated almost every friend she had in the Grants.

Of course, this new constitution was meant to cover the interior counties as well as the seaboard and river ones. But it could hardly have been written in a manner

VERMONT'S DECLARATION OF INDEPENDENCE— from New York—was signed at Westminster, January 15, 1777.

more distasteful to frontier democrats, radical and conservative alike. Nearly every grievance they had against the old royal province was carried over into this new frame of government. It was perfectly clear that the aristocrats, merchants and men of wealth were to dominate the new "revolutionary" state, whether the back country liked it or not. It was Bayley himself who observed that the inhabitants of Gloucester County, formerly reluctant to break away from New York, were "now almost to a man violent for it."

The discordant factions thereupon fell into each others arms. Gathering at Windsor on June 4, 1777, they sat down to listen to a message from Dr. Thomas Young, Philadelphia revolutionary and old friend of Ethan Allen.

"To the Inhabitants of VERMONT," he wrote, "a free and independent state, bounding on the River Connecticut and Lake Champlain." "Vermont" it was to be, for the "new staters" had learned that there was already a district in Pennsylvania known by the name of New Connecticut.

But the convention still felt their position to be somewhat shaky, and they adjourned until July 2nd. In the meantime, letters were sent to all towns asking that delegates be sent to Windsor on that date to select delegates to Congress, choose a "committee of safety," and to form a constitution.

But Burgoyne had begun his invasion of the Champlain Valley, and the worried delegates who gathered on the first anniversary of the colonies' Declaration of Independence were fewer in number, though more popularly elected. Their work was interrupted, however, on July 8th by the shattering news that Ticonderoga had been abandoned, and the rear guard of the retreating American army smashed at Hubbardton by the advancing legions of General John Burgoyne.

COLONEL BAUM, *Hessian Commander of Burgoyne's sortie to collect the Bennington stores, was mortally wounded along with Colonel Pfister, leader of the Tories. They were borne to David Mathews house in Shaftsbury, where both died.* (Painting by Roy Williams).

PLAN OF BATTLE *is set forth on bronze plaque located at site of battlefield, over the border in New York State.*

BENNINGTON BATTLEFIELD *today (top, below). MARKER in Old Bennington (bottom) tells story of expedition.*

GENERAL JOHN BURGOYNE, *dramatist, literateur, was widely known as "Gentleman Johnny."*

AT HUBBARDTON, *the rear guard of Gen. St. Clair's retreating army clashed with advancing British, met defeat, but stopped the pursuit.*

"GENTLEMAN JOHNNY"

The British had used the winter to good advantage, and in the early summer of 1777 were ready to launch the giant blow which would split the new American nation in half. The route was to be the ancient warpath down the Champlain Valley to the Hudson River. There Burgoyne planned to meet General Howe who was to lead his forces up the river from British occupied New York City.

In June the great invasion began, with eight thousand men, composed of British regulars, German mercenaries —Hessians—, Indians and Tories under Colonel Philip Skene, late of Skenesboro and suitably anxious to reclaim his vast estates. The red, blue and green uniforms, the gaudily painted Indians, the scores of banners fluttering in the warm June breeze, all made a strikingly colorful— and awesome—pageant.

The residents of the West-side were panic stricken. Burgoyne had issued an ultimatum, demanding that all the people of the surrounding countryside take oaths of allegiance to the King. Royalists—and many others who had played leading roles in the struggles of the New Hampshire Grants against New York—decided to repair to the royal standard. Among these were Justus Sherwood, Green Mountain Boy, and Colonel William Marsh of Manchester. The latter had been exceedingly active in the conventions of the Grants which had been meeting periodically with the aim of establishing an independent state among the Green Mountains.

Arnold's gallant defense of the Lake had gained for the Americans precious time. But when Burgoyne appeared

before Ticonderoga, the forces cooped up inside were still badly armed and ill-fed—a poor excuse for an army. The commanding General St. Clair ignored certain strategic heights around the Fort, which, when suddenly occupied by the British, made any defense suicidal. One dark night St. Clair began his retreat across to the Vermont side, and headed for Rutland. As rear guard to his frightened, fleeing army he selected Seth Warner's Green Mountain Boys, along with Colonel Nathan Hale's New Hampshire regiment and Colonel Ebenezer Francis' Massachusetts forces.

The British under General Frazer were in hot pursuit, and shortly before sunrise of July 1 stumbled upon Warner's outposts at Hubbardton. In the sharp clash which followed, Colonel Francis fell mortally wounded. His men began to break, and the New Hampshiremen, believing themselves surrounded, threw down their arms. Helpless, a furious Warner organized the retreat over the mountains to the East, toward Rutland. But though the Americans had been defeated, they checked the British pursuit, and probably saved the remnants of St. Clair's army to fight again—at Bennington and Saratoga.

Burgoyne's supply lines, running way down the lakes into Canada, were stretching thinner. The supply problem for his magnificent army was getting more and more difficult. The fear of his Indians had sent the settlers in the Otter Valley and along Lake Champlain fleeing to the south. And in a de-populated country, the British general was finding it increasingly hard to feed his army.

Thus the stores which the Americans were assembling at Bennington began to look increasingly attractive to

CONTINENTAL STOREHOUSE at Bennington, to the defense of which General John Stark rallied his forces (right), is now marked by a marble slab (above), its story worn almost to illegibility.

him. It should be an easy task to gather them in, he thought, as he despatched Colonel Baum with a small force of 800 Hessians to pick them up. Baum was also to make a great circle via Bennington, Manchester, Rockingham, Brattleboro, the Crown Point Road, and back to Ticonderoga.

He never even reached his first destination.

Frantic appeals by Schuyler, Warner, Ira Allen and others had finally bestirred the northern New England colonies to action. New Hampshire drew her brilliant Colonel John Stark from "retirement," and men flocked to serve under the hero of the Indian wars. Then splashing in to Bennington through the spring mud in his one horse shay came the Reverend Thomas Allen, with a large part of his Pittsfield congregation. The "fighting parson" made free to wake the General. We've been called out before, he declared, but never fought. This was the last time. Stark eyed the bristling parson, and pointed to the downpour of rain which was turning the camp into a bog. "If the Lord should once more give us sunshine," he said, "and I do not give you fighting enough, I will never ask you to come again."

There was fighting enough for everyone on the morrow. Baum had paused before he reached the town line, after a clash with the American scouts, and entrenched himself. He then sent back a call for reinforcements. By mid-day the skies cleared, but the air dripped moisture and the men moved in a humid steam-bath. Over the sodden ground Stark launched his attack, and the first shot was fired by the irrepressible Parson Allen. Stark and Warner had gone forward to scout the British guns, which had opened fire on them. To his nervous men, unused to facing cannon, he joked: "The rascals know I'm an officer; they're firing a salute in my honor." And as the tide of battle rose in fury

he is reputed to have told his troops: "There stand the redcoats; today they are ours, or Molly Stark sleeps this night a widow." A declaration for posterity to rank with Ethan Allen's demand for the surrender of Ticonderoga— but probably equally unsubstantiated!

Baum was mortally wounded in the brief but sharp battle which followed, and his troops scattered in wild confusion. The British reinforcements under Breyman were also thrown into retreat by the timely arrival of Warner's Continental regiment, which had been delayed in arriving from Manchester, although their leader had been present throughout the battle.

The unexpected defeat of his crack regiments left John Burgoyne puzzled and greatly dismayed. And well he might be, for his supply lines were open to constant attack from the Grants, "a country," declared "Gentleman Johnny," "which abounds in the most active and rebellious race on the continent, and hangs like a gathering storm on my left." He moved his forces ponderously down toward Saratoga to meet the main American forces. And there, after tangling with the brilliant and tireless Benedict Arnold, he surrendered his entire army in the most crushing British defeat of the war to date.

The surrender had many important effects, not the least of which was the entry of France on the American side. But to the inhabitants on the northern frontier it meant peace and a chance to resume the more tranquil pursuits of tilling the land. For the Grants it meant the virtual end of their military participation in the Revolution. Many times subsequently the British and Indians launched raids into the Champlain Valley and the Green Mountain rivers with frightening suddenness—a re-enactment of the terror of twenty years before. But Burgoyne's was the last major army to invade the northern parts of the colonies.

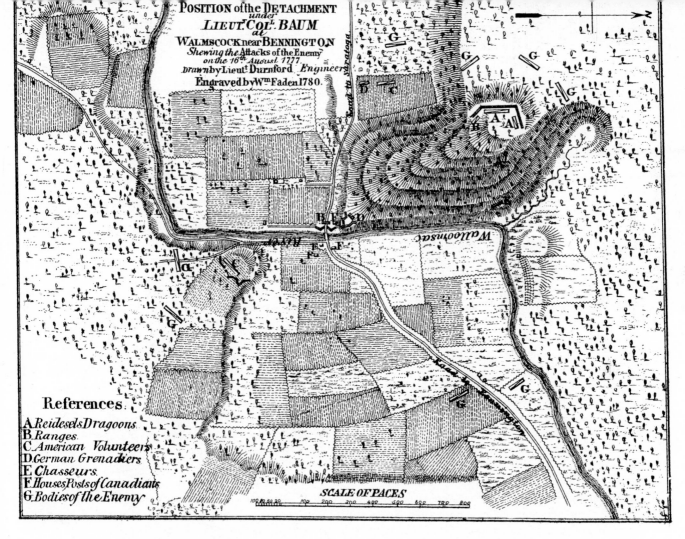

POSITION of the DETACHMENT under LIEUT. COL. BAUM at WALMSCOCK near BENNINGTON Shewing the Attacks of the Enemy on the 16th August 1777. Drawn by Lieut. Durnford Engineer. Engraved by Wm. Faden 1780.

References
A Reidesels Dragoons.
B Ranges.
C American Volunteers.
D German Grenadiers.
E Chasseurs.
F Houses Posts of Canadians.
G Bodies of the Enemy.

SCALE OF PACES

BURGOYNE'S MAP of the action near Bennington, taken from his post-campaign apologia, "State of the Expedition . . ."

SURRENDER AT SARATOGA to American forces ended Burgoyne's threat to split the colonies, and the danger to Vermont's frontier.

FIRST STARS AND STRIPES, carried at Bennington. Now in the Bennington Museum.

Courtesy Fort Ticonderoga Museum →

VI

THE REPUBLIC OF VERMONT

How the Vermonters framed a Constitution and a government for their new nation, and how this independent republic eventually became the fourteenth state.

IT was an exceedingly hot July 2nd, that year of our Lord 1777, and a group of perspiring and thirsty men flooded out of the Windsor meetinghouse in the direction of Elijah West's tavern. They had just spent a weary afternoon listening to the exhortations of the Rev. Aaron Hutchinson, who had been called from his plow in Pomfret to preach the sermon opening the constitutional convention of the new state of Vermont.

The loquacious parson had selected the Golden Rule for his text, but his extemporaneous sermon swerved speedily from the Biblical injunction to a rousing denunciation of the conduct of New York. The delegates could be excused if, after such a trying spiritual experience, they sought bodily refreshment at the nearby tavern.

Rev. Hutchinson had thought that the convention wouldn't gather as scheduled, because of the current threat of British invasion. In fact, the delegates who did come—and they were fewer than at the Windsor convention of the preceding month—were exceedingly uneasy. Nor was their state of mind improved, as they settled down to business, by an urgent call for aid from Seth Warner, watching Burgoyne move down on Ticonderoga.

Unsettled in mind, they turned to the business at hand. Like all the conventions of the Grants, these delegates of independent town governments acted on various matters of common interest, military and civil. But they had been called together principally for the purpose of adopting a frame of government—a constitution—for the new state.

There were four men at the convention who were particularly interested in this item of business. For Heman Allen, Joseph Fay, Reuben Jones and Thomas Chittenden had taken the new state's request for recognition to the Continental Congress in Philadelphia. There, while waiting on a uninterested Congress, they had run across an old friend and neighbor of Ethan, Dr. Thomas Young, now a prominent Pennsylvania radical and intimate of Sam Adams and Tom Paine—whose views he reflected.

It was Young, always interested in the Grants, who had given them Ben Franklin's brand new Pennsylvania constitution, urging them to return home and form a new government. He'd even sent along a message, assuring the new state he called *"Vermont"* recognition, once they'd complied with Congress' May 1776 call upon all revolting colonies to set up new governments, as might be required.

The June convention that followed the commissioners' return had liked the cut of Young's suggestions, even to the name he'd given their state—which was promptly adopted. But slightly worried over its own somewhat informal organization, it had issued a call to all the towns to elect representatives to a real constitutional convention, also to be held at Windsor on July 2nd. And to draft a constitution for consideration by the new convention, a committee was appointed, composed—most likely—of the four ambassadors to Congress, who had in hand, thanks to Dr. Young, a democratic and legal document.

It was this committee which now reported to the assembled delegates at Landlord West's the results of their deliberations during June. They hadn't seen fit to make many changes in the Pennsylvania document, but the convention sat down to see how they liked it. The sweat that stood out on many a leathery forehead, however, was not so much the result of mental labor as the oppressive humidity. Storm clouds gathered outside.

Suddenly the suspense compounded of intent mind and strained atmosphere was broken by the clatter of hooves and a babble of excited voices. Ticonderoga had fallen, and the retreating American forces were under attack at Hubbardton! The message ran through the assembly like wildfire, and consternation spread as rapidly. Men from the West-side, including Chairman Joseph Bowker of Rutland, remembered their farms and families, now exposed to attack by Burgoyne and his Indians. Thoughts of conditions and clauses fled from their minds.

Then, as violent as the storm hanging over the Champlain Valley, another and more literal storm burst upon the Assembly. A sudden cloudburst hedged the tavern with a wall of water. As the worried West-siders hesitated momentarily, their friends prevailed upon them to complete the document, then in its final reading. Deliberations were resumed, the Constitution accepted, and December 24 was set as a date for elections to the new Government. A Council of Safety was designated to act on behalf of the state in the meantime. The delegates from over the mountains then dashed off to the westward.

[S]TORM gathers behind Elijah [W]est's tavern in Windsor, [Ju]ly 8, 1777, as the dramatic [ne]ws of the evacuation of stra[te]gic Fort Ticonderoga reaches [th]e delegates gathered there to [fra]me a constitution for their [ne]w state.

[IRA] ALLEN, politician, diplo[mat,] land speculator, became a [force] of the "new state" move[ment] after the death of his older [broth]er Heman. But he does not [seem] to have been present (his [claim]s to the contrary notwith[stand]ing) at the birth of the new [gove]rnment in Windsor. Minia[ture] below, in UVM's Fleming [Muse]um, is the only contemporary [likene]ss of any of the Allen brothers.

IRA ALLEN

RESTORED CONSTITUTION HOUSE stands on a new site. Porch was added in 1914 restoration.

CONSTITUTION
of the State of Vermont

1777–1947

PENN'S CHARTER, *foundation of the liberal Pennsylvania Constitution of 1776, in turn largely adopted by Vermont.*

Because Vermonters live today under substantially the same basic charter of government as that which came out of the historic Windsor Convention of July 1777, it is worthwhile to stop and examine it in some detail. It is, as we have seen, fundamentally a copy of the Pennsylvania Constitution of 1776. This, in turn, reflects the liberal concepts of government expressed in William Penn's royal charter of 1681 and his subsequent "frames of government," as well as the immediate influence of the American Declaration of Independence. The latter was only eleven days old when the constitutional convention gathered under the presidency of wise old Benjamin Franklin. It is quite significant that a document expressing the radical attitudes of intellectual democrats like Franklin, Young, and Tom Paine, should meet with such whole-hearted acceptance on the frontier.

RIGHTS AND LIBERTIES

The opening of Pennsylvania's ringing "Declaration of Rights" is an elaboration of similar observations in the Declaration of Independence with respect to "life, liberty, and the pursuit of happiness." Citizens are promised certain rights they had not always securely enjoyed: freedom of speech and of the press, right of assembly, prompt and uncorrupted justice, trial by jury, free and frequent elections, and protection from search and seizure. The Vermonters, out of their own experience, added several themselves: the right to govern their own internal police, restraints on writs of attachment, and prohibition of the transfer for trial out of the state of any citizen charged with a crime committed within the state.

However, the most important addition was in the very first clause. Here the Vermonters drew down to earth the fancy language of freedom by forbidding any man to be held in bondage against his will. Vermont became thereby the first state to accomplish the ABOLITION OF SLAVERY [*see* the page from the original Constitution, *right above*].

A second precedent-shattering grant to the people at large was made in the establishment of UNIVERSAL MANHOOD SUFFRAGE—a reflection of frontier democracy absent in the Pennsylvania document.

FREEDOM OF RELIGION was a difficult problem. The Vermonters echoed Pennsylvania's assurance to all men of the right to worship God according to the dictates of their own conscience, without being required to support any specific church. Then they proceeded to destroy the value of the clause, saying "nor can any man *who professes the Protestant religion* be justly deprived or abridged of any civil right as a citizen on account of his religious sentiment." (The words in italics were added to the Pennsylvania declaration but were removed in 1793.) Catholics, Jews, Quakers and others like minded were not deemed worthy of religious rights.

Vermont abolishes slavery in her first Constitution

FRAME OF GOVERNMENT

The prevailing insistence on keeping control in the hands of the citizens is reflected in the provisions for setting up the working bodies of government. The center of power lay very definitely in the legislature, a single house somewhat unrepresentative in character. Each town sent one representative (though towns with more than 80 taxable inhabitants could send two during the first seven years only). So deeply rooted was confidence in the New England town meeting that Vermonters resisted any form of participation in state government which might tend to undermine it. Pennsylvania, which had apportioned representation on the basis of population, abolished her unicameral legislature in short order. But Vermont retained this unique institution until 1836, when after many tries, a majority of three approved the creation of a Senate, whose members were elected from the counties according to population. By this action they also abolished the Governor's Council, which had sometimes acted very much like a legislative body. The Constitution placed the executive power in a Governor and Council, which lacked any veto over legislative doings. But the Council was granted the right to prepare bills for action by the General Assembly, and for a long while exercised this quasi-legislative function. In 1786 the Council was also given the privilege of suspending the application of any law until the Assembly re-affirmed it. As a matter of fact, the Assembly itself was required to submit all bills for consideration to the Governor and Council, and to the general public, withholding actual enactment until the following session, though they might— in "emergencies"—pass "temporary acts." The result was that almost all laws were passed as "temporary" and confirmed as "permanent" the following session. This unwieldy system was abolished in 1786.

This Pennsylvania-Vermont frame of government reflects the current concern for the separation of powers as among the executive, the legislative, and the judicial, combined with an oddly contrary preference for the legislature as most democratic. Yet to nail the issue down securely, the delegates to the next (1786) convention added a specific clause stating that the three departments "shall be separate and distinct, so that neither exercise the powers properly belonging to the others."

Men who had thrown off the confining shackles of both royal and provincial (New York) authority also made sure that their new government would be amenable to change if and when the popular will might desire to undertake it. But they provided that the amending process should originate in a Council of Censors,[1] which, meeting every seven years, should have the additional responsibility of reviewing—without power of veto—all acts of government with an eye to their legality and propriety.

Until it recommended its own abolition in 1869, few of its suggestions of amendment were accepted by the conventions called for that purpose. Its recurrent proposal for the establishment of a Senate, for example, was rejected steadily until 1836, when the recent failure to elect a governor threw considerable doubt on the effectiveness of the single house. A Senate was first refused in 1793, and even by 1813 could muster only five votes in its favor.

SUPREME LAW OF THE LAND

It has been a source of frequent comment by historians that the Vermont constitution was never submitted to the people for ratification. Ira Allen admits that if it had been it would have been rejected. However, it gained some legality by the fact that the July convention was composed of delegates elected by many towns for the purpose of adopting a constitution, and this was done unanimously. The delegates gathered again in December to postpone the scheduled date for elections, at which time they tinkered with the document somewhat and ratified it all over again, along with a diffuse and lengthy preamble[2] which Thomas Chittenden and Ira Allen cooked up in a private session in Williamstown, Mass. It set forth again their complaint against New York as well as royal tyranny.

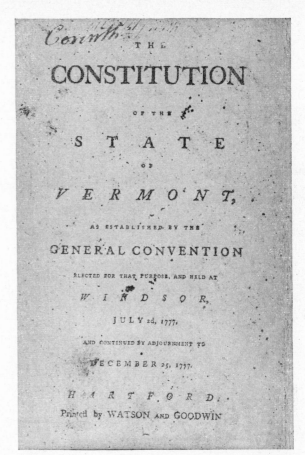

THE

CONSTITUTION

OF THE

S T A T E

OF

V E R M O N T,

AS ESTABLISHED BY THE

GENERAL CONVENTION

ELECTED FOR THAT PURPOSE, AND HELD AT

W I N D S O R,

JULY 2d, 1777,

AND CONTINUED BY ADJOURNMENT TO

DECEMBER 25, 1777.

H A R T F O R D,

Printed by WATSON AND GOODWIN

RARE FIRST EDITION of the Constitution, printed in Hartford, Conn. in 1777. No official manuscript copy is known to exist. Watson did a large quantity of pamphlets for the Allens before Vermont got her own printer in 1778.

Oddly enough, succeeding legislatures acquired the habit of solemnly re-enacting the Constitution, as if that document were not the basis of their own existence. But the reader should remember that written constitutions were new at that time. The modern distinction between a fundamental "constitution" and the "law" made under and in conformity with it, was not so clear then. The forthright declaration in the new U. S. Constitution of 1787 that it constituted "the supreme law of the land" began a new era. And it was a half century before Chief Justice John Marshall firmly established the doctrine of constitutional supremacy (as interpreted by the courts). Unquestionably the whole process of organizing this new state by right of revolution, and in opposition to a multitude of claimants, was irregular. But a handful of skillful frontier diplomats made good their claims of independence in 1791, when all claimants gave in and Congress admitted Vermont to the Union.

1 Another experiment which Pennsylvania quickly shed (in 1790), but which Vermont retained until 1870, when initiative for amending was given to the legislature.

2 This was tossed out in 1793, after Vermont joined the Union.

THOMAS CHITTENDEN, Vermont's First Governor.   *Reconstructed from family portraits and descriptions of contemporaries.*

DIVIDED LAND

The Vermont which opened shop for business in 1777 was not the state we know today, though it even then laid claim to its present boundaries. But within this area the people were split into a number of factions, each group straining restlessly in behalf of its own interests. The people in these towns frequently refused allegiance to the new state which claimed them.

First and most obvious limitation was the fact that the British had forced the new state to withdraw behind a line of frontier forts at Castleton, Pittsford and Rutland. Except for General Jacob Bayley's grim and determined hold on the upper reaches of the Connecticut River, northern Vermont was lost.

On the east-side of the mountains, where the people on both sides of the Connecticut River were drawn together by common economic and social interests, there was violent opposition to any political move that attempted to use the river as a dividing line. And that was just what the proposed new state of Vermont threatened to do. Nothing else counted for much with these valley people, as long as they could stick together. They were willing to go with Vermont or they were willing to go with New Hampshire; they would have particularly liked a new "valley state" of their own. But they did not want to be divided. So instead of accepting the new state of Vermont with whole-hearted enthusiasm, they accepted it with certain local reservations. It was all right if it did not conflict too much with their own interests. Their leader was the ardent patriot and founder of Newbury, General Bayley, generally conceded to be the most influential man on the Grants. Once ready to make his peace with New York, he had now swung over to reluctant and uneasy support of the new state after a long look at the sort of government revolutionary New York intended to impose on its back country. A great many valley people followed the General temporarily into the new state, along with a more limited number of enthusiastic new-staters led by the radical Reuben Jones.

There was not such a strong valley unity further south; settlements on the New Hampshire side had not flourished as vigorously as further up the river. And the people on the west-side of the river were mostly vigorous supporters of New York (with a sprinkling of people who hoped Massachusetts might reassert her ancient claim). There were Yorkers all up and down the River, though influential and Yorkish Col. Nathan Stone—the former leader of "Stone's Rebellion" against the New York courts—lost power in Windsor as that town was swept into the new-state movement. But beginning south of there the towns withheld allegiance to Vermont. Occasionally representatives would turn up amongst the Vermonters, but the Yorkers were in the vast—and vocal—majority. The Cumberland County Committee of Safety continued to function, linked to the New York Committee, though its labors met with increasing roadblocks thrown up by the Vermonters.

The Grants were split not only in a geographical sense, but in a social and economic one. Throughout the territory, many men of property had refused to jump on the bandwagon, either of revolt against the King, or against New York. Old lines, however, became blurred as some like Justus Sherwood and James Breakenridge who had bedeviled the Yorkers, and some like William Marsh who had helped found the new Vermont, went over to the enemy. But most of those with loyalist sympathies hung on until driven from their homes. They were not left in peace long. The new State of Vermont feared that what insecure support it did have might vanish quickly if it attempted to impose taxes for the support of its military effort. So it turned instead to the confiscation and sale of "loyalist" property, (at times even going to the extent of labelling its political enemies as loyalists to destroy them and obtain their estates). At the moment, therefore, there was a widely scattered element of the population on which the Vermonters could not depend for support. As we shall later see, however, when enthusiasm for the Revolution ebbed among the leaders of the new state, many "loyalists" were drawn into the government.

The final group in this kaleidoscope of shifting factions was, of course, the "Vermonters"—for at this time only those who had vigorously prosecuted the new state movement can be reliably so termed. They were composed of a hard core of skillful—and sometimes unscrupulous—frontier politicians. After the death of Heman Allen, Thomas Chittenden was thrust to the fore by the old-timers as a compromise candidate for leadership. It was clear that General Bayley would not support any one of the leaders of the Green Mountain Boys, whom he cordially detested. Chittenden, however, as a newcomer had had no part in the earlier riotous activity, though they knew him well enough to believe him "safe." He did not betray their expectations.

It was Thomas Chittenden, therefore, who served as President of the Council of Safety, which ruled "Vermont" until the new government got under way. And it was Thomas Chittenden who was promptly elected Governor in the first elections.

Only authentic likeness of Chittenden is a silhouette in UVM's Fleming Museum, by the famous American artist Charles Wilson Peale.

Legend has it that Arlington's great pine, plainly visible from the Governor's house and still standing today, was—with the cow, three sheaves of wheat and the distant mountains—drawn into Reuben Dean's original state seal, designed in 1779 by Ira Allen.

ELEAZAR WHEEL-OCK founded the Indian school and college known as Dartmouth, first on the northern frontier. A shrewd politician, he visualized a new northern state for which Dartmouth would be the state university.

Courtesy Dartmouth College

But this maneuver was not accomplished, as Ira Allen candidly admits, without considerable grass-roots politiking. Aware of the tenuous hold they had even on the towns which had thus far consented to join the independence venture, the "Vermonters" made shift to postpone the elections and the first legislature, scheduled by the Windsor Convention for January 1778. The excuse was that they hadn't been able to get the Constitution printed yet—although Ira had gotten through the press a lengthy pamphlet of his own to utilize as propaganda in the coming campaign. They then skillfully saw to it that the printed Constitution was distributed only a few days before the elections, so that the opposition had no time to organize. For there was considerable dissatisfaction, even in the old Allen stronghold of Bennington, over the fact that the document had not been submitted to the people for ratification.

Supporters of the new state were particularly fearful of losing the East-side entirely.[3] Congress had bluntly rejected their application for admission to the union and had denounced Thomas Young's blandishments as "derogatory to the honor of Congress." The Vermonters were advised that no Congressional declaration or resolution could possibly be interpreted so as to supply justification for their secession from New York. The Congressional resolutions were conveyed by the New York Committee of Safety to James Clay of Putney, Chairman of the Cumberland County Committee, who began to circulate copies. Fearful that Congress's disapproval would undermine their support, the Vermonters acted quickly to suppress the news. Clay was seized and jailed. Then Ira Allen, aimed with blank commissions in the Vermont militia, enlistment bounties, and his new pamphlet, set out to stump the East-side for the purpose of counteracting any possible influence Congress's action might have had.

The southeastern towns[4] had already drawn up a "remonstrance"—the first of many to follow—against the movement to form an independent state and forwarded it to Governor George Clinton of New York. This efficient, but stubborn executive had already rejected a plea from New York's brilliant young Gouverneur Morris for a compromise on the land issue. Also he refused to budge from the old policy of ineffective threats against Vermont. At the same time he did nothing to help his own supporters in the grants.

The elections were finally held on March 3rd. Members of the new Council were shrewdly drawn from both East-side and West-side, but of them Bayley alone was not allied with the Allen faction. Ten days later the first legislature assembled at Windsor, also heavily weighted with adherents of the Bennington party. It was perfectly clear to the Valley people whose participation in the new state had been somewhat half-hearted, that the new Vermont was to be run by a tight oligarchy of active and skillful West-side politicians.

As a consequence Bayley and his friends began to revive their old idea of a Connecticut Valley state. In this they received great encouragement from the other side of the river, where at Dresden (Hanover) the learned Eleazar Wheelock had established his new college and Indian school. Now the New Hampshire river settlements were quite as much frontier country as their neighbor towns over across in the Grants. And they were in the midst of an inevitable quarrel with their own government at Exeter over representation in the New Hampshire legislature. With their usual fear of the bumptious back country, the conservatives of the seaboard and eastern New Hampshire had virtually shut out the river towns.

Wheelock was especially anxious to cut loose from the distant seaboard. In a new valley state—or even in Vermont if it included both sides of the river—Dartmouth might become the state university and the cultural center of a new commonwealth. In fact, joining Vermont really meant absorbing it, for the combined valley towns would heavily over-balance the West-side influence. That was all right with Bayley, too.

So the first legislature of the new state of Vermont received a petition to take under its patronage the college at Dartmouth. It complied readily, and appointed President Wheelock a Vermont justice-of-the-peace. The East-side began to perk up a bit at the prospect of carrying some weight in the new state. When the legislature reassembled at Windsor in October there were representatives from 35 East-side towns as against only 26 west of the mountains. And on hand to second the former were delegates from 11 towns *across* the river. It was not surprising, therefore, that 16 Cheshire and Grafton County towns[5] were promptly admitted.

---

[3] And well they might, for an August canvass of Cumberland County by the new-staters showed 480 for New York, 320 for Vermont and 185 neutral.

[4] Weathersfield, Westminster, Rockingham, Hinsdale (Vernon), Newfane, Putney, Brattleboro and Guilford.

[5] Cornish, Lebanon, Hanover (including Dresden), Lyme, Oxford, Piermont, Haverhill, Bath, Lyman, Apthorp, Enfield, Canaan, Cardigan (Orange), Gunthwaite (Lisbon), Morristown (Franconia) and Landaff.

Ira Allen had done his job of East-side persuasion too well. The Bennington faction now watched in dismay as their old enemies ran away with *their* "Vermont." Among the worried group who went into a huddle to discuss strategy was a huge figure which had not been seen in those parts for some time. Ethan Allen was back.

RETURN OF ETHAN ALLEN

At long last, after fretting for over two years in British prison ships, Ethan had been exchanged. But he had not returned immediately to the scenes of his former triumphs. Perhaps it might be well to come back with more than just a harrowing narrative of captivity. So, after he had— as he modestly reports—"landed on liberty ground . . . and received the acclamations of a grateful people," he proceeded to visit first George Washington and then the Continental Congress itself. The Commander-in-Chief liked the bold courage of the man, and wrote to Congress that there was indeed in him a certain "original something which commands admiration." A charmed Congress gave him the brevet rank of Colonel in the Continental Army and voted him back pay. Then, in the distinguished company of the victor of Saratoga, General Horatio Gates, he proceeded homeward.

The good people of Bennington were as glad, on that May 31, 1778, to welcome Ethan as they were the usual reluctant Vermont summer. In his absence, politics, like winter, had been bleak and a new dash of color could now be expected. In celebration they joined him in "passing the flowing bowl."

As always, Ethan did not disappoint his public. Finding this new state of "Vermont," erected in his absence, leaderless and crumbling—or so it seemed to him—he promptly took personal control. Although he held no official position in the new government, he sharpened his quill and began writing vigorously. Soon people began doing their official business as much with Ethan as with the elected officials.

In June Colonel Allen presided at the hanging of David Redding, convicted of correspondence with the British. In July he herded together seventeen loyalists—"atrocious villains"—and drove them off to Albany to be turned over to the British. But these unhappy souls complained to Governor Clinton and General George Washington that their only offense was in not supporting the new state. Ethan himself confirmed their claim in a letter to Elisha Payne in which he admitted that he had extended the legislature's act of banishment to cover "Yorkers as well as Tories." Confiscation of the property of these opponents of the new regime proceeded apace, and Ethan and others bought heavily at bargain prices.

Before the end of summer Ethan took into his own hands the threat of the "Eastern Union." New Hampshire's Governor Weare had written both Governor

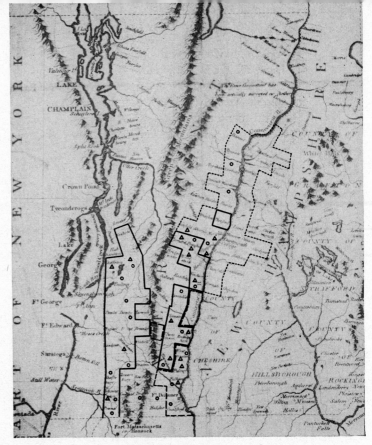

NEW HAMPSHIRE GRANTS – 1777-1778

Base map: section from Conder's 1777 map.

——— "Vermont" towns   ▲ Towns adopting Decl. of Indep., Jan. 7, 1777

◾◾◾ "Yorker" towns

········· "Valley" towns   ● Towns adopting the Constitution, July 8, 1777

Chittenden and Colonel Allen hotly protesting the admission of the Grafton and Cheshire County towns. As it happened, both men were as unhappy as Weare about it. Ethan immediately set out for Philadelphia and there engineered a trade with the New Hampshire delegate. He agreed to "return" the bothersome towns if New Hampshire would support Vermont's admission as a state. Returning to the Vermont legislature, assembled again at Windsor with the New Hampshire towns in attendance,[6] he presented a terrifying report of Congress's anger over Vermont's theft of her neighbor's territory. "Except the State recede from such union immediately," he warned, "the whole power of the United States of America will join to annihilate the State of Vermont, to vindicate the right of New Hampshire, and to maintain inviolate the articles of confederation, which guarantees to each state their privileges and immunities." Somehow this giant trembling in mock terror had conveniently forgotten his own friends' full-throated defiance of Governor Clinton and of Congress over the original —and similar—secession of the Vermont towns from New York in 1777.

---

6 There were 26 representatives from west of the mountains, 35 from the east-side, and 13 from the ex-New Hampshire towns.

The Assembly would not dissolve the union. But on the other hand, after considerable discussion, neither would they reorganize the Vermont counties to include the New Hampshire towns. The Allens had thus won an initial victory. Ethan promptly and joyously wrote Governor Weare, apologizing for the "imbecility" of Vermont in "inadvertently" annexing some of his territory.

Following the action of the Assembly the new State broke in half. Jacob Bayley stomped out of the government, accompanied by two other members of the Council, Lieutenant-Governor Joseph Marsh, and twenty-four legislators—including representatives of ten East-side towns. Eleazar Wheelock's son John then set forth for Philadelphia to protest to Congress.

Ethan had also decided to revisit Philadelphia, to collect on his bargain. Here the two men clashed when Wheelock pointed out to that august assembly that Ethan had no authority to turn the river towns back to New Hampshire against their will. The angry and frustrated Green Mountain Boy promptly denounced the valley leaders to Governor Weare as "a petulant, pettifogging, scribbling sort of gentry, that will keep any government in hot water till they are thoroughly brought under by exertions of Authority." Odd words indeed, from a man with a genius in the arts of stirring up trouble by pen and sword, and with a bitter aversion to "Authority."

When the Vermont Assembly gathered again at Bennington in February 1779, a bare quorum of fifty included 29 from the West-side. Formal ejection of the New Hampshire towns was thus easily accomplished. But "Vermont" had now shrunk again to the few West-side towns which had declared independence in January 1777, plus a few remaining East-side towns. The upper Connecticut towns led by Bayley and Marsh preferred to join with their brothers across the river, either in a valley state or in New Hampshire. To the south lay the lower Cumberland County towns which had never seceded from New York. It was to these latter that Ethan now turned his attention.

To protect a frontier exposed to British attack the Assembly had passed several measures to strengthen its military arm. Among them was a draft law. But certain Yorkers in Cumberland County, refusing to acknowledge the state of Vermont, resisted its application. This was all Colonel Allen needed. Gathering a hundred men behind him and spouting horrible threats, he invaded Cumberland County and arrested 36 Yorkers. The latter were duly impressed, for one of them wrote fearfully to Governor Clinton that the Colonel was "more to be dreaded than death with all its terrors." Ethan prodded a hesitant Court into slapping heavy fines on thirty of the "convicts." A pleased legislature thereupon made the Colonel a Brigadier-General, and Governor Chittenden generously issued a blanket pardon to all.

GEORGE CLINTON *first governor of republican New York, held stubbornly to that state's claim to the Hampshire Grants lands, despite the attempts of other prominent Yorkers like John Jay, Gouverneur Morris and Alexander Hamilton, to compromise the dispute.*

CLINTON AND CONGRESS

Ethan's high-handed conduct in Cumberland County had not gone unnoticed in New York. Obstinate Governor George Clinton fumed helplessly as letters and petitions flooded in upon him from his subjects on the Connecticut River, isolated from New York proper by a group of unruly west-side towns which refused to recognize his jurisdiction. These Yorkers seemed to operate on the hopeful assumption that a petition a day might keep Ethan Allen away. To all Governor Clinton offered only counsels of "prudence" and "firmness." But the Yorkers wanted something more substantial.

The Governor did, however, manage to agitate the Continental Congress with protests over Vermont's unwarranted activities, and succeeded rather thoroughly in sabotaging any moves to admit the little republic to the union. As a matter of fact, no one quite knew what it was Congress was expected to admit, for "Vermont" grew or shrank as her various factions drew together or apart.

Congress was also informed by Lieutenant Governor Marsh and other representatives of the Connecticut River towns that this area would need to be counted in on any deliberations. They hadn't yet formed a central government—as had the towns acknowledging allegiance to the Bennington party—because they weren't sure whether they wanted to join New Hampshire or Vermont, or set up an independent valley state. They had petitioned New Hampshire for admission, and the legislature had agreed to accept them. Perhaps it *might* be a good idea—some began to think—to split the Grants down the middle, dividing them between New York and New Hampshire.

Under constant prodding from New York's John Jay, Congress finally agreed to set aside the urgent business of winning a war long enough to debate the Vermont problem. The upshot was that all three contending states—New York, New Hampshire, and Massachusetts, but *not* Vermont—were asked to allow Congress to set their boundaries. New York and New Hampshire agreed. The rump state of "Vermont" was thereupon ordered to cease all land grants, all sales of confiscated property, and to lay off those residents of the Grants who did not choose to join the independence movement.

FREDERICK HALDI-MAND, British Governor of Canada, endeavored to draw Vermont back into the empire through the agency of the Allens, whose initial desire for statehood shifted to a preference for a Canadian link after repeated rebuff from Congress. Most Vermonters still favored the American cause, however.

The Vermont legislature, assembling in Manchester bright in its colorful October dress, was duly impressed by Congress's orders. The Allens, however, saw control over even what was left of Vermont slipping from them. Ethan began talking; Ira began negotiating. At the end of two weeks they had stiffened enough backs to obtain a forthright re-affirmation of Vermont's independence and her right to be a party to any settlement regarding the lands she claimed. The fact that obedience to the Congressional mandate meant the loss of all sources of revenue —land sales and loyalist estates—no doubt helped.

But Ethan and Ira had not confined their exertions to Manchester. Even before the legislature the sound of scratching quills must have kept the neighbors awake in Arlington and elsewhere. For with the help of Jonas Fay and a newly arrived lawyer named Stephen Row Bradley, they composed and circulated personally three vigourous pamphlets throughout New England and many of the other states. The effect of these polemics was considerable, for the Vermont arguments became widely known thereby.

But again the distractions of war—which was not going too well for the colonies in the South—prevented Congress from taking action. Finally, in September 1780, the delegates sat down to clean up this annoying side issue once and for all. They had new letters from Clinton, and also from Lieutenant Governor Marsh. But they also had one from Governor Chittenden, part of which disturbed them intensely. Since the Vermonters, he declared, were "not included in the thirteen United States, but conceive themselves to be a separate body, they . . . are, if necessitated to it, at liberty to offer or accept terms of cessation of hostilities with Great Britain." Worried doubts swelled into shouted questions as startling new despatches poured in from the fighting fronts. One of the most brilliant and competent of their generals—Benedict Arnold—had gone over to the British, but not before a vast plot to loose the American hold in the north had been uncovered. Congress turned it's attention anxiously toward the northern frontier.

There was good reason for concern on the part of the Continental Congress as to conditions on the northern frontier and as to the conduct of the Vermont leaders. They were definitely up to something with the British.

Let us look back for a moment and see how it all began. After Burgoyne's defeat and the French alliance which followed, British attempts to end the war by conciliation collapsed. They then turned their attention to the possibilities of winning over important leaders or even whole colonies by private negotiations. A number of overtures were made, and almost universally were rebuffed. But two men bent an interested ear to the suggestions of British Colonel Beverly Robinson—Benedict Arnold and Ethan Allen. The discovery of Arnold's plans sent him fleeing to the British lines, but the news of Allen's conferences leaked out more slowly.

Oddly enough, as we know, the two conspirators were bitter enemies. Allen self-righteously informed his old friend Captain Justus Sherwood that he would not be a party to any "damned Arnold plan to sell his country and his honor." Sherwood had come under a flag of truce to talk things over at the request of Governor Chittenden, to whom Ethan had shown Robinson's letters. The ostensible subject of negotiation was a "cartel" for the exchange of prisoners, but Sherwood and Allen soon found a quiet corner to discuss the possibility of Ethan's bringing his Vermont back into the British fold. Ethan was much intrigued, but admitted that the Vermonters would "cut off his head" if they thought he had any such idea. He was right in his judgment as to their temper. Members of the legislature became suspicious, and requested an explanation from Ethan. In a fine show of indignation, General Allen resigned his commission and went back to his books. Governor Chittenden, uneasy at the prospects, also asked to resign, but was persuaded to continue in office. Ethan's "retirement", however, was probably advised by his friends and fellow conspirators, for he was much too outspoken and unaccomplished in the devious arts of diplomacy. Moreover "General" Allen was also a Colonel in the Continental army and would have been hanged as quickly as General Benedict Arnold, if caught.

Thus it was the experienced negotiators, Ira Allen and Joseph Fay, who took over the subsequent negotiations with General Frederick Haldimand, Governor of Canada. In the exchange of sentiments begun in the fall of 1780, these frontier diplomats expressed the hope that Vermont might be permitted to assume a neutral position. But Haldimand quickly rejected that possibility; they would have to choose between coming back into the fold, or remaining enemies of the Crown. Incensed at the Continental Congress, some of those few who were in on the talks began to draw up plans to join the British. But if this were to be done, there must be developed more widespread support. And the Vermont which became a British province certainly ought to be as large as possible.

"GREATER VERMONT"

Ira went first to some old enemies. There were an increasing number of loyalists, as well as Yorkers, along the Connecticut River. Here Luke Knoulton—an unsuspected secret agent of the British—was a leader of the Yorkers, who were increasingly disgusted with Governor Clinton's failure to protect them against the "pretended" state of Vermont. It was not difficult for Knoulton to sell them on the idea of a valley state. Moreover, the towns further up the river on both sides had long liked the idea. But when forty-three river towns gathered in Charlestown in January 1781, Ira Allen was present. Joining hands with Knoulton, he persuaded the assembled delegates to apply again to the Vermont Assembly, which promptly welcomed them with open arms. On April 6 the valley towns, including 35 representatives from New Hampshire, were back in Vermont.

The whole affair seems topsy-turvy. Why were the Yorkers applying for admission to a state dominated by their mortal enemy, Ethan Allen? The answer lies in the widespread belief that the more densely populated Connecticut River Valley towns would have no difficulty in breaking the power of the Allens and taking over the government of Vermont.

Why then did Ira promote such a union? First because he needed as large a territory as possible to bargain with the British. Then too, he counted on additions of strength on the West-side to offset these otherwise unwelcome additions from the East.

Vermont's township form of government looked most attractive to the towns between the Hudson River and the Vermont boundary. After Ethan had paid them a missionary visit they gathered in a convention at Cambridge, New York, and voted to join up with the expanding republic to the East. Despite the opposition of many of the Connecticut River towns, only just admitted themselves, the Assembly voted 33–24 to annex "all lands north of Massachusetts as far west as Hudson's River."[7]

This area had become a source of considerable worry to General Schuyler, commanding the American northern army, for it showed strong loyalist inclinations. But this was what Ira counted on—along with the numerous loyalists of the Connecticut River Valley—to strengthen his hand against the revolutionary party. The Vermont patriots led by Bayley were giving the "junto"[8] numerous sleepless nights, and their position with the legislature and the people was becoming progressively more shaky. Even their hold on Bennington had been broken by a newcomer, Isaac Tichenor, who had just recently entered Vermont as an army commissary. Only the rather considerable and widespread respect for Governor Chittenden, who actually was "in" on it all, saved the conspirators from losing power entirely.

Thus while they still held the reins of power, the "junto" turned to other old enemies for new support. The Act forbidding return of the loyalists was repealed, and loyalists and ex-Yorkers were increasingly brought into the government in order to offset the loss of support of the revolutionary party. As the former rebels donned one loyalist garment after another, leadership of the American cause passed to Tichenor and Bayley, who

---

7 To justify these annexations, the Vermonters revived the phantom province alleged to have been granted to Philip Skene in 1775 (see page 68), which had included this area.

8 Ethan and Ira Allen, Joseph and Jonas Fay, Chittenden, and several other loyal supporters like Matthew Lyon.

GENERAL JACOB BAYLEY, first citizen of the Upper Connecticut towns, urged upon General Washington a campaign against Canada from Newbury. For this purpose he began the Bayley-Hazen Road toward St. Johns in 1776, abandoned at "Hazen's Notch" when the projected invasion was cancelled (see map, page 93). An ardent patriot, he earned the hatred of the Allens, whose negotiations with the British he bitterly denounced. Twice the British sent expeditions to capture and silence him. One was diverted to Royalton, which it destroyed. The other reached Newbury, but missed its quarry. Legend has it that a servant girl held the redcoats at bay while the General escaped (left). Actually he had been warned by Col. Thomas Johnson, a returned captive himself, who recognized some of his former captors skulking near Newbury. By a note dropped in a field he warned Bayley, who escaped across the river (see page 58).

denounced them to General George Washington as traitors.

Washington was not entirely ignorant of what was going on. As early as the fall of 1780 he had received from General Schuyler some of Ethan's correspondence with the British. Lt. Governor Marsh, in the course of protesting Vermont's actions, sent him more. And his secret agents provided him with a steady stream of reports on the negotiations. It was a leaky bag in which the "junto" was attempting to confine its secrets.

Another ardent patriot, disease-wracked and battle weary, heard about the strange doings in his beloved home-land, and painfully made his way back to inquisition his old friend Ethan Allen. Had Ethan been in touch with the British? Allen squirmed and lied. But Seth Warner knew him too well. Faced with the facts of what Warner, Schuyler, and Washington knew, Ethan confessed to the receipt of two letters from Beverly Robinson. He thereupon quickly sent the letters to the President of Congress, intimating that they were the full extent of negotiations, and adding the true but incomplete statement that they had not been answered. He neglected to mention the conversations with Sherwood and the subsequent negotiations under cover of truce. And he could not resist a final note of bravado. Asserting Vermont's right to make a separate peace, he concluded, "I am as resolutely determined to defend the independence of Vermont as Congress that of the United States, and rather than fail will retire with the hardy Green Mountain Boys into the desolate caverns of the mountains and wage war with human nature at large." This was not the Ethan who had two years earlier painted fearful pictures of the consequences of opposition to Congress. Furthermore, he ignored the fact that Seth Warner, not he, now led the Green Mountain Boys.

But his bold action convinced the Vermont Assembly for the moment that all was well.[9] And it also stirred Congress into doing something about the Vermont situation. The time seemed ripe; even New York's Governor Clinton now seemed willing to admit Vermont if she would shrink back into the old Grants territory between Lake Champlain and the Connecticut. This was indeed an about-face, for only five weeks before Clinton had to threaten to dissolve his own Assembly to prevent it from acknowledging Vermont's independence. On June 22, Ira Allen, Jonas Fay and Bezaleel Woodward[10] were sent to Philadelphia to negotiate for admission.

Congress was further stimulated to action by a document forwarded by Benjamin Franklin from Paris. It was an intercepted letter from the British Colonial Secretary, Lord George Germaine, detailing the British plans for receiving Vermont back into the empire.

Congress was understandably upset over what seemed to them confirmation of rumors of treachery on the northern frontier. It might be well, many decided, to attach this troublesome "pretended" state of Vermont to the American cause by admitting her to equal partnership. But it could hardly be the expanded Vermont which had stolen territory from her neighbors—both members in good standing of the Confederation.

Therefore the resolution offering admission specified that Vermont must recede to the lands between Lake Champlain and the Connecticut. To this offer only New York dissented. But the Vermont delegates were somewhat diffident; the Canadian connection—which would take in the whole of "Greater Vermont"—looked increasingly attractive. Furthermore, it was not going to be too easy to get rid of the New York and New Hampshire towns, for the General Assembly was now swelled with delegates from these very towns, and these delegates were not likely to vote to set free the towns they represented. Vermont's only response to Congress, therefore was an offer to arbitrate the matter.

---

9 Chittenden had been asked to produce all the papers relating to the negotiations, but he carefully removed anything incriminating. The Assembly was satisfied with the balance.

10 Woodward acted as Eleazar Wheelock's political agent and executive secretary of the College Party.

FORT VENGEANCE at Pittsford (right), was the northernmost of three forts guarding the frontier against British and Indian raids from Lake Champlain, still under British control despite Burgoyne's defeat. Invasions down Otter Creek made the northern towns uninhabitable. Smaller forts at Bethel and Barnard and blockhouses along the Hazen Road guarded the Connecticut Valley settlements. But Royalton was nearly wiped out by a bloody raid in 1780. For location of Forts Vengeance and Warren, see map, page 93.

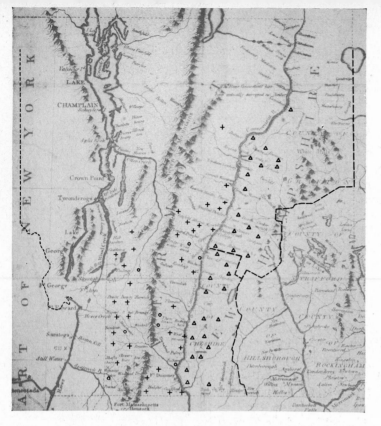

"GREATER VERMONT" – 1781

Base map: section from Conder's 1777 map.

- - - - Most westerly claim   ▲ N.H. towns admitted Apr. 5, 1781
- - - Most easterly claim   + Vermont towns voting for admission
Grafton and Cheshire Counties, N.H.   ● Vermont towns voting against admission

THE PEACE PROCLAMATION

Even before the Vermont Assembly had made its decision, Ira and Joseph Fay returned to British Skenesboro with their terms for Vermont's return to royal allegiance. They requested that Haldimand issue a proclamation granting these terms and offering to accept "Greater Vermont." He was also to send up the lake a force sufficient to threaten the frontier and protect the junto against the patriot groups. Haldimand agreed tentatively, though he had some doubts as to his authority to grant as much as Ira demanded. Allen and Fay, for their part, promised to produce a friendly legislature.

But events conspired to wreck their carefully laid plans. First came rumors that British Lord Cornwallis had suffered a crushing defeat at Yorktown and had surrendered his entire army. Ira hurriedly wrote Justus Sherwood, asking him to withhold the proclamation, though reassuring him of his desire to carry through the scheme at a later, and more favorable time.

But the British had already marched up the lake, and were awaiting the signal to issue the proclamation. Hearing no word, they decided to capture an American scout, and to send by him an inquiry as to how things were going at Charlestown, where the legislature was in session. But the scout died resisting capture. Dismayed,

the British forwarded an elaborate apology to Charlestown. But why should the British apologize for killing an American soldier? The messenger who brought the dispatch broadcast his suspicions. Excited and angry men cornered Ira Allen to demand an explanation. Ira stalled them long enough for the conspirators to forge a new and innocent despatch. This was read to the Assembly which, of course, saw no grounds for special action.

Rumor spread like wildfire through the Grants—and beyond its borders. General Stark took it upon himself to demand from Chittenden the original of the dispatch. The junto decided to ignore his request, but to send a letter of explanation, signed by Chittenden, to General George Washington. Hoping to quiet the clamor by convincing the Commander-in-Chief, they concocted a plausible but incomplete story of the negotiations.[11]

Washington's reply, however, exploded a powder keg under the junto. Agreeing to accept the Governor's explanation for the time being, he suggested that Vermont give evidence of its good faith by shedding the territory stolen from her neighbors—at which time she might reasonably expect admission into the Union.

DISSOLUTION OF THE UNIONS

Now the victory at Yorktown and virtual end of the fighting had tremendously strengthened the hand of the patriots in the legislature. Delighted at the prospect of early admission, the General Assembly hastily dropped both the Eastern and Western Unions.[12] This action caught the junto completely unawares. Ira Allen and Jonas Fay had gone to Philadelphia to announce Vermont's unshakable determination to hold on to the New York and New Hampshire towns. And Ethan had just departed for Hartford to get printed a new pamphlet defending the Unions. The Allen party was left stranded and furious.

Tichenor's triumph—for it was he who engineered it—was shortlived. He was sent with Moses Robinson and Paul Spooner to Philadelphia to complete the details for Vermont's admission. But they found Congress in an ugly mood after conversations with Allen and Fay. Furthermore, it was hopelessly divided on the question. Southern states feared to strengthen New England; states with western lands[13] hesitated to establish a precedent for setting up new governments on the claims of the original states. With respect to this, of course, New York's Governor Clinton vigorously and vocally agreed.

---

11 Many contemporaries—and subsequent historians as well—accepted Chittenden's account as full and correct. But others, like Alexander Hamilton, were not fooled by it.

12 The meeting was in Bennington in the dead of winter, with few from the East-side present. The Bennington party, now led by Isaac Tichenor, controlled the proceedings.

13 Many states laid claim—on the basis of their colonial charters—to great tracts of land to the west of their settled and undisputed boundaries.

Moreover, many delegates held Vermont lands under one type of grant or another, and each voted to confirm the jurisdiction most favorable to his own interests.

It was fundamentally impossible for Congress, loosely organized as it was, to act on the question. This Confederation of states suffered from a basic defect of political organization. It was not, like the states themselves, an effective government, with administrative as well as legislative powers. It was a mere loose league of independent states, able to act only when there was virtual unanimity among its parts. To expect such unanimity on the complicated problem of the New Hampshire Grants was to expect the impossible. Not until the government was reorganized under the new Constitution in 1789 were Vermont's friends in the federal government able to press her case successfully.

PEACE OF PARIS

In the meantime, hopeful that Congress' rebuff might again strengthen their hand at home, the Allens reopened negotiations with Haldimand. Ethan, his patience exhausted, wrote that the "Vermonters" would have no further truck with the United States, and that as for himself, he would do everything in his power to render Vermont a British Province. Haldimand sent loyalist James Breakenridge with a treaty, but demanded ratification by the Assembly. The junto did not dare to submit it. In fact, rumors of renewed negotiations brought a mob to Chittenden's door, and it was only with difficulty that he turned them aside.

But in Paris peace negotiations were proceeding, and Haldimand got instructions to defer any action on the Vermont question. As the negotiations drew to a conclusion the junto anxiously asked Haldimand to intercede with the British government to claim Vermont. But the British were no longer interested, and in setting the boundary along the 45th parallel—the present Canadian boundary—the treaty tacitly recognized Vermont as a part of the United States.

Thus Vermont was separated by an international boundary line from her natural markets in Canada. The Allens, however, never gave up their dream of a political as well as a commercial link with Canada. Ethan repeatedly asserted his preference for the connection with Canada, and Ira continued commercial negotiations in the hope of reviving the dream of an Onion River–Lake Champlain empire. And Levi—the ex-loyalist who had been welcomed back into the family fold when his brothers also turned toward the British—was in London futilely negotiating for Vermont's admission into Canada at the very time she finally joined the Union.

Historians have argued for years as to the intentions of the junto in these negotiations. Afflicted with a pious fear of injury to the state's heroes, some have contended that during the entire course of the affair the junto acted only to deceive the British into postponing an invasion. Actually, Haldimand had no troops to spare for a full scale attack. Present-day scholars,[14] with the amazingly complete British records of the proceedings at hand, are agreed that the motives of the members of the junto varied from one time to another, but that at least during the later stages, the Allens and their friends were quite serious in their intent to return Vermont to the British empire—always providing, of course, that adequate protection for their land and trade interests were assured.

However, in these later years it can hardly be argued that any of them spoke officially for the people of Vermont. Ira was eased out of active participation in the government by 1786, although Chittenden retained his popular appeal until his death in 1797. Ethan had retired to Sunderland to write his *Oracles of Reason*, though he was occasionally drafted as a trouble-shooter. He was particularly available for the familiar task of chastizing Yorkers.

THE "GUILFORD WAR"

It did not take the Yorkers in Cumberland County long to discover that Luke Knoulton had tricked them into supporting first a valley state project and then the state of Greater Vermont. They soon began to revive their old preference for New York, and to pester Governor Clinton and the Continental Congress. Neither paid much attention.

Finally the towns of Brattleboro, Guilford and Halifax, led by the mountainous and talkative Charles Phelps, gathered in a convention and begged New York to re-establish authority over them. The inevitable clash with the Vermont authorities came—as before—over the enforcement of the draft. After several struggles with Yorkers who refused to recognize the state's authority, local Vermont officials called upon Chittenden for military aid. The ever-willing Ethan donned his flamboyant uniform, buckled on his sword, and led a force over the mountains. Storming into the dissident towns he took several captives. But in Guilford he ran into an unexpected ambush. His men beat a hasty and undignified retreat. Such a humiliation was intolerable. Regathering his forces he roared threats at the Guilfordites. "I, Ethan Allen, he thundered, "do declare that I will give no quarter to any man, woman or child who shall oppose me, and unless the inhabitants of Guilford peacefully submit to the authority of Vermont, I swear I will lay it as desolate as Sodom and Gomorrah, by God." There was no further armed opposition, though the Yorkers were far from converted.

14 Dr. Clarence W. Rife, Dr. Chilton Williamson, Henry S. Wardner, and Mary G. Nye have drawn their conclusions from the original sources. John Clement has indicated agreement with Wardner. Of those who have worked from secondary material, Charles M. Thompson accepts the newer interpretation, Frederic F. Van de Water the older one.

A Vermont court tried the culprits and confiscated their property, and the verdict was carried out enthusifastically and violently by General Allen. But the chie-offender, Charles Phelps, had escaped. After voluable protests to Clinton, be betook himself to Philadelphia and unloosed a torrent of language upon the Continental Congress. With incredible persistence he hounded the delegates until finally, prodded also by Governor Clinton and the New York delegation, Congress ordered restoration of the Yorkers' property. Phelps and other fugitives returned in triumph, only to be promptly thrown into jail by the unrepentant Vermonters.

Unrest swelled into raids and counter-raids, and finally into an armed clash between a small body of Yorkers and the Vermont militia. The latter, after losing one man, chased the Yorkers across the Massachusetts line. Again the indomitable Ethan came galloping to the fore with new troops. But finding no enemies at hand, he set about arresting suspects. Again the Court assembled—to try Phelps. He was charged with treason, imprisoned for 60 days and all his property confiscated. The legislature subsequently granted him—and others—their freedom, but not their property. Militia were left in Windham County,[15] but the revolt was over.

---

15 Cumberland was altered to Windham County Feb. 11, 1781.

AN INDEPENDENT COINAGE, minted at Rupert in 1785 by Reuben Harmon (who also cut the Vermont seal for Ira Allen in 1779), was one of several acts of sovereignty by the independent republic of Vermont. Harmon's dies and money scales are in the Vermont Historical Society Museum.

This was the last major appearance of Ethan on the public stage. He was solicited to lead a revolt of the Connecticut settlers in the Wyoming Valley, Pennsylvania, but his reputation and tactics were considerably less successful outside of his own state. He retired to a large farm on the Onion River, but was temperamentally unsuited to the placid life of a tiller of the soil. On February 12, 1789, he died after a night of celebrating with cousin Ebenezer Allen across the ice in South Hero.

His brother Ira resumed his land business, both before and after being eased out as State Treasurer in 1786. His political enemies were not fully satisfied, and attempted unsuccessfully to dig out falsifications in his accounts. In 1789 Chittenden lost the race for Governor because of his close association with Ira, then under fire. But Ira was due for more trouble; the British government in 1796 confiscated a cargo of arms in which he was speculating. He spent eight years, part of it in prison in Paris, before regaining his muskets. By then he dared not return to live permanently in Vermont for fear of imprisonment for debt. Land-poor, he died in Philadelphia in unhappy poverty.

THE CRITICAL PERIOD, 1783-1789

At the end of eight years of revolution and civil war, the colonies were exhausted, though victorious. Suffering from an uncontrollable inflation, with trade blocked at each state line, and subject to a government inherently unable to govern, the new United States was united in little more than name. But Vermont—which had born so small a part of the revolutionary burden, which had financed the costs of both government and warfare almost without taxes—Vermont was relatively well off as compared with her sister states. Indeed, the hunger for new lands, which were being granted profusely by the government, was drawing a new flood of settlers to the promised land. Faced with repeated rebuffs from Congress, Vermont seemed wholly satisfied to let her case rest. In fact, there were many—including ex-loyalists—in the government, who were still hoping for a Canadian connection.

But the frontier was not to escape all the troubles of the "critical period" of American history. Wild inflation of currency in Vermont, as elsewhere, left bitter unrest in its wake. Many of the newcomers had bought land on credit, and many old residents had over-reached themselves. Hard money was scarce, despite Vermont's determination to coin its own as a sovereign republic. When creditors pressed for payment, and Courts began foreclosures late in 1786, riots broke out in Rutland and Windsor. The authorities took immediate and decisive action; in Windsor the mob was broken up by Sheriff Benjamin Waite—one of the Windsor anti-court rioters of 1770. The legislature thanked the militia and promptly expelled a member who had unwisely joined in the Rutland affair. But unlike the merchant dominated legislatures of southern

New England, these farmer-representatives acted to alleviate the source of the trouble by making produce legal tender for payment of debt.

Massachusetts had not done so well by its backcountry. An angry rebellion, led by farmer Daniel Shays, flared momentarily in Worcester and Hampshire Counties, but was bloodily suppressed by militia under General Lincoln. The Green Mountain Boys did not rise to their aid, as some of the hopeful rebels had expected. On the other hand, when Shays and some of his men escaped into Vermont, Chittenden refused to turn them over to Major Royall Tyler, Lincoln's aide, who had come to get them.

END OF THE REPUBLIC

In 1787, in reaction to such riots and to the ways of uncontrolled democracy and unchecked provincialism, conservatives gathered in Philadelphia to form a strong central government under a new Constitution. Vermont, still acting the role of an independent nation, took no part in the epoch-making struggle for ratification. But when the deed was done, and a new government established with George Washington at its head, leading Vermonters hopefully expressed to Alexander Hamilton their federalist sentiments. Speaking through Nathaniel Chipman, they assured him that Vermont could be counted on to strengthen the "Federalist" faction then gathering behind the new Secretary of the Treasury.

Hamilton, a New Yorker, pressed upon a new Congress the desirability of admitting as a state that wedge on the northern frontier which his own state could no longer control. The obstinate Clinton delayed matters a while. But the North was desirous of having a new state to offset Kentucky, which was now clamoring for admission. By mid-1789 New York gave way and addressed an invitation—for the first time—to "His Excellency," Governor Chittenden. Would Vermont care to negotiate outstanding differences?

She would, and did. The commissioners agreed to pay New York the munificent sum of $30,000 for all her land claims. New York, in turn, agreed to withdraw her opposition to Vermont's admission to the Union. On January 6, 1791 a convention at Bennington ratified the Federal constitution 105–4, and made application to Congress. On March fourth the United States admitted the first new state to her union, and thereby began a process which was to swell the numbers of her self governing states from thirteen to forty-eight, and to extend her dominion from the Atlantic to the Pacific.

The Republic of Vermont had disappeared, and there were few who mourned her passing. Only Ira and Levi Allen were left actively to pursue the dream of a Canadian connection, though Chittenden still held secret hopes. Ethan was dead and the Onion River Company was falling apart. New leaders were taking over.

Over the grave of the republic we write her obituary, and inevitably make curious inquiries about the motives of her leaders. Was the original Vermont of 1777, as some have charged, a creation of the Allens and their cohorts on behalf of their land speculations? Such a verdict presupposes a singleness of purpose among different men, and over a period of years, for which there is insufficient evidence. It ignores the fact that the movement for independence, though far from unanimous, gained wide support from men who had no link with the Onion River Company.

This does not mean that the "junto," led by the Allens and their friends, did not endeavor to control to their own ends the course of public policy adopted by the new state. They unquestionably utilized support earned in the cause of the "Grants" and of the Revolution, to promote their dreams of landed empire and commercial growth. They even attempted to retrace the steps of rebellion taken too hastily in 1775, but could not carry their former associates with them. But at no time during their negotiations with the British could they be said to have represented "Vermont." In fact, they used secrecy, forgery, deceit, and duplicity to conceal their transactions from Vermonters, whom they knew would promptly consign them to political oblivion upon discovery of their intentions. They used their influence to introduce into the government loyalists—including old enemies—in order to strengthen their hand, and lent a helping hand to British spies and deserters from the colonial army.

But the Vermonters themselves refused to follow their old leaders, and thereupon raised up new ones. To sectionalism there was thus added factionalism, and the beginnings of parties in Vermont. But this is is another story, and one we shall defer for a bit while we take a look at the social and economic structure of the fourteenth state.

AMERICAN FLAG was altered to 15 stars and 15 stripes after the admission of Vermont (1791) and Kentucky (1792). Original 13 stripes were restored as other states were added later.

VII

LIFE AND LABOR

*How the pioneers broke the wilderness, built homes, sowed crops,
and brought Yankee life and institutions to the northwestern frontier.*

OVER the horizon drawn by the peaks of the Green Mountains, the southern New England Yankee saw a promised land of rich acres and unhampered life. In the last half of the eighteenth century men from all walks of life flooded into the rugged wedge jammed between the sparkling bowl of Lake Champlain and the darker tumbling waters of the seaward bound Connecticut.

First came the restless hunters and trappers, who moved on ahead of the advancing wave of hardy yeomen. Establishing in the wilderness called for ingenuity and unceasing toil. The pioneer usually came first to explore and make his "pitch," erect a crude shelter and make a small clearing in the dense forest which blanketed the hills and valleys alike. If his land lay near the course of one of the many rivers, he then brought his family and few belongings over the frozen ice of early spring, in time to get in the first crops. Inland areas were reached by crude sledges and, occasionally, an ox-cart.

The resources available to the pioneer were almost limitless: virgin soil, the inexhaustible water-power of tumbling streams and thousands of square miles of standing timber, filled with game—this was indeed a rich heritage for the newcomer. But it took both brain and brawn to bend it to human use.

First and most important was the land. The thick woodlands were more a hindrance than a help to the settler. True, the forest provided logs for his first crude shelter, but it also blocked and shaded the land against growing things.

It was on the uplands that clearing first began, for the river valleys were a tangle of brush and marsh land. Underbrush was first slashed out, and the mighty trees—many running more than four feet in diameter—were felled and burned where they lay. Their ashes then served to enrich an already fertile soil. It was slow, backbreaking work; a good man might clear as little as three acres in a year, or the same amount in a month, depending on whether or not he attempted to grub out the stumps, dig out the stones and fence it in. In desperate need of food, many a settler sowed his first crops among the stumps. And even after long years of occupancy of large

tracts, most farmers were unlikely to have more than five per cent in improved land.

The soil was incredibly rich—for a time. The accumulation of rotting leaves, untouched for centuries, produced an amazing yield for these incredulous yeomen, more accustomed to the sparse produce of southern New England. But no effort was made to replenish this rich legacy, which was used up or washed away. There was no rotation of crops, no use of fertilizer, and the manure of animals was lost in the pastures.

The first implements with which the pioneer attacked the wilderness were the gun and axe, the former to keep him alive while he employed the latter to create his farm. But farming itself required additional tools. These were scarce and crude. The land was broken by the wooden plow and harrow behind oxen, which were found to be superior to the horse as a draft animal. The rest of the work was done by hand, from planting to harvesting. All grass crops were cut with a scythe or sickle; grain was threshed with a hand flail and winnowed in the wind. Indeed the painfully slow labor of agricultural production inevitably limited the amount of land a single family could farm. These few acres rarely produced much more than the bare essentials.

The first crops had to be those which would produce the most for the pioneer household. Corn, planted in hills as the Indians had taught, was most widely grown. But wheat also was sown, and unlike corn, it did not need cultivating—a valuable factor. Rye, oats, barley and potatoes came later. The yield, at first, was startling. A

BOTH LIFE AND LABOR in the wilderness began with the need for shelter, and thus with the log cabin (upper left). As the farm expanded, and as neighbors appeared, the pioneer gained help in the building of a frame barn (and perhaps a house too) through a community "barn-raising" (upper right). The barn provided essential storage for the bountiful crops of a fertile land (center left), for there were, for a long time, no stores in which to buy food. After the first subsistence crops came the broad fields of wheat, reaped by hand with scythe and sickle (center right). Winter brought a variety of household tasks to man, woman and child—spinning, churning butter, making and repairing tools and furniture, and obtaining wood for the cavernous fireplace, only source of warmth and illumination (lower left). Later candles, made at home on "candle-dip day," brought better light to the pioneer household (lower right). →

LONG WINTERS were a real problem to the farmers.

MODERN DIVISION OF LABOR as between "bread-winning" and "housekeeping" was less clear-cut on the frontier. Many a woman joined her husband in the fields to get in urgently needed crops, and some ran the farm alone while their men did military duty.

Middlebury pioneer got his first ears of corn two months after planting. Thirty bushels of wheat to the acre was not at all uncommon. Vermont's first historian, Samuel Williams, reported that many a farmer could cover the entire expense of clearing, fencing and sowing his land out of his first crop. This was particularly true later on, when it became possible to market this produce.

No wonder these Yankees broadcast the word that here indeed was a Garden of Eden for the man with a will, a wife, and a strong right arm.

Staple crops were supplemented by gardens, especially turnips, beets, parsnips, and carrots, which could be winter-stored in root cellars. Pumpkins were a particular favorite. Hardy apple trees were set out as soon as possible, for cider was even more essential than the dried apple. Most other fruits were wild, but abundant, as were nuts. Sweetening from honey and especially from the ever present maple, as well as game from the forest completed nature's bounty, leaving only salt and rum as "essential" imports.

The average pioneer came only with his oxen, but acquired other cattle[1] as soon as possible. They were badly needed to lighten the burden of labor, and were seldom slaughtered till very old. Inadequate housing and winter feeding made all except the pigs poor sources of food. By the turn of the century sheep had become the most important kind of livestock, not for their mutton, which was held in low esteem, but for their wool. As a source for home manufacture of clothes, and later as an exportable product, wool took over a very important role in farm life.

---

1 "Cattle" included all four-footed farm animals. Cows and oxen were known as "neat cattle."

INDUSTRY AND TRADE

This all adds up to a picture of pioneer self-sufficiency. The frontier farm was established to provide a living for the typically large frontier family, and not to produce goods for exchange. In fact, the isolation of these people coupled with the lack of adequate transportation made anything else impossible.

As time went on, however, as population grew, as farms multiplied and pioneers found themselves with neighbors, and as houses came to cluster into villages, some facilities for community service began to appear. Mills were the first concern of the farmer: mills to grind his grain, saw his timber, and, later, card his raw wool for spinning. Grist mills were almost always the town's first industrial enterprise, and saw mills were usually established soon after. Abundant streams with a considerable fall were everywhere. Knowing how essential a mill would be, town proprietors often gave land free to anyone who would set one up. Remember Baker accepted such an offer, and thus became a leading citizen of Arlington.

The mill sites usually provided a center around which other village industries grew up. First came the artisan who could do some of the specialized jobs at which the farmer was himself no expert: the blacksmith to shoe his horses and to turn out some few iron tools to replace the wooden ones; the cooper to repair wagon wheels and to produce barrels, pails, and other wooden ware; the shoemaker to work in leather; the physician, preacher and school master, and perhaps eventually a carpenter-builder to erect dignified residences for the prominent leaders of the town. Most of these work-men were farmers first and specialists afterward. But it was not too long before a man could make a good living in his trade.

FOR HEAVY TASKS oxen were preferred in the early days. But Vermonters soon developed one of the finest of all draft horses, the Morgan.

MAP of early roads is taken from Blodget's rare 1789 edition. Lacking complete information, he broke off his roads abruptly.→

Eventually a number of men were employed in certain enterprises, like the tanneries which grew up to service the trade in furs and hides. In addition to the smithies, iron works—like Matthew Lyon's at Fairhaven—sprang up in response to the growing demand for nails and other metal products. And while the making of cloth remained for many decades a household industry, mills to "card" the raw wool and to prepare it for spinning began to appear before 1800. There was a scattering of other businesses, such as paper mills, marble and slate quarries, and brickyards. They were not widespread or influential, but were the beginnings of important Vermont industries. Certain centers like Bennington, Fairhaven, and Vergennes early became engaged in a variety of industrial pursuits.

Like these small enterprises, retail stores arose first to serve local needs, and then to act as go-betweens for a growing trade with the "outside world." From almost the beginning the pioneers had developed a trade in the ashes from their burned trees. But as transportation improved it became more profitable to market the logs themselves. The northern towns on Lake Champlain developed a thriving lumber industry based on sales to the Canadian market. Ira Allen himself had built the first saw mill at the falls of the Winooski, and the first raft of timber we know anything about was launched in 1794. There were a steadily growing number thereafter. Burlington soon became a great lumber port. At the same time there grew up an increasing trade back and forth across the border in a variety of products. The Lake Champlain area felt a very strong commercial link with the trade centers on the St. Lawrence River, into which the lake flowed. This northern orientation held firm until the completion of the Champlain Canal linking the lake and the Hudson River in 1822.

A Map of the
STATE of VERMONT.
As it was about A.D. 1791

On the other side of the mountains the Connecticut, and the many streams flowing into it from both east and west, long served as the main traffic artery. By 1770 small flatboats were added to the rafts and dugouts which had floated down the river since colonial times. It was largely a one-way traffic downstream, except in winter when the frozen surface was used by sleds bringing merchandise to the rapidly multiplying stores in the frontier settlements.

Inland trade, however, was badly hobbled by the abominable state of the dirt roads, many of which were passable only when winter filled in the trench-like ruts. Mostly they had begun as blazed trails, widened first to bridle paths and then to roads capable of accommodating ox-carts. Exceptions were the two great military roads: the Crown Point Road built from Springfield (opposite Fort Number Four on the Connecticut River) to Crown Point, and the Bayley-Hazen Road, begun by General Jacob Bayley in 1776 as a pathway for the invasion of Canada and continued by Colonel Moses Hazen as far as Hazen's Notch in 1779. But even these highways fell into disuse after the war. Like all other pathways hope-

FIRST AMERICAN PATENT, under the signatures of George Washington and Thomas Jefferson, was issued in 1790 to a Vermonter, Samuel Hopkins of Burlington, for a process of making potash. This was easily made by leaching wood ashes from a plentiful raw material—timber. Light and easily transported, it became the earliest "export crop" of the pioneer, and often his only source of cash.

fully sliced through the wilderness, they were given little or no regular care. For the most part the early roads kept to the high ground, avoiding the tangle of brush and marsh in the river valleys. Most roads were built for local purposes, primarily to connect a new frontier settlement with some more heavily populated town nearby. There sometimes were long stretches laid out for particular purposes, like the path cut by Ira Allen in 1772 from Castleton to Colchester, for the purpose of linking his speculative Onion River lands with the settled communities to the south. In 1793–94 a branch was taken off the

Hazen Road and built due north into Canada to serve eventually as part of the Boston to Montreal stage route.

There was, none the less, a growing amount of traffic over some of the routes. Inns and taverns thrived in the service of travelers as well as thirsty local inhabitants. They became as near to community centers as existed, and many of the important meetings—such as the Constitutional Convention at Windsor—were held in the tavern instead of the meetinghouse. As a consequence innkeepers like Stephen Fay at Bennington became respected and informed leaders of the community.

POST-OFFICES were established in 1784 in Benning-ton, Rutland, Brattleboro, Windsor and Newbury.

COIN SILVER was scarce, often because it was melted into safer and more useful table silver.

Trade and travel grew in spite of rather than because of the erratically expanding road system. Assisted by the rivers, commerce with southern New England grew steadily. In fact, before the opening of the lands beyond the Appalachians, New York, Boston and other Yankee cities competed vigorously for the northern frontier markets. Both the Connecticut River canals and the Champlain Canal in New York were built to draw commerce southward away from Canadian outlets. Even bad roads did not interfere with the driving of cattle—and particularly sheep—to Boston markets. The first bridge over the Connecticut at Bellows Falls saw frequent large droves of them. It was not long before regular stage coach routes were established for the convenience of Boston-bound businessmen.

By 1784 the main routes were in condition sufficient to warrant the establishment of a regular postal service. Five offices were set up in the larger towns, with the more isolated areas served by postriders. But high postage rates[2] and unreliable service caused many people still to depend on the courtesy of travelers to carry messages.

The unpredictable money situation was also a great handicap to business. Barter necessarily had been the principal method of the earliest pioneers. With no bulk crops for sale, they acquired little cash, merely exchanging needed items among one another. But merchants also found themselves forced to this same expedient by the scarcity of money, long after the stage of agricultural self sufficiency had been passed. Even when available, money fluctuated so in value as to make exchange and credit extremely difficult. Continental currency depreciated steadily between 1777 and the end of 1780, when it

<hr/>

2 Postage was payable by the recipient; stamped envelopes first appeared in 1847 at Brattleboro, Vermont.

became valueless. Debts paid in depreciated money left creditors with little to show for their loan. The legislature twice, in 1781 and 1787, set comparative values for all contracts in terms of the depreciated currency.

Prices, of course, rose to fantastic levels, and then collapsed when the paper disappeared and prices were again stated in terms of hard money.

The result was continuous resort to the courts. Lawyers flourished in a land which once lumped them disparagingly with land-jobbers and other characters scorned by all good Green Mountain Boys. Much of the unrest during the years following the peace stemmed from taxation, half of which, it was claimed, was employed in the maintenance of courts. Taxes were particularly burdensome, since they had to be paid in hard cash. The amount of suits, court action, and other legal doings indicated that no small part of a man's income went into lawyer's fees.

No less frequent on the records of the period are its many land transactions. Lacking stocks and bonds and all the other modern possibilities for investment, anyone who had any money to spare—and many who didn't—speculated in land. It was a tricky business, but in a period of advancing land values resulting from constant population growth, it proved highly profitable to many—and ruinous to a few. Fortunes were made in the purchase of lands auctioned off for little or nothing at tax sales. Governor Thomas Chittenden used his official position to get an inside track on these sales, in addition to the acres he reserved to himself as a condition for each land grant—quite like Benning Wentworth. The influence of land speculation on politics was tremendous, as we have already seen in the story of the New Hampshire Grants and the Onion River Company.

95

COOPERATION was as notable a characteristic of frontier life as independence. Many difficult tasks, impossible to the individual in a society which lacked modern service enterprises, were undertaken by joint effort—often through "bees." Having themselves faced starvation in a land without grocery stores, neighbors often gathered to harvest a sick friend's crops.

LIVING CONDITIONS

These many economic changes in trade and transportation altered very little the basic self-sufficiency of the farm family. Many products previously unavailable—and particularly improved farm implements—now lightened the burden of life and labor on the frontier but did not change its basic pattern. Almost all the fundamentals of living—food, clothing, and the furnishings of the home—were still provided by the pioneer himself. There is here a marked contrast to the complete interdependence of modern life, in which we buy everything we need and sell nearly all our labor.

The very first settlers existed on what they could trap, catch, shoot and pick, such as woodchucks, fish, moose, berries, roots and acorns. They faced the everpresent possibility of starvation, until crops were harvested and the land began to issue forth its bounty.

Corn was the basis of most meals in the form of samp, Indian meal or mush. No less common were pumpkins, which were, with milk, sometimes the only item of diet in the long winter months. The garden, and in winter the root cellar, supplied vegetables as long as they lasted. Peas and beans were often dried and stored in the loft. If cattle were slaughtered, it was usually after winter had set in firmly so the meat could be kept frozen; there was no method of preservation except salting or drying in other months. Despite the additions of wild berries, honey and maple sugar, the diet was monotonous and not well balanced.

Cooking was done first over the open fire, and then in the great fireplaces which frequently filled the entire end of the rude cabin. Food was handled in large quantities—when available—for the big families, and their utensils seem mammoth to us today. Fire, of course, was fundamental not only to cooking but to existence itself throughout the extended winter. If the fire accidentally went out, another had to be laboriously rekindled from flint. Or perhaps it was necessary to hike a great distance through drifted snow to the nearest neighbor for a burning brand.

We have already noted how apples were treasured more for the cider they made than the food they furnished, how rum along with salt was one of the "indispensable" imports. An enormous consumption of liquor which would scorch the interior of an effete city dweller today, was then quite general. Rum fortified the toiler, minimized the curse of loneliness, defended against cold, and enlivened the social gathering. One wonders, from Ethan Allen's own accounts, how he was able to take time off from "passing the flowing bowl" to accomplish his reckless and colorful deeds of frontier daring. In the expense accounts of the time, paid without question by State Treasurer Ira Allen, were large items for the liquid replenishment of the spirits. There are occasional one shilling meals, but more frequent six shilling drinks.

No less than food was clothing essential to the frontier family. Skins furnished the first rainment for the woods runner. But determined pioneer women were soon spinning and weaving flax from the fields and wool from their own sheep. It was indeed an "age of homespun." Even shoes were first made on the farm from its hides. But store shoes and boots were much desired, and itinerant cobblers soon found it possible to establish a thriving business in a new town. Both shoes, incidentally, were alike, and designed for a lifetime of service. Leather was also in great demand for harnesses, saddlery and many articles of clothing.

Not only clothing, but also all other household items were produced at home. Crude furniture was hewn from the same logs which built the rough cabin, for wood was the universal material. Kitchenwares such as bowls, spoons, paddles, and "trenchers" were whittled or scooped out during the winter days when outside work fell off. The women, in addition to cooking, spinning, and gardening, also joined in the process of manufacture of such necessary things as candles, the sole lighting device available apart from the flickering fire on the great hearth.

The hardships of frontier life are such as to be almost unbelievable to the modern country dweller with his automobile, furnace, radio, automatic stove, bathroom, and the other comforts and labor saving devices of contemporary civilization. But the pioneer, unable to foresee these future contrivances, would have been quite surprised at his descendants' awesome contemplation of wilderness living. He knew exactly what he was getting in for, and it was mostly what everyone did anyway.

Toil was the first and everpresent condition of frontier life. It was essential to existence itself, and the man who dreamed of an estate for his family and himself could plan on back-breaking, dawn-to-dusk labor before he reached his goal.

The first settler in any town could expect also a lonely life, for these tiny clearings were often miles from the nearest other venturesome soul. A hardy pioneer woman might find herself alone for months at a time, and there were even occasions when self-reliant children had to fend for themselves for a considerable period. Isolation was emphasized by lack of transportation and the miserable condition of such roads as did exist. And there was actual and constant danger from wild animals, including wolves and bears.

Shortages of nearly everything dogged the settler's existence. He lacked proper implements for farming or conduct of the household, and those he improvised were crude and costly in sweat and time. By the end of a winter he might even be faced by shortages of food; starvation was never far away for the unlucky or improvident. Good health was a thing to be treasured, for there were few if any doctors available, even in the more settled areas. The inevitable necessities of birth and death were handled by mid-wives or perhaps just by friends. How much help a doctor might have been, however, is an occasion for some doubt as we read of the purging, bleeding, and potent medicines deemed necessary and effective.

As settlers began to nudge each other in the new areas, the restless ones moved on and the solid citizens began to develop the rudiments of community life. Large tasks which were impossible to the individual—like a barn-raising—were handled by neighborhood "bees." Their popularity was such that they were adopted for other social activities, such as husking, sewing, and even spelling bees. A sugaring-off party, a neighborhood wolf-hunt or a wrestling match could also be expected at frequent intervals.

From the very earliest times these independent, freedom loving people gathered in the town meeting to adjust community affairs, such as roads, fences, schools and "preaching." The latter engaged by far the most attention, and after the building of the church, Sunday meeting became an important social as well as religious ceremony.

In the larger settlements the heritage of the New England town began to show itself in the erection of substantial frame houses, the establishment of stores and industries, and even perhaps of a newspaper. It was not long before Bennington, Westminster, Newbury and other important centers began to bear a close semblance to the New England towns whence their settlers had come. Sometimes even the name was the same.

ANN STORY, alone, raises a family, refuses to flee before the enemy.

Life on the frontier bred an indomitable people. The histories of the towns are filled with stories of hardship and of incredible stamina and persistence. There was our old friend, Benjamin Waite, who after sanguinary service with Rogers' Rangers became one of the first settlers and leading citizens of Windsor, tramped to Ticonderoga with Ethan Allen, served in the Revolutionary army, and then, at an age past eighty, set forth again into the wilderness to found the new frontier town of Waitsfield. There was sturdy Ann Story of Salisbury, who, when her husband died beneath a falling tree, took over his back-breaking tasks as well as her own, raised her family and even refused to retreat with the rest of the settlers before Burgoyne's advancing British troops and Indians.

They were a restless, independent folk, a strange and contradictory combination of the visionary and the realist. They were adventuresome, dreaming ever new dreams of rich lands and great wealth just over the horizon. Yet they knew how to buckle down to the dirty, laborious job of drawing a living from the soil. Few of weak will or tender fibre survived; the frontier acted in some respects as a sorting process.

They were, on the whole, a happy people. Visiting preachers and other travelers found them surprisingly cheery despite their hardships and what seemed to the more "civilized" visitor an unkempt, grubby, vermin-ridden existence. Even the Reverend Nathan Perkins, shocked by the irreverence of these rough pioneers, conceded grudging admiration for their hearty hospitality and unsubdued love of life. The wide open spaces of a green and fertile wilderness had indeed entered into and expanded the spirit of its children.

VIII

CULTURE OF THE FRONTIER

*How the pioneers built their homes, churches, schools and libraries, and how Ethan Allen,
Samuel Williams, and others brought literature and printed word into the wilderness.*

THE conquest of the wilderness made larger demands upon industry than upon intellect. It was not odd, therefore, that artistic and intellectual endeavor did not flourish at first on the frontier. Art, music, literature—the world of the mind—were of little concern to the Yankee farmer who pushed forward the line of the frontier and broke open a virgin soil. Even after the end of long and distracting wars, the pioneer found whatever energies remained from dawn-to-dusk toil absorbed by a political fight over the land and its ownership. The land grant struggle produced its own literature of controversy, as we shall see, but an unsettled frontier and an unbroken soil left little leisure for scholarly contemplation or creative effort. Isolation and poor communication kept these preoccupied people aside from the mainstreams of New England cultural development.

"Men must have bread before books," a pioneer preacher observed. "Men must build barns before they establish colleges. Men must learn the language of the rifle, the axe and the plough, before they learn the lessons of Grecian and Roman philosophy and history; and to those pursuits was the early American intellect obliged to devote itself, by a sort of simple and hearty and constant consecration."[1]

It was not surprising therefore that the first flowering of man's instinctive love of the artistic and the beautiful came as an outgrowth of his first necessity—shelter.

Despite the fact that he came from New England towns whose forthright, simple colonial architecture was already taking on elaborate Georgian embellishments, the first settler built a house simple in both structure and function. In the urgency of wresting a living from the land he erected the most available shelter—sometimes merely a bark-covered, three sided shed.

Mostly, however, he was able to manage a log cabin, constructed without thought of "architecture." From the very trees he felled to clear his lands, he selected those of nearly uniform girth, hewed two sides flat, and notched the ends. He then laid them up one atop the other, securing the ends with wooden pegs. He cut a door and windows— perhaps only one, since there was no glass to keep out the weather—and covered his log rafters with bark. Usually

he also laid up a great stone fireplace and chimney at one end, and sometimes split some logs for the floor. But many a cabin boasted nothing but a dirt floor and a hole in the roof to let the smoke out. Practically none of these cabins remain since they were seldom built on a foundation, and soon collapsed. There are a few in Grand Isle County and some elsewhere hidden in a coat of modern clapboards

In all but the most isolated regions sawmills were quickly set up. As soon as boards became available, real building was possible, even if—as was sometimes the case—wooden pegs had to substitute for nails. But it was not a house he first built to replace his cabin, but a barn for his essential livestock. A barn-raising was usually a community affair in the more settled areas, and the huge timbers of the framework were raised with a neighborly heave-ho.

But the frame house came quickly—often while log cabins were still a-building. The pioneer quite naturally tended to copy the family homestead back in his native town in Connecticut or western Massachusetts, which had been built many decades before. Vermont building thus reflected the architecture of a much earlier period than that which was now becoming popular in the more settled area of southern New England. The bulk of the remaining early houses are the larger, more substantial ones, like Parson Jedediah Dewey's or the more unusual Henry House, both in the town of Bennington (see page 105). But most, originally, were the simple gabled story-and-a-half rectangle, with a mammoth central chimney. Since all heating and cooking depended on the open hearth, there had to be a fireplace for each principal room. These rooms were therefore grouped about the chimney, with the parlor on one side and the best chamber on the other, and the great kitchen with its tremendous fireplace and ovens all the way across the back. Steep stairs up from the seldom used front hall clung to the fourth side, into which was often built a smoking oven. Wood was the most common material for all uses, and the "up-and-down saws" then used could turn out boards as wide as the center cut of a great three foot thick pine. Both floors and walls boasted great wide boards measuring two or three times the width possible to modern circular saws. They were commonly left to weather to a rich golden brown, or

---

[1] Quoted in Merle Curti's "*Growth of American Thought,*" (N.Y. 1943), 266.

Grand Isle County is the last place where the earliest Vermont houses can still be seen. Before they had sawmills, the pioneers built log cabins like Jedediah Hyde's, raised in 1783 (above). There was practically no water power on the level islands and consequently logs were used more extensively. This cabin, about to be destroyed in 1945, was moved by the Vermont Historical Society to a new location just outside Grand Isle village on Route #2, for restoration as a local historical center. Picture above shows it on the original site.

Ethan Allen died returning across the ice to Colchester in 1789. The "Sandbar Bridge" now links the Islands to the mainland.   (Way)

Despite the great new bridge to the north, ferry boats still cross from the Islands to the New York shore.   (Beatrice Lowe Haskins)

INTERIORS were usually simple and revolved around the great fireplace. The simple furniture was pine, often constructed by the householder himself.

stained with red and other native colors—as were the clapboards outside. White paint was exceedingly scarce.

The rough, unfinished interior of the log cabin, with its crude hand-made furniture (limited usually to a bed, table, and some stools) had long since given way to more elaborate interior decoration. The same careful architectural detail which appeared on the outside of the Georgian houses of Bennington, Woodstock, Newbury, and other centers of wealth, was repeated on the inside in mantels, cupboards, and window and door trim. Walls were often laboriously stenciled by itinerant artists. A few even obtained the fine imported wallpaper, with its great landscapes and formal French and English gardens, which was well known in the seaboard regions. To this was added simple but tasteful pine furniture—the corner cupboard, the "trestle" table, the "hutch" table which folded up to make a chair or bench, the "Windsor" or the slat-back chair, the blanket chest, and perhaps also a larger drawer chest or high-boy. Sometimes the furniture, brought from the coast, was more elaborate than the homes. Landlord Stephen Fay's desk and his son Jonas' highboy, now in the Vermont Historical Society, would have graced the house of any Boston merchant prince.

The prospective owner—even Parson Dewey—was usually the builder of the house. The neighboring farmer might be a carpenter also, who would help him lay it out. Or, as soon became the case in the "older" settlements, there might be available a carpenter-builder who specialized in this work. These men combined a simple but adequate knowledge of architectural principles with sound craftsmanship and a feeling for beauty and proportion. They were amazingly versatile; they could not only design the structure, carpenter its frame, and lay the brick chimney, but also produce the most elaborate door and window trim, mantels, cabinets and paneling. Some could even turn out an acceptable mural, as in the Chittenden-Hasbrook house in Jericho. In fact, these murals —with the early wall stenciling which was rather widely used—are about the only evidences of early pictorial art.

Men of property started out with a spacious, two story mansion. But many another, like Ebenezer Robinson of Reading, built first the usual 1½ story farmhouse and then, in later prosperity, added to it a fine two story

Georgian front, incorporating all the available elegance. Mostly they were the old simple colonial facades with new Georgian refinements, such as the "palladian" window, a motif which Robinson liked well enough to repeat in his doorway.

These carpenters drew heavily on the building books of the Greenfield architect, Asher Benjamin, whose *Country Builder's Assistant* and other volumes were widely circulated. Benjamin, in turn, was greatly influenced by the more famous work of Boston's Charles Bulfinch, Salem's Samuel McIntire, and, later the English Adam brothers. But the conventional architectural devices shown in the books were freely interpreted by these independent craftsmen. Several became outstanding architects in their own right, such as Lavius Fillmore, who built beautifully detailed churches in Middlebury and Bennington (page 108). Thomas R. Dake, a resident of Castleton, provided the transition from "colonial" and "Georgian" to the newer "Greek Revival" styles (pages 102–103). In addition to his tasteful and original houses in the older style, he designed, in 1840, the Ransom House with five Ionic columns in a massive portico. This elaborate, new style swept the country, though Vermont did not acquire as many Grecian temples as, for example, did central New York, which was just entering its great building period in the early 19th century. Vermont passed quickly into the mid-century Victorian craze, and even older houses were "beautified" with the addition of gables and jig-saw gingerbread.

Mostly the middle-class farmer went on building the simple story-and-a-half farm house familiar to his father and father's father. As families grew the eaves were raised to gain more room beneath the roof, and new homes were constructed in this fashion, losing the careful proportions of the older 18th century structures. A great many boasted what has been termed "continuous architecture"—that is, the barns were connected with the house by a series of sheds to provide a covered passage during the long and bitter winter months. The great chimneys vanished with the more extensive use of stoves, and the fireplaces were often blocked up or torn out in the older houses.

Wood was the most widely used building material. But wherever there were good deposits of clay, brickyards were established, and brick houses were common, as in Bethel. Despite extensive quarries, stone houses are rare, except in the Black River Valley, where there are many fine examples. In the Rutland-Fairhaven area slate and marble went mostly into foundations, and were largely ignored as a structural stone until the monumental urban building of the late 19th century. The same was true of the granite areas to the north.

Some of the finest architectural detail and the most loving attention went into the construction of the "meet-

The superb but simple architecture of another day is one of the significant heritages of the past in Vermont. As population drained away from once prosperous towns, as the land ran out, many of these fine old houses were left to decay as their owners sought a living elsewhere. Now they are coming back to life as homes for new and old Vermonters.

Ebenezer Robinson, Revolutionary veteran, waxed and prospered, and in 1824 built himself a "mansion" in front of his more modest "cabin." His house reflects the good taste in architecture then prevalent, with its palladian window repeated in the doorway, the delicate dentils and interestingly irregular spacing of the side windows.

Late eighteenth century houses—Vermont's earliest— were mostly simple gabled structures built around a great central chimney (above), with a great kitchen fireplace and at least two others for the bedrooms.

Many houses, such as those in Bennington, reflect the Georgian influence even before 1800, but most of the older cabins received their face lifting by the addition of a new two story Georgian front later on.

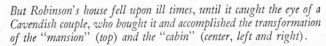

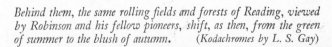

But Robinson's house fell upon ill times, until it caught the eye of a Cavendish couple, who bought it and accomplished the transformation of the "mansion" (top) and the "cabin" (center, left and right).

Behind them, the same rolling fields and forests of Reading, viewed by Robinson and his fellow pioneers, shift, as then, from the green of summer to the blush of autumn.   (Kodachromes by L. S. Gay)

LANGDON COLE HOUSE (1833)

DAKE STAIRWAY: RANSOM GRAINGER HOUSE

FEDERATED CHURCH, CASTLETON (1833)

The genius of one of Vermont's outstanding architect builders is manifest in the work of Thomas R. Dake at Castleton. He showed a remarkable ability to combine traditional Georgian with the new Greek Revival styles, as in the unusual but attractive Langdon-Cole House, (left). In the same year (1833), he built a New England meeting house with a Greek Revival portico and peaked Gothic doors and windows. And yet the overall effect is highly pleasing.

He was equally at home in the realm of careful painstaking interior work. His mantels and stairways are masterpieces of grace and refinement. The crowning achievement of his career was the magnificent pulpit of the Federated Church.

Architecturally one of the loveliest villages in Vermont, Castleton boasts many fine old colonial homes which antedate Dake's work, including the simple cobbler's shop (opposite) probably one of the oldest brick houses in the state. The Jakeman house is representative of some of the solid, somewhat heavy brick homes of the early nineteenth century.

Castleton's homes are opened for inspection on the annual Colonial Day, held normally early in August.

FEDERATED CHURCH PULPIT

AMES HOUSE

*is brick structure, one of
oldest in Castleton is
eved to have once served
a cobbler's shop. It is to
restored as a community
orical center.*

KEMAN HOUSE

*is substantial brick struc-
of interesting lines was
lt shortly after the turn
he nineteenth century. It
epresentative of the many
erb examples of early
mont architecture in
tleton.*

OLONIAL DAY

*nually the people of
tleton gather to celebrate
r historical heritage in a
olonial Day," when
ny dress in costume, and
cs of a by-gone age are
ught out again for one
of new life.*

ing house," whether it emerged with the early chaste simplicity of Rockingham or the soaring, elaborate beauty of Bennington (pages 108–109). But the very earliest structures were frequently rude, functional rectangles, thrown up before the town fathers had much time for the consideration of beauty and refinement. Contrast, for example, Bennington's first meeting-house (page 66) with Fillmore's exquisite Old First Church (page 108), built to replace it in 1806, or his equally beautiful Middlebury church. But most of them were raised, like the houses, by frontier farmer-tradesmen, perhaps under the supervision of a boss builder of some small experience, who was likely the possessor of a handy "Country Builder's Assistant."

FRONTIER PIETY

Religion first entered Vermont in the black robes of Jesuit priests who stayed in the Champlain Valley only until 1759, which was close to the end of the French empire in North America. It was, therefore, Yankee religious as well as political habits which were fastened upon the new land when the colonials and the red-coats came to stay. Rum and religion came to the frontier in the same year (1724), when Fort Dummer imported both liquor for the Indians and a preacher to save their souls— and incidentally to minister to the needs of the garrison.

Piety first took hold among the Green Mountains, however, in the first chartered town—Bennington. Samuel Robinson led the "separate,"[2] or dissenting congregations of Hardwick and Sunderland, Massachusetts into the valley of the Walloomsac in 1761. They were joined here by others from Westfield, whose pastor, Rev. Jedediah Dewey, brought about a formal union of the three churches the following year. Yet an organized migration of congregations was unusual in this period, and even the Benningtonites came more for ordinary economic reasons, than because of persecution. The Coos country, far up the Connecticut, experienced a similar organized pilgrimage when Jacob Bayley led several groups from Newbury and Haverhill, Mass., to establish the new towns of Newbury, Vermont and Haverhill, New Hampshire in 1763. But most of the towns were settled in a hit and miss fashion.

The migration to Vermont was not limited to Congregationalists; in fact, there was an even stronger tendency for adherents of the minority sects—the Baptists, Methodists and Episcopalians—to seek peace and religious independence in a new land. The stout Puritan, Samuel Robinson, sorted them out as they came to him for advice on lands. To the Baptists he described the glories of Pownal and Shaftsbury; for the Episcopalians he located a land of milk and honey in Arlington—saving Bennington

for the adherents of the "true faith." And while Baptists and Episcopalians settled in many other nearby towns, yet their centers were as Sam Robinson had projected.

Thus the Baptist Church had its beginning in Shaftsbury in 1768, though for twelve years the town had no regular pastor. For a decade there was neglect of worship in Pownal, but in 1772 the second Baptist society was organized in this town.

An Episcopal missionary passing through Arlington in 1767 reported that regular services of the Church of England were being held at the home of Jehiel Hawley, who was both lay reader and lay missionary for the Church. Within five years the inhabitants had organized a parish. Respected, beloved, Hawley was exiled as a loyalist, his property confiscated, and his home occupied by Governor Thomas Chittenden. He refused an invitation from his neighbors to return, and died enroute to Canada in 1777. Ironically enough, it was the Governor's missionary brother, the Reverend Bethuel Chittenden of Tinmouth, who carried on Hawley's work. In 1784 an Episcopal Society was organized and a church begun. The foundation laid by Hawley and Chittenden was so strong that even today the Episcopal Church is very nearly the community church of Arlington.

Actually, the principal strength of religion was not on the westside but on the eastside of the mountains. Most all the churches were Congregational; yet after Bennington it was eleven years before another church was set up on the Westside—in Rutland. In fact, by 1780, out of 21 Congregational churches in the State, these were the only two which were not in the Connecticut Valley. Migration, as we have seen, proceeded directly up the Connecticut River, from older settlements possessed of well established churches. The Westside, on the other hand, was largely settled from the restless and distinctly unconventional west frontier of Connecticut. The rigid discipline of the Puritan Church was, therefore, prevalent in the Connecticut Valley, while most of the Westsiders ignored the problems of piety entirely. Jacob Bayley's suspicions of the Green Mountain Boys were based as much upon their noisy irreverence and shocking "deism," as upon disagreements over politics. As late as 1789, the upright Rev. Nathan Perkins reported with horror that a quarter of the inhabitants of the frontier were "deistical" and a large part of the rest had no religion at all. The inhabitants of Vergennes overlooked religion until 1793, when out of a population of 300 only nine gathered together to form a Church. By 1807 they had persuaded only six more. The Congregational Church of Peacham—which by 1840 was the second largest in the state—was not organized until 1794, and then with only fourteen members. At that, it was the first church in Caledonia County.

Religion did not develop spontaneously on the frontier. A great deal of the organizational work came not from

---

2 The "Separate" church had its origin in the protest against the formalized "half-way covenant" of the established Congregational Church, and its roots in the evangelistic "Great Awakening" of twenty years earlier.

STEPHEN FAY'S "CATAMOUNT TAVERN" in Old Bennington served as a gathering place for the Green Mountain Boys. Its substantial bulk, devoid of ornament, is typical of pioneer taverns (where the objective was to gain a maximum of interior space with a minimum of exterior embellishment). It is shown here at the time of Jefferson and Madison's visit to Bennington. (Painting by Roy Williams)

OLD HENRY HOUSE (1769) is said to have been identical with Seth Warner's house nearby. It differs radically in its architecture from the local colonial pattern. It stands next to the famous old covered bridge.

PARSON JEDEDIAH DEWEY'S HOUSE (1763) is probably the oldest existing frame house in the state. It stands simple and four-square, with its massive central chimney.

the settlers themselves, but from missionaries. In 1780 the General Association of Connecticut (Congregational) sent two ministers for service in Vermont. Others, like the pious and stiff-necked Reverend Nathan Perkins, came from time to time thereafter. Many of the early churches owe their origin to these devoted men.

The Methodists were naturally most successful in this evangelistic work. As early as 1788 there were missionaries in the western towns from the New York and Massachusetts "circuits." In 1796 the Vershire circuit was established, including many northeastern towns. Soon there were in operation seven circuits with eleven preachers. These fervent and pious bearers of the Word were not always received with open arms. Eccentric Lorenzo Dow came to the Essex circuit in 1799. But the suspicious people of Stowe, undecided as to whether he was preacher or thief, refused to give him audience. He met with even more violent opposition elsewhere, and left for Ireland the following year.

Even after the pioneers finally "got religion," they were uncommonly slow about building a church and maintaining a preacher. For years, sometimes for decades, they quarreled in town meeting—for it was here that they settled both civil and ecclesiastical affairs—over the location of the meeting house, over how the preacher should be supported, how much he should get, and whether the community was getting its money's worth from him. Although New Haven spawned a Congregational society in 1791, only four years after the town was organized, it was unable to raise money for building or preaching for twelve years. The pious gentleman who was finally obtained to do the Lord's duty found the going hard with bad roads and a scattered and not too conscientious congregation. Complaints began to arise that he was not attending his duty in full, and in 1807 he was dismissed.

In Pomfret, an Eastside town where the need of religious discipline was more strongly felt, the first settlers built a log meeting-house. But they spent the fourteen years from 1778 to 1791—virtually the life span of the Vermont Republic—fighting bitterly over the costs and location of a framed building. By the end of the quarrel nearly seventy inhabitants had joined churches in the neighboring towns.

Their action with regard to a preacher was no less confusing. In 1774 the town joined with their neighbors in Woodstock and Hartford, to support the Rev. Aaron Hutchinson, who took up residence in Pomfret. But there was no consistent policy with regard to his payment; at first they raised money by property and poll tax. But after his five year contract expired they merely undertook to collect individual subscriptions on his behalf. In 1781 they voted that only "the stiddy herers Bee taxed to pay for the last year's Servis."

THE PIONEER PARSON

The Reverend Aaron Hutchinson had a good many "steady hearers" in the three towns he serviced. He was a remarkable man; a graduate of Harvard, he was also awarded a degree by Yale in the same year and honorary degrees from Dartmouth and Princeton subsequently. Profoundly learned in the ancient languages as well as in religious doctrine, he possessed a prodigious memory, and was never known to refer to a Bible for any of his scriptural quotations or readings. Nor was it surprising that the leaders of the new state turned to him to open their Constitutional Convention, for the good parson was as patriotic as he was learned, and could be depended upon to direct the wrath of the Lord upon sinners, Yorkers and red-coats alike.

The life and labors of Reverend Hutchinson were representative of the condition and contribution of the pioneer preacher. Rigid in church discipline, bearer of a gloomy Puritanic doctrine, he was a magnificent specimen of physical as well as mental development. The pioneer parson needed to be, for he spent more time behind the plow than the pulpit. He made most of his living in the same manner as his neighbors—from the land, for his salary was always meager, and was customarily paid in wheat or other produce. The eminent divine, Cotton Mather, observed quite accurately that "there was nothing cheap in New England but milk and ministers."

He covered his parish on horseback or afoot, and split his own wood in order to thaw frozen fingers sufficiently to write lengthy sermons, which he delivered in barns, log-houses, and even in forest clearings. He was, as you see, not only a spiritual man, a learned man, but also a practical man.

Often the parson was the only educated man in the community, and was thus considered the fountainhead of wisdom and knowledge, both religious and general. Often he served as the only teacher before schools; Hutchinson took his pupils as hired hands and taught them as they milked, split wood, or guided the plow.

Because of his learning and spirited conversations, the Rev. Aaron was a coveted prize for dinner. His parishioners frankly bid for his presence, and he quite as frankly inquired as to menus and selected the best offer. One day he accepted a rather modest invitation. When asked to say the blessing he surveyed the supplies and complied:

"The Lord be praised! How I'm amazed
To see how things are mended.
Here's cake and tea, for supper I see,
When mush and milk were intended."

Even the dour divine managed to acquire a sense of humor in the spirited and irrepressible atmosphere of the frontier.

Rev. Hutchinson also acquired a very practical business sense in the course of bartering his services for what the settlers had to pay—produce. Reverend Aaron promoted both trade and industry, and his successor, the Reverend Elisha Hutchinson, took up inn-keeping after ten years of ministering to an intractable congregation. Many a parson served as the only available physician, as a mediator before the advent of lawyers, and often as a lawyer. Many a patriotic parson found himself thrown into politics, like the Rev. Jedediah Dewey of Bennington. Others served in town offices; the distinguished Rev. Leonard Worcester supplemented an annual salary that never exceeded $500 by acting as Peacham Town Clerk as well.

But the pioneer parson flourished as preacher and teacher; as scholar and statesman; and as author and artisan. Most found time for a full and conscientious family life; the Reverend Leonard produced fourteen children, sent six to college, and presented the Congregational ministry with five new Worcesters to take his place when he finally concluded forty-one years of service to the town of Peacham.

CHURCH AND STATE

There was substantial encouragement for the town's first preacher in the Wentworth grants, where, in addition to a right of land for the use of the Church there was also one for the first settled minister.[3]

But he commonly received his main support from a direct tax, laid by the town on the entire citizenry and voted at town meeting. It was witness to the identity of church and state, just as in Connecticut, where the Congregational Church held a monopoly quite as tight as the Church of England did in that latter country.

We have already observed that the Vermont Constitution was somewhat equivocal in its support of religious freedom. But it did make a bow in the direction of those pioneers who had shrugged off the Puritan restraints of Connecticut with more than a little satisfaction. "All men have a natural and inalienable right to worship Almighty God according to the dictates of their own understanding, regulated by the word of God"; it declared, "and . . . no man ought or of a right can be compelled to attend any religious worship."

But this was about as far as tolerance could be stretched. The Constitution limited these rights to Protestants, and declared that everyone must observe the Sabbath and support some religious worship. One of the earliest sessions of the General Assembly made this more specific in 1780 by empowering the towns to exact land taxes for building a meeting-house and supporting a minister—providing no one was compelled to contribute to the established church "contrary to the dictates of his conscience." But in 1783 it was specified that any objector would have to present a certificate from another church that he was contributing to it. Not until 1801 was it possible to evade the tax merely by a declaration that the objector did not "agree in religious opinion with the majority." In 1806 the Council of Censors recommended abolition of all laws uniting church and state, and the next year religion was left to the support of voluntary contribution.

The Constitution had also included a religious test for the holding of office, because of which Ethan Allen obstinately refused to serve in public office. This was dropped in the second revision of the document, in 1793.

The General Assembly had also spent much of its time in legislating the morals of the community. Severe penalties were laid down for violation of the Sabbath, and grand jurymen, constables and tythingmen were enjoined to "inspect the behavior of all persons on the Sabbath." Swearing and cursing were punishable in the stocks, and the death penalty was set for blasphemy. With punctilious concern, specific punishments—including execution—were provided in detailed acts for various sexual crimes.

This excessive concern for the morals of the populace has lead some to question the purity and sobriety of our ancestors. Tumultuous, rough, and irrepressible they were, but not on the average any more lawless than usual on the frontier, where only an independent and self-sufficient soul survived. True, there were vast differences within the population; in general, the settlers in the Connecticut Valley were more conservative, pious and law-abiding than those across the mountains. But one should not forget Stone's Rebellion, or the Westminister "Massacre," or the Guilford War—all East-side events. Nor can we overlook the moderates of Bennington who consistently pressed for a conciliatory settlement with New York, despite the riotious behavior of the Green Mountain Boys, and who selected the stable and respected Seth Warner over Ethan Allan in the revolutionary crisis. Nor can we pass by the conservatives of Arlington, many of whom became loyalists. Yes, there were wide differences, not only regionally but locally.

For the most part they were a joyously intemperate but not sodden people, who confounded the visiting preachers who tried to classify them into saints and sinners. Reverend Nathan Perkins, traveling a hundred miles without sight of a church in 1787, denounced their mode of living as dirty, nasty, miserable, flea-bitten squalor. But, he observed with reluctant but conscientious justice, "woods make people love one another and kind and obliging and good natured. They set much more store by one another than in the older settlements."

They were indeed of sturdy stock and of obstinate but independent mind, for all their rigorous and unconventional way of life.

---

3 Wentworth also reserved rights for the Church of England and its agency, the Society for the Propagation of the Gospel in Foreign Parts, in a vain attempt to fix his church upon the Hampshire Grants.

On the following page: Bennington's "Old First Church" (1806) →

ROCKINGHAM MEETING HOUSE was raised in 1774 with the aid of 40 pounds and "4 gallons of rum." It was replaced in 1787 by this second, larger structure (right). Its severe simplicity contrasts markedly with the delicate and elaborate detailing of Lavius Fillmore's "Old First Church," built over 20 years later in Bennington.

INTERIOR retains the straight-backed solemnity of old box pews and the high pulpit with its sounding board. Restoration was undertaken in 1907. Care of the building originally carried a munificent $2.50 annual salary, with fifty cent fines for delinquency.

SCHOOLS

"I thank God," wrote Governor Berkeley of Virginia in 1640, "there are no free schools nor printing presses here, and I hope we shall not have, these hundred years."

The New Englanders felt differently about the objects of Berkeley's intemperate outburst. That same year Cambridge issued its first volume, the Bay Psalm Book, and Governor Hopkins of Connecticut reported that already "one fourth of our annual revenue is laid out in maintaining public schools." Seven years later Massachusetts passed her famous law ordering that all towns with 100 families should establish "grammar schools" or become subject to increasingly stiff fines. New Hampshire, upon achieving its own government, adopted the same law.

It was some time before any of the frontier communities in the New Hampshire grants had 100 families. But there were many reflections of typical Yankee concern for schooling, particularly among the more conservative communities. Governor Benning Wentworth had included grants for schools in his later charters, along with those for the church. As early as 1761 the proprietors of Guilford set aside three 100-acre lots and a house lot for a school. The new settlers of Bennington showed equal concern for mind and spirit in 1763, voting a tax to build both a schoolhouse and a meeting-house. There seem to have been three schools in operation by 1765.

As in the field of religion, Newbury followed close on Bennington's heels, laying a tax for the support of a school in 1769. Chester, first settled in 1764, took action in 1773 on behalf of both school and church, although the latter had to wait sixteen years for a house of its own. Springfield, settled permanently the same year, opened her first school and first religious meetings simultaneously in the same building, also in 1773. Some of the later towns acted even more speedily. Cambridge was organized in 1785 and got its school the next year—five years before its first grist mill!

But one should not be misled—as some writers have been—into assuming that schools were the very first concern of the pioneer settlers. First clearing the land and then a succession of wars and political controversy engaged their active attention. Moreover, most were young, many just married with no children of school age, and almost all were well isolated one from another. A school, requiring regular attendance from such widely scattered farms was hardly feasible. Actually, schooling preceded schools, for there was no lack of that basic Puritan concern for learning. For a man to know his Bible, he must first learn to read it. To engage in trade—never frowned on by the descendants of John Calvin—he must be able to write and "figger." Considerable instruction was undertaken in the home, and as homes drew closer together, it was not uncommon for children to gather at a single household for instruction by the best educated person in the neighborhood. There was certainly very little evidence of scorn for education as "high fallutin" or opposition to its introduction, phenomena which were quite visible on the mid-western frontier a few decades later. Despite historian Samuel William's promotional enthusiasm, his 1794 statement is probably representative:

"Among the customs which are universal among the people in all parts of the state," he asserted, "one that seems worthy of remark is the attention that is paid to the education of children. The aim of the parent is not so much to have his children acquainted with the liberal arts and sciences, but to have them taught to read with ease and propriety, to write a plain and legible hand, and to have them acquainted with the rules of arithmetic, so far as shall be necessary to carry on the most common and necessary occupations of life. All the children are trained up to this kind of knowledge. They are accustomed from their earliest years to read the Holy Scriptures, the periodical publications, newspapers, and political pamphlets, to form some general acquaintance with the laws of their country, the proceedings of the courts of justice, of the general assembly of the state and of the Congress, etc. Such a kind of education is common and universal in every part of the state, and nothing would be more dishonorable to the parents or to the children than to be without it. One of the first things the new settlers attend to, is to procure a schoolmaster to instruct their children in the arts of reading, writing and arithmetic. And where they are not able to hire an instructor, the parents tend to it themselves. No greater misfortune could attend a child than to arrive at manhood unable to read, write and keep small accounts. He is viewed as unfit for the common business of the towns and plantations, and in a state greatly inferior to his neighbors."

It is obvious that Vermont had schools before she had school laws. But the first Constitution laid out a very thorough plan of education (largely copied from the Pennsylvania model) from the primary school right up through a university. "A school or schools," it ordered, "shall be established in each town *by the legislature* for the convenient instruction of Youth, with such salaries to the masters, paid by each town, making proper use of school-lands in each town, thereby to enable them to instruct youth at low prices. One grammar [secondary] school in each county and one University in this state ought to be established by direction of the General Assembly."[4]

Vermont's Constitution was not unique in its concern for education, though only three other state constitutions included any similar provision. But it was unusual in that it proposed a system from the grades through college.

---

[4] This provision echoed the familiar custom of Massachusetts and Connecticut, placing primary responsibility on the town, but reserving supreme authority to the legislature.

The legislature, distracted by the needs of war and split wide open by political controversy, had all too little time for cultural and educational matters. But it did, in 1778, begin the process of reserving one right of land for a county grammar school and one for the university in each town granted by it. In October 1781, the first law was passed to implement the constitutional direction as to schools; the towns were authorized to lay taxes for the building of schoolhouses, churches and bridges. The following year they passed the first comprehensive school law. Towns were authorized to divide into school districts, each district to raise its school money by taxation or subscription under the direction of a committee. But there was nothing absolutely required; everything was left to the towns—indeed, to the school districts. Already the legislators were ducking the forthright constitutional provision that "schools *shall* be established in each town *by* the Legislature." Their position was written into the revised Constitution in 1786, which announced in mild tones that "a competent number of schools *ought* to be maintained in each town."

Schools there were to be, but with the Constitution of 1786 the dream of a complete educational system disappeared. Not until 1797 did the legislature get up courage enough to order the towns to support schools and teach the three "R's"—reading, writing, and arithmetic.

We noted that Vermont had schools before it had school laws. And the development of schooling now continued in much the same manner as before, except that towns which could support more than one school divided into districts. Some had done this before 1782; Woodstock set up five districts in 1779 and voted to "raise four pence on the pound for the advantage of schooling." But no action was taken; the pressure of other problems distracted the town fathers until 1782, when a tax was voted in conformity with the legislative act. They then set about building a schoolhouse. Next door, in Pomfret, the freemen were more blunt; in 1778 they voted *not* to build a schoolhouse. A school was finally organized by subscription in 1786, and 26 scholars immediately bent over their books in a tiny log shop—the only building available.

SCHOOLHOUSES AND SCHOOLMASTERS

The schoolhouses when built were small, low, rude, and often erected in great haste. They were seldom well maintained, and were a constant subject of complaint by schoolmaster and scholar alike. The stone fireplace heated so poorly that in St. Johnsbury the ingenious master converted a makeshift stove out of a mammoth potash kettle, and improved things greatly.

The frontier schoolmaster needed to be ingenious—and philosophical as well. The conditions of work and the strain of dealing with unpredictable local opinion made the job a sacrificial one. Pay rarely exceeded ten dollars a month, and might run as low as four for a "school marm" —plus "board." The board was supplied by farming the teacher out to the various families, his stay being conditioned on the number of pupils supplied by that family. The system had its good points: the master gained greater insight into the character of his pupils, and himself served as a refining influence in the household. But it was a trying experience at times. One master reporting in on Monday enjoyed a hot baked gander, but became steadily less interested in the bird as it reappeared each meal up to Wednesday's supper. Hot johnnycake that meal left him "greatly revived," but for Thursday's breakfast it was "cold gander again; much discouraged [his diary reports] to see the gander not half gone." On Saturday he "weighed and found had lost six pounds the last week; grew alarmed; had a talk with Mr. B. and concluded I had boarded out his share."

The qualifications of these men varied widely. James Hicks, who started teaching school in Newbury within a decade after its first settlement, had been well and broadly educated in London. There were many scholars like Dr. Jonathan Ware of Pomfret, well trained in astronomy, mathematics, the classics and ancient languages, who shared their knowledge freely. But the experience of some towns indicated that many of the roving masters—who bargained only a term at a time—were the worthless ones thrown off by the more settled areas of southern New England. Most were young, and almost all labored on the farms or in village shops between terms, of which there were two. The winter term began right after Thanksgiving, and extended for 10-12 weeks. A slightly shorter summer term began in May or June.

Discipline was the first requisite of an acceptable teacher, and severity was generally held to be a virtue. Schooling was carried on to the tune of the hickory stick, and under the legend "spare the rod and spoil the child."

STEPHEN DAYE PRESS, now in the Museum of the Vermont Historical Society, is believed to be the original press brought from England to Cambridge in 1638. From it came the first printed word in what is now the United States, and it later issued the first Vermont imprints.

The materials when available, were crude. Paper came in large coarse brown sheets, unruled and unbleached, often folded and encased in a wallpaper cover. The modern "lead" pencil got its origin from the pioneer's "plummet," which was a pencil of lead obtained by pouring hot lead into a shallow groove or crack in the floor. The pen was a slit goose quill; the Gillot steel pen did not appear until 1830, and at 25 cents was even then deemed too costly for widespread use. Desks were rough boards, and the benches a split log on legs, flat side up. But all this could be endured, with good will, for a proper dose of "book larnin'."

GRAMMAR SCHOOLS AND UNIVERSITY

Land grants by Vermont made provision for county grammar schools—the equivalent of our modern high schools. These were visualized in 1777 as part of a state system, but like the lower schools, were turned loose in 1786. Most were opened under private auspices, the first being Clio Hall in Bennington, incorporated in 1780 at about the same time as Massachusetts' first private academy, Phillips Andover. Others followed.

At the peak of the 1777 educational plan stood the state university—a pet dream of Ira Allen. But the 1786 document omitted all mention of it, and in this omission we can find some explanation of the educational about-face executed by the legislature. The reader should recall that there was at this time in Hanover on the Connecticut River, a flourishing college, which had been taken under the patronage of the General Assembly when the New Hampshire towns were temporarily absorbed by Vermont. Even after the permanent exclusion of these towns from the new state, founder Eleazar Wheelock's son, President John continued to carry great influence in the legislature of Vermont. In 1785 these hard-headed, and often tight-fisted men delivered to Dartmouth an entire township, which has ever since been known as Wheelock, (and whose scattering inhabitants still pay rents to the New Hampshire college). Emboldened by his success, Wheelock proposed that all the lands reserved by the legislature in the various towns, for grammar schools and for a university, be turned over to the college. For its part Dartmouth would take over the entire educational system, and be responsible for its development and maintenance at all levels. This seemed like a bit too much, and the General Assembly decided to keep some hold on the Vermont system.

In the meantime, patriotic advocates of a new state university mobilized their strength, and in 1791, under the leadership of Ira Allen, obtained a charter for a University of Vermont, to be located in Burlington. Some previous proposals had been considered; Elijah Paine of Williamstown had offered £2000 toward a university to be located in his home town. But Allen gave £4000 and raised £1650 more. However, Ira soon departed for Europe, and never resumed permanent residence in Vermont. Without his enthusiasm and influence, the project languished. It was not until 1800 that a President and a faculty were appointed—all incorporated in the person of Rev. Daniel C. Sanders. The first university building was also begun the following year.

In the meantime a Middlebury group, judging the chartered state university still-born, projected a college in that expanding town on Otter Creek. They had been greatly encouraged by President Timothy Dwight of Yale. Under a charter granted in 1800, they began immediate operation with a President—and a tutor as well. By 1813 funds, chiefly from Gamaliel Painter, had been raised for a home for the new institution. Painter Hall, built in 1815, is today the oldest college building in the state, and is still in constant and useful service.

LIBRARIES

Few would have proposed that the enlightenment of the populace be confined to the schools, for most of these Connecticut people were well acquainted with libraries in their native state. In 1800 the General Assembly passed a law authorizing the establishment of these useful bodies. Brookfield had already established a library in 1791, as had Peacham in 1799. Now Pomfret, on Christmas Day 1804, took time off to organize one also, in keeping with the Act. Shares were sold at $1.50 each, and annual dues were 25 cents. A stiff and detailed schedule of fines for all kinds of damage was drawn up—for books were scarce, and exceedingly precious.

By 1810 there were all of twelve circulating libraries in the state. But even by that date few volumes had been actually printed in Vermont, and imports of books took second place to badly needed tools, cloth, and other household requirements.

THE PRINTED WORD

Canny President Eleazar Wheelock of the new college at Dartmouth was thoroughly sold on the power of the printed word. In fact, he thought that if he could only get a printer into town, he could easily convince the people of Vermont that the whole Connecticut Valley—including his private province of Dresden—might well be a part of that brand new state. So in 1778 he persuaded that eminent Connecticut printer, Timothy Green, to send him a protégé—one Alden Spooner.

As the autumn leaves drifted downward, Spooner loaded aboard an ox-cart his types and an old press the Greens had brought from Boston years before—outdated, but still mighty serviceable. A reputable press, too, for it had had the honor of giving to the continent north of Mexico its first printed word, "The Freeman's Oath," in 1639.

And then, on October 15, 1778, in Dresden, Vermont,[1] he began work. That same month came appointment as

printer to the State of Vermont. But when the towns east of the river were unceremoniously booted out of the new state early in 1779, the state printer found himself back in New Hampshire. Nevertheless he persisted in his intention of starting a newspaper, and in May of 1779 there appeared the first on the northern frontier: the *Dresden Mercury*.

Alden was unable to make up his mind whether he ought to accept Vermont's invitation to move to Westminster. But his brother did so, and in company with Timothy Green IV, put out in December, 1780 the first Vermont newspaper, the short-lived *Vermont Gazette, or Green Mountain Postboy*. When the new firm failed, Alden picked up the pieces and began anew at Windsor. Here, in addition to the state printing, he began the *Vermont Journal and Universal Advertiser*, still in circulation.

But Spooner had delayed too long. The Benningtonites had brought to that town Anthony Haswell, who in June 1783 issued his own *Vermont Gazette, or Freeman's Depository*, the state's second newspaper. He was also granted a share of the state printing.

---

[1]The New Hampshire towns east of the Connecticut River had been admitted to Vermont June 17, 1778.

Even more significant was the founding in Rutland, December 8, 1794, of one of the state's greatest modern papers, the *Rutland Herald*. Its editor, a distinguished Harvard professor and scholar of international reputation, Samuel Williams, had fled to the frontier to escape financial difficulties. Six years of frustrating labor as a preacher had brought him only one convert—his wife. In company with a Rutland judge of—oddly enough—the same name, he produced a newspaper notable for excellence of style and a rare lack of personal animosity.

Not satisfied with his weekly paper, he also published for a brief period during 1795–96 the state's first periodical, the *Rural Magazine*, devoted to literature, popular science, and history. The good doctor's historic talents had already been demonstrated by the publication in 1794 of his *Natural and Civil History of Vermont*, a surprisingly well balanced narrative.

His tremendous energy and intellectual talents had also involved him importantly in the founding of the University of Vermont, and in many philosophical and scientific inquiries. He sold the *Herald* in 1805, and died in 1817—one of Vermont's most brilliant intellects.

Samuel Williams was a rarity in his times, an editor who was not a printer. Most were, like Alden Spooner and Anthony Haswell. And in those days of poor communication, few books, and widespread illiteracy, your printer-editor was the intellectual center of the region in which he resided. It was no coincidence that Alden Spooner served for many years as postmaster at Windsor, and that Anthony Haswell became the new state's first Postmaster-General. For the mails were the principal means of spreading information, the printer its principal source.

With the coming of the printed word, and its widespread circulation, began a new phase in the cultural history of Vermont.

DR. SAMUEL WILLIAMS, *minister, scientist, philosopher, editor, historian, had made an international scholarly reputation before he came to Rutland to preach, and then to edit a weekly paper.*

THE PAMPHLETEERS

Ethan Allen knew, as well as Samuel Williams, the importance of the printing press to literature. But Ethan's chief output was not of a self-conscious literary kind; it was merely vocal thunderings reduced to paper. He engaged in a running battle of words with Governor Tryon and the New York "land jobbers" led by James Duane, frequently reducing his arguments to pamphlet form to give them wider currency.

One of them, entitled *Animadversory Address . . .* , drew grudging admiration from Duane himself. "Ethan Allen, he wrote, "has commenced author and orator. A phillipic of his against New York is handed about. There is quaintness, impudence, and art in it." Which was a very apt characterization.

As one might expect, there is an effusive, strident quality about this early controversial literature, whether issued by Ethan or his friends. It is writing born of an overwhelming urge to defend a cause—the same impulse which gave rise to Jefferson's memorable Declaration of Independence. But unlike the Declaration, there was here a strong element of self-interest; the Allen pamphlets were, in part, tracts in defense of a speculative business enterprise threatened by equally unscrupulous competitors.

But Ethan, at least, was more than just an 18th Century

FIRST NEWSPAPER in Vermont was printed in Westminster, possibly also on the Daye Press. Note the motto, below the masthead.

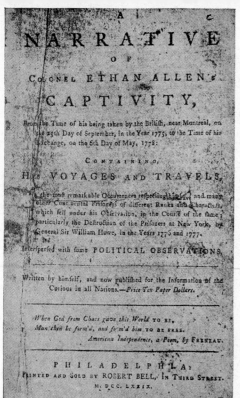

publicity manager for a contemporary business enterprise. He was an odd mixture of man of action and contemplative philosopher. Upon return from England he wrote and published his rough-hewn *Narrative of Col. Ethan Allen's Captivity*, a popular thriller which ran through several editions. It was in this volume that he attributed to himself the famous demand for the surrender of Ticonderoga (surely the supreme moment for a man of action) "in the name of the Great Jehovah and the Continental Congress."

Doubtless many must have mumbled that it was an odd sort of an ultimatum, for Ethan was thought to be on bad terms with both parties. The reason for speculation as to the state of cordiality between Ethan and Jehovah arose from his quite vocal criticism of the "priests" of the Congregational Church, and more particularly from a philosophical treatise on religion, completed in 1782, though not published until 1784.

ETHAN ALLEN'S BIBLE, presented to his new bride.

The *Oracles of Reason*, as Ethan called his magnum opus, was actually begun thirty years before, when he was still a youth in Salisbury, Conn. Across the New York State line dwelt a learned doctor, Thomas Young by name, who found great pleasure in long discussions on complex subjects. Young had at least a smattering of knowledge of the English and French rationalists. He was an avowed "deist" in religion, and soon infected young Ethan with his enthusiasm for a rational investigation of "revealed" religion. Their discussions took the form of extensive notes for a projected book on the subject. But when Young moved away, he took the material, probably to put it in a finished form. That was logical, for Ethan had no formal training in the King's English. He had been headed for college, but upon his father's death gave up all plans for higher education to run the family farm. Yet he was no backwoods yokel, and his mind was as inquiring as his tongue was effusive. In the preface to his *Oracles* he apologized for his presumption in rushing into print:

In my youth I was much disposed to contemplation, and at my commencement in manhood, I committed to manuscript such sentiments or arguments as appeared most consonant to reason . . . . This method of scribbling I practiced for many years, from which I experienced great advantages in the progression of learning and knowledge, the more so as I was deficient in education, and had to acquire the knowledge of grammar and language, as well as the art of reasoning, principally from a studious application to it . . . . But [I am] confident nevertheless that I have struck the outlines of a consistent system, which I recommend to abler writers to perfect.

It was probably not Ethan, however, but Thomas Young who "struck the outlines of a consistent system." Careful analysis of the text has shown extensive medical references and, in sections, Latin words and phrases which were foreign to Allen's experience. The book is a mixture of Young's ponderous, logical reasoning and Allen's more vivid but ambiguous comment. Ethan obtained the manuscript from Young's widow, and, after revising and expanding it to suit his own argumentative caste of mind, issued it under his own name in 1784. Despite its joint authorship, such a work by a rude, untutored soldier of fortune was somewhat of a phenomenon. It was one of the first works of philosophical literature produced in the new

United States—years before Thomas Paine's similar *Age of Reason*—and it came not from the intellectual centers of Boston or Philadelphia, but straight off the frontier.

Of course, it made a great stir among the horrified New England clergy, who denounced it as "deistical, heretical, and blasphemous." Even the printers had been scared of it. The manuscript lay in the hands of Ethan's old Hartford printers for two years. They had been willing to defy the government of New York, but the Congregational Church was a different matter. So Ethan rescued the book and took it to Anthony Haswell, who had lately set up shop at Bennington. Haswell agreed to do it, if Allen would pay for it as work progressed. Ethan agreed but had to sell his Sunderland home to Ira to keep up payments. It finally appeared in 1784, and the proud author presented the first copy to his new wife. He also dispatched copies to all his friends, and even mailed one to his acquaintance, St. John de Crèvecoeur, in Paris, with a request that he lay it before the Academy of Arts and Sciences of Paris, "by whose sentence," he added hopefully, "I expect to stand or fall."

Bad luck dogged the philosopher Ethan. He lost nearly the entire edition when a bolt of lightning destroyed Haswell's shop. It was the Lord's verdict on the blasphemer, said the clergymen in a chorus of pious triumph. So, they thought, was the old war-dog's untimely death only five years later, on February 12, 1789, just as Dartmouth President John Wheelock sat down to pen him a compliment on his "philosophic and contemplative tone." The news traveled fast; President Ezra Stiles of Yale made a notation in his diary for the 13th: "Died in Vermont the profane and impious Deist, Gen. Ethan Allen, Author of the Oracles of Reason, a Book replete with scurrilous Reflexions on Revelation. 'And in Hell he lift up his Eyes being in Torment.' " It was only a few weeks later that the traveling parson, Nathan Perkins, "arrived at Onion River falls, and passed by Ethan Allen's grave. An awful Infidel, one of the wickedest men that ever walked this guilty globe. I stopped and looked at his grave with a pious horror." If Ethan was not as preoccupied as President Stiles assumed, he must have been vastly amused at Perkins' characterization.

To the modern reader, with a century and a half of the secularization of religion behind him, Ethan Allen's Bible seems less shocking than tedious. But the deep sincerity and conscientious soul-searching of the author emerges none the less from a mountain of wearisome prose.

Ethan Allen was not the only scribe for the Green Mountain Boys. Ira equalled him in output, and Stephen Rowe Bradley and Jonas Fay sometimes assisted. But perhaps the most widely appreciated of all—in the Grants at least—was Thomas Rowley, who rhymed his opinions against the Yorkers to the vast delight of the frontiersmen:

"We value not New York, with all their powers,
For here we'll stay and work; the land is ours."

But Vermont's most distinguished writer was a Brattle-boro lawyer, Royall Tyler. By virtue of the performance of his play, *The Contrast*, in 1787, Tyler was already in excellent repute as a playwright when he issued the printed version and moved to Vermont, both in the year 1790.[1] He now became closely identified with the new state, serving in progressively more important legal positions until he was appointed Chief Justice of the Supreme Court in 1807. His pen was ever active, and his witty and informed comment on law and politics appeared frequently in contemporary magazines. In 1802 his *Algerine Captive*, a two volume novel, was widely seized upon as a genuine narrative of a pirate captivity, though it was entirely fictitious. It was among the earliest American fiction, and was one of first to be republished in England.

Tyler's fame, however, rests primarily on his play, *The Contrast*, the first American comedy to be performed professionally in an American theatre. It had a significance all its own, for its characterizations served to dramatize the widening gulf between the Englishmen of the old world and those of the new.

We have spoken of the literature of the frontier—what of its art, its music? Such as existed was auxiliary to other activities. There were itinerant portrait and landscape painters, most of whose work is cloaked in anonymity. Some merely carried stock canvasses with the bust nearly completed, to which only the sitter's features were added. In Windsor, however, there was an engraver of some force and originality—Isaac Eddy by name.

Music, so far as we can tell, was limited to hymns and folksongs. There must also have been many folk tales repeated around the fireside. Certainly the events of this concluding half of the eighteenth century provided a rich heritage of material for the pen of subsequent writers of folklore. The exploits of Ethan Allen and the Green Mountain Boys have passed into the realm of the folk legend, along with those of Paul Bunyan and Johnny Appleseed. Yet in the folklore of the period lies a vast unexploited reservoir of material for the understanding of the joyous, uninhibited and unpolished culture of the Green Mountain frontier.

---

[1] The reader will remember that he appeared in the state once previously, in pursuit of Daniel Shays and his men.

Washington was an advance subscriber to the printed play (left,), first performed in 1787 (below, right).

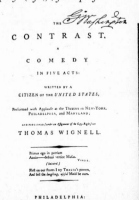

"THE LION OF VERMONT"

The State House portrait of Matthew Lyon (above) was painted at the bequest of the late Zenas Ellis of Fairhaven, indefatigable Lyon enthusiast, and is based on an original "primitive" portrait of Lyon once in Ellis's possession.

IX

YANKEE RADICALS

How Vermont democracy spawned a multitude of causes and isms until emigration and exhaustion gave the state a new and conservative outlook.

THE Revolutionary radicals of '76 had been unable to organize a stable government when fighting ceased. The economic distress and political confusion of the period which followed gave conservative business men and other "friends of order" both an excuse and an opportunity to frame a tightly knit, federal Constitution for the new nation. But these "Federalists" wanted to control the new government on behalf of the well born and well-to-do—to the considerable distaste of Thomas Jefferson and other quite vocal democrats. From this opposition grew a new faction—the Democratic-Republican party, and all over the country democratic societies began to spring up.

MATTHEW LYON had a stormy career as Vermont's representative to Congress. Here a contemporary cartoon pictures a fight on the floor of the House, Lyon armed with fireplace tongs.

So when the scientist-statesman Jefferson appeared with his friend James Madison at Bennington in June of 1791 on a "botanical tour," it was not odd that he conferred with prominent anti-federalists on this, the "radical" side of the new state.[1] Nor was it coincidence that vigorous democratic societies soon sprang up in Bennington, Rutland, Castleton, Middlebury, and Middletown—none of them, notice, in the pious, conservative and more densely populated Connecticut Valley. The societies were the first new enthusiasm of a volatile people, who were to hatch

many "isms" before emigration and exhaustion gave the state its more familiar conservative caste. Many prominent Benningtonians, including the influential Robinsons and the fiery editor-printer, Anthony Haswell, took up the Republican-Democratic[2] cause. But of them all, the Federalists had no more outspoken or bitter foe than the Irishman Matthew Lyon, friend and fellow conspirator of Ethan Allen, pioneer industrialist and founder of Fairhaven. Among his varied enterprises, Lyon published a rabidly republican sheet called *The Scourge of Aristocracy*, which kept up a running battle of words with Samuel Williams' more scholarly and conservative Rutland *Herald*. Elected to Congress in 1796, Lyon broadcast

---

[1] Turn back to Roy Williams' painting of Jefferson's arrival in Bennington (p. 105). Jefferson and Madison are third and fourth from the left in the group.

[2] Jeffersonians were known as both "Republicans" and "Democrats."

a steady stream of bitter denunciations of President John Adams and his Federalist colleagues. He thereby ran afoul of the new and infamous "Alien and Sedition Acts," which provided a jail term as well as fines for "disloyal" criticism of the government. Lyon, consigned to a bleak cell of the Vergennes jail, immediately became a national hero. In far off Virginia funds were collected to pay his thousand dollar fine, but a lottery in Vermont had already raised four times that amount. In 1798, while still in jail, he was reelected with only one vote less than the total received by four opposing candidates, including Samuel Williams and the learned Nathaniel Chipman. A triumphal procession the following year celebrated his release and return to Congress, where his irrepressible tongue kept the House in a recurring uproar.[3]

The opposing Federalists were led by Isaac Tichenor and Nathaniel Chipman, who had done so much to undermine the hold of the Allen brothers on Vermont politics. Their services in bringing Vermont into the Union, as well as the national prestige of the Constitution makers, gave the Federalists a strong hold on the affections of the people. But Tichenor was unable to loose the firm grip which Thomas Chittenden had upon the governorship. It was true that Chittenden had been associated with the questionable pro-British policy of the Allens—so bitterly fought by Tichenor—but the voters made a practical judgment on the years since 1777, and decided that however devious the policy, the results had been good. During Chittenden's administration, Vermont had remained largely free of war and war debts, had eventually been admitted to the Union, and a general recovery from the economic tumult of the "Critical Period" had been made. As a result Chittenden's position—like Washington's—was felt to be that of an elder statesman, above factional politics. Upon his death in 1797, however, Tichenor became chief executive. Extremely popular and an expert politician, he retained the governorship[4] long after the Democrats won control of the legislature.

The division of political sentiment was visibly along geographical lines; when Thomas Jefferson captured the national government in 1800, he carried every Vermont county west of the mountains, and lost every one to the east.

Jefferson was immediately faced with the epic struggle between the British and Napoleon's France over the control of Europe. America was divided between French sympathizers (the Republicans) and British protagonists (the Federalists). But American expansionism and British

violations of neutrality at sea produced a rising sentiment for a renewal of the war against England. The Vermont legislature resolved 169–1 to back the President in strong measures. But Jefferson, determined to avoid armed conflict, chose economic means to bring the British to a recognition of American rights. Late in 1807, Congress ordered an "Embargo" on all trade with that nation. It bore heavily on seafaring New England, but inland Vermont was not affected until early next year, when the embargo was extended to the Canadian trade—which was vital to Vermont. The Collector of Customs at the Canadian border promptly informed his superiors that it could not be enforced except with soldiers. Evasion was a daily occurrence along the border where friends and relatives, merchants and customers, lived on both sides of the line. All kinds of dodges were worked, even to the extent of rolling goods down hill across the border. Boats plied the Lake, among which was the famous "Black Snake," whose capture cost three lives. Trials of the smugglers before the Supreme Court, Chief Justice Royall Tyler presiding, created great excitement, and the execution of Cyrus Dean brought out an audience of 10,000. General dissatisfaction with the Embargo policy gave the Federalists their chance, and in 1808 Tichenor recaptured the governorship—lost in 1807 to Republican Israel Smith—though the General Assembly stayed Republican. Tichenor's dissatisfaction was so great that he cocked an interested ear toward Canadian suggestions that Vermont lead New England back into the British fold. But the voters gave the dissatisfied Federalists little opportunity to perfect any schemes, returning Republican Jonas Galusha to the governorship the very next year.[5]

Led by its western "War Hawks," a Republican Congress voted war against England in June of 1812, with three of Vermont's representatives in accord with the decision. The fourth, Martin Chittenden, son of the first Governor, dissented vigorously, and soon delivered to Congress petitions against the war signed by thousands of Vermonters. New Englanders generally were bitterly opposed to the conflict, and the Connecticut Valley settlements in Vermont shared the sentiment of the maritime states. It was at Windsor that the Federalists assembled in 1813, to nominate Chittenden for Governor. The popular vote in the election gave Galusha a slight edge, but not a majority, throwing the election into a Federalist Legislature, where Chittenden was elected by a margin of just one vote! The Republicans had been seriously weakened by opposition to the administration's embargo policy in the northern towns, usually pro-Republican.

The War did not put an end to smuggling; if anything, it increased. Smugglers even drove routes through wilder-

---

[3] Haswell also ended up in jail for blasting the administration editorially for Lyon's conviction. Lyon migrated first to Kentucky, whence he was again returned to Congress, and then to Arkansas, where he again ran, probably was elected, but died before he could serve his term.

[4] 1797–1807; 1808–09. Israel Smith—who had been removed as Chief Justice because he was a Democrat—unseated him in 1807.

[5] Galusha served until 1813, and again from 1815 to 1819. Governor Chittenden's son-in-law, he was opposed by Thomas' son, Martin Chittenden, who served as Governor 1813–1815.

ness areas to avoid the customs officers. "Smuggler's Notch," on the side of lofty Mt. Mansfield, saw hundreds of cattle headed northward for Canada to feed the British armies. The Canadian Governor-General reported back to England that "two-thirds of the army in Canada are at this moment [1814] eating beef provided by American contractors, drawn chiefly from the States of Vermont and New York."

The British again attempted to divide their enemy by sending an army down the Champlain Valley, with the new hope that, unlike 1777, anti-war sentiment in New England might break off that area with some ease. But Vermonters flocked to the colors at Plattsburg. Chittenden seized this moment to order the Vermont troops home, reserving them for the states "own defense and protection." But their officers flatly refused to comply. "An invitation or order to desert the standard of our country," they replied indignantly, "will never be obeyed by us, although it proceeds from the Governor and Captain-General of Vermont. . . . We consider your proclamation as a gross insult to the officers and soldiers in the service. . . ."

The British invasion was turned back on the Lake, however. Young Lieutenant Thomas MacDonough, with a makeshift fleet constructed at Vergennes during the winter of 1813–14, defeated a superior British fleet in one of the nation's memorable naval battles. Fearful of being trapped without control of the Lake, the English withdrew hastily into Canada.

Federalist control in Vermont, based on Yankee dissatisfaction with the conflict, ended with the war. Vermonters turned down the invitation to join the New England secessionist meeting at Hartford in 1815, and hoisted Galusha back into the Governor's chair. As in the nation, the Federalists—their obstructionist policy descredited—declined steadily. The country entered a period of "good feeling," with party strife at a minimum. But this was not a normal state of affairs, and by 1824 the Democratic-Republicans had split into two wings, with Andrew Jackson leading one and John Quincy Adams the other. In Vermont the conservative "National" Republicans showed the greatest strength. Their dominance was challenged, oddly enough, not so much by the Jacksonian Democrats as by a new party—the Anti-Masons.

ANTI-MASONRY

Vermont spawned many "isms" during the first half of the nineteenth century. But it was an imported "cause" which had the first direct effect on politics. Far to the west in New York State one William Morgan, author of an "expose" of the secrets of Masonry, disappeared in 1826. It was charged he had been murdered by Masons to silence him. A wave of anti-masonic sentiment burst the borders of New York State and swept over New England.

Even though most of her distinguished leaders[6] were Masons, the indignation reached its height in Vermont. The principal strength of anti-masonry lay in the new counties to the north, and among the more democratic religious sects like the Baptists, who were strong there. In the secrecy and selectiveness of the Masonic order they saw a threat to the new democracy, and Free Masonry soon became the whipping boy of the democratic press. The rising protest against the monopoly of offices by a few leaders was channeled into a new "people's" movement, with anti-masonry as its central theme. Essential to the spread of the excitement were newspapers, which had multiplied rapidly in the years following 1820.[7] Editors dipped their pens in vitriol and assailed the Masonic aristocracy. Fired by this undercurrent of social protest, anti-masonry soon became the dominant issue in religion and politics, dividing churches and political parties alike. Politicians unable to breach the citadel of National Republicanism recognized a bandwagon when they saw it, and jumped aboard. A political convention was held in 1829, and Heman Allen of Burlington nominated for Governor. He polled a surprising total of nearly twice that of the Democratic candidate—aptly named Doolittle—though only half that of Republican Governor Samuel C. Crafts. But the Anti-Masons did elect a Congressman in the Fifth District.[8] In 1830 the contest had to be decided by the legislature, and in 1831 William A. Palmer won the Governorship and held it for four years on the Anti-Masonic ticket. And in the national election of 1832 Vermont—alone of all the states—gave its electoral votes to the Anti-Masonic candidate for President. Even an unprecedented "Union ticket" of Republicans and Democrats failed to unseat Palmer in 1833. However, the very success of the party undermined it. Stunned at the virulence—and success—of the attack, Masonic lodges closed their doors. Deprived of its enemy, the party began to fall apart. In the election of 1835, Palmer ran up a good margin over both opposition candidates, but missed a majority of the total. As many times before, the decision was thrown to the legislature. Sixty-three ballots failed to elect a Governor, and Lieutenant Governor Silas Jennison, a moderate Anti-Mason, served out the term as Acting Governor, achieving election himself on the next round. Led by William Slade—later Governor—most of the Anti-Masons trooped into the new Whig party. The more determined democrats joined the Jacksonian party of that name, while the more excitable elements looked about for some new object of social and religious concern.

---

6 Ethan and Ira Allen, Matthew Lyon, Thomas and Martin Chittenden, Jonas Fay, Anthony Haswell, Isaac Tichenor.

7 1820–30: 26 new weeklies were started; 1830–40: 53; and 1840–50: 44—totaling 123.

8 Roughly Orleans, Essex and Caledonia Counties. Contrast Vermont's five Congressmen in 1829 with 1949's one.

JOSEPH SMITH, Sharon born prophet of Mormonism.

THE REVIVAL OF RELIGION

For a generation democracy and free thinking went hand in hand among the citizens of the young republic. Even Vermont's admission as a state did not end its frontier period, nor what shocked clerical visitors termed the "reign of infidelity." But the excesses of the French Revolution went a long way toward discrediting the philosophical deism which had been the religion of revolution. In this country, the Democrats had won their political battle in 1800. Moreover, without the formal organization of church membership, the free-thinkers lacked cohesion and direction. Thus there was little vocal opposition when a new evangelical revivalism replaced the old radical deism as an emotional outlet for the frontier.

The revival of religion got its impetus in 1801 from two main sources—the new evangelical sects which arose in reaction against the gloom and fatalism of Puritanism, and a new missionary effort from within the Congregational Church.

The most influential of the various new sects were the Free-will Baptists, the Christians, and the Universalists—all of whom emphasized the possibility of salvation through daily good works. Intensely democratic, they found many recruits among the newer northern counties where the frontier was still in the making. But the Methodists, working through their circuit riders, gained the most converts of all. Their ministers of the Gospel were common people, and the warm, intimate, personal appeal of their message had many takers.

Supplementing the revivalists was an awakening within the Congregational Church, and an attempt to regain its old hold upon the people. Vermont, as a stronghold of "infidelity," was the immediate subject of concern to the Connecticut Missionary Society, founded in 1798. By 1801 the evangelical tide began to flow through the Green Mountains. In the ten years which followed, churches gained hundreds of new members, and there were recurring revivals in various towns. The distractions of war and politics, however, resulted in a slackening of evangelistic fervor after 1810. With the end of the fighting—military and political—in 1815, there was a new surge of religious interest. Revivals were frequent in 1816 and 1817.

But more significant were the hundreds of new religious societies organized for moral reform during the twenties. A young Bennington editor named William Lloyd Garrison found the outlook highly pleasing on New Year's Day, 1829: "A new impulse has been given the friends of religion. Stupendous enterprises have been planned to elevate our country, and are now in a train of successful operation. . . . In fine, the year 1828 has been one of the brightest for Christian effort since the appearance of the Messiah on earth."

Indeed, the planning of "stupendous enterprises" for reform was part of the new religious outlook. Many of the reformers became fanatical in their enthusiastic devotion to moral and social causes. A great revival swept the country in 1830–31, bringing thousands of converts; but its very excesses brought exhaustion and reaction. Religious reform broke apart into many causes: temperance, prison and educational reform and abolitionism. But the over-all effect was to introduce a new strain of social humanitarianism into the harsh moral code of the Puritan Church.

There were a number of religious sects which emerged out of the intense evangelical ferment of this period. Some were led by frauds, others by sincere religious fanatics confident of their divine inspiration. An example of the former were the Dorrilites, whose leader preached communism of property, but complete obedience to his divine direction. He later confessed having set up the whole thing in his own behalf. Neighbors generally denounced the fanatic excesses of these sects: the Dorrilites were accused of bacchanalian revels, and under the influence of one fraudulent evangelist, two girls—feeling the presence of the devil in their clothing—shed it and sped naked over the winter snow to the top of a nearby hill. The "Pilgrims" migrated from lower Canada to South Woodstock in 1817 under a leader who preached a doctrine of primeval living, in which filth was a virtue.

Equally condemned in his own time was John Humphrey Noyes, prophet of "Perfectionism." In 1838 Noyes founded, at Putney, a Christian community based on the spiritual communism of Jesus. Shedding the conventions of sex among others, the Perfectionists aroused the righteous indignation of their conservative neighbors, who threatened violent measures. Unhappy, but determined to carry through with their experiment, the Perfectionists fled in 1847, only to reassemble later at Oneida, N. Y., where they developed their plans with surprising success.

Joseph Smith, Sharon born prophet of Mormonism, also fled before the lash of enraged public opinion, leading his Latter-day Saints from Palmyra, N. Y. to Carthage, Illinois—where he was murdered. The role of leader was assumed by another Vermonter, Brigham Young, who led a part of the faithful across the prairies to found a new city of Zion on the barren wastes beside the Great Salt Lake in Deseret (Utah). Young's Church of Christ of the Latter Day Saints is today one of the nation's most prosperous and vigorous religious organizations.

But the greatest disruption of religious life was caused by the revelations of a sincere but fanatical Bible student. William Miller first imbibed deism from the library of seditious Matthew Lyon, then like many others, fell victim to religious revivalism. Carefully calculating from the Bible, he predicted the second coming of Christ for 1843 or 1844. As the date approached, interest ran high, and many converts swarmed to the banner, especially from the evangelical sects—the Baptists and the Methodists. Even some of the Baptist clergy—one with the bacchanalian name of Chilian Wines—joined up to await the millennium. When the appointed day passed without divine action, the calculations were reassessed, and October 20 announced as the Day. Fervor increased as the hour approached, and donning white robes, many climbed high hills to be ready. But again nothing happened. The movement fell apart, though many could never again readjust themselves to everyday life and sank into various fanatical excesses.

THE TEMPERANCE MOVEMENT

Despite its excesses, religious revivalism provided the impetus for many social and humanitarian reforms, as the crusaders moved from moral into social problems. When the evangelists found that liquor made permanent conversions unlikely, they quickly awoke to the necessity of a drive on the evils of drink. That the movement achieved a statewide prohibition law in 1852 was a testimonial to the effectiveness of the crusade. It involved a great reversal of public opinion, for liquor had been considered the friendly companion of the frontiersman and the worker, and was one of the principal items of commerce. The reformers had to buck not only "the liquor interests," but also a firm convention of the times. Moving from moral persuasion to legal action against the sale of liquor, the Vermont Temperance Society (founded in 1828 as an off-shot of the Boston-bred American Society for the Promotion of Temperance) drew to its leadership men like industrialist Erastus Fairbanks, afterwards Governor. It also met vigorous opposition, not only from the average man who enjoyed a friendly glass, but from men like Episcopal Bishop John Henry Hopkins of Burlington,[9] who had been sorely tried by the dizzy gyrations of over-enthusiastic radicals. Nevertheless, the temperance reformers accomplished one of the most amazing social revolutions in American life when they succeeded in making "the drinker an exception instead of the rule, and sobriety a virtue, not an oddity."[10]

SOCIAL HUMANITARIANISM

Temperance was far from occupying the whole of energies available for social reform. There was a multitude of projects to ease the sufferings of the poor, the sick, the insane, and yes, even the criminal.

Prison reform came in part as a reaction against the cruel and drastic code of punishments provided by the first legislature for both major and minor offenses. Actually, the hanging, whipping, branding and clipping of ears then prescribed were seldom invoked by easy-going law enforcement authorities. But it was unlikely that the legal situation would be altered until imprisonment was possible as a substitute. A State Prison at Windsor was finally opened in 1809, but the situation there soon was such as to provide discomfort equal to or in excess of the old corporal punishment. A widespread revulsion against the disgusting conditions of prison life inspired numerous calls for an end to overcrowding and exploitation of prisoners at Windsor. An addition in keeping with advanced prison ideas was finally provided in 1830. By 1843 Miss Dorothea Dix, the famous Vermont-born humanitarian, found conditions considerably better. Reform took another tack in the pressure for abolition of imprisonment for debt, finally accomplished in 1838. Furthermore, increasing maturity brought the state automatic relief. As frontier turbulence subsided, Vermont found herself with less rather than more criminals than her neighbors.

Relief for the insane was also provided during this period by the foundation, through private bequest, of the Vermont Asylum for the Insane in Brattleboro, in 1836. Assisted by small annual appropriations from the state, the "Brattleboro Retreat" acquired an outstanding

---

9 Bishop Hopkins was one of the most talented men of his times. Formerly a successful businessman, he was also a gifted architect, artist and musician.

10 The full story of the legal ups and downs is told in Ludlum, *Social Ferment in Vermont*, 63–85, and on a broader canvas in Krout, John A., *Origins of Prohibition*.

FIRST NORMAL SCHOOL in America was founded by Samuel Reed Hall at Concord Corners, Vermont, in 1823. Here he also introduced for the first time the now familiar blackboard and wrote the first manual for teachers: "Lectures on School Keeping." Over in Middlebury Emma Willard opened the first women's seminary in 1807, then later moved it to Troy, N. Y.

record. Yet proper care and housing was a palliative, not a cure. In 1850 the Census listed 550 cases of insanity— one for every 366 persons—the highest average of any state in the Union.[11] But people had at least been infected with a sense of public responsibility to these unfortunates.

Care of the poor was universally left to local action, and was as universally neglected. There were occasional charitable societies organized, but to little effect. Some relief was provided by success in temperance reform—a graphic illustration, said the moralists, of the degradation that had been due to liquor. But this was in turn increasingly offset by the influx of a new element of foreign-born people, handicapped in experience, education and training. They constituted over one third of those on public charity in 1850—far more than their proportion of the population as a whole. This was one of the many resentments which gave rise to the shameful intolerance of the nativist "American for Americans" movement— which had many supporters in Vermont.

---

11 The insane, and financial support of public institutions for their care, still constitute, in 1949, one of the state's most nagging problems.

EDUCATION

Probably the most significant advances of the period were made in the field of educational reform. Insistent agitation resulted in the creation of a State Board of School Commissioners, but real power over the schooling of youth remained in the hands of the local school districts —hundreds of little educational republics, each with different standards, each jealous of its independence, and most of them determined to provide the bare bones of schooling at the least possible cost. There were in 1845 2,750 districts, averaging 37 students each!

The great American battle for free, tax-supported, state-supervised, non-sectarian schools was begun in neighboring Massachusetts by Horace Mann. His disciple in Vermont was Thomas Palmer, of Pittsford, who was later seconded by William Slade, ex-Congressman and Governor, 1844-45. In the latter year, the Vermont General Assembly passed an act of emancipation for the schools, providing for town overseers, county superintendents and at the top, a State Superintendent of Education. Horace Eaton, first occupant of the position, began an immediate statewide survey of educational conditions. He discovered unbelievably decrepit, ugly and unhealthy schoolhouses, no equipment, a "Babel-like confusion of books," a woeful lack of competent teachers, and an "appalling" record of absenteeism. Only one half of Vermont youth was in regular attendance. Thus it was that 1850 saw only the beginning—but at least that—of the great common school revival then sweeping the nation.

The Vermont Constitution had prescribed not only common schools for each town, but a "grammar school" for each county. These multiplied rapidly during the first half of the century—testimony to an increasing demand for additional grades of education. Most of the early ones were private academies, but a number of sectarian schools[12] were established, especially by the Methodists.[13] Many of them fell by the wayside, however, after educational reformers added the high school to the public school system, though some have continued a precarious existence into the present, or have been converted into preparatory schools or junior colleges.

The year 1819 saw the founding of Captain Alden Partridge's[14] "Literary Scientific and Military Academy" at Norwich, which later moved to Northfield, Vermont, and evolved into the modern Norwich University, still a

---

12 Parochial schools, now common in most large cities, were not started in Yankee Vermont until after the French Canadians and other immigrants brought the Catholic religion.

13 Most prominent of these were Newbury Seminary, moved later to Montpelier, now Vermont Junior College; and Troy Conference Academy at Poultney, now Green Mountain Junior College —both still with Methodist connections.

14 Partridge was a former Superintendent of the U.S. Military Academy at West Point.

military school. Middlebury and the University of Vermont continued a hand-to-mouth struggle for existence, but made some progressive changes in their course of study. Medical colleges sprang up at Woodstock and Castleton, but their existence was relatively brief though they contributed many distinguished graduates to the profession.

ECONOMIC REFORM

It was inevitable that the tide of reform should wash over into the erstwhile placid ponds of economic life. There were almost no evidences of urban socialism—the radicalism of the frontier was an agrarian one, linked to the philosophy and program of Thomas Jefferson. But the same democratic impulse which inspired the "democratic societies," and which gave an odd "leveling" touch to the intolerance of anti-masonry, also sought to put real weight behind Jefferson's call for "equal and exact justice to all"—an economic democracy growing out of political equalitarianism.

There were numerous "Workingmen's Societies" organized in 1830-31, with constitutions incorporating demands for most of the humanitarian and educational reforms already reviewed. To these they added several modest economic requests, such as abolition of licensed monopolies and equal taxation on property. But as the great wave of social reform swept on, more unusual projects were suggested. Furthermore, the crippling blow to the American economy, administered by the 1837 depression, turned the eyes of many from moral to economic reform. The economic communism of the French economist Fourier had many exponents in Vermont, but no colonies were established there. There was, of course, a spate of blueprints—changed daily—for the perfect society. More down-to-earth, however, were the proposals for land reform which would have opened land to the little man and limited the amount of acreage any one person might hold. When an attempt to legislate the change in Vermont was blocked, the land reformers were swept into the new Free Soil Party. And Vermont sent to the U.S. Senate Justin Morrill, who paved the way for the Homestead Act of 1862—which opened the great West to a flood of little people, Vermonters among them.

Farmers who did not migrate to solve their economic problems frequently joined in cooperatives to market their produce—mostly wool at this period. But the movement did not take firm hold until the struggle against the giant milk distributing companies forced the dairymen together in the 20th Century.

In 1848 Governor Carlos Coolidge noted with pride "eminent success in the experiment for the enlargement of the happiness of the race." However, by this time the many calls for reform had been united into one great chorus of furious protest—the results of which brought neither peace nor prosperity to any one.

ANTI-SLAVERY CRUSADE

Vermonters do not easily forget that theirs was the first state constitutionally to abolish slavery. They readily recall that one of the most distinguished cultural leaders of the early frontier was the negro Lemuel Haynes. They recollect how in November 1777 Captain Ebenezer Allen freed Dinah, the slave of a fleeing British officer, giving her a certificate of emancipation which was duly recorded in the Bennington town clerk's office. They remember how Supreme Court Justice Theophilus Herrington, faced with a demand for the return of a fugitive slave, requested as evidence of ownership "a Bill of Sale from the Almighty." These hill people, inhabitants of a land ill-suited to slave labor, acquired a vigorous distaste for an institution which was gradually becoming riveted upon the cotton kingdom of the deep South. Vermont, observed a New Hampshire leader, had "no seaport for the importation of slavery, or the export of its own republicanism." When in 1828, therefore, a slender, thoughtful young man by the name of William Lloyd Garrison began hurling violent blasts against slavery in his *Journal of the Times* at Bennington, it was not odd that he found a receptive audience.

Garrison soon left in search of a broader audience for his impassioned orations. But the tide of anti-slavery sentiment continued to rise alongside the multitude of other "isms" which swept the state in the '30's and '40's. Vermonters—among them ex-Governor Samuel Crafts, Secretary of State Clark, and the Quaker Rowland T. Robinson—organized in 1834 the first state chapter of the new American Anti-Slavery Society. Like many other reforms, abolitionism had its roots firmly planted in the church, especially among the more liberal sects. Nevertheless, the churches suffered severely from dissensions within, as ardent reformers disagreed bitterly over the not-too-obvious course to be taken in combatting the obvious evil. It was not until 1846 that the abolitionists within the powerful but conservative Vermont Congregational Church could obtain a forthright condemnation of slavery as "utterly sinful before God." And in the nation the great Baptist and Methodist Churches were shattered into Northern and Southern segments by their failure to agree. But in Vermont, by 1846, all churches were officially on record opposing slavery, and preachers everywhere denounced the South's "peculiar institution."

Even before this, however, many of more radical reformers—church and laymen alike—began advocating political as well as moral action. The Garrison abolitionists were bitterly opposed to any participation in a government which sanctioned slavery, and fought furiously against political action. But Garrison's energies had been diverted into a multitude of "isms," and the majority of the Vermont abolitionists preferred a single edged attack. A new "Liberty Party" polled very few votes in Vermont—or anywhere—in 1840, but its political clubs grew

RAID on St. Albans by Confederates from Canada in Oct. 1864, stirred Vermont. Raiders robbed bank, then fled back into Canada.

in influence, and took over much of the work of the Anti-Slavery Society, which itself had severed connections with the Garrison-dominated American Anti-Slavery Society in 1841. Their threat was enough to inspire prominent Whig abolitionists like William Slade in endeavors to make their party a real national anti-slavery party. In 1844 Slade, who had been a prominent opponent of slavery in Congress, was elected Governor.

Nationally, the Whigs attempted to straddle the issue, and even Slade became disillusioned. The new Free Soil Party drew his allegiance in 1848—as it did that of many others. The Free Soilers, advocating a moderate program of opposition to the expansion of slavery, satisfied most of the advocates of political action, and polled a larger vote than the Democrats. But it was a new anti-slavery party, the Republican, which really drew the affections of Vermonters in 1856—and they have never deserted the "Grand Old Party" since.

The Legislature itself began to speak out boldly during the forties. Vigorous opposition to the annexation of Texas—a new slavery state—was expressed. In 1849 the assembled members pronounced slavery a "crime against humanity," and in 1856 they appropriated $20,000 for the relief of the free-state men in embattled "Bleeding Kansas."

The southern response was immediate and bitter. Georgia demanded that a ditch be dug around Vermont and that the pestiferous state be floated out to sea. As late as 1880 a southern newspaper suggested that the nation trade off Vermont to Canada "in payment of some ancient fish indemnity" or that at least it "be put on exhibition, as a fossil annex, at some future world's fair, if well fenced in and properly guarded."

The new Republican party rapidly gained strength in the North as the two sections drew further apart. This strength was nowhere so surely demonstrated as when, in 1860, an obscure Illinois lawyer named Abraham Lincoln polled four times Stephen Douglas's vote in Vermont. And Douglas had just completed a triumphal tour of his native state.

The net result of a generation of sectional bickering between North and South was civil war within the Union or—as Southerners preferred to call it—War Between the States. With logic and enthusiasm, Vermonters threw their energies as vigorously into the military struggle as they had into the moral and political battle. Both towns and individuals pledged large sums of money toward the state's war effort, railroad and steamship companies offered free transportation for troops and munitions, and companies started drilling on town greens throughout the state. The legislature promptly appropriated a million dollars to arm and equip its militia.

During the course of the war, sixteen Vermont Regiments were enrolled. The Second Vermont suffered particularly grievous casualties, losing forty percent of its men in killed and wounded—eight times that of the Union Army as a whole. In a single afternoon at the Battle of the Wilderness, the Vermont regiments suffered more than a thousand casualties.

Vermont soldiers compiled an outstanding record of gallantry and their descendants still quote with pride the order issued at Gettysburg: "Put the Vermonters in front and keep the column well closed up." Their sacrifice is implicit in the figures of the state's contribution of men and money to the cause. One out of every two able-bodied men shouldered arms, and Vermont's casualties exceeded the Union average by a considerable amount. In proportion to population Vermont gave the lives of more of its sons to the Union cause than any other state. And the state and towns together expended more than ten per cent of the total value of all property in the state.

Towards the war effort Vermont had given much, emotionally as well as physically. The war drained off a substantial portion of those turbulent energies which had sparked so many reform crusades. Interests were diverted into new channels; agricultural Vermont embarked upon a new industrial development and, as in the nation at large, found the economic problems of the new industrial age absorptive of all its energies. Americans were finding the practical philosophy of scientists like Darwin and thinkers like William James more suited to the new era. Vermonters likewise found little room for the naive emotionalism of their pre-Civil War crusades. The change was signalized in the shift in the Republican Party; the crusading anti-slavery party became the party of the new industrialists, and Vermont the citadel of Republicanism.

More important, even, than the exhaustion of war was the slow drain of human resources by emigration. Let's have a look, therefore, at the economic picture in Vermont at the time people first began leaving their native state, and see how this trend affected the economic development of Vermont.

LEMUEL HAYNES IN THE PULPIT OF THE OLD FIRST CHURCH AT BENNINGTON. FROM THE
PAINTING IN THE BENNINGTON HISTORICAL MUSEUM BY WILLIAM TEFFT SCHWARZ

*The career of the distinguished preacher, Lemuel Haynes, is a tribute to the heights to which a
colored man could rise in the days of early Vermont, before slavery, civil war and reconstruction
of the South set the races apart. An illegitimate child, he was abandoned by his parents, and then
adopted into a white family. He was a common soldier in the days following Lexington and
Concord, and enlisted for the perilous expedition to Ticonderoga under Ethan Allen. He fell in
love with a member of his white Connecticut congregation, but so reticent was he, that it became
necessary for the girl to propose to him. With the whole-hearted approval of his ministerial
colleagues, he married in 1783. Shortly after, he came to Vermont, and administered to the people
of the Rutland West Parish for thirty years. A man of devastating wit, he was nonetheless widely
beloved and universally respected. After filling a pulpit in Manchester and one in Granville,
N. Y., he died in 1834. He ranked with Samuel Williams and Royall Tyler as one of the most
learned men on the northern frontier. (Note in the painting the old box pews.)*

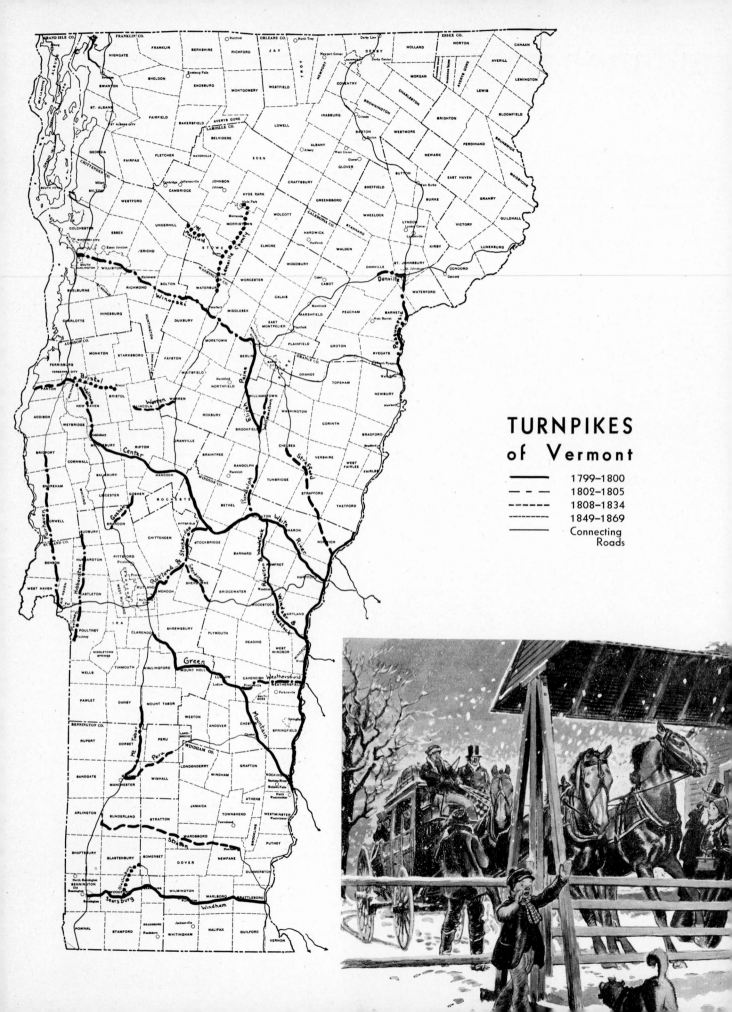

TURNPIKES
of Vermont

————————	1799–1800
– – – – – –	1802–1805
–·–·–·–·–	1808–1834
··········	1849–1869
————————	Connecting Roads

X
PROLOGUE TO EXODUS

*How inventions and industry, wool and waterways, failed to keep
Vermonters from leaving their native state to people the west.*

For her first hundred years Vermont was an agricultural state, devoted to the cultivation of the Green Mountain lands. Yet there were a surprising number of small industries and craftsmen serving the needs of the rural dweller: mills to grind his wheat or saw his logs or card his wool; smithies and forges to shoe his horses and make and repair his tools; tanneries, cabinet shops and potteries. There were also the tiny beginnings of what later became large industrial units— the woolen mills and the stone working shops, for example.

The first decades of the new century saw the end of the "age of homespun." As mills and factories multiplied, home crafts declined. The early neighborhood barter and local self-sufficiency gave way to a money economy and trade across town and even state lines.

Home life changed as the burden of production shifted from the family toward outside manufacturers. The woman's burden of toil was eased somewhat, though families were still large because of the need of extra helping hands, in both household and barnyard chores. The log cabins gave way to more substantial frame houses. Stoves were introduced to improve winter comfort. And as the massive old central chimneys and their fireplaces disappeared, the architecture of the story-and-a-half farmhouse changed. Ceilings rose, as did eaves, and the old, careful colonial proportions disappeared. Rooms no longer had to be grouped around the hearth, and this new architectural flexibility lent itself to the "Victorian" craze for odd shaped structures and elaborate carpenter's "gingerbread."

With the growth of trade and a money economy, many new businesses sprung up. In 1818 banks were established at Windsor and Burlington, and ten years later the first fire insurance company—the Vermont Mutual—was founded in Montpelier. And just as our first century ends in 1850, Dr. Julius Y. Dewey (father of the famous admiral) joined with others, including Henry Clay, to found the great National Life Insurance Co., now the state's largest. Montpelier is still famous for its many insurance companies.

But most new businesses grew out of Yankee ingenuity and craftsmanship. Farmers and laborers devised shortcuts and labor saving devices to ease the burden of rural toil. A flood of applications for patents poured out of the Green Mountains following the nation's first, issued to Samuel Hopkins of Burlington in 1791. But most of these men were not self-conscious inventors, and often did not attempt to protect their ingenious devices legally.

The smithies, as workers in iron, were especially productive. In 1817 Silas Howes of Shaftsbury devised the first steel square out of a couple of old saw blades, and as the demand rose for this now indispensable carpenter's tool, established The Eagle Square Manufacturing Company. Over in Windsor Lemuel Hedge laid the foundations for the machine tool

Pat'd 1826   Replica of S. Morey's Liquid Fuel Engine

Carburetor

By F. I. MUSSELMAN STUDIOS, PHILA.

*SAMUEL MOREY, steamboat inventor, also perfected a
liquid fuel, internal combustion engine sixty years before the auto.*

industry of New England with his ruling and measuring devices. Here he was joined by John M. Cooper and Asahel Hubbard, inventors of the rotary pump, as well as the gun makers who devised and put into operation the system of interchangeable parts—foundation stone of the modern American machine industry. In St. Johnsbury Thaddeus Fairbanks devised the first platform scale and based a great new industry on this and other inventions.

But many of these men were too far ahead of their times, and failed to found successful businesses upon their inventions. Thomas Davenport, "the Brandon black-

and modern times, the greatest the world has ever seen, the greatest the world will ever see. . . . Friendship, esteem, and the mysterious love between the sexes is founded on the same principle with which Mr. Davenport runs his wheel."

The eminent New Haven professor, Benjamin Silliman, commented with equal awe: "Science has most unexpectedly placed in our hands a new power of great but unknown energy. . . . Nothing since the discovery of gravity and of the structure of the celestial systems is so wonderful as the power evolved by "galvanism."

THOMAS DAVENPORT, like most Yankee inventors, had little to work with. He wrapped the magnet for his electric motor with the silk from his wife's wedding dress. JAMES WILSON of Bradford, (left) quit farming to learn copper engraving. In 1810 he made the first American globes, and soon had quite a business. Many of his methods are still in use today in globe-making.

smith," was one. Intrigued by the possibilities of "electromagnetism," he virtually laid aside his blacksmithing—much to the distress of his family—to experiment. Without scientific books or contact with what others had done before him, he devised an electric telegraph which he showed to an impecunious portrait painter named Samuel F. B. Morse. The latter had already been stimulated by the work of European experimenters and the counsel of Joseph Henry of Albany. By 1837 Morse applied for a patent for his telegraph—evolved from the ideas and advice of many others, including Davenport.

Davenport's most significant contribution, however, was the invention of the electric motor, with the aid of a fellow blacksmith Orange Smalley. This he successfully demonstrated in 1834 and again in 1837 in New York. Its significance was immediately recognized; an enthusiastic *New York Herald* reporter labeled "this most extraordinary discovery probably the greatest of ancient

To promote his invention, Davenport began publication in 1840 of a New York newspaper, printing it on a press driven by one of his own motors. "The power of electricity is far superior to steam," he asserted, "and must and will triumphantly succeed." But he was unable to prove the immediate practicability of his device, or to disprove the contention that it was excessively costly—compared to steam—as a source of power.

Distressed over the lack of interest in his motor and Morse's failure to acknowledge his contribution to the telegraph, Davenport returned to his forge in 1842. He died in 1851—his doctor said—of a broken heart. It was nearly a century before the electric motor replaced steam as a main source of power for industry and transportation.[1]

[1] Many men were working on similar projects in this period of great scientific and intellectual ferment. Wareham Chase, a Calais farmer, ran an electric motor in Montpelier in 1841. The armature is now in the Museum of the Vermont Historical Society.

Similar obscurity befell the efforts of Samuel Morey, of Orford, New Hampshire and Fairlee, Vermont. As early as 1793[2] he ran a paddlewheel steamboat on the Connecticut between these two places, and endeavored to interest Fulton and Livingstone in it. The New Yorkers were greatly intrigued, and carefully inspected his engine. Their enthusiasm seemed to cool in 1806, and Morey discovered the reason the following year when Robert Fulton ran his famous "Clermont" up the Hudson. Morey died believing his invention had been stolen, though Fulton seems to have drawn upon a number of the

southern New England had a firm grip on the market, and the tide of migration from Vermont was sweeping across the northern hills. Inventions did not necessarily mean industry.

In the face of Yankee ingenuity and enterprise, and abundant power, it is surprising that industry did not take better hold. Perhaps the answer lies in part in the prosperity of agriculture in Vermont, and the opportunities in industry elsewhere. Immigrants were those seeking new land; seekers after opportunity in New England commerce and industry looked rather to the flourishing

ALVIN ADAMS established the first American express service between Windsor and Woodstock in the 1820's. Adams Express Co. later merged with the Railway Express Co.

CANAL at Bellows Falls was one of country's first. Built before steamboats, it lacked necessary width and few could get through. Oxen dragged the "William Hall" around the falls in the early 1830's.

early experimenters, including Fitch, Stevens and Morey.

Perhaps even more significant was his invention in 1826 of an internal combustion engine, complete with carburetor. From Morey's specifications, a working model was constructed in 1931 at the instance of Charles Duryea, who had built the first roadable gasoline automobile in 1892. Duryea acknowledged Morey's achievement as epoch making[3]—as it was. But like Davenport's electric motor, it was submerged for a half-century.

While the embargo and war from 1808 to 1815 shut off foreign imports, manufacturing flourished in Vermont, as elsewhere in the youthful nation. For a time it seemed as though the Green Mountain state might join her seaboard neighbors in the building of an industrial New England. The total value of her manufactures in 1810 exceeded five million; but by 1820 it had toppled below the million mark—an 80% decrease! It was not until 1840 that output passed the mark set in 1810, but by that time

mills of Lawrence and Lowell, the trade of Boston and New Bedford, or the factories of Springfield and Hartford.

Furthermore, Vermont lagged in the development of transportation adequate for the growth of industry; in the age of water transportation, she could not open her Connecticut River pathway to important traffic, and her interior lay out of reach among the Green Mountain forests. She was too distant from the principal marts of trade, and her road system did not encourage overland travel. By the time the railroad finally breached the mountain fastness, southern New England had already forged a network of rails tying her industrial and commercial centers together.

2 John Fitch had run a boat with steam operated paddles on the Delaware River as early as 1786.

3 Goodwin, K. R., and Duryea, C. E., "Samuel Morey, Precursor of Motor Power Development," *Vermonter*, 36, 134–142. A miniature boiler of Morey's, dated 1792, is in the Museum of the Vermont Historical Society.

BURLINGTON, at mid-century, was the center for a thriving lakes trade in lumber and produce. She first exported lumber to Canada, then, as forests gave out, began importing it. Railroads sounded the death knell of a lively water commerce.

WATERWAYS AND PATHWAYS

Certainly Vermont tried hard enough to improve her transport facilities. The experiments of Morey and his contemporaries resulted in Robert Fulton's commercially successful Hudson River steamboat, the "Clermont," in 1807. Only a year later John and James Winans launched their "Vermont," and in 1809—just two hundred years from Champlain's first canoe trip up the Lake—steamboats began operation on the waters named for him.

Lake Champlain was a busy waterway even before this, however, as lumber from the forests bordering the lake and the Winooski River floated down the Richelieu River to Montreal and Quebec—some of it destined for Britain. Trade with Canada in beef, hides, potash and other products of the frontier was still vigorous in this northwest area. Geography and transportation still linked it more intimately with the British province over the border than with neighboring states.

The beginning of a shift in the course of Champlain trade began in 1823 with the opening of the Champlain Canal south to the Hudson River, Troy and the port of New York. It was appropriate—because of the active shipbuilding industry on the Lake—that the first boat through was the St. Albans built "Gleaner," whose progress down the new canal was celebrated with cannons and jubilant merrymaking. The Erie Canal to Buffalo and the Great Lakes was christened two years later, and the

Great West as well as the port of New York was thereby opened to the inhabitants of the lake shores, and to cities some distance up the Winooski River and Otter Creek. Marble from the Rutland quarries floated north down the Otter, and then south to Troy, to avoid the shorter but more difficult overland haul.

The year 1826 saw the establishment of the Champlain Transportation Company, which—with new and improved craft—placed steamboating on a commercially profitable basis until rail and motor competition beat it to the ground 106 years later.

In 1842 the British author, Charles Dickens, whose dyspeptic account of his American travels often verged on the libelous, found the "Burlington" "a perfectly exquisite achievement of neatness, elegance, and order." His opinion of a Connecticut River trip was something less than enthusiastic, however. He found the boat crude, dirty and unbelievably small. "We all kept the middle of the deck," he commented "lest the boat should unexpectedly tip over."

It was true that the Vermonters on the East side had had little success in perfecting transportation on the upper reaches of the great Connecticut waterway. It wasn't that they had not begun early enough.

In the same year—1791—that Samuel Morey began his boat experiments further up the river, a company was chartered to build a canal around the rapids at Bellows

132

For 140 years, from the launching of the "Vermont" (right) in 1809 (only two years after Fulton first ran his steamboat up the Hudson) to the present day, Lake Champlain has seen a procession of picturesque sidewheelers. The "Ticonderoga" (below) is the last of the great white fleet.

Courtesy National Life Insurance Company

Kodachromes by R. N. Hill

STAGECOACHES were the principal means for passenger travel before the railroads, but they were impractical for freight.

Falls. This—the first canal for navigation in the United States—was to be one of a series which would open the river to traffic from above the Great Oxbow at Newbury to Long Island Sound. Capital came largely from British and Dutch investors. The Bellows Falls canal was completed in 1802, and others to the north and south by 1810. Oddly enough, the last built (in 1829) was the furthest down, at Windsor Locks, Connecticut.

The canals largely failed of their purpose—the building of a great river trade. True, for many years rafts and flatboats took produce down the river. The flatboats could be laboriously poled back up, but rafts were split up and sold for timber. It was mostly a one-way traffic.

Great hopes were placed in the new steamboats. With the completion of the canals, the "Connecticut River Company" built the "Barnet" in 1826, in confident expectation of opening regular steam transportation as far north as that upper Connecticut town. But the boat never got past Bellows Falls. A new and narrower "Vermont" reached Hartland in 1829, and two years later the "John Ledyard" made it to Wells River, where she grounded on a sandbar. Other boats were built at Wells River and White River Junction, and plied the upper reaches for a short time. Difficulties of operation resulted in high freight rates that diminished traffic—which did not pay for itself. By 1832 the company failed and steam navigation of the upper Connecticut was abandoned. For nearly a century the Connecticut north of Hartford, Connecticut, has been bare of river traffic, and her canals and dams have served instead as sources of power for developing industry.

The impulse to build canals was not limited to residents of the Connecticut Valley, however. During the canal "craze" of the eighteen twenties, interior towns laid elaborate plans for artificial waterways connecting them with Lake Champlain or the Connecticut. One of the most constantly agitated was a cross-state connection.

One such proposal would have cut a channel from Barnet to a tributary of the St. Lawrence River via the Winooski and Wells Rivers. "We most earnestly hope," a Montpelier committee declared in 1825, "that the fever will not abate until the cooling waters of the Connecticut shall meet and mingle with those of Lake Champlain."

None was any more fantastic a project than that proposed to connect the Hudson and Connecticut via the Hoosac and Deerfield rivers in Massachusetts—which would have required cutting through the mountain range (finally done for the railroad by the Hoosac Tunnel).

The canal craze was abruptly deflated in the forties, as over-land rails seemed a cheaper and quicker method of bringing transportation to back country New England. Yet the search for water routes had begun because of the abominable state of land transportation, where road improvement had failed to keep pace with the growth of commerce.

TURNPIKES AND SHUN-PIKES

Vermont's road system had developed to a surprising extent by the turn of the century. In 1810 Surveyor-General James Whitelaw revised his great map of the state, first published in 1796, and careful students will find on this (and on his later revision in 1824) many roads which do not even exist today. But the extent of the system was no guide to its usability. Even the main highways dissolved into a sea of mud in the spring, and they hardly became negotiable again until late fall. Winter frost hardened them, and well packed snow provided a smooth surface for sleighs and sledges. But even so, a blizzard could bring transportation and communication to a standstill for days.

With public roads under town maintenance (which was unpredictable), it was virtually impossible to obtain satisfactory through routes. "Turnpikes" were the first response to the rising demand for adequate means of transportation for the new trade in the produce of farm and factory. Turnpikes were financed by private capital, and tolls were therefore collected at gates placed at strategic points. In 1799 the Green Mountain Turnpike was started at Col. Enoch Hale's toll bridge at Bellows Falls[4] and extended northwestward up the Black River to a connection in Clarendon with the main Bennington to Burlington road. (See the map on page 128.) Within the two years 1799–1800, two additional cross-state

[4] Built in 1785, this was the first bridge to be thrown across the Connecticut, and was the marvel of its day. Windsor built her bridge in 1796.

turnpikes had been built—between Brattleboro and Bennington, and between Hartford and Middlebury. Additional shorter stretches were built at the same time, and the next decade saw the entire southern and central portions interlaced with them.

But as the newness wore off and maintenance deteriorated, toll collections became increasingly unpopular. Stretches of road were built to by-pass the toll gates—and were appropriately tagged "shunpikes." One by one the turnpike companies gave up the ghost, and transferred their properties to the towns. The last of the old turnstiles—Peru Mountain—was opened for free passage in 1917.

In the north part of the state new public roads were built. The old Hazen Road saw less and less use, and in 1815 a new road was opened from St. Johnsbury to Barton, joining with the old stage route from Montpelier to the Canadian line at Derby.

Few advances were made in improving roads. "Corduroy" surfaces lamed the horses and jarred wagons to pieces; plank roads soon rotted out. The vehicles which used these primitive pathways were gradually improved as the old springless stage gave way, by 1828, to the famous Concord coach. There were also the phaeton, chariot, gig, laundau and chaise for private travel. Yet no one traveled for pleasure; Washington Irving wrote plaintively: "There is a certain relief in change, even if it be from bad to worse; as I have found in traveling in a stage coach that it is often a comfort to shift one's position and be bruised in a new place."

Commercial stagecoach lines operated through Vermont, most of them headed for Montreal. Two of the four lines northward from New York passed through Bennington and Fairhaven respectively. The turnpikes provided, for a while at least, excellent routes to Boston via Hartford, Windsor, or Bellows Falls. The trip from Middlebury to Boston took two days—if you left at 4 A.M.! Two days and a night got you to Troy. All this required frequent changes of horses at "relay" stops.

Freight moved even more laboriously, by sledge in winter—the most favorable time—and by carts and wagons at other times. The latter were pulled by as many as ten horse teams. There had been little change in the past thousand years of land transportation.

It was not odd therefore that farmers endeavored to convert their produce into commodities which could get to market under their own steam. They fed their grain to livestock, which they then drove to the great slaughterhouses grouped around Boston. Other products were converted to a more transportable form: timber was burned for ashes; potatoes were reduced to starch and whiskey, and apples to cider. These products moved to market, and in return came imports of tea, coffee, salt, chocolate, hardware, cloth and other things the farmer could not make—or no longer cared to.

WOOL was one of many "crazes"; silk-raising was another.

AGRICULTURE

The old days of self-sufficient agriculture were now rapidly drawing to a close. As men ceased to barter locally, and as trade and the supply of money increased, the household made less and bought more. Farmers were forced, as a result, to change over to crops which would bring them in actual cash. The trend was a source of no small alarm to observers of the New England scene, who begged in vain for a return to "republican simplicity."

Another factor which drove Vermonters to seek new agricultural pursuits was the progressive exhaustion of natural resources. Forests shriveled before the onslaught of the pioneer's axe and the demands of the lumber and potash markets. As the woodland cover disappeared, streams dwindled. The little local mills ground to a stop during dry seasons, and the land washed away in flash floods. But even more important, the soil began to wear out as heedless farmers failed to fertilize or renew the land. Grain crops increasingly suffered from recurrent disease and pests. Vermonters, who once raised as many as forty bushels of wheat to an acre, began to import flour for their own bread.

The new cure for all troubles was wool. Vermont's first experiment in the raising of sheep dates back to 1811, when enthusiastic William Jarvis retired as Consul at Lisbon. He brought back with him to Weathersfield a flock of prize Spanish Merino sheep, and sold his neighbors on sheep raising. Flocks dotted the pastures of southeastern Vermont, but when wool fell from $1.50 a pound to forty cents at the end of the War of 1812, the bubble burst. However, the set-back was only temporary; wool production began again ten years later. Favored by high tariff protection during the decade which followed, textile mills paid good prices for wool. Between 1824

People continually ask how
abandoned lands, the deserted home
the "back beyond" in Vermont ca
into being. Simple reasoning about
and lightning, remoteness and dar
can become over-simple. For one th
there is the matter of actual soil
forest to be considered. Lands clea
of woodlands all too soon prove thin
the ledges show gauntly through. C
tivation is hard and endless and the
sult slim. But the major reason lay
the several migrations from Verm
hill country of the back-lands. In
days of the opening West, well bei
gold was found at Sutter's Mill,
westward fever came to these part:

At the end of the Civil War
westward trend was heightened an
less in a frenzy was nevertheless so
times enough to drain a whole Vern
valley, and depopulate a whole
township. Most readers have let
from ancestors who were, in the e
1830's and 1840's, in Wisconsin
Iowa and "moving on west."
second great migration came with
industrialization of the '80's, and '
when the railroads reached the exte
their penetration of the hills and l
men to the factories and girls too. F
Cabot and Cavendish, Elmore
Woodbury, families treked to the r
of Lowell and of Claremont, to q
family records. The third migra
came with World War I, when the
hangers-on lost their sons to
gentler life of the towns. Part
parcel of this migration was the
creased number of modern tech
gadgets which made life easier
which would not function where t
were no electric lines. The automo
was a prime mover in more ways
one, of hill people to valley villa

It is however another type of m
tion, embracing parts of all the otl
which also helps to account for the
beyond. This migration came wi
certain dying out of the pioneer s
That is not unique in Vermont but
here a more concise laboratory
ample. It was actually when
changed from the satisfaction in
ing a living to the actual need of
ing *money*, that the Vermont pic
became obsolete. Home spun, I
grist, home cobbling, and abov
home entertainment gave way to
chases with "cash money."

It is the modern trend from bar
tangible income, from services sl
to services purchased, that has
moted the "other Vermont"—the
Beyond.

← *HERITAGE of a century of*
migration: the deserted fields,
cellar holes, and abandoned
homes of the "Back Beyond."

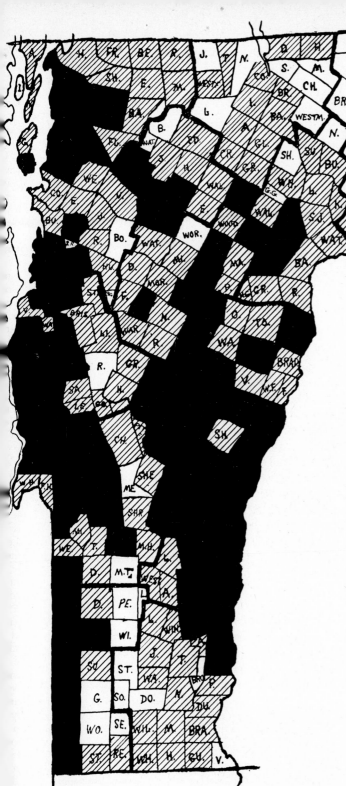

1000—5000

Over 5000

Map by L. D. Stilwell

forties. Prices fell to twenty-five cents a pound, and by 1849 flocks were being ruthlessly sold off for hides and mutton. In 1850 there were a third less sheep in the pastures, and the decline was steady thereafter.[4]

The sheep craze took such hold that little was done otherwise to revitalize Vermont agriculture. There was consistent production of grains—oats being the most important—if only as a basis for livestock and dairying. Yet there were less than a tenth as many dairy cows as sheep, and for a time there was even a small decrease in the former. But as the sheep boom collapsed, farmers began to give more attention to other kinds of livestock. Dairy products increased twenty times in the decade 1840–1850, as farmers shifted from beef to butter. But the dairy industry was not yet in a position to supplant the sheep industry, and husbandmen found little comfort in other lines of agricultural activity.[5] They began to look about for other remedies.

EMIGRATION

One of the easiest solutions to the economic dilemma of these days was to get out. Better land on the frontier—the same magnet that had drawn the Yankees into the Green Mountains—sent them chasing westward as the frontier moved across New York into the old Northwest.

and 1840 the number of sheep quadrupled[4]; by the latter date there were six sheep for every inhabitant. Vermont rapidly shifted to a single crop—wool. In Addison County flocks averaged 373 to the square mile. But the depression which followed 1837 and the loss of tariff protection in 1841 and 1846 brought real distress in the

---

4 See the chart on page 201, as well as the map, above.
5 Farm land in New York ($29.00) was worth twice Vermont's.

YOUNG VERMONTERS, like Horace Greeley, left the state to make their fortunes. Greeley is still quoted for his advice "Go West."

The exodus began even before the turn of the century, but it was a forced emigration of loyalists and Yorkers, caused by political persecution. It was a negligible loss alongside the great influx of expectant pioneers, who skyrocketed Vermont's population from 85,000 to 218,000 in the twenty years between 1790 and 1810.[6]

But Vermont's troubles began in 1810. The impact of the embargo, the hectic hot-house of the war years, and the collapse of prices which followed, disrupted the state's economy. Natural disasters multiplied her woes; the appalling floods of 1811 were followed by epidemics of spotted fever and tuberculosis. And the year 1816 forgot its summer; snow, frost and ice in June killed the new plantings, and the following months were cold and dry. "Eighteen hundred and froze-to-death," chilled and starving inhabitants labeled that year; many families survived the following winter only by frantic borrowing from neighbors who had little to share.

Accumulated afflictions and misfortunes made dreams of western paradises all the rosier. Newspaper advertising and letters from friends sung the praises of the flat, fertile farmlands between the Ohio and the Mississippi. Spotted fever was succeeded by "Ohio Fever," less virulent perhaps, but more widespread. Other fevers were in the land also, as we have seen. Recurrent social ferment kept people stirred up, loosened old ties, and frequently —as in the case of certain religious sects—produced actual organized migrations.

---

6 Only the amazing natural reproduction of a youthful population kept population on the increase to 1850, when it leveled off. In the first decade of the 19th century, over a half of the population was under 16. Eight families in Clarendon had 113 children among them. Population growth is charted on page 201.

Nothing was quite so important, however, as the discouraging outlook for agriculture. As the best land filled up, New England Yankees turned their eyes westward past the Green Mountains. Immigration petered out, for there were no alternate industrial attractions. Already a reversal of the old current began as youth of both sexes moved off to "down-country" employment in mills and offices. In fact, agriculture had only to stop growing, to start the exodus. The children of pioneer parents were too many to share the family farm, and many drifted west or south. From 1840 to 1850 Vermont's population increased only 7% while Massachusetts— older, yet also sending forth emigrants—grew by more than a third.

The West side suffered most severely in the beginning, but soon the exodus began in almost all southern towns. The north parts, more recently settled, continued to grow until 1850. The stream first poured into western New York, and then, joining with other New Englanders, west into Ohio, Indiana, Illinois, Michigan and Wisconsin. Vermont names appeared first in New York, and then elsewhere. Some in the northern towns moved over into the Eastern Townships of Canada, and a few even wandered down into the Old South.

Mostly they were farmers in search of new land. But there were also artisans and craftsmen of all types, schoolmasters, and even professional men such as lawyers and doctors. Almost all of them were young men, with a growing contempt for the drab, monotonous drudgery of grubbing a bare living from the soil. Some were unduly drawn by dreams of great wealth in land or trade; in 1849 the lure of gold sent many Vermonters on the long trek to California. Emigration companies were organized, and by 1850 over a thousand Vermonters had actually reached the West coast. Many tried the mines, but most made a tidy sum at their old trades, and then came home. Frederick Billings of Woodstock made a fortune merchandising in San Francisco before he turned to railroad building.

Among the migrants were many of the nation's greatnames-to-be. Horace Greeley and George Jones left Poultney for New York, and founded, respectively, the great metropolitan New York *Herald* and New York *Times*. Thaddeus Stevens deserted Danville and Peacham for Pennsylvania politics, and became the fierce, embittered leader of the Radical Republicans in Congress, following the Civil War. Stephen A. Douglas departed from Brandon for the mid-west, where he built a political reputation that nearly led him to the presidency. He afterward observed that Vermont was a good state to be born in, but a good state to get out of.

More and more Vermonters began to feel the same way.

Thus, amid the frustrations of thwarted industrial growth, delayed transportation, and hectic, disheartening agricultural shifts, Vermont's youthful zest and ebullient radicalism began to peter out.

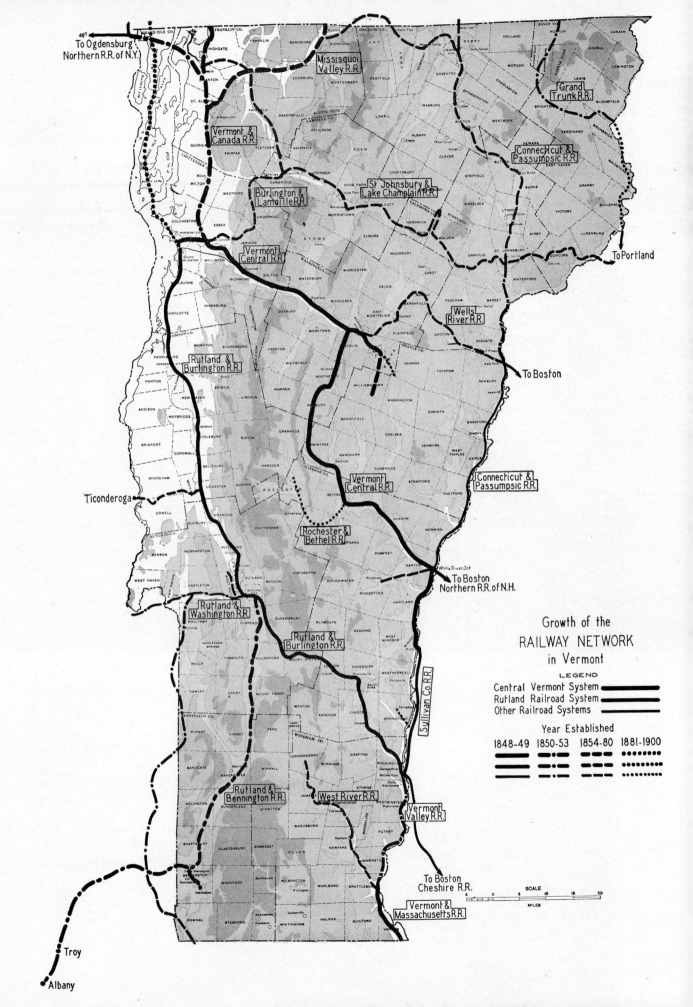

Growth of the
RAILWAY NETWORK
in Vermont

LEGEND
Central Vermont System
Rutland Railroad System
Other Railroad Systems

Year Established
1848-49 1850-53 1854-80 1881-1900

SCALE
5 0 5 10 15 20
MILES

To Ogdensburg
Northern R.R. of N.Y.

Missisquoi
Valley R.R.

Grand
Trunk R.R.

Vermont &
Canada R.R.

Connecticut &
Passumpsic R.R.

Burlington &
Lamoille R.R.

St Johnsbury &
Lake Champlain R.R.

Vermont
Central R.R.

Wells
River R.R.

Rutland &
Burlington R.R.

To Boston

Ticonderoga

Vermont
Central R.R.

Connecticut &
Passumpsic R.R.

Rochester &
Bethel R.R.

White River Jct
To Boston
Northern R.R. of N.H.

To Portland

Rutland &
Washington R.R.

Rutland &
Burlington R.R.

Sullivan Co. R.R.

Rutland &
Bennington R.R.

West River R.R.

Vermont
Valley R.R.

To Boston
Cheshire R.R.

Vermont &
Massachusetts R.R.

Troy

Albany

Courtesy National Life Insurance Company

Courtesy Canadian National R.R.

48–1948

the Yankees
hed their lines
th through
mont, run-
their first
n in June,
8 (above)
adians pressed
hward from
St. Lawrence,
ht) to com-
the impor-
Boston-
treal connec-
in 1851. A
mmoth Jubi-
attended by
dent Mill-
Fillmore,
iel Webster
other celebri-
was staged
at occasion.

XI
COMING OF THE IRON HORSE

*How the iron rails spanned the Green Mountains and raised new industrial and
political leaders, sending many of them west to build the nation's railways.*

RAILROADS were slow getting started in Vermont, as compared with southern New England. Laying the iron bands across a difficult and mountainous land took a lot of cold cash, and most of that was in Boston. The Boston bankers were more interested in linking their own city with the "Great West"—as well as with the industrial cities of interior New England—by building toward Albany.

Excited over the prospects of the "iron horse" (and finally convinced that canals were not feasible in their hilly country), Vermonters hatched many optimistic—and often fanciful—schemes in the thirties. Here was born the great dream of a band of rails from Boston to Ogdensburgh, connecting with the Great Lakes steamers from the Mid-West. This was first projected as a covered road all across Vermont, so that snow might not stop the trains! The three great systems (Vermont Central, Rutland, and Connecticut and Passumpsic) were all chartered in 1835, but no rails were laid for a decade.

However, by 1845 the Boston financiers had completed their link to Albany through the great Hoosac Tunnel—only to find a shrewd empire builder named Cornelius Vanderbilt in the process of linking the upstate New York railroads leading to the West into his Hudson River Railroad system. This, of course, diverted the choice traffic down river to an ancient rival—the port of New York City. The northern route began to look better to Boston money.

There were two prominent Vermont businessmen ready and anxious to press the matter. Governor Charles Paine, owner of a large

woolen mill and great deal of land in Northfield, was one. Judge Timothy Follett, a prominent Burlington merchant already involved in Lake Champlain boat transportation with Thomas Hawley Canfield, was another. Each obtained new charters in 1843—Paine for the "Vermont Central," and Follett for the "Rutland and Burlington." The Governor also joined in the "Northern Railroad of N. Y." project, which extended the Vermont lines from Rouse's Point on Lake Champlain to Ogdensburgh on Lake Ontario. Four years later John Smith of St. Albans organized the Vermont and Canada R. R. to build north from the Winooski River to Rouse's Point. These, with the New Hampshire lines then building, and the Great Lakes steamers, completed the northern route to the West.

As the year 1845 drew to a close, first ground was broken for the Vermont Central at Windsor, and the lines pushed steadily toward Northfield, which Paine had made headquarters for the road. By June, 1848, the line was complete to Bethel, and on the 26th a train of cars left White River for that town—the first train to run in the State of Vermont.

Overland travel took on new life as the iron rails spread over the state. Farmers who had found it cheaper to ship by water to distant New York, now found nearby Boston a better market. New England, previously cut off by its mountain wall, thus made a new bid for its share of the flood of produce moving eastward for export and local consumption. And the northern Yankees at last gave up their century-old hope of a navigable Connecticut River.

*POSTER to drum up interest in a projected West
River Railroad. (Vermont Historical Society)*

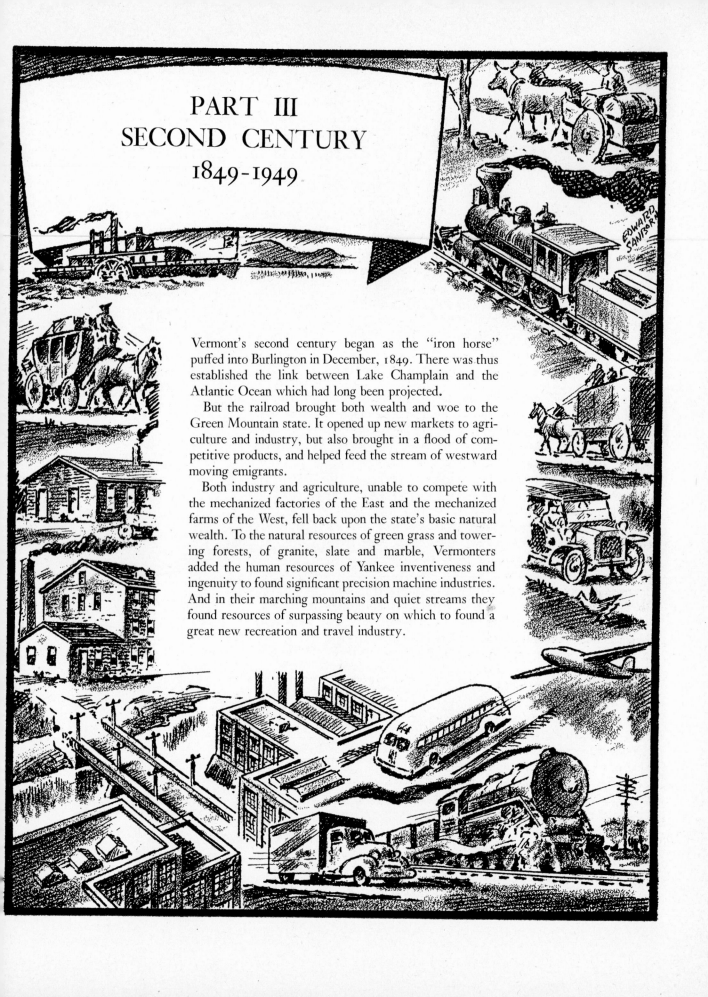

PART III
SECOND CENTURY
1849-1949

Vermont's second century began as the "iron horse" puffed into Burlington in December, 1849. There was thus established the link between Lake Champlain and the Atlantic Ocean which had long been projected.

But the railroad brought both wealth and woe to the Green Mountain state. It opened up new markets to agriculture and industry, but also brought in a flood of competitive products, and helped feed the stream of westward moving emigrants.

Both industry and agriculture, unable to compete with the mechanized factories of the East and the mechanized farms of the West, fell back upon the state's basic natural wealth. To the natural resources of green grass and towering forests, of granite, slate and marble, Vermonters added the human resources of Yankee inventiveness and ingenuity to found significant precision machine industries. And in their marching mountains and quiet streams they found resources of surpassing beauty on which to found a great new recreation and travel industry.

LAMOILLE RIVER BRIDGE, on the Vermont and Canada R.R. *"FLOATING BRIDGE" across Lake Champlain to Rouse's Point.*

As with so much of the State's development, geography determined the course of railway construction in Vermont. (See map, opposite). Railroad builders had to contend with the same rugged topography as the Indians, the colonial soldiers, and the pioneers—and took the same pathways. The Vermont Central Railroad choose the White–Winooski River gateway while the Rutland group selected the Black River–Otter Creek route—path of the old Crown Point Road.

Counting upon connections to Boston via the New Hampshire railroads then building, Paine's and Follett's rival groups began a race from the Connecticut River toward Burlington. Though the Vermont Central had the honor of the first train, the Rutland group got to the Queen City first. On December 18, 1849, salt water from Boston Harbor was mixed with fresh water from Lake Champlain. On New Year's eve the Vermont Central came steaming in, pursued by angry investors from Montpelier. For Charles Paine, in order to bring the trains through his home town, had diverted the road through Roxbury gulf, leaving both the capital city and industrial Barre to one side!

In the meantime, John Smith of St. Albans was constructing his Vermont and Canada Railroad southward to connect the new lines with the Canadian railways as well as with the Northern Railroad of New York, which was building west to Ogdensburgh, N. Y., port for the Great Lakes steamers. A high bridge was built over the widening Lamoille River (above, left), but crossing the upper end of Lake Champlain to Rouse's Point N. Y. was a tougher problem. These ingenious Yankees contrived a unique floating bridge for the trains (above, right), which, to the surprise of everyone, worked.

Smith hitched on his lines at Essex Junction instead of Burlington, much to the disgust of the Rutland group, and the inhabitants of the Queen City, who found themselves at a dead end. Not until 1900 did the Rutland Railroad extend its northern lines across the lake and up through the Islands to a Montreal connection.

In the meantime, Erastus Fairbanks, of St. Johnsbury, in 1850 pushed another projected Boston to Montreal line north from White River Junction to his own St. Johnsbury. It was fifteen years later,

however, before the "Connecticut and Passumpsic Railroad" reached Newport and the Canadian line. He also promoted another scheme to connect Portland, Maine and Montreal, by a cross-state line—also through St. Johnsbury, of course. The Vermont section later came to be known as the St. Johnsbury and Lake Champlain Railroad, or, as its modern critics have tagged it "slow train to yesterday."

Built as parts of a projected transcontinental system, it was logical that these Vermont lines should one day fall under the control of the Great Eastern railroads. The Vermont Central (now Central Vermont) has become a part of the Canadian National System. The Connecticut River railroads have fallen to the Boston and Maine and the Canadian Pacific, and the Rutland Railroad has tottered from one crisis to another, in and out of the Central Vermont and the great New York Central system. Note, on the map below, how the Vermont railroads have become strategic links in the important northern "alternate" route to the Great West, known in railroad circles as a "differential route."

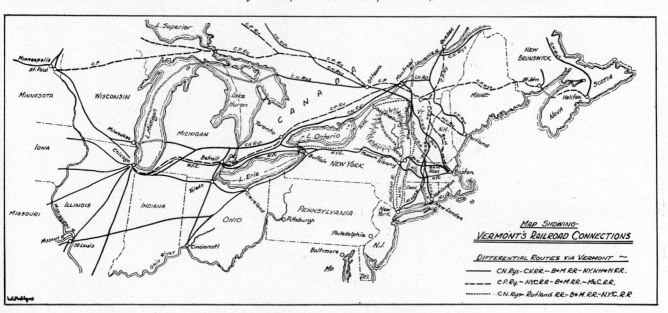

MAP SHOWING
VERMONT'S RAILROAD CONNECTIONS

DIFFERENTIAL ROUTES VIA VERMONT ~

—— CN.Rys~ CV.RR. ~ B+M.RR~ N.Y.NH+H.RR.

---- C.P.Ry.~ N.Y.C.RR~ B+M.RR.~ M&C.R.R.

······· CN.Rys~ Rutland RR~ B+M.RR.~ N.Y.C.R.R.

RAILROADERS — GOVERNORS

The power of the new railroads was soon manifest in the election of their Presidents as Governors. Charles Paine, as Governor 1841–43, played a large role in the building of the first Vermont Central Railroad, later went to Texas and died there promoting a southern Pacific railroad. Erastus Fairbanks of St. Johnsbury, promotor, scale manufacturer, and President of the Connecticut and Passumpsic Railroad, served twice as Governor, 1852–53 and 1860–61. In 1863 John Smith's son, J. Gregory, became Governor, and afterward President of the Vermont and Canada and Vermont Central. He it was who joined hands with Frederick Billings of Woodstock and Thomas Hawley Canfield of Burlington, to project the spectacular Northern Pacific Railway to Puget Sound. Both Smith and Billings served as Presidents of that famous railroad, which they hoped to join to their Vermont lines as parts of a vast transcontinental network. J. Gregory's son, Edward C., extended the unbroken domination of the Smiths over the CV's destinies down to 1928, serving, of course, as Governor for a spell (1898–1900). Canfield had been associated with the Rutland group, as was John B. Page, who in 1867 became both Governor (after six years as State Treasurer) and President of the Rutland Railroad. Percival W. Clement of Rutland also served both as Rutland President and Governor, 1919–21. And there were many others.

In more modern times Vermont has continued to furnish leaders to American railroads. Charles A. Prouty of Newport, served long as the head of the Interstate Commerce Commission. Colonel William J. Wilgus of Ascutney, organized the French railroad system for the AEF in 1917–18, laid out the colossal Grand Central Terminal in New York City, and accumulated an imposing list of other outstanding feats of railway engineering. He has lately completed a survey of the growth of transportation in Vermont.

← And of all these none was more beloved than Daniel Willard, who began as a section-hand on the Connecticut and Passumpsic and became one of its best engineers. Ascending the ladder of railroad success, he went from the Vice-Presidency of the Burlington Railroad to the Presidency of the Baltimore and Ohio. He is here shown (left) as he liked to remember himself—in the cab of his favorite locomotive, the "W. K. Blodgett," on the Connecticut and Passumpsic Railroad. (*Courtesy Baltimore and Ohio R.R.*)

Governor CHARLES PAINE

Governor J. GREGORY SMITH

FREDERICK BILLINGS

Governor JOHN B. PAGE

DANIEL WILLARD

WILLIAM J. WILGUS

145

There have been numerous others who served their apprenticeship (often as manager or President) on Vermont railroads and then went West to head some great national system. Henry Keyes, of Newbury, President of the Connecticut and Passumpsic, became head of the great Atchison, Topeka and Santa Fe Railroad in 1869. In 1881 William B. Strong of Brownington, succeeded to this position, with Albert A. Robinson as his Vice-President and General Manager. Edmund Rice of Westfield, rose from farmhand to the Presidency of the St. Paul and Pacific Railroad. And then there were: George T. Benedict, President of the New Orleans, Texas and Pacific; Charles J. Ives of Wallingford, President of the Burlington, Cedar Rapids and Northern; Henry C. Nutt of Montpelier, President of the Atlantic and Pacific; and, of course, there was also "Jubilee Jim" Fiske, speculator and railroad wrecker.

SPECTACULAR WRECKS were common, like this one on the Vermont & Canada R.R.

Vermont's railroad lines were mostly built in a single period of twenty-five years. The last main line was extended in 1900 by the Rutland R. R.—left at a dead end in Burlington—across the Champlain Islands toward an independent link with Montreal. Branch lines were added from time to time in an attempt to connect outlying communities with the main line., but were later abandoned.

As in most parts of the country, the railroads overextended themselves and fell into almost immediate financial difficulties. Stock-holders led a revolt against Charles Paine, complaining that on top of a salary three times that of any other railroad president in the state, he received special commissions, expense accounts and fat profits from personally owned car-building shops in Northfield, to which he routed VC business. In 1852 he drew $43,619 for "incidentals." He was forced out the following year, and went to Texas—where he died trying to promote a transcontinental road. The Smiths took over, and promptly moved the shops and offices to their own bailiwick, St. Albans. The Vermont Central passed through re-organization after re-organization, emerging finally as the Central Vermont—still under the control of the Smiths. Charges and counter-charges rocked the state, and votes were bought and sold in the legislature—much as in other states. Old recriminations between the Rutland-Burlington groups and the Vermont Central were revived. Particularly infuriating to the former was the deal by which the Rutland was left at a dead end in Burlington by Smith's connection with the VC at Essex Junction. Burlington residents joined the chorus of accusation, and the general public got a sour chuckle out of a widely circulated poem entitled "The Lay of the Lost Traveler:"

With saddened face and battered hat
  And eye that told of black despair,
On wooden bench the traveler sat,
  Cursing the fate that brought him there.
"Nine hours," he cried, "we've lingered here,
  With thought intent on distant homes,
Waiting for that elusive train,
  Which, always coming, never comes;
Till, weary, worn, distressed, forlorn,
  And paralyzed in every function,
I hope in hell, their souls may dwell
  Who first invented Essex Junction!"

The Rutland R. R. suffered no less than the Central Vermont from financial difficulties, but seems to have been freer of financial shenanigans. However, it never recovered from its initial failure to establish a stable Canadian or western connection, and for a while was absorbed into an expanded Central Vermont system. Staggering from crisis to crisis, the Rutland completed its first century in the hands of a semi-permanent receiver, with recurring doubts of the road's ability to continue running.

The Vermont railroads met their greatest test in 1927, when a disastrous flood wiped out the main lines and threw even the normally prosperous Central Vermont into receivership. It was over four months before full service was restored. Unfortunately, two roads were rebuilt— from Bethel to Rochester and up the West River—which might better have been left buried. They were abandoned for lack of traffic shortly after, as the motor truck displaced rail freight for short hauls. But the main line rails still ring with the flow of traffic to Canada and the West, and there were few signs, at the opening of their second century, that the railroads were likely to be soon displaced as bulk freight carriers.

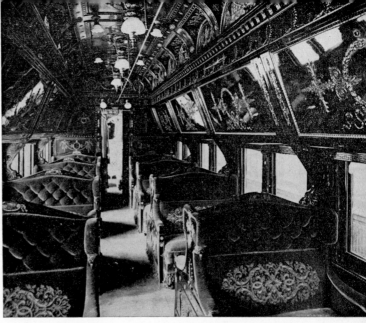

THE WOOD BURNING "STRANGER," at the unique St. Albans train shed. A model is in the Vermont Historical Society.

EARLY SLEEPING CAR on the Boston-Montreal run. More lavishly "elegant," but not very different from the cars in use today.

RAILROAD STATIONS are not greatly different today. Most were built early and have survived a century of railroading. Above is the old Sheldon Springs Station.

Early railroaders were quite ingenious. The odd car below is actually track inspection locomotive "St. Lawrence."

← LOCOMOTIVES and road-beds have changed vastly over 100 years. Here the Central Vermont fast freight south No. 490 crosses steel bridge below Northfield, Vt. as it highballs up Roxbury Mt. Lead engine is a Northern type from the C. V.'s parent railroad, the Canadian National, while the rear engine is one of the huge C. V. Texas type freight haulers. (Philip R. Hastings).

XII

INDUSTRIAL GROWTH

*How underground resources and the ingenuity of Yankee
inventors changed the economy of an agricultural state.*

VERMONT's first industries grew originally out of
the needs and wants of her own inhabitants, and
were fundamentally a supplement to a self-
sustaining rural economy. The early grist mills, woolen
mills, saw mills and forges provided necessary food,
clothing, building materials and iron for tools. But as the
nation began rapidly to shift from an economy of barter
and regional trading to a money economy involving inter-
regional exchange of specialized products, Vermont
changed slowly also.

In their first attempts to provide goods for export,
Vermonters turned to their most accessible natural
resources—timber, stone and agricultural produce. The
pioneers stopped burning the trees for potash and began to
ship lumber down Lake Champlain to Canada. As the first
growth timber thinned, the tide turned and lumber began
to stream up the Lake from Canada to Burlington, which
soon became one of the nation's great lumber finishing
centers. Out of the business of milling lumber grew the
extensive wood-working industries of modern times—
some large, but most of them small and scattered. Yet as a
whole, they now employ 10,000, and constitute an
important element in the economy of the state. Some, like
the large Cushman factory at North Bennington, produce
furniture for a national market.

Concentration on special products, such as chair seats,
bobbins, wood bowls or toys, has often created small
woodworking shops which are the largest of their type
in the country. In 1929, with only 200 employees, the
C. E. Bradley Co. of Brattleboro was reputed to be the
largest wood turners in New England.

Another use of timber developed as paper came to be
made from wood pulp in the 1840's. For many years
during and after the Revolution, Bennington mills supplied
Albany and Troy with their needs for *rag* paper. But wood
pulp mills went to the sources of raw material. The
Mississquoi Pulp and Paper Company built a large business
in bristol board in Sheldon; the Gilman Paper Company,
on the upper Connecticut, was for many years a major
producer of newsprint; and further down at Bellows Falls,
where logs could be floated from the great forests up river,
were concentrated pulp and paper mills.

Of the underground resources, iron was the most

needed—and the first worked commercially. But the
deposits were not extensive, and were mostly abandoned
when the railroad brought in cheap western pig and
finished iron. Copper deposits were tapped, abandoned and
mined again. Even gold was once washed from the streams
of Plymouth, after the enthusiasm of '49 set men seeking
it everywhere. But the greatest resource of all, stone—
marble, granite and slate—was quarried only incidentally
for use in foundations, etc. Not until after 1849 did the
business begin to develop commercially, and here,
particularly, the railroad provided the "open sesame" to a
national market.

Agriculture provided the basis of some industry. We
have already seen how the sheep craze provided a great
quantity of wool and stimulated the growth of carding and
fulling mills to process it, first for home weaving, then for
factory production of cloth. When sheep disappeared, the
mills turned to the West for raw materials, and developed
an integrated industrial process to turn out finished cloth
for sale to national markets.

Nor should one overlook the industry built upon one of
the states smallest but sweetest products—maple sap.
The great Cary Maple Sugar Company in St. Johnsbury—
maple capital of the nation—has been supplemented by
other processing plants in Burlington, Barre and elsewhere.
Production of sugar for industrial use, such as tobacco
sweetening, was for many years an important aspect of
the business. But recent price increases have boosted
maple into the luxury food category, and limited industrial use. The demand is greater than Vermont's own
supply of raw materials, and Cary imports large quantities
of syrup from Canada and neighboring states.

Finally, there are the companies milling grain for
commercial sale. The St. Albans Grain Company was one
of the first large scale grist mills; the Bailey Grain Company in Montpelier is one of the best known.

YANKEE INVENTORS FACE THE WORLD

The second category of Vermont industries includes
those based on the native ingenuity and skill with tools of
the pioneer inventors and craftsmen. The actual business,
however, was more often than not built by men other than
the inventors themselves. There were exceptions; inventor

Thaddeus Fairbanks and his brothers built a great industry on his original platform scale. In Brattleboro, Jacob Estey organized the Estey Organ Company, and by 1890 was employing 500 men to produce 1200 organs a month. The tool makers of Windsor wandered south and west to found a national machine tool industry, but in Springfield James Hartness and his associates founded *and* developed three companies out of the original Jones-Lamson plant. Yankee skill with iron provided the basis for many hardware plants like Wallingford's American Fork and Hoe Company. And the early interest in printing continued into the nineteenth and twentieth centuries. Brattleboro, in mid-century, began to produce in quantity the "stereotype" editions of standard books which flooded the market and made mass circulation possible. It is today, with Burlington and Concord, N. H., one of the three great Northern New England printing centers, catering particularly to the university presses, publishing houses, foundations and other consumers of high grade but quantity printing.

BRANCH PLANTS

Most all of the basic industries of the state were founded and developed by Vermonters. But the twentieth century trend has been a different one. Very few new industries of size have been founded by citizens of the state, though the thirties and forties saw a concerted effort to revive back country towns with small craft industries. Most of the industrial growth has come as the result of the establishment in Vermont of branch plants by large national concerns. The Bell Aircraft plant in Burlington, taken over by General Electric in 1948, is one major example; the National Carbon plant at St. Albans and the American Optical Company at Brattleboro—all recent comers—are others. The underwear and cotton clothing industry of Bennington has largely passed into the hands of national firms. Low overhead and a reliable labor force as well as the intangible appeal of the state, have been important factors in the trend. Even old established industries have fallen prey to the nationalization of industry; E. & T. Fairbanks Company was absorbed by their booming Chicago branch, Fairbanks-Morse and Company, and in December 1948 the great Cavendish woolen mills of Gay Brothers very nearly passed into the hands of "down-country" operators.

FAMILY INDUSTRY

Until the most recent times the dominant characteristic of Vermont industry has been its "family" continuity. The great American capitalist ideal—of business founded on hard-work, conservative financial policies, the plowing-back of profits, and the continuing control by sons and grandsons of the founder—actually existed in Vermont long after it had passed, nationally, from the realm of actuality into the advertisements and pamphlets of the arch-conservative National Association of Manufacturers. Family continuity may still be seen in the scale, the machine tool, and the marble and the woolen industries, and in a multitude of other small businesses which have been passed down from generation to generation.

This has resulted in a closer relationship of employer and employee than is customary in the great mass production industries to the south, and a consequent minimum of industrial strife. It has also produced both a larger degree of benevolent paternalism in place of unionization on the one hand, and a generally low standard of wages as compared with national union levels, on the other. The latter has been partly but not entirely offset by materially lower living costs. In some cases workers have not been uprooted from the soil as in great industrial centers, and have retained a greater degree of independence—and company loyalty—as a consequence. During the depression period, however, unionization made great headway, and by 1949 union labor wielded great political and economic influence in such industrial centers as Barre, Springfield and Burlington.

As in the nation at large, industrialization had a widespread influence in changing the economic, social and political habits of the people. The shift to an economy of "purchase and sale" from one of production for use, caused people to live, eat, think—and vote—differently. The newly prominent leaders of industry and transportation swiftly made inroads on the lawyer's domination of state politics. Four Proctors became governor; the Fairbanks family occupied the executive chair three times, and the Smith family twice. Besides J. Gregory and Edward Smith, the railroads provided Charles Paine, John B. Page, Percival Clement and others. And most of the other Governors since 1849 have had extensive industrial interests. Despite Vermont's basic rural economy, despite control of the legislature by farmers, only one governor has had even a slim claim to have stepped from behind a plow into the Chief Executive's office.

As Vermont's second century drew to a close, industry, its allied businesses and dependent trades played an ever increasing role in the life of the state. Even though the major part of the population continued to reside in semi-rural communities, these villages have become tributary to the industries of the larger cities, as well as to scattered, small local businesses.

In view of the considerable role and influence of industry in the growth of modern Vermont, it is worthwhile to examine in greater detail several of the principal businesses. We will turn first to the two great extractive industries—granite and marble; then to the more scattered but significant woolen mills, and then finally to the two outstanding economic heritages of Yankee inventiveness, the scale and machine tool industries.

QUARRY *by Marcelle Beaudin*

BARRE COSMOPOLITAN CITY *and* Granite Center of the World

THE most cosmopolitan city in Vermont produces one-third of all the public and private memorials erected in the United States. These memorials are skillfully designed, quarried and produced by workers-in-stone from many lands.

When General Lafayette passed through Barre, Vermont in 1825, he was enroute from Boston to Burlington, Vt., and he and his coterie were guests of the Old Day Tavern in South Barre on the post road between the two cities. At that time Barre was little more than a country hamlet of a few hundred souls, and its granite hills were but lightly scarred by surface quarrying for millstones, doorsteps and foundation stones.

When General Grant was elected President in 1868, Barre had discovered her enormous mineral resources and a great industry was in the making. Its population was then 2,079 and its quarries had already furnished the stone for the state Capitol building in Montpelier and a few other buildings in the district, as well as paving stones for several cities.

When Admiral Dewey returned to his native Montpelier, Vermont, in 1899, after the victory of Manila, Barre had more than trebled its population and was rivalling famed Quincy, Massachusetts, as a major granite center, with virtually all its production in monuments.

When President Roosevelt visited Barre in 1936, during his tour of flood control operations in Vermont, the city had become the center of Memorial Art in America, and the most cosmopolitan community in the State of Vermont with a "district" population of nearly 16,000 and an income of nearly 15 million dollars a year.

The story of Barre is one of the epics in the annals of art and industry in America.

Beatrice Lowe Haskins

Quarried stones—running often over 20 tons—were drawn laboriously first by yokes of oxen, then by teams of horses from the quarries to the building site or the railroad. Today they move directly by rail up the valley from Barre toward the main line of the Central Vermont, whence they go to all parts of the world.

Ammi B. Young's classic state house—in its simplicity considered one of the nation's best—was thoroughly gutted by fire in 1857. Its granite walls were taken down, but the six great columns and portico left standing. A new and larger shell—again of Barre granite—with a new, higher and gilded dome, was built behind it, and stands today, a tribute to the men who designed it, as well as to the men who cut and raised its great stones.

Barre Guild Memorials, the creative work of talented designers, are produced in plants emphasizing ideal working conditions, with the health hazards of bygone days virtually eliminated. Circular and gang saws cut quarry blocks into slabs, the first step in the fabrication process.

Barre's vast underground resources lay untouched for forty years after her charter was granted in 1778. Granite outcroppings provided great blocks for house foundations, and for mill stones. But no commercial use or production were visualized until Robert Parker returned from the wars in 1815, joined hands with Thomas Courser, and opened the first quarry in Millstone Hill.

These early producers of granite received their first big order in the form of a contract for blocks for the new state capitol building, which began to rise in 1836 on a neighboring Montpelier hillside. At the same time, the "Greek Revival" in architecture which was beginning to sweep the country, along with expanding finance and industry, opened a new field for the construction of monumental buildings, for which granite was particularly suited. In contrast to its present cost, the stone was then cheap and available for a wide variety of uses. One of the earliest contracts was for ten million paving blocks for the city of Troy, New York.

Progress was slow for many years, for it was exceedingly difficult to move the weighty stone. The State House blocks had been laboriously moved behind straining oxen over the brief ten miles which separated the quarries and the capital city. But such a system was hardly practical for long distances.

The hope which the railroad brought to many industries flamed in Barre, but turned to simmering anger when Charles Paine brought the rails up Roxbury Gulf through his home town of Northfield in 1849, leaving both Barre and Montpelier to one side. In fact, it was nearly twenty years before the Central Vermont finally extended a spur into the granite center. This opened new markets to the finished product, but provided no solution to the problem of getting the rough stone from the quarries to the sheds.

In 1890 Barre herself built what was known as the "Sky Route" (now the Barre and Chelsea R. R.), with a grade of 250 feet to the mile up Millstone Hill.

At last the industry began to flourish, and to attract workers from outside. It was the period when the tide of immigration from Europe was rising to flood proportions. Skilled Italian designers and sculptors from the quarries of Florence and Carrara, thrifty Scotch artisans whose heritage of stone working dates back to the eleventh century, as well as laborers from France, Spain, Norway, Sweden, Finland and England, all poured into Barre seeking opportunity to ply the trade they knew best. This Yankee town soon became one of the most cosmopolitan cities in New England.

These workers arrived as mechanization began to invade American industry. A trade which involved so much of art and individual craftsmanship was bound to resist—sometimes bitterly—the introduction of pneumatic carving tools and other labor-saving machinery. None the less, the use of modern tools has not removed the stimulus to fine craftsmanship as it has in many industries. The granite workers have displayed ingenuity and resourcefulness in the fields of design and production.

The most recent reflection of this is the establishment of the Barre School of Memorial Art, under the supervision of the Barre school system and the watchful eye of the Barre Guild.

THE BARRE GUILD

The Guild was organized by the several quarriers and manufacturers of granite. Unlike the marble industry, there has been little absorption of small units by a single giant of industry. Both the quarrying and finishing of granite are still largely carried out by different firms,

Columns and urns are turned on lathes, but the capitals are carved by skilled artisans using pneumatic chisels. Deft workers cut the rubber stencil sheet, upon which the design and lettering have been transferred, preparatory to the abr... carving of the 'sand blast' machine and the work of the hooded shape-ca...

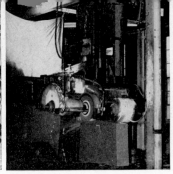

Slabs are steeled or polished with these high speed machines. Rough surfaces are smoothed by the pneumatic hammer of the surfacing machine. The abra- *sive wheel of the Contour grinder, guided by templates, forms curved monument tops and sides. Checks and flutes are added with the Abrasive Edger.*

though some large companies like Rock of Ages have perfected the industrial-commercial chain from quarry to consumer. Because of the huge costs involved, quarrying has gravitated into the hands of a half-dozen or so companies and the small quarries in Calais, Woodbury and further south in Bethel see little activity any more. But there are over 150 manufacturers scattered throughout Washington County, and the Central Vermont spur from Barre to Montpelier Junction came to be lined with granite "sheds."

The Guild itself is more of a promotional than an industrial association. It has eschewed the price-fixing and production coordination attempted by many like organizations founded to evade the federal anti-trust laws. It is patterned somewhat after medieval ideals and objectives, and maintains standards for the entire industry through a staff of inspectors, who can award or withhold the hallmark of the Guild. It has also increasingly taken on the job of advertising and promotion of the memorial use of granite. This has become necessary because the industry's principal competitor—marble—is concentrated under single ownership. The Barre firms found it better to sink intramural quarrels in favor of cooperation against a mutual business adversary. The granite industry has long since lost the building stone market to marble, which is more easily worked and can, under present conditions, be delivered at the site for less cost. In 1948, despite a desire on the part of the State Building Commission to build its new State Office Building of granite to match the State House, the Library and Courts Building, and the nearby National Life Insurance Company offices, current costs made its use impossible despite close proximity of the quarries. Officials then turned to marble, at a saving of over a hundred thousand dollars.

A new threat to the memorial industry has recently arisen from a limited reaction against the costly commercialization of death and burial. Cremation, the establishment of monument-less cemeteries ("memorial parks"), and the movement toward "living memorials" in the form of parks, hospitals, scholarships, and educational, scientific and charitable foundations—all have presented a challenge to the industry's salesmanship.

Barre's own cemeteries display some of its craftsmen's best work.

The granite companies have led the stone-working industry in the development and installation of protective measures for the health and safety of workers. Barre was among the first of the mineral industries to install dust-removing equipment to combat silicosis. Yet the industry has suffered perhaps more than any other in the state from industrial strife. This is, however, a relative statement, for Vermont has not experienced anything like the industrial warfare of her neighbors. Moreover, many of the granite strikes have been called in response to the orders of the national union, which maintains its headquarters at Quincy, Massachusetts, although Barre long ago outstripped that city in stone production. Strikes

Master carvers bring significance and symbolic beauty to Barre Memorials today as they have for more than sixty years. Sculptors, trained in studios, *ateliers, and stone centers here and abroad, working from plaster models, interpret the creation of the original artist in Barre's world-famed granite.*

Planning Drill Patterns

Channeling with 16 Ft. Rods

Lyner Drills are Dust-Controlled

Squaring a Block

Grout—75% Waste

QUARRYING BARRE GRANITE
for a NATION'S MEMORIALS

All uncredited photographs by *Harris Palmer*

Slope Channeling   DERICK

Derricks Handle Blocks up to 60 Tons   EMERSON

25 Tons on a Wire-rope DE

Splitting with Wedges

Low-level Railroading

Granite for a Nation's Monuments

BARRE'S two civic monuments have earned wide acclaim. Jenne-wein's "Youth Triumphant" graces the City Park soldier's memorial.

The statue of Robert Burns, with its exquisite bas-reliefs from the poet's works, was presented by the city's Scotch stone workers.

have therefore sometimes been more closely related to conditions in Massachusetts than Vermont.

Before we turn to inspect the marble industry, we should also examine the slate regions where the Vermont–New York boundary bisects a major deposit. Thus Poultney, Fairhaven, Wells, Pawlet, Rupert, Vermont, and Granville, N. Y. are the centers of a very considerable industry, second only to Pennsylvania's extensive quarries. Slate had long been cut out for foundations, and split off for roofs. The use of slate for roofing spread as railroads made shipment possible, and as the industry expanded, Welsh emigrants flocked to the quarries. In 1877 150 workers from a single district in Wales came in a body.

Asbestos, of which northern Vermont is one of the most significant producers, has grown as its use for insulation and fire-proof boarding has expanded in the mid-twentieth century. Soapstone, used in colonial times

for stove backs, is now powdered and sold as talc, widely used in the paper and cosmetics industry. Between them, Vermont and New York produce more than two thirds of the nation's talc. In years past, too, Vermont held high hopes for the production of iron and gold, but neither proved commercially profitable for long. Between 1820 and 1860, the iron industry gave employment to several hundred persons in Brandon, Pittsford, Bennington, Tinmouth, and Plymouth. But both iron furnaces and gold streams in Plymouth lie deserted today. On the other hand, the defunct copper mines of Strafford have been revived in the last decade, principally as a result of critical war needs. Production from a rich vein has been continued to meet post-war demands.

Thus the resources underneath the feet of Vermonters serve in modern times, as in years past, as a principal support for her industrial prosperity.

SLATE is split by hand, as in colonial days, but modern aerial carriages lift the great blocks from the Poultney quarries.

VERMONT MARBLE

ARBLE quarrying in Vermont dates back to the early pioneers. But for over a century only small businesses operated with varying degrees of success. Then in 1880, Redfield Proctor founded the Vermont Marble Company. This was a union of two of the more important marble producers of that time. During the following thirty years other Vermont firms in the industry were purchased by the Proctor company.

The Vermont Marble Company is one of the State's largest industries. It employs some 1300 workers, most of them in Rutland County. Its annual payroll in the State is more than two and a half million dollars. Sales offices and auxiliary plants are widely spread over North America.

The company is self-contained to a rather unique degree. It manufactures its own electric power at five hydroelectric stations and sells a substantial amount of excess electricity. It operates a railroad, several machine shops, carpenter and plumbing shops, a fleet of trucks and auto-

mobiles, employees' clubs and an excellent hospital, and was the first industry in the country to have a "visiting" nurse.

To supplement its own marbles with colored stones not obtainable in America it imports from Italy, France, Spain, Sweden, Belgium and South America and has become the country's largest marble importer.

Numerous markets have been found for the by-products and wastes of the marble business. Crushed and ground marble are used for land improvement and in a wide variety of industrial processes, including paper making, rubber, floor coverings and paints.

During the war the major part of the company's Vermont plants were converted to making war products—machine tools, steam engines, winches and steamboat whistles, power cases, radio parts and other items.

Aristide Piccini is one of Vermont Marble's finest carvers. Born in Carrara, Italy, he is a graduate of the famous Academia di belle Arte there. Here Piccini carves a statue of St. Joseph and Child from a plaster model. Piccini carved the recent replica of the Mead statue of Ethan Allen, on the State House Portico. →

MARBLE IS SAWN into thin slabs and rectangular blocks by gang saws—a series of steel blades set into a swinging chassis. Here a quarry block goes into a gang at West Rutland.

Charles Raksanyi brings out the beauty of a Vermont Marble monument with an electric polishing machine. Raksanyi, born in Nagy Acsad, Hungary, is one of many Vermont Marble workers who originally came ← from Europe.

Industrial diamonds find important use in marble cutting. This saw with diamond teeth cuts swiftly through the stone. →

A rubbing bed is a cast iron disc some fourteen feet in diameter. As it revolves a mixture of sand and water "rubs" the marble to its desired thickness. Carl Carlson, the operator, came from Sweden.

Opposite: MAMMOTH CRANE IN PROCTOR YARDS

INTERIOR of one of the marble plants in Proctor. This building is four hundred feet long and a hundred feet wide. It is used entirely in the production of marble memorials.

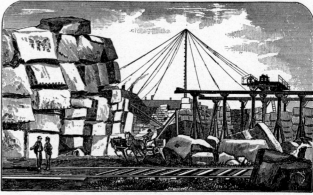

The first marble quarry in North America was not opened at the spot where the industry centers today, at Proctor, Vermont. It was rather at Dorset, in the year 1785, that Isaac Underhill first exploited the great underground deposits of the age-old stone.

Of course, the pioneers had split off slabs from exposed marble ledges for door steps and fireplace hearths. And they chiseled out crude but appealing headstones which still stand doggedly against the elements in the old hillside cemeteries. Even before that, the French had taken marble from the deposits on Isle La Motte to make lime for use in old Fort Ste. Anne.

Marble was later found along the whole range of the Taconic Mountains bordering Lake Champlain, as far south as Bennington, and with isolated deposits as far north as Swanton and Isle La Motte. Yet quarrying stone was not an easy task, with near-primitive tools. Even after Underhill's venture, the growth of the industry was slow and halting. But quarries were opened in Pittsford before the century ended, and the Rutland area saw its first activity in 1807.

Getting out the stone was only half the problem. Once out, you had only a rough block, hardly suitable for elaborate memorials. And even if it were to be finished elsewhere, how were you to get it to that point? There were no railroads and road transportation was difficult enough for light traffic; heavily loaded vehicles moved across the countryside ponderously or often not at all.

NEW MECHANICAL METHODS

The first move that began a revolution in the struggling marble industry was the introduction of efficient saws. Utilizing the power at the falls of Otter Creek, Dr. Ebenezer Judd in 1805 set up a mill with 65 saws, which he operated quite profitably. Other mills, however, did not do so well, until considerably later when the "gang" saw was introduced. This was a series of saws which sliced the huge blocks into manageable slabs. The original Dorset area was still the most active one before the Civil War, and here were to be found eleven mills of 62 "gangs," employing over 300 men. Later quarrying itself was simplified by the use of "channeling" machines, which sliced the quarry floor into uniform blocks.

The Dorset area was early stimulated by new demand for marble as a building stone. In 1837 the blocks for the new U.S. Bank building in Erie, Pennsylvania, were quarried and laboriously dragged behind oxen to Whitehall. From here they went down the new Champlain Canal and across the Erie Canal to the Great Lakes. If land transportation could be avoided, however, it was. The Middlebury mills sent their product down Otter Creek into Lake Champlain, and then way around by the St. Lawrence River and the Atlantic Ocean to eastern seaboard cities—all this to avoid as little as 50 miles of land transportation. It gives you a little idea of how difficult the latter really was.

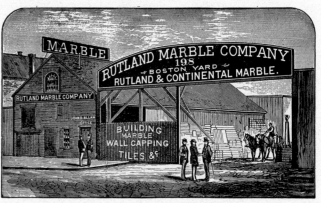

COMING OF THE RAILROADS

It might be expected, therefore, when the railroad came up through Rutland and Pittsford in 1849, that there would be a second revolution in the marble industry. There was; for the railways brought not only improved transportation. They had also helped stimulate industry all over the nation, which then promptly felt the need of great temples for its places of business and palaces as homes for its leaders—to rival even those of ancient Rome. This was welcome news to the marble men.

Before the railroads, there were only five localities with very much activity: Swanton, Isle La Motte, Middlebury, Dorset, and the Pittsford—Rutland area. And the tremendous possibilities of the latter were still mostly unrealized. But with its fine new railway connections in the fifties, activity began to boom. Through the activities of the Ripley and Clement families and Governor John B. Page, several firms were built up, both to quarry and finish the stone. The largest of these was the Rutland Marble Co., owned mostly by New York financiers, but its expansion was slowed by a habit of paying out all its profits in dividends. Just north was another company, the Sutherland Falls Marble Co., which was doing just the opposite. Its president, Redfield Proctor, had invested every cent he could gather to buy up a bankrupt mill and quarry in 1870. He then proceeded to plow back every dollar he made to expand and strengthen the new company. Impressed by the competition of this newcomer, the New Yorkers asked Proctor to manage the Rutland firm, and in 1880 he merged the two into a new corporation—the Vermont Marble Company.

VERMONT MARBLE COMPANY

No less important than machines and improved transportation in revolutionizing the industry were new methods of business organization. The leaders of the new industrial age were seeking means to regulate the distribution and prices of their product to their own liking. One of the first methods tried, before it was outlawed by the government, was the "pool." In Vermont, the new marble company joined hands with several of its smaller competitors in a pool to sell jointly, at a set price, all of their marble. Each company contributed a fixed amount, over half being allotted to the Vermont Marble Co.

Like most of the "pools" of the time, it had a short duration. All over the country the big firms were getting bigger, and they soon preferred to swallow up their competitors instead of joining in pools. The Vermont Marble Co. followed a similar course, absorbing the smaller firms one by one over the course of years until it assumed undisputed dominance over the industry. Today, it has extended its sway over quarries and mills throughout the nation. And in Proctor it has taken over or built up all the auxiliary services necessary to its huge plants there.

Gov. Redfield Proctor   Gov. Fletcher D. Proctor

PROCTORS IN POLITICS

Behind this amazing expansion lay the organizing genius of Redfield Proctor and his sons. His single-minded devotion to the growth of his company and his careful investment policy created a new giant of industry.

Like other contemporary American industrialists who found it desirable to promote their manufacturing interests by participation in politics, Redfield Proctor mounted the steps from local politics to the governorship in 1878. Ten years later he served as Chairman of the Vermont delegation to the Republican National Convention. For his services there, and at the petition of the state legislature, he was appointed Secretary of War in the Cabinet of President Benjamin Harrison, a position he filled with distinction. At the death of Vermont's great U. S. Senator George F. Edmunds, Proctor was appointed to fill his unexpired term, and was reelected regularly thereafter.

Upon entering national politics, Redfield passed on the presidency of the Vermont Marble Company to his son, Fletcher D. Proctor, who guarded its destinies until his death in 1911, having served as Governor 1906–1908. The present president is Redfield Proctor, Jr. who became Governor 1923–24. Also active in its present affairs is Fletcher's son, Mortimer R. Proctor, who was elected Governor in 1945. Each of these men had extensive service in the legislature before stepping up to the governor's chair. And during its entire existence the Vermont Marble Company has played an influential role in state politics as the state's most extensive industrial enterprise.

Gov. Redfield Proctor, Jr.   Gov. Mortimer R. Proctor

FROM THE MAIN SHOPS at Proctor, building marble and memorials go out to customers all over the country.

PRESIDENT FRANKLIN DELANO ROOSEVELT specified "a plain white marble monument to be placed over my grave" at Hyde Park, New York.

FIRST STEP: EXPLORATION—A diamond drill cuts a core from a cross section of a marble ledge. The cores are polished and examined. If the quality and quantity of the marble warrants, a quarry may be opened here. Soil must first be cleared away.

END PRODUCT: THE SUPREME COURT BUILDING at Washington is an outstanding example of the many Vermont marble buildings in the nation's capital. A thousand carloads of the Vermont product were used in this great Grecian temple of justice.

THE HOLLISTER QUARRY in Florence (Pittsford) *extends over three hundred and fifty feet below the surface of the ground. The first quarry in this area was opened about 1795.*

SHADOWS UNDERGROUND *(right, above). In the "West Blue" quarry at West Rutland John Molaski runs a channeling machine back and forth along a movable track, cutting the marble layer into blocks.*

TOWERS OF MARBLE *(right, below). Blocks are piled high in the West Rutland storage yards. These white blocks are from Vermont quarries. Stored here also are marbles from Italy, France, Spain, Belgium, Sweden and South America.*

COLUMN BASE *for the Supreme Court Building (opposite page) is being fluted by a carborundum wheel. It was first turned in a lathe.*

CHAMPLAIN MILLS of the American Woolen Company are by far the largest in the state, and the only mills producing worsted.

THE WOOLEN INDUSTRY

MAN's first concern is for food, shelter and clothing. Thus, the pioneer first cleared the stumps from fields, and planted some crops. He built a roof over his head and brought his family to the new home. And on the ox-cart there was likely to be a spinning wheel, for how else in the wilderness were father, mother and children to be clothed?

It was no coincidence therefore that the first industrial units in Vermont were grist mills, followed shortly by saw mills, to turn out lumber for the much wanted "frame house." And after that these enterprising Yankees began to put their racing streams to work to provide them with the makings of clothing. Out of the age-old hand spinning and weaving came new mechanical methods—"carding" mills to put the wool in shape for weaving, "fulling" mills to improve the finish of the woven cloth. Bennington boasted a woolen mill before the Revolution, and by 1781 had a fulling mill in operation.

But the industry got a more permanent start up on the Ottauquechee River, where a spectacular drop promised abundant water power. In 1771 Jonathan Burtch bought the old saw mill there and added to it a fulling mill. He was so successful that he was able to sell out only six years later for the very neat price of $10,000.

In 1794 power was applied to the carding process, and only fifteen years later there were 139 carding mills supplying wool for nearly 15,000 hand looms—which in turn could turn out a million yards of cloth.

Then came the Jeffersonian Embargo and the War of 1812. Imports of foreign cloths were virtually cut off, giving a tremendous stimulus to domestic manufacture. Perhaps nowhere else than in textiles was the activity so vigorous. Factories to produce both woolens and cottons sprang up. But the boom collapsed after peace came in 1815. English woolens flooded the markets at $8.00 a yard, while the Vermont product went begging at half that. There still was a vast difference in quality and appearance.

But a gentleman from Weathersfield—Consul to Portugal William Jarvis—was preparing a new revolution for the Green Mountain state—and, as a matter of fact, for the country as a whole. He brought back from Europe a number of merino sheep, whose long fibre wool was of much finer grade than that of the native American sheep.

EFFECTIVE CONTRAST to the Tunbridge mill is this artist's combination of the great Cavendish (left) and Ludlow (right) mills of the modern Gay Brothers plants. In the rear runs the Black River and the Rutland Railroad, both important factors in the growth of the woolen industry in this area.

ORIGINAL MILL in Tunbridge was purchased and developed by Stearns Gay and his father in 1869. This painting by Arthur B. Wilder depicts the building as it was about 1845. Improved facilities and transportation lured Gay to Cavendish in 1886.

FOUNDERS

Albert Gallatin Dewey (left) and Stearns Gay (right) founded two of the "family" enterprises which have survived economic tribulations over nearly a century. Their firms are now two of the most important units of the Vermont woolen industry.

Merinos were widely introduced after that, especially in Vermont. The availability of this excellent wool gave new stimulus to the woolen industry. In fact, in Windsor the Essex Merino Association enlarged an old carding mill into a woolen factory of considerable size. Windsor experienced an industrial boom from 1812–15, but the Association folded in the deflation which followed.

But the experiment had a lasting effect in improving the quality of American wool, and in laying the basis for the extension of sheep raising. Within fifteen years the Vermont farmers began throwing over all other crops in favor of wool. Soon Vermont took first place in the production of raw wool, and her green slopes were crowded with sheep. Not even in the South was there so much devotion to a single crop.

The new protective tariffs of the late 1820's had stimulated an industrial revival and the growing textile mills of southern New England were ready and willing to absorb all the wool the Vermonters could produce. But by this time Vermont herself had seen a considerable re-establishment of woolen manufacturing. Yankee will-power and water-power combined in establishing over 100 factories, to help consume the annual "clip" of three million pounds.

Markets were still few, scattered, and hard to reach, however. The industry, after its first boom, fell into doldrums in the forties. Although the capital investment shot up from 1½ to 2½ million dollars, and employees from 1500 to 2100, actual output remained the same!

By the fifties railroads had breached the Green Mountains, opening new markets. But they had been in operation in southern New England even longer, and the competition of the mammoth new Massachusetts mills discouraged new enterprise in Vermont.

There were several firms, however, which were steadily expanding by the process of plowing back into the business modest profits from dawn-to-dusk labor. Most of these firms originated in the family earnings of a mill worker, carefully husbanded to purchase second-hand machinery.

Such an enterprise was the Dewey Mills at Quechee. In 1836, enterprising young Albert G. Dewey set about the building of a mill at the falls of the Ottauquechee. At first he was not too successful, and at the end of three years, he was $15,000 in debt. But in 1841 he installed a patent rag-picking machine which had been constructed by inventor Reuben Daniels of nearby Woodstock, under Dewey's supervision. And here in Dewey's Mills, Vermont, was made what was probably the first American "shoddy"—that is, re-worked wool.[1]

But transportation was then a major problem. Weekly a team left for Boston with cloth, returning with raw materials. Thus the coming of the railroad to neighboring White River Junction in 1848 made an immense difference. By 1856 Dewey had all his debts paid, and by 1870 had increased his capacity to 1300 yards a day. At his death in 1886, the firm was taken over by his sons—inventive, mechanically ingenious John J., and shrewd, financially minded William S. Dewey. The mills are now in the hands of the third and fourth generations, a typical family enterprise.

Similar in nature was the growth of the Gay Mills. Young Stearns Gay, an expert carder, brought his father and family from Connecticut in 1869 to establish, by dint of hard labor, a small mill in Tunbridge. Materials made in the shop were distributed locally by trading with the local

---

1 Made from wool rags, tailor's clippings and new threads.

farmers for raw wool. But they were many miles from the railroad, which failed to come up the Tunbridge branch of the White River—as many had hoped—on its way to Barre and Burlington. Furthermore, the Black River Valley, further south, was rapidly becoming the center of the woolen industry in the state.

Now, the people of Cavendish were faced with an idle mill, built in 1832 but gutted by fire and abandoned in 1869. This they decided to offer to the Gays, with six tenement houses, tax free for ten years. It was too tempting an offer to resist, and the business moved to Cavendish in 1886.

Its subsequent growth under the careful ministrations of successive Gays has been unspectacular but steady. Today one of the state's most modern and largest mills employs—in both Ludlow and Cavendish—over four hundred people and produces over a thousand *miles* of cloth a year. Here again a family dynasty has guided the fate of a growing business by hard-headed business administration. And like Dewey's mills, it came into the hands of brothers: Leon Gay, with his aptitude for facts, figures and public contacts, and Olin Gay, specialist in plant and processes.

Only the branch plants of the American Woolen Company in Burlington and Winooski are larger. These "Champlain Mills" had their origin also in the untamed water power at the falls of the Winooski River—coveted years before by Ira Allen. Parts of the plant date back over a hundred years, but the great expansion of these massive mills is largely a development of modern times. During World War II over 2800 people were employed, and the figure stands at 2200 in 1948—four times as many as its nearest competitor. In fact, it is thus the largest single firm of any kind in the state, and the only textile mill producing both woolens and worsteds.[2]

There are many other large woolen manufactories in Vermont, mostly in the Black River Valley. At Springfield is the John T. Slack Corp., one of the largest shoddy mills in the United States. In Ludlow, along with Gay Brothers, are the Jewell Brook Woolen Co., the Verd Mont Mills, and the Mountain Woolen Mills, all with over a hundred employees, and several smaller firms as well. At Quechee, as well as A. G. Dewey Co., is the Harris Emery Co., which dates back to some of the earliest mills in that area. This firm also runs an even larger branch at Penacook, N. H. Further up the river is the Vermont Native Industries at Bridgewater. This was one of the first firms to undertake—in 1925—direct retail sales from the factory, a practice now adopted by most of the other companies.

Large mills also operate at Hartford, Northfield, North Montpelier and at Bennington, where began some of the earliest textile firms. From its first underwear factory in

2 Woolens are produced through "carding" wool, worsteds through "combing," using only long staple product.

RAG PICKER *stands at the beginning of the woolen process, for many fabrics include a substantial proportion of reworked wool.*

CARDING MACHINE *prepares the wool for spinning and weaving into cloth.*

WEAVING MACHINE *produces the actual cloth, though it normally must go through the "fulling" process before ready for use.*

1802, Bennington has developed into one of the nation's important producers of knitted goods.

The textile industry in all of contemporary New England has suffered from southern competition. Low taxes, cheap labor, and (with cotton) proximity to raw materials has drawn many plants into the deep South. But Vermont manufacturers still claim many advantages. While water power has ceased to be an important factor since the advent of electricity, abundant, good water is needed for processing. New England mills lost the advantage of proximity to raw materials when sheep raising moved westward. But mills no longer obtain raw wool direct, scouring it themselves. Instead they buy scoured wool in large lots from the great Boston market—first in the nation—which is close by. And while federal taxes are the same everywhere, state taxes have traditionally been modest in Vermont. And even more important, local communities of which the mill is often the economic mainstay, have refrained from heavy taxation, chiefly through conservative valuation of the industrial properties.

But most important has been the labor element. Like their employers, workers in the woolen mills have often remained for generations, building up a vast reservoir of skilled and generally contented laborers. Northern New England has suffered much less than Southern New England from the modern industrial migrations.

Furthermore, the relatively small size of the plants and their scattered locations has largely avoided the creation of conditions which caused industrial strife in metropolitan centers. When, however, depression hit Vermont in the 1930's, insecure workers turned to labor unions— though less violently and enthusiastically than elsewhere.

The great mills at Winooski were well and completely organized by the new CIO Textile Workers Union, which is now very influential in the area. In the Black River Valley unionization came more slowly. The Gay Brothers did not welcome all the implications of union activity, but gave in to the inevitable. In a statesmanlike manner they endeavored to build a cooperative policy, and when they wrote their 75th Anniversary history in 1944, the union had a hand in the labor chapters.

Unionization ran up against a stone wall at Quechee, largely because of the policy of benevolent paternalism practiced by the Dewey's. The company village provides comfortable housing at extremely low rentals—which go uncollected if the mill shuts down. The company provides benefits equal to those granted by the unionized companies, including vacations with pay, health and accident in-

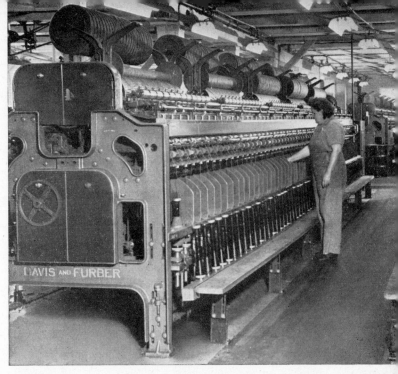

SPINNING MACHINE provides effective contrast to the old spinning wheels of the pioneers, used well down into the 19th Century.

surance, and free pension trust and retirement benefits— all at the expense of the employer. The record of continuous employment is high; nearly half have been there over five years, and some over twenty-five.

Industry is playing an increasingly large role in the over-all economy of the state, and the woolen industry, with over 6000 men and women, constitutes 15% of the total manufacturing employment. The industry today has entered a new era—unstable, competitive, with large advantages for the "big" enterprise. And the end of World War II, plus an increasing public preference for worsteds, brought serious distress to woolen mills in 1948.

MILLS of the A. G. Dewey Co. at Quechee Gorge occupy a site of spectacular beauty. Company homes of the workers are grouped nearby.

SHOWROOM and restaurant at Quechee won for the architects an Annual Award from the magazine "Progressive Architecture." Built for the A. G. Dewey Co., it features their finished woolens as well as those of other producers. It represents the increasing tendency of the Vermont mills to take their colorful product directly to the consumer.

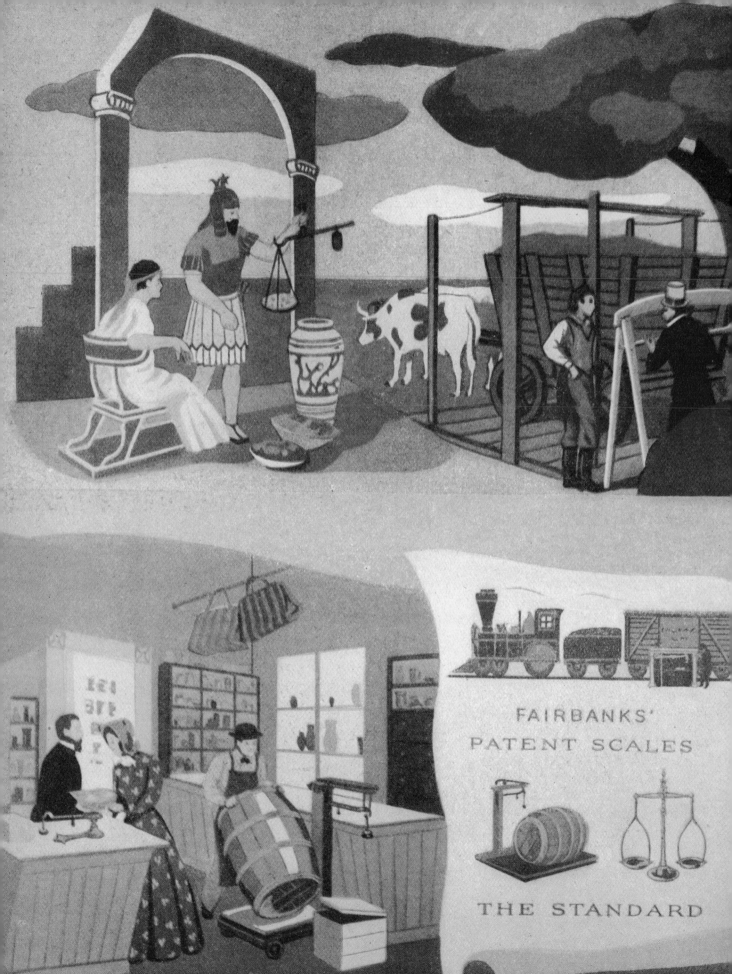

FOUNDER→
Thaddeus Fairbanks supplied the inventive genius for a great new Vermont industry in 1830 through his invention of the platform scale.

←BUILDER
Charles C. Morse, also from St. Johnsbury, built a midwestern industrial empire, and eventually absorbed the parent company.

BIRTH OF THE MODERN
SCALE

MANY a Vermont mechanic anticipated the modern miracles of the machine age in his own ingenious fashion. But none of them built permanent industries around their inventions—except one.

Young Thaddeus Fairbanks came to St. Johnsbury in 1815 with his father and two brothers, Erastus and Joseph. Immediately the youth began experimenting. His brother Erastus joined him in 1824, and the two went about manufacturing wagons, stoves and plows. Within two years Thaddeus had taken out a patent for a revolutionary new iron plow. Farmers were skeptical, claiming it would surely break with use. But the Fairbanks plow is substantially that in use today.

It was another ingenious device, however, that was to provide the basis for a major new industry. In 1829–30 Vermont was seized with one of her recurrent crazes—this time for hemp. The unwieldy apparatus used for weighing hemp was a challenge to Thaddeus's inventive genius. He quickly devised a method of transmitting the weight from a platform to a "steelyard"—familiar Roman weighing device (see drawing opposite page and right, and model, right). It then became possible to place great

loads on the platform, but to read the weights readily off the steelyard arm. The year 1830 thus saw the birth of what came to be known, logically enough, as the platform scale. It brought about a revolution in the fields of trade and merchandising, for goods of any bulk could now be sold by weight instead of by count or by guess.

←MODEL *of Fairbanks' original platform scale. Drawing below shows its use.*

←*From the original steelyard of the ancient Romans, (upper left) came the platform scale in 1830 (upper right). It quickly became the most common possession of every tradesman, and was put to use weighing loads of both great and small size.*

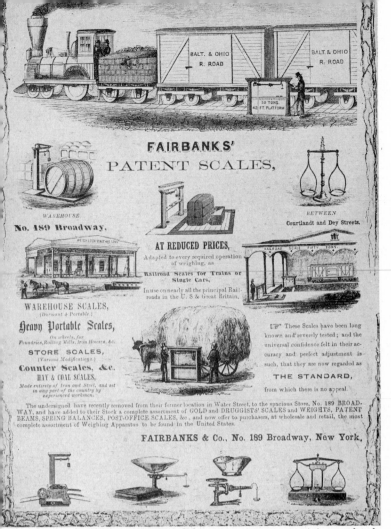

ADVERTISEMENT *for 1856 demonstrates varied uses of scale. E. & T. Fairbanks were among the earliest large scale advertisers.*

CENTENNIAL PAGEANT *presented at St. Johnsbury in 1930.*

Fairbanks soon adapted his principle to the weighing of colossal loads such as canal boats and railway trains, as well as to store use. Note on the poster (left) the various commercial uses to which the new product was quickly put.

In 1834 the three brothers founded the firm of E. & T. Fairbanks and Co. Erastus, an indomitable personality and thorough administrator, served as head of the firm. Joseph displayed marked talents in the field of finance and public contacts. Thaddeus, a retiring soul, gave his undivided attention to the mechanical department for over fifty years, until his death in 1886 at the age of ninety.

It was a typical family enterprise, and like most, was the principal industry of the town in which it developed. The Fairbanks family dominated the life of St. Johnsbury, though always in a benevolent fashion. St. Johnsbury Academy, St. Johnsbury Athenaeum (the first privately endowed free library in the state), the Music Hall, and the Museum of Natural Science were all gifts of the three brothers and their children. Unlike many a ruling dynasty, they seem to have been well liked in the community they ruled. When Erastus Fairbanks was elected Governor in 1852, he carried St. Johnsbury 416 to 184. His margin was even greater in 1860—456 to 73. His son Horace was drafted to run for governor in 1876, and he equaled his father's record, 826 to 176. In October, 1875, a curious New York *Evening Express* reporter inquired of a scale worker as to the secret behind Fairbanks' success. The man replied: "Best material, best machinery, best wages, best management, best credit, and best markets."

From 1842 through 1857—when a nationwide depression hit all industry—business doubled every three years. This was due partly to a superior product, partly to the vigorous sales activity of the brothers. Thaddeus made numerous trips into Maine, Erastus attacked the Boston and New York markets, and Joseph set forth down the

FAIRBANKS SCALES reached China as early as 1846. Here a Chinese mandarin weighs his precious jade. →

← *FAIRBANKS SCALE WORKS in the sixties.*

Mississippi River to Cuba, where he established a profitable West Indian trade. The platform scale was soon in world-wide use.

FAIRBANKS–MORSE

One of the company's most active sales agents was a St. Johnsbury boy, who like many another, went west to make his fortune. Charles H. Morse had worked for the Fairbanks as an apprentice, but afterward left for Chicago —where he shared lodgings with another anxious and enterprising young man named Marshall Field. After the Chicago fire of 1871, he established the firm of Fairbanks, Morse and Co. and subsequently studded the west with branch sales offices. He had already taken on many other products as sidelines, and as his business prospered he obtained control of the sources of such new but critical needs of an expanding West as windmills, pumps and engines. Eventually—in 1916—he acquired all the stock of the original parent company. Fairbanks Scale was then absorbed into a great new industrial empire of plants producing mammoth pumps and the new diesel engines as well as railroad locomotives and equipment.

THE HOWE SCALE

The original platform scale was balanced on knife edges. In 1856 Frank M. Strong of Vergennes patented a ball-bearing platform which the very next year took first premium at the Vermont State Fair in competition with the other older and more established scales. Manufacturing was begun in Brandon, where John Howe established the Howe Scale Company. But fire destroyed much of the plant in 1873, and four years later it was moved to Rutland. Here was built the state's second great scale company, which today employs nearly 800 people.

During World War II, Howe pioneered in the design and manufacture of scales for weighing aircraft. The largest of these was made to weigh the famous B-24 bomber and had a capacity of 250 tons. On it the bomber can be weighed by 30 men in 30 minutes, to within an accuracy of 1/40 of one percent.

Howe has also produced the longest track scale in the world; scales for balancing airplane propellor blades; aluminum scales so light that they can be carried in cargo planes for weighing cargo at ports where no scales are available; trailers for carrying hot ingot bars and the immense hot ladles used in the steel mills, besides many other adaptations of its regular line of scales and warehouse trucks. The latter developed out of trucks built for use in the plant, which were of such good design that they were put on the general market.

Together Howe and Fairbanks supply nearly three-quarters of the nation's scales, and have retained for Vermont for over a century leadership in the manufacture of this precision product.

MODERN PRODUCTION LINE at St. Johnsbury turns out a platform scale remarkably like Thaddeus Fairbanks' original one.

HOWE SCALE Company in Rutland is one of state's largest industrial enterprises, employing over eight hundred people.

HOWE AIRPLANE SCALES weigh a flight test model of the great Boeing Stratocruiser, emphasizing the capacity of modern scales.

Hubbard's "Revolving Hydraulic Engine" of 1828.

Yankee Tool Makers

LEMUEL HEDGE, *Pioneer Inventor*

THE first tool makers were those who hammered out, in crude forges, essential implements for frontier farming. Many of these shops developed into neighborhood industries, of which Matthew Lyon's mills at Fairhaven were a good example. By mid-19th century the iron industry had played a considerable role in the economic growth of the state, and already was on its way out.

Yet Yankee ingenuity and skill with tools began and kept alive a machine tool industry which has withstood, for over a century, competition from the mammoth plants of southern New England and the mid-West. And the men who built this industry and devised its tools provided the mechanics and engineers for great new machine tool plants all over the nation.

It all began in the little town of Windsor, already famous as the birthplace of the state of Vermont. Industries were tried at an early date; recall, for example, the Essex Merino Association experiment which failed in 1818. Yet the little village, isolated from sources of supply and available markets, soon drew to it several men of remarkable inventive genius. Several founded businesses to capitalize on their inventions, but unfortunately only a few displayed commercial talents equal to their mechanical ingenuity.

Many of these men were cabinet makers, and

174

From the painting by ALLEN SAALBURG   SPRINGFIELD, VT.   *Courtesy Fellows Gear Shaper Co.*

From the anvils of New England's village blacksmith shops, and from the corner workbenches of ancient sawmills, came pioneer inventors and mechanics with new ideas about machine making. Finding in the Windsor–Springfield region abundant water power, these natural mechanics applied ingenuity and enthusiasm to a series of machine building enterprises which led directly to the present machine tool industry in this section.

The range of inventive genius was wide in spread and logical in sequence: from ruling machines to firearms; from dividing engines to musical instruments; from steamboats to water pumps; and finally to the development of the rotary gear pump.

Here, in this quiet Vermont valley,—through the manufacture of interchangeable parts and precision tools like the Fellows Gear Shaper (right)—began the American system of mass production.

Against a background of America from the days of the water-powered mill to the modern industrial age, the artist has depicted stages in the development of the contemporary machine tool. In the home workshop was perfected the hydraulic pump, with parts made from an early metal turning lathe. With the assistance of local gunsmiths, large quantities of mass-produced firearms were turned out to arm the frontiersman, the 49'ers, and the Union Army. In the process, the were produced a wide variety of machines. Specialization followed the intro duction of the first automatic indexing turret and the high and flat turret lathe and finally the modern Fay automatic—all of which have been indispensable i the manufacture of the automobile, the airplane, and the streamliner.

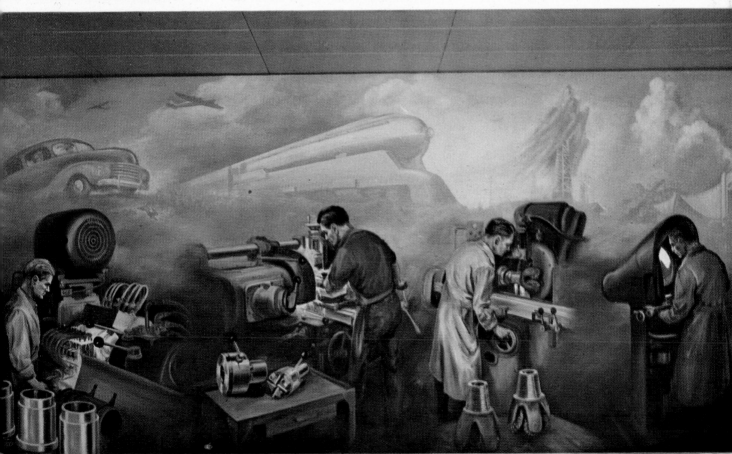

The STORY *of* MACHINE TOOLS

as told in a series of murals by BERNARD F. CHAPMAN
for the JONES AND LAMSON MACHINE CO.

These precision machines, product of Bryant (above) are typical of the output of this Vermont industrial center.

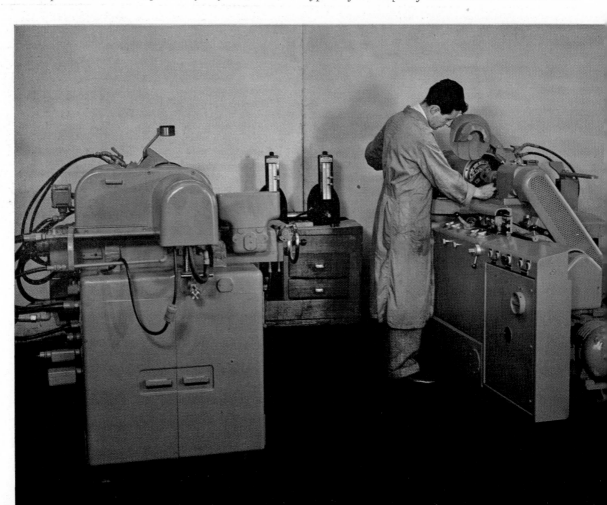

it is interesting to note the translation of one skill into another. One of the first was Lemuel Hedge, who began a remarkable career with a machine for ruling paper, and in a lifetime multiplied invention after invention, including such everyday items as the band saw and the carpenter's two-foot rule. Another was John M. Cooper of Guildhall, who patented a rotating pump in 1827. Defects caused the failure of his company, but the following year Asahel Hubbard perfected a workable pump (see page 174), with tremendous sales possibilities.

The citizens of Windsor, burned once in the collapse of Cooper's venture, backed away from investing new money. So Hubbard set out for Proctorsville, about 20 miles west, where he sold the idea to influential Jabez Proctor. Even before his son Redfield organized the powerful Vermont Marble Co., the Proctors had political influence, and Jabez obtained for Hubbard appointment as Warden of the State Prison—conveniently located in Windsor. He also got the state to install a stationary steam engine and machine shop. Then, utilizing prison labor for which they paid the state twenty five cents a day, they began production in 1830 as the "National Hydraulic Company." The Company, immediately successful, developed agencies all over the United States. But one sale, to the infant city of St. Louis, presented just one small difficulty—the pioneer town couldn't pay. Hubbard went to collect, picked up some cash, and settled the balance for a spirited white saddle horse, which he proudly rode back into the streets of Windsor.

Working in Hubbard's plant was an alert young gunsmith, Nicanor Kendall by name. "Cain" became enamored of the boss's daughter, whom he drove out one day for a bit of "sparking." As he withdrew his gun from beneath the robe to shoot a squirrel, he accidentally caught the exposed hammer, discharging the gun. The shot blasted his hand and whistled through the hair of his intended. Shocked and frightened at the narrow escape, Kendall devised an "under-hammer" rifle, which was soon added to the company's products. The first big order for the new gunshop came from the new-born Republic of Texas—which deeded 2000 acres of that state to the company in payment. Hubbard sold out to his son-in-law in 1839 and departed—along with hundreds of other Vermonters—for Iowa. One wonders if he rode his great white horse back west. . . .

ROBBINS AND LAWRENCE

The third of these founders of the Windsor machine

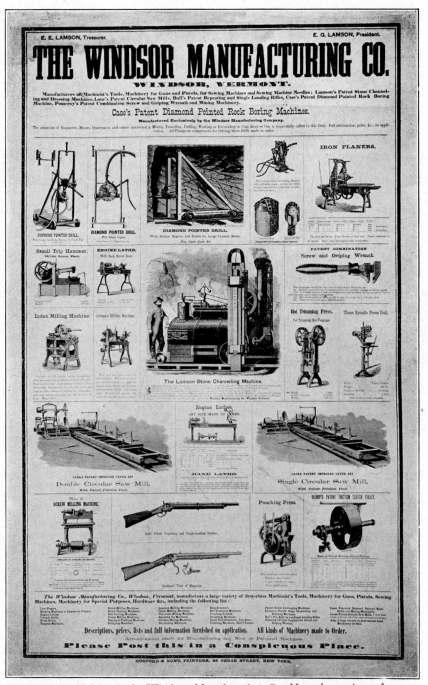

CATALOG of the Windsor Manufacturing Co. Note the variety of products, ranging from stone, metal and wood-working machines to guns.

tool industry was a Chester boy—Richard Smith Lawrence—who went to work for Kendall in 1838 and joined him as a partner five years later. Displaying uncommon salesmanship, he immediately obtained a contract to supply the government with rifles at the unbelievable price of $10.90 each. But something new had come out of the Windsor armory which made this possible—*interchangeable parts*. Pioneered by Eli Whitney and Lemuel Hedge, this system of building a product from uniform, standard parts received probably its first large scale industrial application in the shops of tiny Windsor. It has since become the most significant element in the growth and success of American manufactures. (Note the R&L shops, above, in 1849.)

Lawrence's high-powered business techniques left his partner somewhat abashed, and Kendall withdrew to join his father-in-law in Iowa. The new firm of Robbins and Lawrence[1] found a ready market for these cheap and excellent rifles among the forty-niners, and even the British sent missions to examine them. The company was given a contract for machinery for the new English armory, as well as for 25,000 rifles. But at last the little plant had gotten over its depth. Failing to fulfill its contract, it was taken over by the British in 1856. Its tribulations had only begun, though during the Civil War five thousand men were kept working night and day to arm the Union soldiers. In 1870, however, Ebenezer Lamson sold off the gun machinery and afterward, with Russell

Jones, re-equipped the plant as a cotton mill, with the machine tool plant as a supplement. But by 1888 the firm had tottered to the brink, and was purchased by a group of Springfield promoters, who moved it to that nearby center.

Dismayed, the Windsor mechanics banded together to establish the Windsor Machine Co., but the depression of 1893–96 nearly wrecked the infant enterprise. In keeping with a trend we have already noted in Vermont's recent industrial growth, the plant in 1915 passed into the hands of the National Acme Mfg. Co. of Cleveland, which immediately doubled its size, building in the midst of "colonial" Windsor what was then the largest workers' apartment house in New England. The firm's superintendent, Frank L. Cone, promptly resigned to begin the manufacture of a multiple-spindle automatic lathe of his own design, and at the time of his death just twenty years later, his company had grown to a working force of 400. During World War II employment soared to 2400, while output increased ten times.

JAMES HARTNESS

To manage their new version of an old company, the Springfield directors of Jones and Lamson promptly brought in a 27-year-old mechanic and designer. James Hartness saw great possibilities in the isolated Black River town, which, unlike Windsor, hadn't even a rail connection.[2] At the end of the first year, the directors

---

[1] A branch plant established in Hartford, Connecticut, is the progenitor of many of that city's mammoth tool companies.

[2] In 1896 an electric railway—the only one left in the state today—linked Springfield with the main Connecticut River line.

saw few signs of new life, and nearly let him go. But the youth was quietly planning a consolidation and rejuvenation of the sixty-year-old firm. He finally got the company to shed all its products except one—the turret lathe—and that in one size only. Hartness foresaw the growing trend toward specialization in industry, and insisted on the need of concentrating on a single item of manufacture. By 1898 he was President of Jones and Lamson.

Hartness's emphasis on specialization lies at the origin of several other tool plants which have grown up in Springfield. Young Edwin R. Fellows joined Hartness as a designer in this new Vermont venture, and then left the firm in 1896—accompanied by his friend's blessing—with blueprints for a new method of cutting and shaping gears. The Fellows Gear Shaper subsequently played a large role in the development of the new automotive industry.

Fellows was succeeded by W. J. Bryant, who in turn left the parent firm in 1909 to form the Bryant Chucking Grinder Co. His successor, Fred P. Lovejoy, developed a special cutting tool, and Hartness helped him found the Lovejoy Tool Co. A fourth plant, a foundry, was later established by two of the machine tool companies to supply necessary castings.

The leading name in Vermont's modern machine tool industry is another country boy who later married the boss's daughter, Helen Hartness. Ralph Flanders, starting work in 1911, rose to the position of General Manager of Jones & Lamson, and became president in 1933. A brilliant engineer, he displayed marked business and commercial talents as well, and was later made Chairman of the Federal Reserve Bank of Boston. While his plants increased production for wartime purposes sixfold, and employees increased to 3200, Flanders served constantly as consultant to various federal production, rationing and priority agencies. Despite an unsuccessful campaign in 1940, he was sent by Vermont to the Senate in 1946, where he immediately assumed a prominent role in national politics. His father-in-law, James Hartness, also had his fling in politics as Governor. His name is still something to conjure with in Springfield. A business autocrat in some respects, he was nevertheless god-father to several other enterprises which he might have dominated, had he wished. The various machine tool plants, however, are complementary to each other, rather than competitive, for each produces—and promotes—a special product. There is today, in fact, a considerable interchange of personnel and talent.

The machine tool business of late years has suffered from alternations of feast and famine. From depression doldrums in the thirties, production began to climb under the stimulus of re-armament orders from Russia, Japan and the western allies. After the United States joined the struggle late in 1941, the demand for the machines that make machines became tremendous. In 1943 the three principal Springfield companies did a business of 70 million dollars, and their labor force at its peak (along with Cone Automatic in Windsor) reached a combined total of well over ten thousand men and women. Workers commuted daily from distances as great as fifty miles, and hundreds of handy mechanics, tradesmen and farmers went to work in the plants. Here, in fact, mushroomed without plan the oft-discussed combination of farm and factory employment.

While it also holds true elsewhere in Vermont, the modern highly industrialized machine tool plants have underlined a significant element in the state's labor picture —the near absence of the hopelessly dependent worker. Multiple skills, individual home—and often farm—ownership, and the absence of overwhelming concentrations of mass production industry have all served to limit the usual inroads upon the economic independence and free choice of the worker. The predominantly rural character of life and labor in Vermont has modified many national trends toward concentration of industry and de-personalization of the productive process, but has not by any means left the state entirely outside the mainstream of American industrial development. Its leaders, however, have endeavored to retain the personal element in production as well as in industrial relations.

Inspecting a casting for a turret lathe.

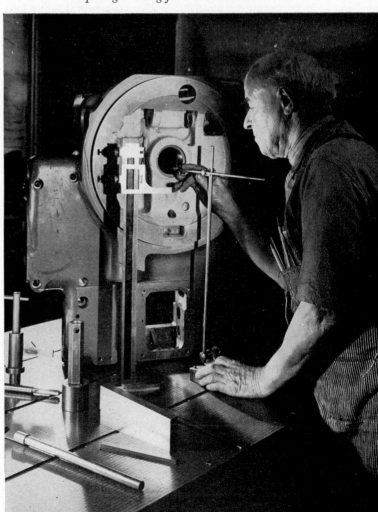

XIII

DECLINE AND REVIVAL OF AGRICULTURE

*How emigration and western competition wrecked Vermont's rural economy,
and how it was restored by cows and concentration on quality produce.*

THE ubiquitous Iron Horse gave great new stimulus to the growth of manufacturing in Vermont. But it very nearly wrote out a death warrant for a more significant part of the state's fundamentally rural economy—agriculture.[1]

True, the immediate effect of railroad building was to open new markets in southern New England to the Vermont farmer, and to reduce the burdensome cost of transportation. But this was, for some time, confined to the few farms along the iron rails. Extra cash income came from the sale of timber for ties and bridges—which disappeared when building ceased—and from the sale of fuel for the wood-burning locomotive, which later turned to coal.

At the same time the railroad opened up the markets of southern New England to Vermont, it did the same to the great expanding midwest. It was, in a sense, ironical that Vermont's own railways were built as a part of the grand plan to provide a commercial link between Boston and the West. For over these rails—as well as the even more important ones spanning New York and Pennsylvania—came a rising torrent of western produce. The hill country of northern New England could not compete with the level, fertile fields of the Ohio country—or even of central New York, for that matter. The Vermonters—and other Yankees—who had migrated westward now began to compete with their old neighbors, and even with their relatives, who had stayed behind.

Moreover, these same rails carried more and more Vermonters west, accelerating the drain of population out of the hill country. And those who went, as we have seen, were predominantly the youth needed to maintain the vitality of rural life in their native state. Western railroads consciously stimulated this emigration, advertising the attractions and fertility of the West in the newspapers and in broadsides, and the Vermont lines joined them in a short-sighted attempt to crack up passenger traffic.

Then, too, the very stimulus given industry proved an indirect set-back to agriculture. Instead of making the things they needed, both rural and urban families turned to commercial, ready-made products, now made widely available by improved transportation. This destroyed the market for village industries, which had provided local markets and supplementary employment for the farmer. Even more important, out of the concentration of industry rose the big cities.

And thus to the lure of the West was added the lure of the city—an attraction which was to become even more potent than western lands. As the great plains filled up, the tide of emigration turned toward the city. Between 1850 and 1900 Vermont-born residents of New York State decreased by half, while they doubled in the rest of New England. The ancient tide of immigration from east to west was reversed; the grandsons of the pioneers who came up the Connecticut River from Massachusetts and Connecticut, now descended it to the factories of Boston, Worcester, Springfield, Hartford and New Haven. Boys who once would have gone West now went to the city.

There were other special causes for this drain of population. Vermont's enthusiasm for the Union cause sent 34,000 of her best young men to the battlefields of the Civil War. Not one-half of these returned. The death toll was heavy, but most stayed away because they found the opportunities greater elsewhere, having once been brought into contact with the waxing currents of national growth.

And there were special things about which many Vermonters complained. Taxation, as always, was one; the burden of taxes, it was claimed, was disproportionately heavy on farm property as compared with other kinds of wealth. But this was part of the vicious circle; high tax rates were largely caused by the constantly decreasing amount of taxable property—in turn caused by emigration from the hill towns. And then the tax burden on those left merely encouraged them to leave also.

But, characteristically, the greatest amount of com-

---

[1] And yet it was the railroad in the 20th century which enabled the restoration of agricultural prosperity through quick delivery of perishable dairy products to nearby urban markets.

NO WORDS can illustrate the problem of Vermont agriculture as well as a map of the land classified according to its visible adaptability to commercial agriculture. Note the great band of green—land suitable only for forestry. →

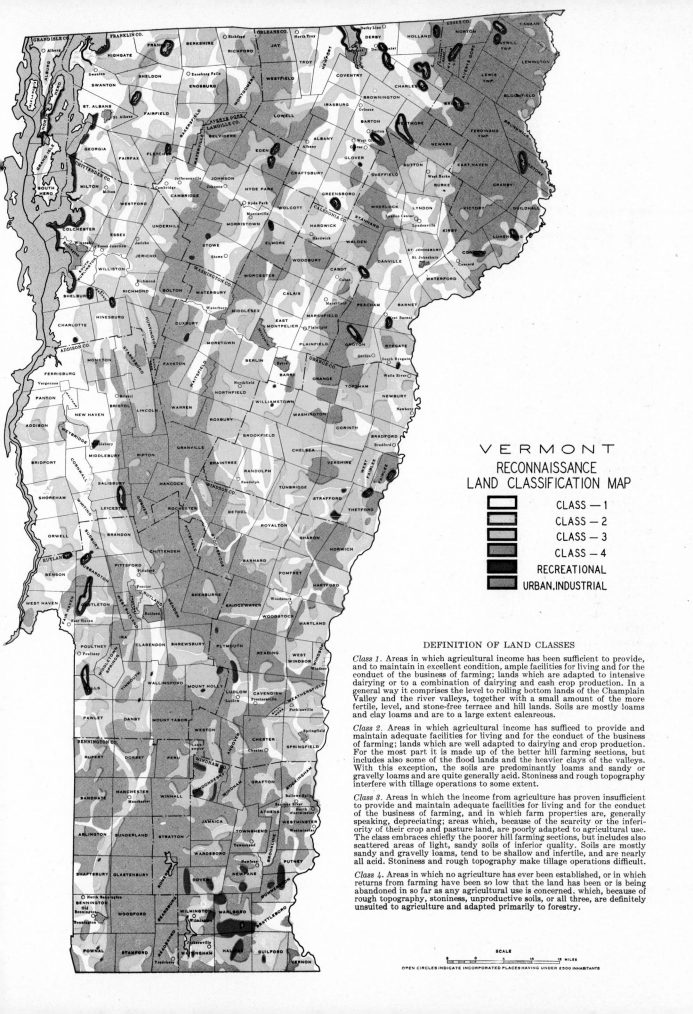

VERMONT
RECONNAISSANCE
LAND CLASSIFICATION MAP

- CLASS — 1
- CLASS — 2
- CLASS — 3
- CLASS — 4
- RECREATIONAL
- URBAN, INDUSTRIAL

DEFINITION OF LAND CLASSES

Class 1. Areas in which agricultural income has been sufficient to provide, and to maintain in excellent condition, ample facilities for living and for the conduct of the business of farming; lands which are adapted to intensive dairying or to a combination of dairying and cash crop production. In a general way it comprises the level to rolling bottom lands of the Champlain Valley and the river valleys, together with a small amount of the more fertile, level, and stone-free terrace and hill lands. Soils are mostly loams and clay loams and are to a large extent calcareous.

Class 2. Areas in which agricultural income has sufficed to provide and maintain adequate facilities for living and for the conduct of the business of farming; lands which are well adapted to dairying and crop production. For the most part it is made up of the better hill farming sections, but includes also some of the flood lands and the heavier clays of the valleys. With this exception, the soils are predominantly loams and sandy or gravelly loams and are quite generally acid. Stoniness and rough topography interfere with tillage operations to some extent.

Class 3. Areas in which the income from agriculture has proven insufficient to provide and maintain adequate facilities for living and for the conduct of the business of farming, and in which farm properties are, generally speaking, depreciating; areas which, because of the scarcity or the inferiority of their crop and pasture land, are poorly adapted to agricultural use. The class embraces chiefly the poorer hill farming sections, but includes also scattered areas of light, sandy soils of inferior quality. Soils are mostly sandy and gravelly loams, tend to be shallow and infertile, and are nearly all acid. Stoniness and rough topography make tillage operations difficult.

Class 4. Areas in which no agriculture has ever been established, or in which returns from farming have been so low that the land has been or is being abandoned in so far as any agricultural use is concerned; which, because of rough topography, stoniness, unproductive soils, or all three, are definitely unsuited to agriculture and adapted primarily to forestry.

SCALE

0   5   10   15 MILES

OPEN CIRCLES INDICATE INCORPORATED PLACES HAVING UNDER 2500 INHABITANTS

WESTERN RAILROADS sent in land agents, and advertised extensively in Vermont newspapers to promote migration to the West and thus increase their passenger revenues. With surprising short-sightedness, Vermont railroads joined the chorus, singing the praises of western lands. (Broadside, above, from Vermont Historical Society).

plaints were over the weather. Even natives resented the length of winter, and the resulting brief growing season. There were too few days for open grazing, too many when livestock needed warm cover and stored fodder. Too much of their energy was consumed in combatting the cold, or getting ready for it. Vermont burned off her forests, not merely to make potash, to keep her locomotives running, or to boil down sap, but also to keep warm. Cord wood was a family-produced, family-consumed agricultural product. Winter had social as well as economic drawbacks—a bleak isolation which weighed particularly on the farm wife. "The thing one resents about winter," wrote one, "is its inactivity, the perpetual same-ness of ice armored hills and snow blanketed woods. . . . There is no life but in the swing of the winds, the mad dance of eddies, the arrival of still more snow."

"Everyone talks about the weather," one Connecticut Yankee said, "but no one does anything about it." Many Vermonters did; they got out.

There was also in the grim attitude of the hill country farmer an element of puzzled frustration. Had he been deceived by this green land? In many cases he had. To avoid the marshy tangle of the valleys, the pioneer went to the hillside, with its deceptively fertile cover of rotted leaves. That transportation was difficult bothered little in a self-sufficient life. But the thin layer of mould disappeared with the trees and a few decades of cultivation, leaving angular fields, studded with rocks. And as the economy shifted away from self-sufficiency, the hill farmer found himself isolated from the main lines of valley transportation and the village industries which grew up there.

Even when the valleys had been drained and cleared there was all too little of the fertile river intervale land, and the late-comers were forced into the hill country between.

Thus it was the location of Vermont farms which produced the most fundamental cause of agricultural decline—the attempt to carry on farming in areas where poor land and lack of essential facilities made continuously profitable operation unlikely, if not impossible. Perhaps the soil had not permanently lost its fertility, but it had declined steadily in productive capacity. And the lay of the land was such that even large farms were broken up into small and scattered fields, suited to the scythe but not to the new agricultural machinery. And in the midst of a swelling tide of doleful predictions as to the future of New England agriculture, many recognized that abandonment of back country farms was an inevitable and perhaps wholesome readjustment of an uneconomic situation. Furthermore, they pointed out that despite the clamor of pessimists, the condition of the hill farms was not representative of the entire situation of agriculture in the state, which on lands that warranted it, *was* shifting gears and altering its outlook and production to meet the challenge of urban demand and western competition.

EFFECTS OF ABANDONMENT

The effects of western competition and emigration was, of course, reflected in abandoned farms, a decrease in the amount of improved land, a sharp drop in farm values, a decline in agricultural production, and a leveling off of population growth.

The impact of western competition was greatest in the staple crops—particularly wheat. In the first half of our second century, 1849–1899, production of wheat declined 92% (see chart). Today it is a negligible element in the state's agricultural economy. Corn took a more modest

(Continued on page 189)

"ONE-MAN FARM," owned and run by Kenneth Walker of Weston, (above) is about 200 acres, including the sugar bush and wood lot. He keeps about 50 head of stock, and milks 14 cows. Fixing fence is only one of the endless tasks of the farmer, whose day begins with chores at 5:00 A. M. and ends with chores at 7:00 P. M.

TRACTOR is necessary equipment for even a one-man farm. Here Walker has hitched it onto his manure spreader. White stuff on top of the manure is lime. Walker owns and tills this meadow land, but buildings in background are part of another farm. Mountain in the background is part of Mount Terrible, dividing Weston from Andover.

VERMONT FARMS run the gamut from the "one-man" variety to highly mechanized units. Here, in pictures, are examples of each.

MODERN "MECHANIZED" FARM is run by John Pratt (*center, below*) of North Clarendon, with the aid of his sons Richard (*left*) and John Junior (*right*). His herd has varied between thirty and sixty milkers, but the total cattle runs to twice that figure. Portrait was at 4:15 P. M.—milking time.

AUTOMATIC POTATO PLANTER is typical of the highly mechanized equipment Pratt needs to farm his 400 acres. It digs the trench, puts in the potatoes and fertilizer, covers them, and goes on, allowing 3 men to plant an acre in 1 ½ hours. It takes as much capital as for a small factory to set up a large farm.

MILKING MACHINE of this type is hung from cows' back with strap, and does not rest on floor. Walker has two.

CHILDREN raise their own calves, instead of getting a cash allowance.

MACHINE has to be supplemented by hand stripping.

FOOD for the animals is the ever-present necessity. Here Beverly Walker helps her father prepare hot mash for the pigs. Boiling water is poured over the grain and stirred.

FARM BREAKFAST is always a hearty one, yet no one takes on excess weight. Agricultural labor is hard, and requires a larger proportion of energy foods like bread and potatoes than city life. The Walker children get lots of milk, yet on many small farms where it is the only cash crop it is all too often absent from the table.

COWS on the main highways are a familiar sight (*below*). Many pastures, like Walker's, are separated from the barns.

Walker is married and the father of four fine youngsters, the oldest of which is 8. The two oldest go to the village school about half a mile away. Mrs. Walker, formerly a first rate school teacher in one of the state's outstanding schools, if also followed through her day in the house, would keep to a busy schedule as active as that of her husband.

Walker's father was a farmer before him and his mother lives with him on the home place. His brother is a school teacher in the south, and his sister works in a neighboring city. Their farm is on the edge of a village, so they have advantages of both farm and village life. They attend the Methodist Church, and Walker is a member of the town's Planning Board and a Justice of the Peace.

The Pratt farm in North Clarendon is largely typical of the larger Vermont farms. John Pratt bought this place when he moved from Shrewsbury before the first World War. In comparison to Walker's, which lies in the hills at an elevation of 1400 feet to 2000 feet, Pratt's establishment is in a lush valley along Otter Creek. Pratt has ploughed back everything he has ever made on the farm, which is his way of saying he has not taken the profits out and invested them in stocks and bonds. As a result he owns today a piece of fine looking property which would probably fetch upwards of $50,000—several times what he paid for it.

The hay and cow barn on the Pratt place, as the illustration (right) graphically demonstrates, is a huge structure holding over 200 tons of hay and capable of tying up 60 head of cattle. Everything on this farm is highly mechanized. In use are 3 tractors, 4 wagons and trailers, 2 ploughs, 2 harrows, 1 manure spreader, 1 corn planter, 1 potato planter, 1 potato grader, 2 cultivators, 2 mowing machines, 1 rake, 1 corn harvester, 1 insilage cutter, . . . just to give a brief idea of the major field equipment needed on a farm of this type. There will soon be one of the new motorized stable cleaning machines which will automatically clean behind the cows and into the spreader outdoors where it will be spread over the land daily the year around. No more manure piles. This approaches the point where almost everything is done by machine.

Top. John Pratt (*left*) plows as his brother Richard harrows. Photo (*center*) shows only part of the huge haymow necessary to store hay for winter's operation. View below shows the herd at the end of milking as John Pratt empties the milking machine.

Moriarity

NEW-MOWN HAY lies in meadow before gathering. After experiments with wheat and other bulk crops, Vermont farmers fell back on the natural grass crop, best suited to Vermont's terrain and soil. Hay is the mainstay of the dairy industry, now the source of the state's principal agricultural product—fluid milk.

MECHANIZATION has invaded the process of gathering hay. For a century and a half the Vermont farmer loaded his wagons by means of a pitchfork and a strong right arm (below). Today most of the medium and large size farms have a tractor mower to cut the grass, a tractor-drawn rake to draw it into wind-rows, and a buck rake to scoop it up and carry it directly to the barn. A motor driven hay fork lifts it to the hay-mow.

Carleton

drop of 30%. With the decline in staples, and the complete abandonment of many farms, the percentage of improved land slipped from 63% to 45%.[2] Land values tumbled—in the face of a national trend the other way. In just twenty years, from 1870 to 1890, farm property dropped from a total worth of nearly 135 million dollars to little more than 100 million. Land could be bought for as little as three dollars an acre, including the buildings. Very few acres brought more than ten.

The drain of population continued until many Vermonters complained that the only place growing was the cemetery. In this same half-century, less than two-thirds of those born in Vermont stayed there, and in each decade two out of five natives left. The tide of population decline in Vermont towns moved steadily north, even as the northern parts began their first growth. In the years 1870–80, three fifths of the towns were losing population; in the following decade it was four fifths. As a result, the growth in the North—and in urban areas—was cancelled out by decline in the South. In face of a tremendous national increase, Vermont's population remained about the same.

One other element in the population picture was significant. In the last two decades of the 19th century, the numbers employed in agriculture dropped 10%. One should not assume from this that Vermont was becoming urbanized. In contrast to New England's total, over one half "urban,"[3] Vermont laid claim to only 7% in 1890. Yet the trend had begun. We have already noted the destructive effect of industrial concentration and rapid transportation on local industry. Some of its former employees migrated to the factories of southern New England, but others merely moved into the larger towns, which could not yet be classified as urban.

No less significant than the economic results of emigration and abandonment were the social effects. It was a selective migration, in that it drained off the more vigorous elements—the youth. Those over 50 years of age increased from 14% to 21% in the years 1850–1900. With the loss of the young'uns, it was increasingly difficult for the old folks to carry on. Those left behind were less fitted and less inclined to make the radical readjustments necessary to keep the state's economy healthy. And the loss of vitality combined with a cessation of growth had a numbing effect. The buoyancy which accompanies growth disappeared, and Vermonters began to assume the characteristics and conservative temper of a static society. The spirited radicalism, the readiness to experiment so typical of Vermont's first century, evaporated in an aura of despondency. In rural areas a shiftless neglect of land and buildings, of roads and schools, became contagious.

There resulted, moreover, an actual degeneracy of the

vigorous old New England stock. The most energetic and enterprising elements left, and those who remained in increasing back country isolation deteriorated with the countryside, from in-breeding. Feeble-mindedness, immorality and excessive illegitimacy were the results. Vermont was presented with not only the appearance but the population for a "Tobacco Road" like that of the South. And the burden upon public welfare and private charity, upon mental hospitals, and correctional institutions in the next generation was heavy.

Of course, this demoralization was neither general nor widespread. The majority faced up to the critical problems confronting them, often with reluctance and a stubborn disregard of facts, but finally with typical Yankee determination. And there were influences working in their favor.

RURAL REHABILITATION

Survival under highly competitive and rapidly shifting conditions required both the efficiency and flexibility of a good business man. But the Yankee farmer, though a sharp trader, was not an "entrepreneur." His experience was in production alone, and it was only a short time that he'd had to deal with any problem of marketing at all. Normally industrious, he was not quick on his feet, and change regularly caught him off balance. The development of new aptitudes and ideas suitable to the changing scene required an extensive amount of both agricultural and commercial education—which he often resisted stubbornly. He had an inbred scorn for "book farming," until the success of those who practiced it became self-evident.

There were an increasing number of agencies ready and willing to provide the farmer with information and assistance. The almost spontaneous growth of county agricultural societies in the fifties was the first move in the direction of cooperative activity. These years saw the hey-day of the old country fair, sponsored by these societies. Later came local groups—"Farmers' Clubs"—a more informal sort of neighborhood gathering for the exchange of information. But even more widespread in influence were the agricultural periodicals, of which *The New England Farmer* was the best known. The state even had, for a brief moment after 1877, its own *Vermont Agriculturalist*. The first movement toward official state aid came with the establishment of the Board of Agriculture in 1871, "for the improvement of the general interests of husbandry and the promotion of agricultural education throughout the state." Its initial functions were few beyond the publishing of its "report"—a compendium of useful but not widely read information. Its irregular efforts were strengthened in 1908 by appointment of a Commissioner of Agriculture, who soon acquired regulatory functions of licensing, registration, quarantine, etc. In 1910–11 the department ran "Better Farming Specials"—exhibit trains—all over the state, to

---

2 There was some alteration of the census definition of improved land during the period 1850–1900.

3 In cities of 2,500 or more.

an estimated audience of more than twelve thousand. Under a progressive and efficient Commissioner, Elbert S. Brigham, from 1912 to 1924 the department gained stability and direction, and by 1917 all state agricultural activity was consolidated under his jurisdiction. This state agency is today a vital element both in providing agricultural information and in enforcing agricultural controls.

Oddly enough, it was federal action—urged and sponsored by Vermont's distinguished Senator Justin Morrill—which ultimately provided the beginnings of an effective educational program, under state guidance. The Morrill Act in 1862 set aside a portion of the public lands on behalf of agricultural colleges in each state. Vermont took early advantage of the opportunity, establishing in 1865 the Vermont Agricultural College, in conjunction with the state university at Burlington. But no agricultural courses were given for nearly a quarter century thereafter.

Being on a college level, they reached few who really needed agricultural education. The State Superintendent of Education observed wryly that the only way a boy could get training was commit a crime, whereupon he would be committed to the Industrial School at Vergennes, where secondary school agriculture was taught. In 1910, however, the legislature converted the Randolph Normal School into a State School of Agriculture.

Particularly significant were the federal grants begun in 1888 to assist in maintenance of the state Agricultural Experiment Station established at the college two years earlier. But most effective in terms of actually reaching the dirt farmer was the Farm Extension Service, also begun with federal cooperation. The agricultural college reached a minority of well-to-do farmers' sons, many of whom never returned to the farm. The valuable work of the Experiment Station was seldom converted into practical counsel for the individual. But the Extension Service actually managed to translate learning from library and laboratory into concrete practical advice, personally slanted by its agents. The first American units were established in New York and Vermont, in 1911, with three agents for Bennington, Windsor and Caledonia counties. It was a year'round, realistic service of personal consultation and neighborhood meeting. Its effectiveness was demonstrated in the twenties by the Windsor County agent, whose campaign to combat soil acidity resulted in a seven-fold increase in the use of lime within five years.

The County Extension Agents were soon followed by the Home Demonstration Agent and the County Club Worker offering similar ideas and training for, respectively, housewives and children. For the latter there were organized the now famous 4-H Clubs, each with a definite project. Begun in 1914, the clubs had multiplied to 450 within fifteen years.

The work of the County Agents has been closely linked with the activities of an unofficial but highly influential organization—the Vermont Farm Bureau. It was first organized to give local assistance to the County Agent, but its activities have widened into many fields of agricultural education and politics. Officially non-partisan, the Vermont Farm Bureau, tied in with its national organization, has played a vital and influential role in forwarding the interests of the farmers in both state and federal politics. Despite opposition from nearly every newspaper in the state, Farm Bureau influence over the vast rural vote is credited with electing George D. Aiken first to the governorship and then to the U. S. Senate—the latter over the opposition of industrialist Ralph Flanders."[4] It has also played a significant role in the strengthening of the liberal wing of the state's Republican party.

Another—and older—organization is the State Grange. After establishment of the first unit at St. Johnsbury in 1871, growth was rapid. But after 1910 membership leveled out.[5] Its original strength was in the Mid-West, where it entered into an active battle against monopoly railroad and industrial interests. Reflective of this early concern for economic action was the Vermont Grange's attempt at cooperative buying. But there were too many puzzling commercial problems for the inexperienced farmers—who, with typical independence, failed to trade with the Grange whenever better buys were available elsewhere. The large farm supply outlets under-cut just long enough to ruin the experiment, and then raised their prices again. Discouraged, and perhaps a bit wiser, the Grange shifted to social and educational activity, which provided an important social outlet for the isolated farmer before the radio, the automobile, the telephone, and the movie.

NEW INVENTIONS—NEW CONTACTS

Although the extension—for a while—of branch railroad lines into the interior helped some, it was not until the advent of 20th Century mechanical wonders of transportation and communication that most Vermont farmers were brought into contact with the outside world. As much as the formal educational efforts of official agencies and volunteer organizations, these inventions brought about a revolution in, and to some extent a rehabilitation of rural life and labor.

After the turn of the century—and with the beginning of road improvement—Rural Free Delivery service was extended much more widely, bringing news and market quotations. These same years saw the invasion of the

---

4 Flanders later joined Aiken in 1946, when Senator Warren Austin was promoted to the position of U. S. Representative to the United Nations.
5 The Grange is much stronger in the other northern New England States. In 1930 Maine boasted 55,000 members and New Hampshire 28,900, against Vermont's 14,300.

L. B. Puffer

Donald Whitney

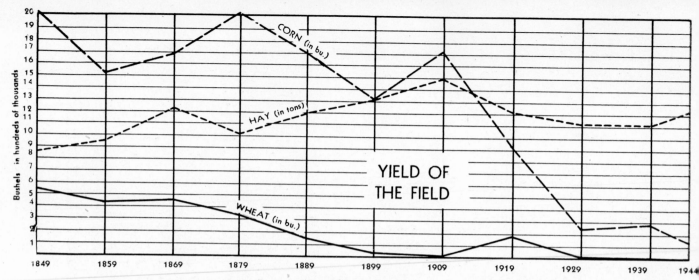

YIELD OF
THE FIELD

rural areas by Alexander Graham Bell's new and startling telephone, which had been in use in the villages as early as the seventies. By 1930 61% of Vermont farms had phones—about the New England average but way above the national figure of 34%. The "party line" became one of the institutions of rural life; it has been aptly observed that farm families learned how to "tune in" before radio.

The new "wireless" was the third great change in communication which broke open the pall of loneliness that enveloped back country life. It brought entertainment and news, and more than that, valuable weather reports. The first broadcasting station was set up in 1920; by 1949 there were seven stations. Receiving sets multiplied as the price came down. Some were battery sets, but most were dependent upon the new "high line."

Electricity promised the greatest revolution of all for the farm. It brought not only more reliable illumination, but power—power to run appliances which lighten the load of both household and barnyard chores. The milking machine and the milk cooler were supplemented by the electric refrigerator, freezer, vacuum cleaner, iron and a score of other small kitchen appliances. Yet these were all dependent on the "high line," which stretched with discouraging slowness into the rural areas. The commercial companies found profits higher in the more densely settled areas, and the construction of lines to isolated single farms was a costly proposition which the individual countryman could not finance. Eleven percent of farm families had current in 1920; 30% in 1930; 93% in 1948. After 1930 cooperatives built a grid of lines in the rural areas, and the private utilities hastened to follow suit.

The greatest revolution in American life was brought about by the new "horseless carriage." At first a rich man's toy, it saw little service among rugged and rural Green Mountains. Vermont consistently lagged behind the rest of the United States; in 1920 a quarter of the farmers had an auto, as compared with nearly a third nationally and better than a half in states like Illinois and Wisconsin. But Henry Ford's tough, economical Model T was more adaptable to rutted, recalcitrant country roads, and was within reach of the farmer's purse. Within ten years nearly two-thirds of the farmers had acquired a car. Even those who did not buy a vehicle of their own profited by the revolution in transportation. Mails traveled faster, milk was picked up by regular trucks, and busses provided passenger transportation. The automobile broke the last bonds which chained the farmer to rural isolation; it gave him a freedom and a flexibility previously unknown, both in social and commercial contacts. It brought the city and the country closer together,

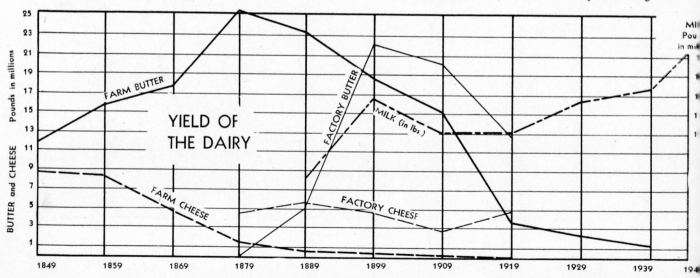

YIELD OF
THE DAIRY

opening the urban markets to the farmer's potatoes, maple sugar, fruits and vegetables, the retail stores to his wife, and the city high schools to his sons and daughters. The "hick from the sticks" and the "city slicker" mixed on the sidewalks of the city and on the roads of the state, and it became increasingly difficult to tell them apart. The automobile was a healthy and cosmopolitan educator.

The effect of these new inventions was to lessen loneliness, stir lethargy and quicken rural life. At the same time new attitudes and new people were brought to the countryside by a number of new trends.

Attempts to restore to the hill country its agricultural population began early. The first Boards of Agriculture initiated publicity campaigns to that end, and were soon issuing lists of "Desirable Farms." There were special attempts to encourage European—mostly Swedish—immigration, with the thought that these people, accustomed to the restricted over-worked farms of the old country, might be less demanding than the optimistic, expansive Americans. At the same time, fear was expressed by some over the influx of French Canadians, who, they smugly contended, might depress the standard of rural life in Vermont! But the best the European campaign produced was 27 families, and the Canadians mostly passed on to the industries of southern New England—though a considerable number gathered in the factories of Burlington and Winooski, and along Lake Champlain.[6]

Likewise, a concerted "back-to-the-land" movement just after the turn of the century brought meager results. Emphasizing the vices of city life as portrayed by the "muck-raking" writers of that time, many of these proponents of the virtues of rural living had high hopes of re-populating the abandoned farms with the surplus industrial population of the teeming cities. But most of these workers were in cities by virtue of their own choice, and there was little evidence that hill farms could provide a better living for inexperienced newcomers than it had for hard-headed Yankee farmers. Furthermore, the fear that any reduction of the rural population would constitute a fundamental dislocation of American economic life overlooked the fact that the food needs of the nation could now be supplied by vastly fewer hands.

The repopulation of the hill regions began in the 20th Century, mostly as a result of the great development of the state for summer recreation and vacations—which we will examine more closely in a later chapter. The hill farms usually provided exactly the isolation, wide sweep of view and rolling countryside which was wanted by the prospective summer resident. While the new influx by no means offset the continuous migration of youth to urban centers, it did accomplish the re-occupation of abandoned farm units and their more suitable re-use.

6 In 1920 only 10% of the farm population was foreign born, with another 18% of foreign or mixed parentage.

Much more significant than any of these ameliorating influences of an educational or promotional character, was the fundamental economic re-adjustment made by the farmers themselves. As a result of competition from cheap western wool—and perhaps also because of the ravages of dogs—the sheep industry slipped into a steep and steady decline. By 1900 there were less than 300,000 sheep in Vermont, about one-fifth of the number in the peak year of 1840. Unable any longer to compete in the field of staple grains or livestock, the puzzled and distraught Yankee groped for a solution. In his dilemma he turned again, as had his pioneer ancestors, to the basic natural resources—the green grass and the towering forests. Let's see first what he did with the grass.

Grass makes hay, and hay—like the staple grains—is a bulky crop of low value, not easily transported. So the farmer converted his grass into saleable merchandise by feeding it to cows, who converted it into milk. But milk was too perishable, so it was in turn converted into butter and cheese. The latter reached a production peak of nearly nine million pounds as early as 1849. The first cheese factory was set up in Wells in 1854, but it was not until 1879 that factory production made serious inroads on farm output. By this time more and more milk was being converted into butter, and combined farm and factory cheese began a steady decline. From the churns of Vermont housewives came a waxing stream of golden five pound crocks of butter, totalling over 25 million in 1879. Just as with cheese, however, creameries began to account for an increasingly larger share of total output; by 1899 factory production outstripped the farm. But the sum of the two increased steadily, until large fluid milk shipments began at the turn of the century.

An examination of production figures for the period 1849-1899 shows how fast dairying became the principal occupation of Vermont farmers. In 1894 the Board of Agriculture could report it as the state's leading industry. And the preceding Census (1890) had already shown Vermont to be the only eastern state to produce over 200 gallons of milk for each inhabitant. In all the United States she was surpassed only by Iowa. As a result of this concentration on cows, more than half of Vermont's farms were dependent on them for their principal support—as against 22% specializing in livestock and only 7% in grains.

There were several factors which made this change over from wool to milk possible. Most important was the rising demand for dairy products in the great and growing cities of New York and New England. Other things helped; dairying made it possible to use the entire family to better advantage, although it was a much more confining and painstaking operation than sheep-raising. In fact, Vermonters changed over with great regret; for years there were many debates—at first heated and then increasingly wistful—over the relative merits of the two.

Most helpful to the farmer when he finally made up his mind was the rise of "associated" dairying. Beginning with the first cheese factories, creameries multiplied, and farmers sent more and more of their milk in for factory processing—as we have seen. In the '90's, St. Albans, center of the rich Franklin County dairy region, boasted the largest butter creamery in the world, producing over two million pounds a year. It was a much more reliable market for milk than selling one's own butter and cheese.

The farmer, assisted by the rising flood of agricultural advice we have already examined, began to develop more efficient means of production, storing hay in silos and purchasing western grain to make year 'round dairying feasible. Breeds of milk cows were improved, as farmers gave up the idea of trying to raise a combined milk and meat animal. New equipment of great importance was introduced, such as the centrifugal separator and the Babcock butterfat tester.

FLUID MILK

The farmers' problems were not over when he finally accomplished his conversion to dairying. Soon the same old bogey of western competition again raised its head; the great dairy farms and creameries of Wisconsin and Minnesota began pouring a flood of butter and cheese over the improved and speedier trains of the twentieth century. This competition—plus the continued abandonment of farms—caused a decline in milk production in the early decades of the new century. But by 1929 production had been almost restored to its 1899 peak of more than 140 million gallons—a figure more than twice Maine's output, and nearly four times New Hampshire's.

The principal factor which made possible this revival was the great and increasing demand for fluid milk in the urban areas to the south. There was also a tendency to convert pasture and hay lands near the cities to the production of truck crops—fruits and vegetables—as land values rose. This meant that big city milk dealers had to go constantly further afield to supply the growing demand. The area upon which the Boston dealers drew was known as the Boston "milk shed." This extended its boundaries rapidly, until by the first decade of the new century it began to take in southern Vermont. But since northwestern Vermont was the ideal dairying region, it was not long before this area was dispatching as much or more milk to Boston as the southern parts of the state—almost half again as close. As early as 1920 Vermont was supplying a half of Boston's needs,[7] and had a wedge into the New York City market.

This extension into more distant regions was made possible by the development, first, of insulated railroad tank cars, and later, of tank trucks, which were able to transport this highly perishable commodity 300 miles or more and still keep it quite fresh. Furthermore, as the big city milk dealers got bigger—and fewer in numbers—they were better able to extend their sources of supply.

The great increase in consumption of milk was itself due in part to its increased availability, but even more to its improved quality. Vigorous efforts were made by leading dairymen to eradicate bovine tuberculosis. As city health authorities became more particular, a sanitary inspection service was begun. In 1912 the Creamery Inspection Act provided for a semi-annual examination by state inspectors. Vermont was most active, perhaps because she was the most dependent upon her dairy herds. By 1920 she had more people than any other state engaged in dairying, and led the nation in the value per capita of her dairy products.[8]

This meant that the problems of production, shipping, and marketing in this new agriculture were of particularly critical importance to Vermont farmers.

The problems of production were primarily those of ironing out seasonal variations in output. This meant more emphasis on winter dairying and thus, as we have seen, greater dependence on western grain—which required a cash outlay. After the perfection of the dairy milk train, shipping problems revolved mostly around the difficulty of getting the milk to the creamery. Individual hauling was a time-consuming and costly operation. Improved roads and new tank trucks made it possible for the creameries to set up regular milk collection routes—which in turn left the farmer at the mercy of the creamery.

Indeed, it was the farmers' increasing dependence on the great milk distributing agencies which brought them their most sizeable problem. It seemed to the average dairyman that he received all too small a portion of the amount collected from the Boston housewife. But how could he obtain a larger share? He had no chance of entering into direct competition with the companies himself—no way of taking his product direct to the consumer. His only remaining weapons were cooperatives and the "boycott."

In the long and bitter "Boston Milk War" of 1910 the Yankee farmers used the boycott with some degree of success. Organizing themselves as the Boston Cooperative Milk Producers Company, they managed to withhold three-quarters of the milk normally supplied. The Boston dealers turned to New York State, but the milk from these irregular sources was, according to the *New England Homestead*, "old enough to vote before it leaves New

---

[7] At the same time Vermont supplied nearly two-thirds of New England's butter and four-fifths of her cheese.

[8] $77.20 per capita, as compared with Wisconsin's $68.00, Minnesota's $32.00, and Maine and New Hampshire's $23.00 each. By 1930 3/5 of Vermont's farms were dependent on their cows for 40% or more of their income. Milk checks provided the necessary cash for taxes, insurance, interest, cars, trucks and other mechanical equipment, plus the normal commercial purchases.

York City." In a revival of the techniques of their Green Mountain Boy forefathers, farmers spouted fearful threats against non-cooperating neighbors. Before five weeks had passed, the dealers knuckled under and granted the dairymen's demands. In this instance, it was maintenance of a uniform, year 'round price. Their triumph was short-lived; the next year the BCMP ran afoul of the anti-trust laws, and quickly fell to pieces. The hard-won benefits were soon lost, and prices began again to fluctuate widely.

The next step was the organization of the New England Milk Producers Association in 1913. Each member tossed ½ of 1% of his total milk checks into a common pot to finance the work of the Association. But it was not a marketing organization, only a "collective bargaining" agent for the farmers in their negotiations with the dealers. By 1920 it had 20,000 members, and controlled about four-fifths of New England's milk. Obviously it was the dominant influence in the Green Mountain dairyland. But it too succumbed to a growing disorganization of the market, largely brought about by the addition of large numbers of new, small producers willing to undercut.

"New England Dairies"—a super cooperative of coops —was the next expedient, but had little more success. It was thus with some relief that the usually independent, Republican Vermonters turned to the AAA codes set up under Franklin Roosevelt's New Deal in 1933, in order to stabilize production and markets.

SPECIALIZATION

Obviously our Vermont farmer has been making a slow, often painful, but quite definite shift from *extensive* agriculture to *intensive*. He was discovering that he could profit more by using a little land thoroughly than by spreading his efforts thinly over a greater acreage. He was, in effect, like his industrial neighbors, being pulled toward the specialization which seems so characteristic of our machine age. And he wisely decided to utilize any geographical advantages he might have.

As we have seen, he turned principally—though not entirely—to dairying. There were other perishable products, like eggs, where the Vermonter had a definite advantage of proximity to the urban markets and fast rail and truck transportation. Production of eggs more than doubled in the fifty years before 1930. Some attempts were made to revive cattle raising, but the cost of winter grain was just too much. Some sheep were brought back to the hill farms, but profits were too small compared with the income from dairying. There was an increasing amount of truck gardening, especially for Vermont's own growing cities, and potatoes soon became an important crop. But apart from dairying, forest products was the principal area in which new prosperity was found. And so, from grass, we turn to trees.

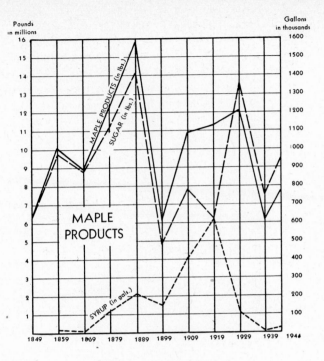

FOREST PRODUCTS

Men, women, maple sugar and horses;
The first are strong, the latter fleet;
The second and third exceedingly sweet,
And all are uncommonly hard to beat!

Thus the Vermont poet, John G. Saxe, characterized the four chief contributions of his state to the nation. Surely of them all, maple sugar has accumulated the most fame—and folklore.

It is true that Vermont leads the nation in maple production; yet it is actually less than 3% of the value of the state's total agricultural produce. On the other hand, because of its national fame and consequent publicity value, it has a value to the state all out of proportion to its contribution to agricultural income. The maple industry has seemed unusually important because of the romance which surrounds it in the average American's mind. But it has traditionally been of special importance to the Vermont farmer. Sugaring is undertaken at the time of year when little else can be done. It brings in a tidy sum of cash—a matter of some 2 million dollars annually— which has long been called "tax money," for it comes just in time to meet the demands of annual taxes. Actually, if one were to count in interest and depreciation on equipment—like spouts, pails, evaporators, etc.—as well as the labor, he would quickly discover that the farmer "theoretically" loses money on each gallon. But the theory is ignored in favor of the tangible cash. Still, there are a multitude of problems involved in the operation of a successful sugar orchard.

Colonel Fairfax Ayres

BY NORMAN ROCKWELL

When the steam begins to rise each Spring from hundreds of sugar houses all over Vermont, there's sap a'boiling inside.

Sap gathered by oxen and sledge or by pipe lines, boiled down to syrup and spread on snow, makes a familiar delicacy.

Sap, like milk, is a warm-hearted host to bacteria and sap can not be left around the sugar house until the farmer gets good and ready to boil it down. Neither can it be left in buckets on the trees. A good tree will give up about 10 gallons of sap a season (and contrary to the city fellow who feared so, it doesn't hurt trees to take out some sap), and your sugar bush, as we call a defined group of maple trees, is scattered over hill and dale. Getting around fast, with a sled and team to draw the gathering tank, wallowing through deep snow to take down and empty hundreds of buckets of sap into the tank, hauling the tank to the sugar house, cutting cords and cords of wood before-hand to keep a brisk fire going under the evaporator pan all night, proves that sugaring is more than a process . . . it is fast, coordinated and unceasing labor until Nature, a fickle element, decides to give up no more sap that year.

This process, up to a few years ago, had been carried on in about the same manner as it was 150 years ago. The wooden buckets and tanks of course have changed to tin, and pipe line systems are beginning to be set up, though many argue they are more trouble than they are worth. And the big iron boiling kettles, barbecue style in pioneer days, have given way to the long shallow partitioned pans, called evaporators. But the general principle has remained static, until, a couple of years before the last war, an outlander, Colonel Fairfax Ayres, brought science to the sugar bush.

Sugar Orchard, Weathersfield   *John Lovely*

Newton Farm, Felchville   *Vic Edwards*

Ayres invented what he called a "hydro-therm," which enabled the producer to make sure that his syrup weighed the proper—and legal—eleven pounds to the gallon.

Much more controversial, however, was his campaign to lift maple into the luxury class, and thereby provide a more substantial return to the farmer. The price of syrup did skyrocket upward during the forties, but this resulted principally from special war-time factors—including both an artificial and natural shortage of sweets of all kinds. Oddities in price control during the war caused the commercial processors to divert syrup into specially packaged and profitable maple candy. Syrup rose to fantastic levels in the "black market." Two successive poor crops in 1945 and 1946 added to the shortages, and with the end of government controls, the retail price settled down at six dollars or so—over twice pre-war.

But the farmers became accustomed to getting six dollars *net* from retail sales, and would not sell to the processors at the old one and two dollar rates. As a result, the use of sugar for industrial purposes, such as tobacco sweetening, dropped from nearly three quarters of the total to less than a half. As more and more syrup—including the inferior grades previously sold in drums to the processing plants—went directly onto the retail market, it became increasingly difficult to protect the prestige and long standing national reputation for quality held by the "Vermont" label. The latter had been appropriated by some processors and dealers in adulterated and spurious maple products. Apprehensions over the indifferent policy of labeling and distribution of off-grade products resulted in an urgent appeal to the 1949 legislature for legally enforceable standards as a protection to the industry. And in the meantime, processors turned increasingly to cheap imports from Canada and New York State to supply their needs, expanding their output of blended maple syrups.

Sugar production today has many potentialities. Only one half the available trees have been tapped, despite the loss of many maples to the woodsman's axe during the forties, when high labor costs and a rigid OPA price ceiling made sugaring less profitable than lumbering. In the long run it was short sighted, but the need for ready cash and the temptation of sky-high prices being paid for hard-wood timber were too much for many farmers.

But whether production increases or decreases, maple sugar is likely to remain the state's most famous product.

Another tree crop which has been widely developed of late years is the apple. Until about 1875, apples were used mostly for cider. When this was displaced as a national drink, the small orchards were neglected. Changes of taste and diet, however, brought new uses in cooking and eating. Production became profitable and commercial orchards multiplied again, particularly in the temperate area around Lake Champlain. But even the hill regions could profit, for it was a crop that did not need level ground. To stimulate the industry, the state exempted new plantings from taxes for fifteen years. Today, Vermont MacIntosh apples command top recognition in the metropolitan market places of the northeast.

Vermont's apple crop will normally run to more than a half million bushels a year, and in the favorable years of 1937 and 1943, production nudged the million mark.

Not only the fruit of the tree, but the tree itself has been a crop of great value. The "woodlot" is essential to any going farm, for fuel and lumber. But for many it has also provided a profitable source of extra income in the winter—when time is most available. The cutting of evergreens for Christmas trees, for example, has reached considerable proportions. By 1930 six hundred carloads were leaving the state by train, and as many by truck.

Of course, the great tree crop of Vermont remains in the natural growth of her wooded hillsides. Almost all of the original "first growth" timber is long since gone; the great era of clearing the land for crops reduced the state to its lowest proportion of forest land as early as 1800. When abandonment of hill farms began, the green tide moved back across the land, over-running the fields wrested from the forest so short a time ago. First scrub, then second growth timber, it lacked many qualities of the old. But it provided pulp for the great new paper mills of northern New England, and lumber for woodworking.

The restoration of Vermont's woodlands came mostly by natural regrowth. But in the twentieth century, at last convinced that the Green Mountain slopes were better suited to trees than tractors, Vermonters turned to scientific reforestation. In 1904 the Board of Agriculture appointed a Forestry Commissioner, and by 1909 the program was underway in earnest. Uncultivated lands newly planted with trees were exempted from taxation for ten years. State forests were established, where scientific reforestation was begun under the direction of the State Forester. Today, Vermont has learned that in these abandoned lands there lies a great new potential for agricultural prosperity.

DIVERSIFICATION

Specialization brought new life to Vermont agriculture through dairying. At the same time, the state again risked the danger implicit in concentrating on any single product, whether wool or milk. Today, every shift in the fluid milk market sends shivers up and down the agricultural backbone of the state.

There was no sign in 1949 of any marked decrease in the demand for fluid milk. Nor have the western states been able to solve the problems of transporting such a perishable product, and thus to offer crippling competition, as was the case with butter and cheese. Yet many farm experts were already advising a greater diversification of agricultural output. Retain the proven values of speciali-

THE MORGAN HORSE *at the W. J. Bryant Farm, on the Black River*

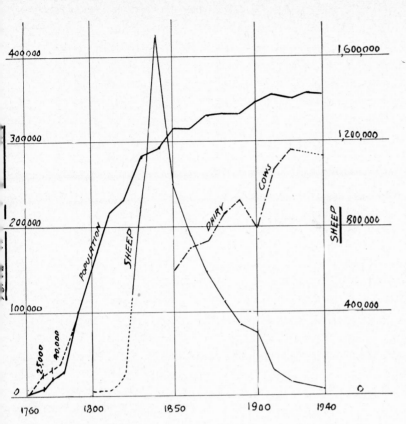

Population and Livestock

POPULATION

1771- 7,000		85,925	154,465	217,895	235,891	280,652	291,948	314,120	315,098	330,551	332,286	332,422	343,641	355,956	352,428	359,611	359,231
1776-20,000																
1783-30,000																

SHEEP

| 1824 475,000 | 1,638,819 | 1,014,122 | 752,201 | 580,347 | 439,870 | 333,947 | 297,521 | 118,752 | 62,756 | - | 17,425 |
| 1828 700,000 |
| 1837 1,100,000 |

DAIRY COWS

| 146,128 | 174,667 | 180,285 | 217,033 | 231,419 | 199,603 | 265,483 | 290,122 | - | 281,883 |

1800 1850 1900 1940

Graph axis labels: 400000, 300000, 200000, 100000, 0 (left); 1,600,000, 1,200,000, 800,000, 400,000, 0 (right); POPULATION, SHEEP, DAIRY, COWS, SHEEP; years 1760, 1800, 1850, 1900, 1940; 25000, 40000

| St.Lawrence R. | Hudson R. | Connecticut R. |
Basin	Basin	Basin
1 Burlington 27,686		4 Brattleboro 9622
2 Rutland 17,082		8 St.Johnsbury 7457
3 Barre 10,909		10 Springfield 5182
5 St.Albans 8037		12 Bellows Falls 4236
6 Montpelier 8006		13 Windsor 3402
9 Winooski 6036	7 Bennington	
11 Newport 4902	7628	
14 Waterbury 3074		
85,732	7628	29,879
70%	6%	24%

123,239
(34% of State Population)

VERMONT
Decennial Increases of Population

	Before 1760 - 1771	7,000
Initial Rise 1760-1783 (25± yrs)	1771-1776 ...	13,000
	1776-1783 ...	16,000 Rev. War
	1783-1790 ...	55,425
	1790-1800 ...	69,040
II - Marked Rise 1783-1830 (45± yrs)	1800-1810 ...	63,430
	10 - 20 ...	17,996 War of 1812
	20 - 30 ...	44,761
	30 - 40 ...	11,296 Panic of 1837
III - Lessened Rise 1830-1870 (40 yrs.)	40 - 50 ...	22,172
	1850 - 60 ...	978 Panic of 1857
	60 - 70 ...	15,453
IV - Stationary 1870-1890 (20 yrs.)	70 - 80 ...	1735 } Panic of 1873
	80 - 90 ...	136
	90 - 1900 ...	11,219
V - Small Rise 1890-1910 (20 yrs.)	1900 - 10 ...	12,315 } World War I
	10 - 20 ...	⊖ -3528
VI - Stationary Again 1910-1940 (30 yrs.)	20 - 30 ...	7,183
	1930 - 40 ...	⊖ - 380
		+ 363,139 -3908
180 Years, Total	...	359,231

THE MORGAN HORSE, opposite, was first bred in and has g been associated with agricultural activity in Vermont. The S. Government maintains a Morgan horse farm at Weybridge. Vermont's hill farms machinery will probably never entirely lace the horse. Some farmers even argue in favor of—and keep— n, particularly for sugaring and lumbering.

zation, they urged, but specialize in a greater number of high quality products, exploiting the magic of the name "Vermont," long associated in the public mind with the best in maple sugar, turkeys and apples. As the state's second century drew to a close, expanded production in these and other quality products, seemed to such experts the best promise of a secure farm future.

XIV
EDUCATIONAL AND CULTURAL GROWTH

*How Vermont pioneered many educational advances, but lagged behind herself, and
how native Vermonters contributed to the literature and art of state and nation.*

VERMONT has ever been a pioneer in the field of
education, but has, unfortunately, failed in most
instances to build a stable and satisfactory school
system upon the ground-work laid by those who first
showed the way. Her first Constitution was unique in its
provision for a complete and integrated educational
system, from the grades through college. But subsequent
legislatures shot the dream full of holes within ten years.
At Concord was established the country's first normal
school, but for over a century local jealousies prevented
the building of a first rate institution for teacher training.
Vermonters pioneered the kindergarten, but there are less
than a dozen in the state today. What lay behind this odd
and contradictory situation?

The effect of a continuing exodus of Vermonters from
their native state was reflected in all fields of activity.
Education was not the least of these. While population
increase as a whole merely leveled off because of new
growth in the cities, there was a marked decline in rural
population. This, combined with the increase in the age of
those remaining, meant fewer and fewer pupils in rural
schools which had been established to care for many more.
And "school rates" became increasingly burdensome for
their parents.

Originally
towns were sub-
divided into
school districts—
over 2,600 of
them in 1851. In
the days of slow
and inadequate
communication,
the school dis-
trict was an eco-
nomic and neces-
sary unit, reflect-
ing typical Yan-
kee democracy in
education. By
1850 it had be-
come uneconom-

ic; indeed, many school districts were vacated entirely
because of hillside emigration. Others labored on with a
half-dozen pupils in a school built for five times that
number. In 1870 the General Assembly gave formal
recognition to this situation by authorizing towns to
consolidate their district organizations, if they wished. In
the next twenty years, forty towns did so—although
fifteen soon went back to the district system. Not until
1892 could the advocates of reform, led by State Superintendents Justin Dartt and Edwin Palmer, persuade the
legislature to make the town system compulsory.

The opposition was reflected in the 1885 report of
Town Superintendent Wheelock of Milton. "The schoolhouses . . . try one's nerves", he admitted, "more than the
'mene, mene, tekel upharsin' of poor old Belshazzar."
But "Mr. Buckham, Dartt & Co. are trying to make
capital out of facts similar to these and induce the people
to adopt the town system, so called . . . . [which] would
not only be a wicked blow to our poor children . . . but
would result in the fatal 'R's'—Robbery, Revolution and
Ruin." But the progressives won out.

The next step was the joining of towns into union
districts, which had been permitted as early as 1841.

In no other
field of govern-
mental enterprise
has local pride,
jealousy, and fear
of outside control
expressed itself
more vigorously
than in public
education.

Even after the
firm establish-
ment of the town
system in 1896,
there remained
gross inequalities
in school taxes
and educational
facilities. In 1890

←NORWICH UNIVERSITY at Northfield is one of the highest rated military schools in the United States.

MIDDLEBURY COLLEGE (above), founded in 1800, is one of the state's most venerable and distinguished institutions. Its language schools are nationally known.

VERMONT ACADEMY at Saxton's River was founded in 1876 to provide individualized preparatory education impossible to overcrowded high schools. Here was held the first "Winter Carnival." →

the legislature had acted to impose a state tax for distribution among the towns, to help equalize the burden. This was the beginning of "state aid" to the common schools.

A good deal of the educational progress during the period 1850 to 1900 can be attributed to the yeoman work of the State Superintendent of Education, an office established in 1845.[1] But the sort of state control over education envisioned by the first Constitution of 1777 was still nowhere in evidence, even as the twentieth century began. However, many reforms had been made. In 1894 free textbooks were made available all over the state by legislative direction—as far as grade 8, at least—though selection remained in the hands of the local school boards, as it does today. As early as 1867 Vermont adopted a compulsory school attendance law—the second state to do so.[2] Children between the ages of 8 and 14 "of good health and sound mind" were required to attend the public schools, unless equivalent education was being provided privately.

In 1886, Vermont permitted the addition of the "kindergarten" to her school system—again the second to do so—at the urging of Burlington's George P. Marsh, U.S. Minister to Italy, who brought the idea back from Europe. And it was another Vermonter, Lucy Wheelock, who took up the campaign for its national adoption and established the famous Wheelock School for the training of kindergarten teachers in Boston.

Despite many readjustments, Vermont's school system, too often linked to a declining local prosperity, failed to keep pace with the national advance. From sixth place among the states in 1880, she had slipped to twentieth by 1920. The critical state of public education became obvious to even the farmer-dominated legislature, and it finally consented to an impartial, expert survey of Vermont's needs.

In 1912 the General Assembly set up a Commission to investigate, which in turn invited the Carnegie Foundation to make a thorough educational survey. Its experts recommended change in almost every aspect of the state's educational system—including a reorganization and strengthening of the State Department of Education. Many of these recommendations were carried into law by the epoch-making School Act of 1915. Most significant changes were the establishment of "union" superintendents for groups of towns, and a Commissioner of Education appointed by the Board of Education, rather than elected by the legislature. It was a positive step toward more efficient—and more centralized—operation of the state school system. But Mason Stone, who had long served as elected Superintendent of Education and who was now reappointed as first Commissioner, resigned in the face of such a "bureaucratic" trend. There was much other latent opposition to such radical change, and by 1923 legislative opponents of the new order managed to clip the department's wings and abolish the union superintendents. But the obvious value and economy of such cooperation across town lines brought their restoration again in 1934. Today, only the most populous towns retain their own individual superintendent of schools. The effects of the Carnegie Investigation were lasting; moreover, it was the first such state-wide investigation of a school system, and became a model for similar surveys elsewhere.

Despite the increasing trend toward more centralized control over schools, Vermont managed to leave the

---

[1] From 1856 to 1874 the office was known as "Secretary" of the State Board of Education. The title "Commissioner" was established in 1915.

[2] Massachusetts was first. In 1867 Vermont also got her first Child Labor Law, which forbade any child to work in a factory unless he had attended school for two months.

greatest responsibility—and burden—for their maintenance on the local level. This is reflected in the figures for state aid to schools; the proportion of support supplied by the state in 1940 was only 13.3%, about half the national average. This percentage was even less than it had been in 1912 (16.6%), and even the extensive increases made in 1947 left it at less than 16%. Moreover, Vermont applied only slightly more than a third of her total tax revenue toward schooling; only six states had a lower percentage.[3]

Economic factors made even more difficult the task of providing good schooling. Never well paid,[4] teachers were increasingly attracted by the expanding opportunities for women in the fields of business and other "white collar" occupations. And even those girls ready to make the financial and social sacrifices demanded of a teacher preferred better paid positions in neighboring states. In an effort to stem the tide, the 1947 Legislature upped state aid to the towns, increased minimum salaries, and provided funds for a campaign of teacher recruitment. Yeoman work by the Department of Education began to produce results by 1949, but officials admitted freely that only further increases in minimum salary levels—and consequently in state aid—could attract first rate teachers.

Greatest handicap was the inability of towns to raise the increased revenues necessary to provide adequate primary schools, to say nothing of extending secondary education. The only solution seemed to lie in consolidation of wasteful, small and scattered one-room schools. Fear of losing neighborhood schools and problems of transportation have slowed what seems an inevitable development. Yet opponents of the trend have argued that consolidated schools have provided better facilities, but not necessarily better schooling. They point to the increasing trend on the part of cities which rushed into the construction of great educational factories, to return to the "country day school" as a better setting for the training of youth. And, they say, the rural school is merely a rough-hewn version of the swankier country day school.

TEACHERS AND TEACHER TRAINING

Vermont's difficulties in common schooling harked back in part to the inadequacy of her teachers, which was in part due to the absurdly low salaries paid, to the social restrictions imposed by the community, and to the miserable equipment and facilities provided by the town fathers. But it was also due to poor training in the arts of teaching. The state's normal schools suffered, like the primary schools, from local jealousies. That the state which

produced the first normal school should lag so was ironic.

The first official recognition of the need for teacher training came just as our second century opened—in 1849. The General Assembly of that year made an appropriation for teachers' institutes, annual gatherings with speeches, demonstrations, etc. In 1866–67 three of the county grammar schools—in Castleton, Johnson and Randolph— were converted into normal schools, when their continuance as secondary schools seemed no longer possible. (It was significant also that there was one in each Congressional district.) As we have seen, the Randolph unit was converted into the State Agricultural School in 1910, but Lyndon Institute was later subsidized to provide teacher training.

On no subject have educational experts agreed more unanimously than on the need for a single, competent teacher's college. A special investigation in 1921 recommended a single institution in Burlington, and the Carnegie Foundation offered $100,000, supplemented by $200,000 from the University of Vermont, to found it. Though approved by the Senate, local jealousies in the House killed the proposition, and Vermont returned to her three normal schools. Revived efforts in the 1947 Legislature obtained for the state teacher's colleges at Castleton and Johnson, but other communities insisted on a similar status for Lyndon, which was granted. However, the Department of Education detached one of its outstanding men, John C. Huden,[5] to serve as first President of Castleton. By 1949, though handicapped by inadequate funds and facilities, Huden had begun the laborious process of building a state teacher's college more nearly comparable to that available in other states.

HIGHER EDUCATION

After nearly a century of groping, of financial difficulties, of educational ups and downs, the state's principal institutions of higher education finally achieved a measure of stability in the twentieth century, as a greater proportion of the population sought college training.

Middlebury had had a particularly difficult careeer. Despite religious squabbles which nearly ended the struggling institution, she reached a total attendance of 168 in 1836. But decline again set in, and in 1871 less than fifty students were in attendance. In 1883 women were admitted for the first time. Middlebury's great period of expansion came under President John M. Thomas, who tripled both endowment and plant from 1908 to 1921, and laid the cornerstones for nine modern buildings.

The University of Vermont had fared little better. When the Vermont Agricultural College was established in 1864, the Legislature provided for consolidation with

---

[3] Vermont's rank among the states with respect to education:
For *ability* to support education: 17th among 48 states.
For *effort* in supporting education: 29th among 48 states.
For *adequacy* of support of education: 22nd among 48 states.
[4] As late as 1896 male teachers averaged $36.00 per month, and females only $25.00.

[5] Huden had served as a practicing teacher, high school principal, State Supervisor of High Schools, and Director of Research and Guidance in the State Department of Education.

GILEAD SCHOOL, Bethel, a representative one-room schoolhouse

Earle Newton

SPAULDING HIGH SCHOOL, Barre, typical of the massive buildings of the late 19th Century.

Bosworth

GODDARD COLLEGE, emphasizes coordination of classroom and work experience. Above, a student "task force" on campus.

MARLBORO COLLEGE, launched in 1947 as the state's newest institution of higher education, began in a restored farmhouse.

it of all the state's institutions of higher learning. Middlebury and Norwich refused,[6] but Vermont accepted. The two were merged the following year. The Medical School, revived in 1853,[7] was also taken under control of the University trustees in 1899. UVM's great period of expansion, however, came in the twentieth century under President Guy Bailey. But Bailey's handling of the University's finances and endowment resulted in serious difficulties, and the state stepped in to reorganize the institution in 1941.[8]

The entire problem of state aid to higher education has been an exceedingly touchy one. The Legislature has long been in the habit of making appropriations for this purpose, but has insisted on dividing available funds between the various institutions. This policy has prevented the creation of a state university providing free college education for Vermonters, as in most states.[9] The question erupted in 1947 when Catholic St. Michael's College[10] applied for assistance, which was refused on the grounds that the institution was sectarian. Large appropriations were, however, made for the erection of badly needed buildings at the University.

As a matter of fact, appropriations of any sort for higher education were called into question by the Carnegie Investigation of 1912, in view of the state's inadequate support of primary schools. The experts pointed out that the total grants to colleges were then greater, in proportion to population, than anywhere else in New England, or even in New York.

The trend in college education—as in other fields—has been toward specialization to achieve recognition among the welter of highly endowed universities elsewhere in the country. Middlebury has placed her principal emphasis on the liberal arts, and her language schools are widely recognized as among the nation's first. Norwich as a

military school—consistently one of the highest rated by the Army—has concentrated on engineering and allied subjects. And UVM offers special colleges in agriculture, education, medicine, and engineering.

One of the state's most famous colleges is one of its youngest. Founded in 1933 as an experimental college for girls, Bennington College has made a national reputation in the cultural arts. Her schools of the drama and the dance have made outstanding contributions to these fields.

Bennington, however, was only one of an influx of new educational institutions founded within the last fifteen years. Goddard Seminary in Barre removed to Plainfield in 1938, and reorganized as a college, with special emphasis on the coordination of classroom and work experience. Marlboro College opened its doors in 1947. Several of the old academies blossomed out as junior colleges:[11] Troy Conference Academy at Poultney became Green Mountain Junior College, and Montpelier Seminary, Vermont Junior College. In 1947 citizens in Rutland organized their own Junior College to provide a municipal institution of higher education.

Rehabilitated, many of the old academies found new

---

[6] An earlier attempt to merge Middlebury and UVM fell through in 1847.

[7] It had operated briefly, 1821–36.

[8] The Legislature now elects nine trustees to sit with the nine elected by the alumni. The 1949 legislature received an offer from the University to reduce its trustees to six giving the state full control—in return for increased state aid.

[9] Many Vermont youths find it far less costly to attend state universities in other states—even as far away as Alabama—than in their own.

[10] Founded in 1904, St. Michael's expanded rapidly following World War II, accepting veterans in greater numbers, proportionately, than any other Vermont college.

[11] The increasingly important role of the junior college was emphasized by the resignation in 1949 of Commissioner of Education Ralph E. Noble to accept the Presidency of Vermont Junior College.

BENNINGTON COLLEGE, progressive center for the study of the fine arts, expresses the same spirit in its informal dormitories.

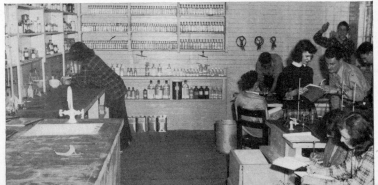

PRIVATE SCHOOLS like the Woodstock Country School (below) have become increasing common in recent years, provide new enterprise.

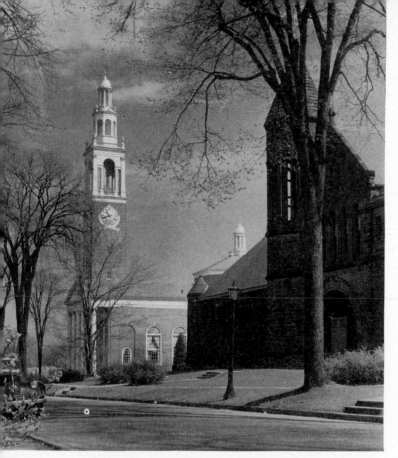

UNIVERSITY OF VERMONT *provides a striking architectural contrast between its "academic Georgian" Ira Allen Chapel (left) and its older "Richardson romanesque" Billings Library (right).*

life as preparatory schools. These were supplemented by new private secondary schools, often of an experimental character. The Newton School in Windham, the Putney School, and the Woodstock Country School are recent examples.

This amazing evidence of new enterprise in private education reflects the increasing popular interest in Vermont as representing unique philosophical attitudes toward life in general, as well as toward education in particular (about which we shall have more to say anon). But this renaissance has served to bring, each year, a new crop of youngsters from all over the country into the state, and thus has introduced Vermont to a vast multitude of friends and parents as well. It has also, in another sense, constituted important new business enterprise, very much like the summer camps, which we will also want to look in on in our next chapter.

STUDENTS *come from all over the country; these girls at Vermont Junior College represent New Jersey, Hawaii, Mississippi, Florida and New York.*

THE FOURTH ESTATE

From the earliest days Vermonters have depended quite as much upon the printed word as upon schools for their education and information. In the seventy years since the first newspaper was established, thriving little weeklies had sprung up all over the state. But the daily—an indispensable part of modern life—did not appear in Vermont until 1848.

In that year the new electric telegraph[12] reached Burlington—over a year ahead of the railroad—bringing the ceaseless chatter of national and international news which had previously arrived laboriously, unreliably and irregularly by letter or word of mouth. Editor Dewitt Clinton Clarke of the Burlington *Free Press* seized the opportunity to provide his home town with a daily paper —for, after all, the "Queen City" had now reached a population of seven thousand.[13] But the first year was pretty rugged; paper, ink, telegraph fees and other costs, according to Clarke "pretty near made an end of us." In 1853 Clarke sold out to the Benedicts, father and son, promoters of the new telegraph, and set out for Texas to build a railroad—like many another Vermonter. But, unlike most of them, he came back five years later and started the Burlington *Times*. Within two years its circulation exceeded that of the daily *Free Press* by half. But the weekly *Times* was not as well established or as profitable as the weekly *Free Press*, and could not absorb the deficits of the daily. Clarke sold it in 1860, and the new owners finally passed it on to the Benedicts in 1868. George W., the elder, was a UVM professor, but a hard headed businessman withall. He enlarged the paper and installed the city's first power press—key to successful production of a daily. Its first motive power was a stout Irishman, later supplanted by a steam engine. George G., the son, a distinguished man of letters and Civil War reporter, assumed the editorship after his return from the battlefields, and remained actively connected with the paper until his death in 1907. He had, however, sold the controlling interest ten years earlier to Willard B. Howe, whose son, David W. Howe, is the paper's present publisher.[14]

Burlington acquired a second permanent daily in 1894. Still published under the same name, the *Daily News* underwent a radical lifting of face and spirits in 1942, when Publisher William Loeb added it to his St. Albans *Daily Messenger*,[15] acquired the preceding year. Loeb brought a crusading—and often strident—note to Vermont's conservative and sometimes stodgy journalism.

---

12 "Tell-lie-graph," it was labelled by its enemies.

13 Which seems to have been the minimum population necessary to support a daily. Several dailies which started in smaller towns quickly collapsed.

14 In 1947, Howe was elected President of the American Newspaper Publishers Association—a signal honor for a small newspaper.

15 The *Messenger* began its daily editions in 1863.

BURLINGTON FREE PRESS.

VOLUME I. BURLINGTON, (VERMONT,) FRIDAY MORNING, JUNE 15, 1827. NUMBER 1.

Left: the first issue of the weekly. Note prospectus for the new paper.

Center: Vermont's first daily, 1848.

Bottom: Even before the daily, there were "extras."

PROSPECTUS

WEEKLY NEWSPAPER, TO BE PUBLISHED AT BURLINGTON, VT. AND ENTITLED THE **BURLINGTON FREE PRESS.** BY LUMAN FOOTE.

commencing the publication of a new paper in this vicinity, the Editor has no way to offer but the demands of the public. These have been too often and too loud pressed to be misunderstood, and it is an obedience to them that he incurs the responsibility of assuming the direction publick journal. Influenced by a conviction of the wants of this section of State in this respect, his leading object conducting "THE PRESS," will of course to supply those wants ; to diffuse useful mation, sound moral and political principles ; to cherish pure, social, and benevolent sentiments, an ardent love of rational liberty and an exalted national feeling ; in short, effecting upon the publick mind the objects of discovery and invention, of literature, science, history, and philosophy, to tribute to the advancement of the great of social improvement.

...

THE DAILY FREE PRESS.

Volume 1. Burlington, Vt., Saturday Evening, April 1, 1848. Number 1.

The Free Press,

Published every evening,
By D. W. C. CLARKE.

TERMS:

To village subscribers, per month,
To those who receive it by Mail, for 3 months, $1.00
Or per annum, $4.00

"PRESS ON."

BY PARK BENJAMIN.

Press on! there's no such word as fail!
Press nobly on! the goal is near—
Ascend the mountain! breast the gale!
Look upward, onward—never fear!
Why should'st thou faint? Heaven smiles above,
Though storm and vapour intervene;
That sun shines on, whose name is Love,
Serenely o'er life's shadowed scene.

...

The Lost Glove.

BY MRS. JANE C. CAMPBELL.

...

Free Press Extra.

BURLINGTON, Tuesday, 1 o'clock, p.m., March 28, 1848.

Further News from Europe.

Arrival of the Caledonia. Overthrow of the dynasty of Louis Philippe fully confirmed.

The French King, Royal Family and Ministers fled to England!

A Republican Provisional Government Established in France!

and recognised by Foreign Representatives in Paris.

All Europe in a Ferment.

Metternich Resigned!

The fires of Republicanism spreading, and Monarchies trembling to their fall!

"Fiat justitia ; ruat Coelum!"

Troy, March 28, 10 1-4 o'clock, A. M.
New York, " 9 1-2 o'clock, A. M.

The Steamer Caledonia, arrived at Boston last night. The Revolution has spread throughout France. All the departments have engaged in it. The Republic is confirmed and has been recognised by the representatives of the U. S. Eng. Belgium, and Switzerland.

Great Tunnel under Liverpool.

...

KIT CARSON.—In the correspondence of the Baltimore Patriot we find the following paragraph. The letter is dated Washington, June 29, 1848:

...

RUTLAND HERALD *has annually taken prizes for its distinguished format. In 1947 it won the Ayer Award over all U.S. papers.*

The Rutland *Herald*, watching the flounderings of its Burlington contemporaries, postponed its daily until the Civil War brought an insatiable public thirst for up-to-the-minute news. Rutland had now passed the seven thousand population mark.

With the rush of war news and the insistent demands of daily deadlines, the old days of leisurely and personal journalism disappeared. The publisher-editor found more and more of his time involved in the urgent details of getting the paper out. He had less and less time for tilting lances with his fellow editors on the burning issues of the day. And newspaper publishers thence set forth on the path which led them into the fold of big business.

Vermont today boasts ten dailies,[16] and forty-two weeklies, including the Middlebury, Norwich and UVM student newspapers. But there were several suspensions in 1947, when papers in Waterbury, Middlebury, Brandon and Bristol gave up the ghost, and a new, second daily in St. Johnsbury failed to complete its first year. Still, the

small independent journal survives in Vermont despite the national trend toward its elimination in favor of widely distributed big city papers. Even here, in the cities, Boston and New York papers sell almost as many copies as the local sheets, and the Vermont papers have never attempted to compete with the massive Sunday editions.[17]

Newspaper editors have individually played a large role in state politics. G. G. Benedict of the *Free Press* and E. P. Walton of the Montpelier *Watchman* have their modern counterparts in Howard Rice of the Brattleboro *Reformer* and Robert Mitchell of the Rutland *Herald*. Rice, for many years a state senator, wielded great influence in state politics, and Mitchell played a large role in the liberal rebellion of 1946–1948 which thrust the young war veteran, Ernest W. Gibson, into the Governor's chair over the violent objections of the older politicians and the party machine—including a majority of the state's newspapers.

On the whole, the state's small population failed to provide an adequate basis for magazine publication. Brattleboro became a great New England book printing center in the second half of the 19th century, and a flood of the new and cheap stereotype editions poured out over the East from her busy presses. It was here that George E. Crowell established the women's magazine *Household* in 1868. But its subject matter was general, and it could operate out of Boston as easily—which it did following 1891. More specifically native in origin and character was the illustrated *Vermonter*, founded in 1895 by Charles Spooner Forbes of St. Albans. Moved to White River Junction under the editorship of Charles R. Cummings, it eventually fell upon declining days, and expired with his death in 1945, on its fiftieth anniversary.[18] The following year saw the first issue of the state sponsored quarterly, color illustrated *Vermont Life*. Building on the nostalgic affection of Vermonters everywhere for their native state, plus an increasing national interest in Vermont's unique philosophy, the magazine skyrocketed to a circulation of 50,000 in its first year—considerably greater than that of Vermont's two largest daily newspapers combined. Its first editor was Earle Newton, Director of the Vermont Historical Society.

Gofyn wyf am galon hapus, Calon onest, calon lan.

NATIONAL CULTURES: THE WELSH

The predominant Yankee strain has been modified by small accessions of various nationalities—Scotch and Italian in Barre, Polish and Hungarian at Proctor, French-Canadian at Winooski. The Welsh slate workers express the finest aspects of their cultural background in one of the state's outstanding choral groups, led by Evan Williams (upper left). In the Poultney Welsh Presbyterian Church (lower left) and in concerts all over the state they join to sing their native Welsh songs, such as "Calon Lan" ("A Clean Heart Forever Singing"). →

---

16 Burlington *Free Press*, Burlington *Daily News*, St. Albans *Messenger*, Rutland *Herald*, Barre *Daily Times*, Montpelier *Argus*, Brattleboro *Reformer*, Bennington *Banner*, St. Johnsbury *Caledonian*, Newport *Express*.

17 In 1948 the Burlington *Daily News* began issuing its Saturday afternoon edition on Sunday morning. A color comic section had earlier been added to the Saturday paper.

18 An attempt to revive it in 1946 failed after one issue.

ROWLAND ROBINSON, blind author of Ferrisburg, wrote some of the best character sketches of early eighteenth century Vermont.

LITERATURE

The affinity of editors for the field of history was early demonstrated by E. P. Walton, lively and influential editor of the Montpelier *Watchman*, who compiled an important ten volume documentary history and served actively in the early publication committees of the Vermont Historical Society—as did George G. Benedict, who wrote the story of Vermont's participation in the Civil War as well as a multitude of historical addresses. He served as President of the Society, as did Governor Hiland Hall, whose *History of Vermont* was for seventy years the standard volume on the early period of the state's growth. Hall was a name which graced a great deal of historical writing of the period; Benjamin Homer Hall's two volume *History of Eastern Vermont* was a careful, searching treatment of the early period, and Henry Hall of Rutland wrote a life of the colorful Ethan Allen. With the exception of B. H. Hall—a Yorker—all injected a strong pietistic flavor into their work. While each undertook much independent research of his own, all owed the bulk of their source materials to the indefatigible energy of Henry Stevens of Barnet, the bookseller and antiquarian, who combed Vermont and the East for private and public documents. These he either bought, "borrowed," or laboriously transcribed, with the assistance of his sons,

Benjamin Franklin and Henry junior, both of whom later became famous London booksellers. He founded the Vermont Historical Society in 1838, though it did not become an active organization until after the Civil War, under the leadership of Walton, Benedict and Governor Hall.

One of the most prolific of Vermont historians was Montpelier's Daniel P. Thompson,[19] also a newspaper editor but better known as the author of the fictional bestseller *The Green Mountain Boys*. One of the most widely read books of its time, it set the scene for writers on early Vermont history for decades to come. It "was a home grown product, if ever literature saw one, as unpretentious as a log cabin . . . a Yankee tale as brisk and wholesome as any mountain ballad. It was a border song in prose."[20] Thompson's later historical work was highly colored by the speculative, romantic flavor of his many novels. Many of his stories of the early founders and heroes have passed into both history and folklore.

Similarly intrigued with the heritage of his native state was Rowland T. Robinson of Ferrisburgh. Although he contributed a formal but lively historical volume to the "American Commonwealths" series in 1892,[21] his principal and sympathetic concern was for the people themselves. Robinson had a keen perception and great love of nature—human and botanical. His *Danvis Folks* and other similar titles reproduce faithfully both the dialect and way of life of a generation now past. An artist as well as a writer, he illustrated his own works. He spent many of his adult years as a New York editor, but in 1886, afflicted with failing eyesight, returned to Ferrisburgh to compose his best books. After storing his mind with memories of the world about him, he was able to continue writing even after darkness closed in upon him in 1893. Several volumes were published after his death in 1900. His works were a contribution to literature, history and folklore.[22]

Theodora Peck, author of the popular *Hester of the Grants*, was another native Vermonter who drew upon the Vermont heritage for her material. Dorothy Canfield Fisher, who knows and writes about Vermont with insight and understanding, has published a series of widely read novels from 1900 to the present. Her deep concern for the problems of little people, reflected in her writings, has allied her with a multitude of charitable and educational endeavors, which of late years have reduced her literary output to the vanishing point. In 1949 she reached

---

19 See portrait, page 44.
20 Van Wyck Brooks, *Flowering of New England*, 415.
21 *Vermont: a Study in Independence.*
22 A temporary acquisition for Vermont was the Britisher, Rudyard Kipling, who married a Vermont girl and in 1892 settled down to write the *Jungle Book* and other well known titles. Quarrels with his brother-in-law sent him packing after only four years, but his odd, Indian-influenced home, "Naulakha," still stands near Brattleboro.

THOMAS WATERMAN WOOD (self portrait, left) took special delight in executing interpretative paintings of Vermonters, like his well-known "American Citizens" (above).

ART AND ARCHITECTURE

While native Vermont authors like Thompson, Robinson, Cady and Dorothy Canfield Fisher wrote freely about the things they knew and saw at home, Vermont artists looked beyond its borders for inspiration and livelihood. Brattleboro produced two remarkable sets of brothers: William Morris Hunt, the painter (1824–1879) and Richard M. Hunt (1828–1895), the well known architect, as well as Larkin G. Mead, the sculptor, and William R. Mead, architect and partner in the McKim, Mead & White combination, whose Georgian architecture has dominated modern educational building. None made their home or career in Vermont. Neither did Hiram Powers of Woodstock, famous sculptor, who took up residence in Florence, Italy. One exception was Thomas Waterman Wood, who returned to his native Montpelier to paint his neighbors, after roaming Europe for years.

The situation in general was in striking contrast to modern times, when Vermont has supplied the inspiration for so many painters of national reputation. Many southern towns have become summer art centers where eager devotees of paint and palette nearly outnumber the natives.

the age of seventy, still as vitally alive, interested and active as when she threw herself vigorously into war work in France thirty years before.

Of Vermont poets there were many, but few of permanent national reputation. Forty editions of the poems of John G. Saxe—another newspaper editor—were published both in this country and in Europe. But he is no better known today than his good friend and fellow editor and rhymester, Charles G. Eastman. Julia C. R. Dorr had a similar vogue during her writing career from 1849 to 1912, but her name is not now recognized by most students of American literature. Daniel L. Cady's homely dialect *Rhymes of Vermont Rural Life* (1919–1926) were widely quoted as authentic Vermontiana; but the author's affections lay as strongly in France, at his beloved Carcasonné, where he spent as much time as possible. The greatest and most authentic interpreter of Vermont life was an adopted Vermonter, Robert Frost, whose dry, sparse lines mirror a rugged sanity in the northern New England character. In free verse, Walter Hard has caught many of the same values, enlivening them with a salty appreciation of the odd quirks of Yankee personality. In modern times some of the best verse is being written by a Norwich University English professor, Arthur Wallace Peach, whose knowledge and love of the state emerges from heartfelt poems and essays, scattered throughout a multitude of publications.

JUSTIN MORRILL, Vermont Senator and distinguished statesman, was one of many famous American statesmen who sat to Thomas Waterman Wood for their portraits.

MAIN STREET, MONTPELIER

by Thomas Waterman Wood
(1823–1903)

From his home "Athenwood," high on the hill above the capital city, no view was more familiar to the artist than this one down Montpelier's principal business street, with its many church towers looming in the background. Note the early engine of the Montpelier and Wells River Railroad (center, right), and the covered bridge over the Winooski River, torn down in 1897. This is Montpelier of the "Gay Nineties." Wood wandered all over the world, copying the work of the masters with meticulous and loving care. But despite his national reputation, he always returned to his native town, and his best work is of the people and places he knew there.

GREEK SLAVE *by Hiram Powers*

WILLIAM CZAR BRADLEY *by Larkin Mead Jr.*

VERMONT SCULPTORS

Hiram Powers (1805–1873), Woodstock born sculptor of the famous "Greek Slave," graduated from a wax museum to Italian studies under the sponsorship of Nicholas Longworth. The latter soon sent to join him a Brattleboro youth by the name of Larkin Mead Jr. (1835–1910), whose snow-sculptured "Recording Angel" had attracted widespread attention. Powers remained in Italy, but Mead returned and contributed some of his best work to Vermont. His heroic statue of Ethan Allen stood on the portico of the State House and his "Ceres" surmounted its dome until recently when, weather-worn, they were replaced by copies. His bust of the Vermont statesman, William Czar Bradley, is in the Vermont Historical Society Museum. Herbert Adams, born in Concord in 1858, also left Vermont early for art study in Massachusetts and France. His "Nymph of Fynmere" (right) won the National Academy medal in 1916, but he is best known for his monumental statues like that of poet William Cullen Bryant in Bryant Park, New York City (left).

←WILLIAM
CULLEN BRYANT
(Bryant Park, NYC.)

NYMPH→
OF FYNMERE
(Cooperstown)

VICTORY AT MANILA. Artist's sketch for the diorama depicting Admiral Dewey on the flying bridge of the Olympia. The diorama was erected in the Museum of the Vermont Historical Society on the fiftieth anniversary of the battle. Made by the Pitman Studio of Cambridge, Mass., its foreground is sculptured in three dimensions, fading imperceptibly into a circular painted background.

GREEN MOUNTAIN *Admiral*

Admiral George Dewey of Montpelier won for the United States the battle of Manila Bay in 1898, and became thereby the most celebrated naval hero in American history.

XV

"UNSPOILED" VERMONT

*How the twentieth century brought a new industry, new
population, and a new way of life to the Green Mountain land.*

HALFWAY around the world, the crash of guns in response to a Vermonter's laconic order—"You may fire when ready, Gridley"—opened the twentieth century. George Dewey, by his destruction of the Spanish Far Eastern fleet at Manila Bay, May 1, 1898, launched the United States on the path of empire, and cast the nation upon a world stage—from which there has been no "exit." A country which had bent its energies toward a half-century of furious and unprecedented internal expansion, now raised its head and flexed its muscles. The vast current of expansionism which had touched the Pacific Coast and filled in the last frontier, overflowed the borders of continental United States and sought new fields to conquer in Asia and South America.

America's pride in her new role was nowhere so joyously shown as in the hero's reception given Commodore Dewey on his return. Triumphal arches, a jewel encrusted sword from Congress, a silver loving cup cast from schoolchildren's dimes, a home, and the four stars of an Admiral of the Navy were only a part of the gifts laid at his feet. No naval officer has since held that rank—which would today rate six stars in the naval hierarchy.

But George Dewey's native state remained largely apart from the frenzied expansionism of the new era. Drained by emigration, her agriculture undermined by high-powered competition, and consigned by geography to a secondary industrial role, the little Green Mountain state sought anxiously for the means to stabilize her economy in a world where the values of careful thrift and hardy self-reliance seemed increasingly less important than ruthless assertiveness and grasping ambition.

But she could not stand entirely aside from the vast current of change initiated by the industrial revolution in America. As split-second communication, rapid transportation, and expanded commercial exchange drew people

GEORGE DEWEY

closer together, they also became more and more dependent upon one another. Although Vermonters retained an undiluted, stubborn independence, and although their land never saw the creation of a helpless proletariat, yet Vermonters, like Americans in general, became dependent upon other Americans for the basic health of their economic life. Their social life, under the influence of the radio, magazines, and motion pictures became also part of the common pattern; their social and economic history in the twentieth century is therefore substantially that of the nation as a whole.

That is not to say that Vermonters were no longer influenced by the traditions of their Green Mountain forbears. Qualities of thrift, self-reliance, independence, and stubborn resistance to change still managed to keep bright green a tiny wedge in the vaster jig-saw puzzle of the American states—where most of the pieces had assumed a shade of well smoked grey.

THE RECREATION INDUSTRY

It was the very green-ness of this land which provided the basis for a great new source of income for the Green Mountain state. Jaded souls sought rest and relaxation among its quiet hills and along its sparkling streams. By the turn of the century, the business of catering to the traveling public had already assumed considerable proportions and Vermont—in 1911—was the first state to establish an official Publicity Bureau.

The business was not a new one. "Mine host" had plied his trade since the time the first white men arrived in the Hampshire Grants. Indeed, the very state of Vermont came into being in a series of taverns. Conceived in Landlord Fay's Catamount Tavern at Bennington, Vermont was born at Cephas Kent's in Dorset, and christened in Elijah West's ordinary at Windsor, now the "Old Constitution House," which, after restoration in 1914, appropriately hung out its shingle again and began

THE OLYMPIA, Commodore Dewey's flagship at Manila Bay.

SWORD and loving cup (above) presented Admiral Dewey by Congress and an admiring public, now in the Chicago Historical Society. At right is his birthplace, still standing in Montpelier.

ANOTHER VERMONTER, Captain Charles E. Clark of Bradford, took the "Oregon" on its spectacular trip around Cape Horn in time to arrive for the great naval battles in Cuba. The exploit emphasized the need of a canal connecting the Atlantic and Pacific Oceans.

serving food—but not drink—to weary travelers.

There have been three principal phases to the growth of the resort and vacation business. The first travelers came in search of health as well as recreation. Even before 1800 people began flocking to Clarendon Springs for the "water cure," and a hotel was built as early as 1798. For nearly seventy years the mineral springs at Highgate, Sheldon, Middletown, Plainfield, Guilford, Brunswick and Brattleboro prospered, and large hotels were created to serve the eager crowds. One doctor combined medicine and hospitality at Brattleboro. In 1844 he built there a big hydropathic establishment and published the *Green Mountain Spring Monthly*, a periodical of over 30,000 circulation. But these resorts suffered severely in the lean years that followed the Panic of 1873, and the "Springs" never recovered their clientele.

The railroads first opened the valleys to the tourist and the resort visitor. Before the auto invaded the furthest recesses of the Green Mountains, huge hotels were erected at resort centers, to which hundreds of weary New Yorkers and Bostonians peregrinated by rail and stage.

The second phase—at its height in the "Gay Nineties" and thereafter—also produced large resort hotels, this time centered around scenic attractions. In 1858 determined promoters dragged timber up Mt. Mansfield to build the first Summit House. Although a trail had been cut a few years earlier it was not until ten years after that date that a road up the steep slope was begun. It was completed in 1870, opening a new era for the Stowe-Mansfield region. The Summit House still stands, although it has lost its porch several times to the gales which whip around the "Nose" of Mansfield. The highway up the mountain was rebuilt for motor traffic in 1923, at a cost of $80,000, and is now a toll road, as are the more recent highways up Mounts Equinox and Burke.

Manchester began its career of catering to the "carriage trade," and the imposing Equinox House, begun before the Civil War, grew steadily. Woodstock constructed its great Inn in 1892, and numerous other hotels sprang up— particularly in towns having access to the railroads, which ran regular excursions. Especially popular were

THE LONG TRAIL, 261 mile "footpath in the wilderness," was built by members of the Green Mountain Club, section by section, during the years 1910–1929. The Club, sparked by the enthusiastic James P. Taylor, then principal of Vermont Academy, gradually increased its membership until it passed the 1500 mark, and achieved financial stability. Maintenance of the trail is good, and shelters are provided at strategic points. From the headquarters in Rutland prospective hikers can obtain a guide book giving maps, descriptions and useful suggestions for the journey. In twenty years the Long Trail has become one of the state's outstanding recreational attractions. →

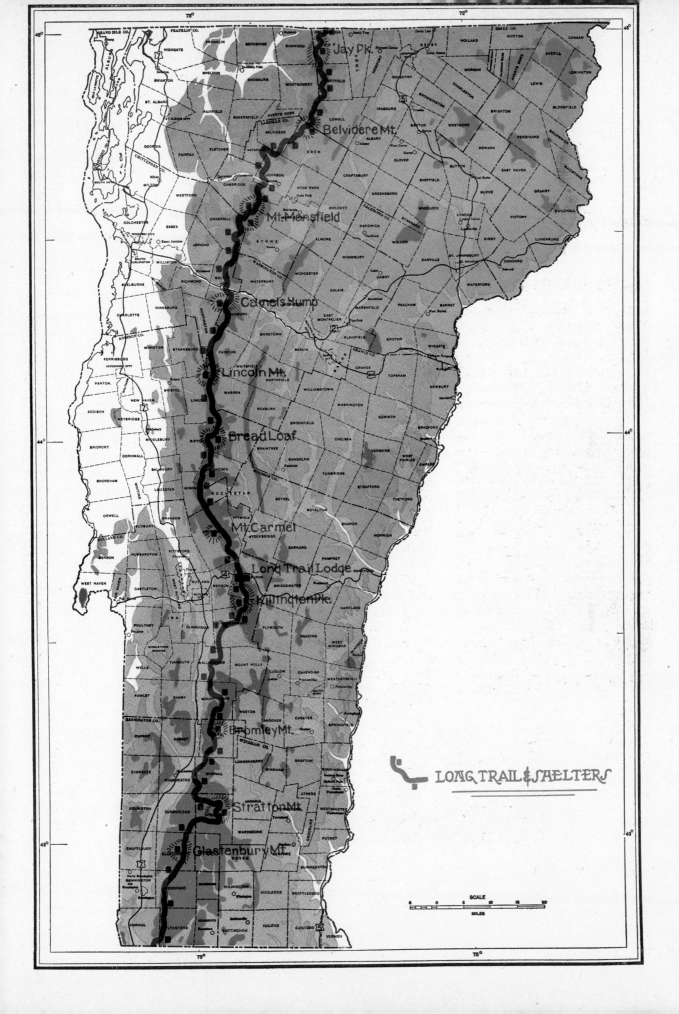

LONG TRAIL & SHELTERS

FOREST CAMPS were stag favorites in the "gay nineties." C.H. Quimby's lodge (shown above in 1896) has now evolved into a modern family resort, still featuring fishing and hunting.

LAKE STEAMERS like the "Ticonderoga" (shown in old photo, above) served not only for scenic boat trips, but also as freight carriers. Champlain Transportation Co. (founded 1826) lasted until 1932.

boat trips on Lake Champlain; this was the heydey of the steamers "Maquam," "Chateaugay," "Vermont" and "Ticonderoga"—of which only the latter still maintains a precarious existence (see page 133). Another and entirely different sort of influx came with the religious gatherings and camp grounds—mostly Methodist—such as those at New Haven, although Vermont had nothing like the activity which characterized the Finger Lakes region of New York and the Pocono Mountains in Pennsylvania.

The third phase proceeded gradually out of the first as the vacationists demanded more and more in the way of "activities." Boating, bicycling, and picnicking were old-time pleasures; to these were added many others, chiefly of a vigorous nature. Hotels with facilities for water sports forged ahead of those which had depended largely on restful verandas. The thousands of twentieth century travelers seemed more intent on extracting active enjoyment from each minute of their limited vacations, than upon retiring to the mountains for months of quiet relaxation.

The new trend was a reflection of a basic social change taking place throughout the nation. As wage scales increased and hours decreased, the great and growing middle class was added to the ranks of vacationists. Limited in both time and money, they sought out the smaller, more modest vacation spots with active recreational programs. The big society hotels, catering to the "carriage trade," suffered increasingly as small resorts, tourist homes and camps sprang up to serve the new clientele. But Vermont was more fortunate than her neighbors; New Hampshire and New York had built gigantic, lavish resort hotels which soon fell upon evil times. Vermont had come into the tourist business more modestly, and was able to build most of her recreational "plant" to serve a predominantly middle-class, auto-borne clientele.

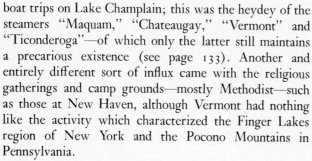

LAKE CHAMPLAIN's shores have provided an ideal site for summer camps and resorts. At Basin Harbor (left), the Beach family has developed one of the state's largest summer resorts. To the old stone homestead (center foreground) they added a large hotel (left foreground, hidden in trees) and many cottages. The harbor is tailor-made for water sports.

The products of the Green Mountain Forge, at Wallingford, are representative of the work of an increasing number of small establishments employing maybe five, ten, or perhaps only one or two people, making special products of unusually high quality. Vermonters have habitually fought shy of mass production for fear of its effect on craftsmanship. It is this tradition which has made the word Vermont a trademark for quality throughout the country.

Pictures through the courtesy of the Vermont State Arts and Crafts Commission.

When the first white men came to the land which is now Vermont, they found a virtual paradise of fish and wild game —which then constituted one of the principal natural resources of the area. Before a crop could be drawn from the earth, the forest had to be cleared; fish and game were therefore the chief support of the early settlers.

Depletion of the supply began almost immediately through abuse of water and forest resources. The cutting off of the woodlands dried up many streams, reduced the level of the water table and raised water temperatures. The erection of impassable dams, the destruction of the young by millwheels, increasing stream pollution, and particularly fishing too much and at the wrong seasons, were cited by the first Fish Commissioners in 1867.

The possibility of artificially restocking streams had been the original stimulus for the appointment of these commissioners, though there was still some ridicule of the idea. Nevertheless, continual experimentation went on, and fish hatcheries were set up. By 1947 there were four of them operated by the State Fish and Game Service: at Roxbury, Salisbury, Canaan and Bennington, with a rearing station at South Vernon. In joint operation with the U. S. Fish and Wildlife Service are stations at St. Johnsbury, Pittsford and West Milan, N. H.

In order to promote natural propagation, experiments began in the partial closing of certain streams. It was soon discovered that absolute cutting off swift mountain streams—already overpopulated with undersized fish—was useless if not detrimental. There has since been general adoption of what is known as the New Haven River Plan, under which certain areas are closed and posted in agreement with the owners. These are normally staggered along any given stream.

Attempts to conserve, as well as replenish this natural resource began with the earliest laws, many of which had to do with fish and game. But the first integrated legislation came in 1876. Enforcement of the laws was originally in the hands of the town wardens, then passed to county wardens. Today an expanding force of state wardens combines policing with conservation activities.

Native fish are no longer, as in the early days, a significant or critical part of the population's food supply. But they remain among the state's most important natural resources, if only for their role as a recreational asset. Both state authorities and those who fish the hundreds of lakes and rivers of Vermont are today acutely conscious of wise old Ben Franklin's saying: "Forever taking out and never putting anything in soon exposes the bottom of the barrel."

FROM THE HIGH LAND *surrounding Big Averill Lake, Essex County stands out as a land of virgin wilderness, a paradise for the fishing and hunting enthusiast. This "unspoiled" land is one of the state's principal assets in terms of its offerings to the visitor. It also contains a vast reservoir of timber for pulp and paper.*

LAKES *provide opportunity for recreational developments suitable for family vacations, in addition to the forest camps. Quimby's, on Big Averill (right) and Forest Lakes, is one of the oldest and best known of Vermont's fishing lodges and vacation resorts.* →

THE ROLLING HILLS—*ideal for horseback riding—are almost unbroken forest. There are over 60,000 acres— nine tenths of it woodlands—in the unorganized townships of Averill, Ferdinand, Lewis, and the two "Gores," Wilson's and Avery's. None of these have population enough to warrant individual local governments.*

*Kodachromes
courtesy Quimby's*

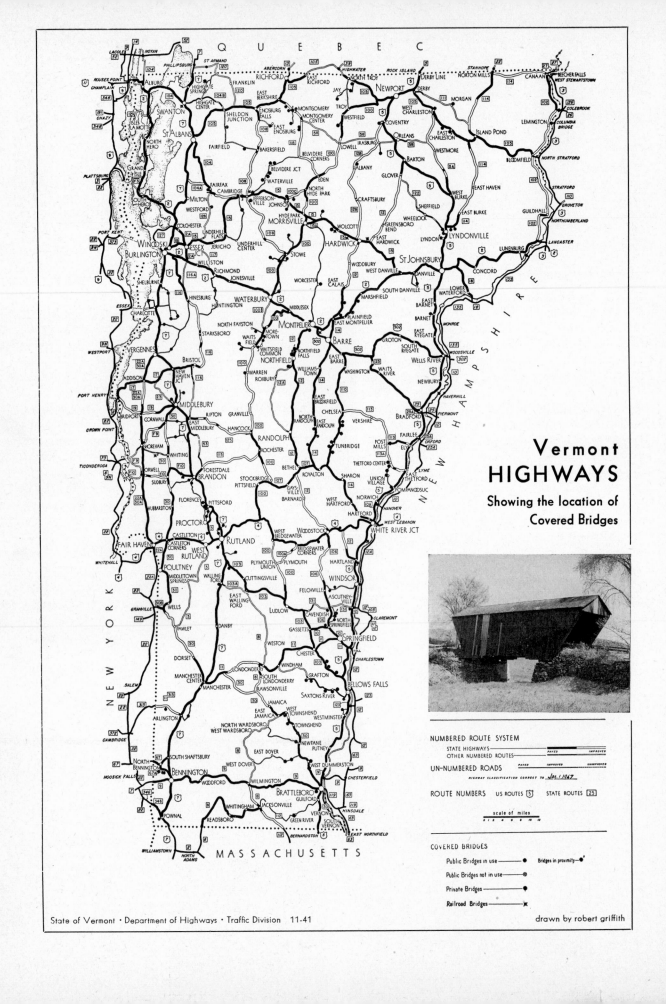

Vermont
HIGHWAYS

Showing the location of
Covered Bridges

NUMBERED ROUTE SYSTEM
STATE HIGHWAYS
OTHER NUMBERED ROUTES   PAVED   IMPROVED

UN-NUMBERED ROADS   PAVED   IMPROVED   UNIMPROVED

HIGHWAY CLASSIFICATION CORRECT TO Jan. 1, 1947

ROUTE NUMBERS   US ROUTES ⑤   STATE ROUTES ②⑤

scale of miles

COVERED BRIDGES

Public Bridges in use ————●   Bridges in proximity—●°
Public Bridges not in use ————⊗
Private Bridges ————●
Railroad Bridges ————✕

State of Vermont · Department of Highways · Traffic Division   11-41   drawn by robert griffith

WINTER complicates highway problems. Before autos, snow rollers packed the roads for sleighs. Now plows are necessary for cars.

REVOLUTION IN TRANSPORTATION

It was indeed the automobile, as much as the rising standard of living, which revolutionized the vacation business. The first cars were uncomfortable and unreliable. But as they gradually improved, adding self-starters, hard tops, and balloon tires, the popularity of the camping trip grew. Extensive sight-seeing awaited good roads, however.

Vermont had built a vast network of roads along its hills and valleys before the new railroads provided an alternate and superior means of transportation. It was not until 1892 that the state undertook to give direct assistance to local road building. However, until after World War I, little was done to improve the surface of even the main highways, and the lack of service stations and garages made auto travel a risky business.

But automobiles became more popular during the prosperous twenties. In Vermont motor vehicle registrations tripled, from 30,000 to 90,000, within that decade. Agitation for hard surfaced roads grew steadily, and by 1943 nearly ten percent of the total mileage (14,338) had been paved, and over half graveled. In addition road beds were improved, new bridges built and curves straightened. This was made possible in part by federal aid, but the chief burden was now the state's; by 1949 the Highway Department's budget exceeded $8,000,000, raised from license fees and gasoline taxes.

Vermont's highway problem has been especially difficult because of the extensive mileage of her road system as compared with her population. Moreover, those roads are mostly over difficult terrain, and are unduly costly per mile. As an agricultural state, she maintains over 9,000 miles of strictly rural roads on behalf of her scattered farms—most of which mileage is badly in need of improvement, though lightly traveled.

The heavy burden of traffic comes on the principal highways connecting major cities, where suburban and commercial vehicles combine with inter-state traffic (see map of traffic flow, page 226). Yet if funds were spent in proportion to traffic use, the back roads would get little or nothing.

Public and private vehicles sounded the death knell of a special type of rail travel—the inter-urban electric trolley. Of the many miles once in operation, only the Springfield to Claremont segment still runs, carrying freight from the industrial centers to the rail terminal.

As the railroads pulled in their out-stretched tentacles, limiting their traffic to the main inter-state routes, busses and trucks increasingly took over the task of intra-state transportation. They consequently added greatly to the burden upon the main highways.

Moreover, as on the rails, an increasing amount of the traffic is of a "pass-over" variety, originating and ending outside of the state—as much as 45% in the summer.

Main roads which dissolved in spring mud hampered early touring.

Same road (Route 7) today, offers the tourist an all-weather surface.

Recognizing the growing importance of the tourist traffic, advocates of a scenic highway proposed, in 1937, a "Green Mountain Parkway" along the ridges of the mountains. Although it was to be built with federal funds, Vermonters in a popular referendum turned it down—preferring to keep their wilderness regions "unspoiled." They did designate Routes 8 and 100 as a central state scenic highway, although after ten years the southern sections were still in primitive condition.

The airplane invaded the state early; the first flight in the state was launched at St. Johnsbury in 1910. In July 1916 industrialist James Hartness organized the first Aero Club in Vermont, and shortly thereafter built the first airfield at Springfield. Fred Harris, of winter sports fame, was exhibiting equal enthusiasm at Brattleboro for air flight, whether by plane or skis.

But the lack of great urban centers slowed the development of passenger or freight transportation by air. When Vermont finally acquired regular scheduled airline flights, it was as a stop on the main New York to Montreal and

Burlington airport (above) is center for air travel. Vermont Transit busses (right) cover most of the state's main roads (below).

TRAFFIC FLOW is heaviest between urban centers, but is supplemented by tourist and inter-state commercial traffic on the main through routes, most of them north and south-bound. ↓

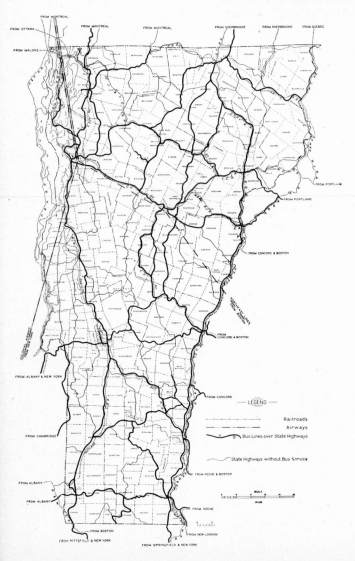

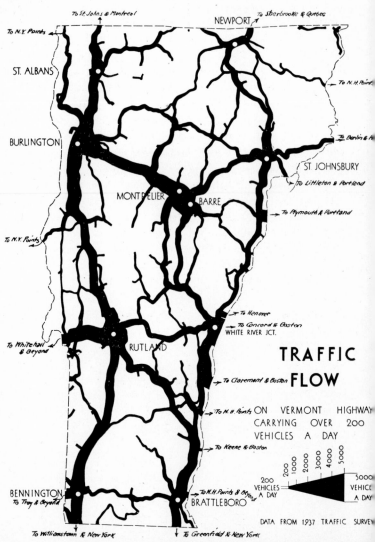

TRAFFIC FLOW ON VERMONT HIGHWAYS CARRYING OVER 200 VEHICLES A DAY

200 VEHICLES A DAY — 5000 VEHICLES A DAY

DATA FROM 1937 TRAFFIC SURVEY

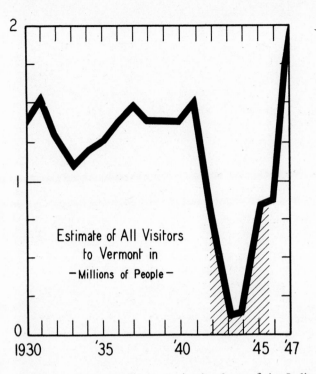

Estimate of All Visitors
to Vermont in
—Millions of People—

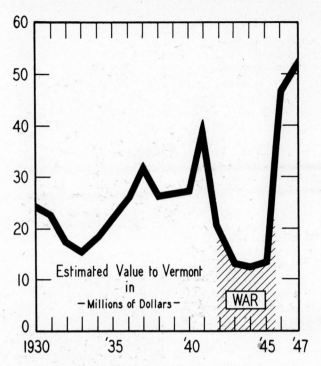

Estimated Value to Vermont
in
—Millions of Dollars—

WAR

Boston to Montreal lines. As in the days of the Indians, or of the railroads, her role was that of a bridge between more heavily populated areas.

Vermont's rugged terrain was not ideally adapted for airfields, but major airports have been built at Burlington, Barre-Montpelier, and Rutland to serve the two regular airlines, with a fourth at Newport, as yet without scheduled service. Ten sod fields elsewhere provide facilities for light commercial traffic and a growing number of personal planes. The Vermont Aeronautics Commission under Edward F. Knapp has laid plans for the development of a pattern of 28 airports, strategically located so as to bring the largest part of the population within ten miles of an airport. Yet for Vermont's residents as well as her visitors, the hedge-hopping helicopter seems to offer the most likely lift into the "wide blue yonder." In the decade of the fifties, Vermont had good reason to expect that personal air transportation would complete the revolution begun by the privately owned automobile, placing Vermont's green-clad beauty in the back yards of nearly every resident of metropolitan or suburban New York and Boston. With their eyes on Coney Island and the Catskills, Vermonters began to wonder how successful they would be in keeping their land "unspoiled." The rejection of the Green Mountain Parkway was the first fearful reaction to the unpleasant possibilities of an uncontrolled invasion. How was the state to balance off its desire to expand an increasingly important segment of its income, against its own independent determination to retain its individuality and special brand of charm? Few pretended to know.

PROMOTION AND PUBLICITY

A second force nearly as significant as the auto was the active intervention of the State on behalf of the vacation business. Vermont had early experience in promotion; before the turn of the century the State Board of Agriculture had embarked upon an extensive campaign to sell abandoned farms. They advertised widely and issued booklets on the attractions of the state—in a largely futile attempt to stem, or at least compensate for the drain of population out of the Green Mountains. In 1912 promotional work was formally established as a division of state government activity, with a Publicity Bureau in the office of the Secretary of State. Walter H. Crockett was its first director.

Today the Publicity office, now a part of the Vermont Development Commission, carries on a direct advertising campaign in metropolitan New England and New York City newspapers. It also sends out thousands of pamphlets annually in response to these ads. Total expenditures for these purposes have risen steadily, even during depression years when travel slumped slightly, and during the war years 1942–45, when gasoline rationing almost eliminated touring. But in the years of inflation following 1945 the publicity dollar bought less and less. Furthermore, Vermont lacked tax revenues comparable to her neighbors, from which to appropriate equivalent advertising funds. Consequently, her modest appeals have tended to snuggle inconspicuously alongside big display ads bought by New York and the other New England states. Still, in 1937, Vermont stood in eighth place among the vacation states, with total receipts from tourists about $30,000,000 (as

Warren Dexter

TRAIL RIDE

Over in Woodstock, Vermont, in the late August of every year there is a sudden influx of people in jodhpurs, dungarees, riding boots—and of cars drawing trailers. It's time for the Green Mountain Horse Association's annual Trail Ride.

Back in 1926 a few enthusiasts gathered together to organize an Association to encourage the breeding and raising of good saddle horses, and to develop a system of bridle trails over the back roads that criss-cross Vermont's hills and valleys.

Over a thousand miles have been mapped and marked for riding purposes. Little country inns and old farmhouses have been designated as over night stopping places on the trails, and it is therefore possible to take equestrian vacations

varying from a few days to a few months over sections of the state little traveled by and often inaccessible to motorists. Vermont was the first state in the union to have such an organized system.

But the activity for which the Association is best known is its annual Trail Ride. Actually there are two of them: the 100 mile Trail Ride and the 50 mile Pleasure Ride. This is not meant to imply that the first is not a source of joy to the contestants also, since officials insist neither is a race nor gruelling endurance contest. But the Fifty Mile Ride is for the beginners and tenderfeet who'd rather start out more modestly.

The 100 mile Trail Ride is one of the best known horse events in the country, and is the parent of a couple dozen other

hundred-mile trail rides held annually throughout western and mid-western states. It draws not only from Vermont, but a dozen other states as well. In 1947 there were sixty-five horses entered from as far away as Illinois.

The general objective of these rides is to stimulate greater interest in the breeding of types of saddle horses that will possess great stamina and hardiness as mounts for trail rides. It serves to educate both with regard to the selection of horses for long rides, and also as to the proper methods of training and conditioning for them. In the course of a couple of tries, the average rider learns a great deal about good horsemanship, as well as about the needs of his mount during and after a long ride.

compared with Michigan's $330,000,000 and Maine's $105,000,000). By 1947 income from this source exceeded $50,000,000.

New, indirect and less costly methods of publicity were added in 1946. In the hope of reaching thousands of people through normal magazine channels, a state sponsored, color-illustrated quarterly *Vermont Life* was begun in the Fall of 1946. Within a year its circulation reached 50,000, or close to a quarter-million readers per issue. Its chief publicity value lay in its ability to turn the legions of ex-Vermonters all over the country into self-appointed publicity agents; it also served a useful educational purpose within the state. Furthermore, *Vermont Life* returned to the state up to ¾ of its cost from sales. In 1948 experimentation also began in the field of motion pictures with the issuance of three publicity films for general circulation.

In 1947, too, the Commission began a campaign to induce small industry and branch plants to locate in Vermont. But shortages of power and labor hampered publicity efforts along these lines.

CAMPS AND CAMPING

Under the influence of the auto-borne middle class, the recreation business in Vermont changed materially. All over the state there sprang up enterprises to serve and sell the peregrinating stranger. Garages, gas stations, roadside restaurants and stands multiplied almost overnight. And alongside the big resort hotels arose hundreds of tourist homes and cabins. Here was new enterprise not only for the businessman planning a motor camp, but also for the main road farmer, who rented the vacant rooms in his traditionally large, rambling rural homestead. And with the arrival of winter sports, homes in strategic snow areas blossomed out under the winter sun as ski lodges.

The large hotels and resorts with progressive management and a well developed schedule of activities survived the swing to tourist vacations. Most representative of the development from past into the present is famous Hyde Manor on Lake Hortonia in Sudbury, nearly 150 years old. Equally well known is the Beach family's Basin Harbor Lodge, on Lake Champlain. Energetic Allen Beach combines a vigorous program of swimming, boating, surf-boarding, tennis and golf with nightly entertainment of a more restful variety. His resort is a self contained unit, raising much of its own food, building its own woods-enshrouded cabins, and carpentering its own furniture.

Up in forest-clad Essex County attractive, red haired Hortense Quimby now runs the hunting lodge established by her father over fifty years ago. An ardent conservationist and one of the state's best businesswomen, she has developed Quimby's into a family resort, with facilities for the care of children, and guides for the adults who find

PROMOTION is carried on directly by space advertising in metropolitan newspapers (above), and indirectly through the state magazine. At right is its first issue.

the wilderness around the Averill lakes (see page 223) a paradise for fishing and hunting.

While many of the great hotels which once graced the lovely Vermont lakes are gone, many still draw a large clientele with a modern activity program. Lakes Morey, Bomoseen, St. Catherine and Willoughby are medium sized bodies of waters with thriving resorts. Newport has great plans for the development of Lake Memphremagog, lying astride the Canadian border. The shores of Lake Champlain, and particularly the islands to the north, are thoroughly developed with resorts and camps, and most of the small lakes are plastered with private summer camps, which have suffered—and dealt with—the "menace" of the motorboat.

Apart from the resort life, many summer visitors came to indulge special enthusiasms. Hiking was one of the earliest of these. The famous Long Trail along the crest of the Green Mountains was begun in 1910 by the Green Mountain Club under the leadership of indefatigable James P. Taylor, then principal at Vermont Academy at Saxton's River. Two hundred and sixty-one miles long, it was laboriously cleared section by section until its completion in 1928 (see the map on page 219). Shelters have been erected at strategic points, and the Green Mountain Club, now boasting over 1500 members, issues a pocket guide for novices. The enthusiasm of the hikers for their mountain trail was no small element in the defeat of the proposed Green Mountain Parkway in 1938.

Horseback riding has at least as many devotees, and Woodstock is their chief stamping ground. But the thousand miles of bridle paths laid out by the Green Mountain Horse Association wind their way through most of backcountry Vermont. The big annual event is the TRAIL RIDE (spelled in capital letters) described in more detail on the opposite page.

The waterfront at Camp Kill Kare on St. Albans Bay, with its boating and swimming facilities, is representative of Vermont summer camps.

Boys at Camp Abnaki, North Hero, get a particular kick out of sailboating, always a popular water sport.

Everyone joins in the Indian pageantry at Grand Isle Camp, on South Hero Island in the middle of Lake Champlain. Group activities characterize camp life.

SUMMER CAMPS

Girls' camps are as well equipped as boys'. Horseback riding (left), canoeing (above) and sailing and swimming (below) are all featured at Ecole Champlain, on Lake Champlain at Ferrisburg.

Eighty-six summer camps for boys and girls, fifty of them located on lake shores or river banks and others hidden away in woodland areas, open annually for an eight to ten-week summer season in Vermont late in June.

The well over 6000 youngsters who experience summer camp life in Vermont each year range from pre-school to college age. Twenty-one of the camps are for boys and girls, thirty-three for girls alone and 32 more for boy campers. In all, 3524 girls and 2947 boys may live the out-door Vermont life at camps which accommodate from one to as many

as 290 boys and girls. Staff members and counsellors number 1838, in addition to 615 camp employes.

Besides tutoring, language-study camps, and others designed for special interests, Vermont camps provide horseback riding, swimming, boating and canoeing, fishing, nature study, logging, gardening, farming, fishing, hiking and scouting. Popular camp sports include tennis, archery and baseball. Most camps offer, as well, crafts and shopwork, and some provide for language instruction, cooking courses, dramatics and special music study.

Kodachromes by MACK DERICK

Hunting and fishing are two ancient occupations-become-diversions, which attract natives and outlanders alike. The first day of open season usually sees offices well vacated, and onlookers in October often have difficulty in deciding whether the deer or the hunter is the safer in the woods. But Vermonters are as deadly serious about their hunting and fishing problems today as when those activities were essential to their livelihood. Each session of the General Assembly bickers endlessly over a multitude of bills regulating fishing in streams and ponds, or the taking of does. Legislators have jealously but consistently refused to grant to the Board of Fish and Game the right to formulate a uniform system designed to conserve wildlife. But conservation has gone on, as we describe on page 222.

Vermont—along with its neighbors—has boasted not only the beauty of its waters and forests but the abundance of their contents. However, of late years, the state has realized that it has over-sold hunting and fishing, and by 1949 the Publicity and Fish and Game Directors joined hands to soft pedal this aspect of Vermont's attractions, for a time at least.

No less important to the state than the visitors to resorts, the hikers and hunters, the fishers and riders, are the campers. Over five thousand youngsters invade the state annually, bringing a million and a half dollars in trade with them. Most become enthusiastic propagandists for Vermont, and among them are many future residents. In addition to the regular recreational camps, there are special ones like the Thorpe Camp for crippled children at Goshen, or the Elfin Lake Conferences where the youth of all nations gather to discuss their common problems.

While the old fashioned "family camping" has been partly replaced by the touring vacation, public facilities for it have increased greatly with the multiplication of forest parks. By 1922 there were thirteen state forests of nearly 30,000 acres, but these were devoted to the promotion of good forestry practices rather than to recreation. The depression of 1930–1940 failed to stop people from vacationing, but did shift the emphasis toward free, public recreational facilities. Furthermore, the public works and relief programs of President Franklin Roosevelt provided the funds and the labor to obtain them. Assisted by the federal Civilian Conservation Corps, the State Forest Service began the construction of recreational facilities in state forests and the laying out of state forest parks. By 1949 there were 20 of the latter, and ten of the 25 state forests had recreational facilities. Attendance reached a peak in 1941, but slipped considerably during the war years. As travel restrictions lifted, the influx began again, and in 1948 more than 300,000 Vermonters and travelers used these handy and well cared for short-cuts to the heart of Vermont.

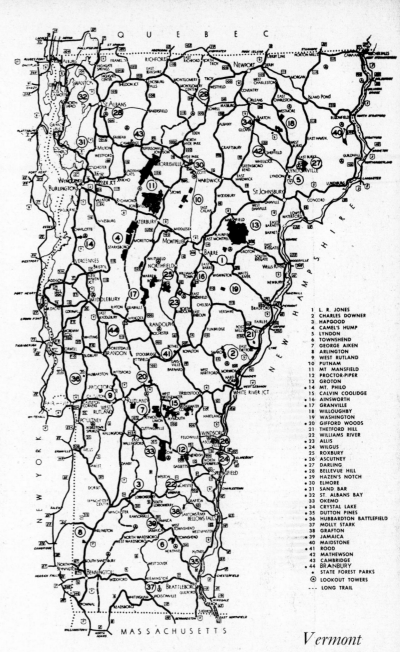

HUNTING attracts many visitors in fall, but overwhelming majority of hunters are natives.

Vermont
STATE FORESTS AND FOREST PARKS

1 L. R. JONES
2 CHARLES DOWNER
3 HAPGOOD
4 CAMEL'S HUMP
5 LYNDON
6 TOWNSHEND
7 GEORGE AIKEN
8 ARLINGTON
9 WEST RUTLAND
10 PUTNAM
11 MT MANSFIELD
12 PROCTOR-PIPER
13 GROTON
14 MT. PHILO
15 CALVIN COOLIDGE
16 AINSWORTH
17 GRANVILLE
18 WILLOUGHBY
19 WASHINGTON
20 GIFFORD WOODS
21 THETFORD HILL
22 WILLIAMS RIVER
23 ALLIS
24 WILGUS
25 ROXBURY
26 ASCUTNEY
27 DARLING
28 BELLEVUE HILL
29 HAZEN'S NOTCH
30 ELMORE
31 SAND BAR
32 ST. ALBANS BAY
33 OKEMO
34 CRYSTAL LAKE
35 DUTTON PINES
36 HUBBARDTON BATTLEFIELD
37 MOLLY STARK
38 GRAFTON
39 JAMAICA
40 MAIDSTONE
41 ROOD
42 MATHEWSON
43 CAMBRIDGE
44 BRANBURY
● STATE FOREST PARKS
Ⓐ LOOKOUT TOWERS
--- LONG TRAIL

The federal government entered the picture also in the thirties. The Green Mountain National Forest comprises 166,000 acres of the rugged and largely deserted mountain areas of south central Vermont. In general the U.S. Forest Service has acquired by purchase only lands not suited for agriculture or summer residence. But within its bounds are many spots ideal for summer and winter recreation, and its wooded slopes have great potentialities for lumbering, under sound timber management.

THE TOURISTS

The improvement of her main roads, leading through a predominantly rural and restful countryside, has made the state a mecca for the tourist seeking a constantly changing

FROM MOUNT ASCUTNEY   *Vic Edwards*

LAKE NINEVAH, MT. HOLLY   *W. J. Bryant*

panorama of rolling hills and peaceful valleys, talkative streams and inviting lakes. Vermont's central asset has always been her quiet beauty; appreciative comments appear in the earliest narratives. And this, of course, is the usual objective of the modern traveler. The fresh promise of late spring, the lush realization of a green summer, the unbelievable color riot of fall foliage, even the crisp white mantle of winter—all have their devotees. It is not that these are not to be found in other states. But in Vermont, its adherents proclaim, you will find them everywhere, for here there are no slums, no industrialized wastes, no highways where occasional scenic glimpses are blotted off by a steady procession of billboards proclaiming the merits of modern civilization's well advertised luxuries-become-necessities.

Yet Vermont, too, has her problems, and billboards are not the least of them. Unconscious of the threat until recent years, the state suddenly awoke to the fact that as traffic grew, the boards sprouted also. Under the leadership of a Springfield artist, Horace Brown, the Vermont Association for Billboard Restriction has waged an as yet moderately successful campaign to bring down the big boards and control the little ones. Brown has enlisted the help of others like Samuel R. Ogden, Chairman of the state Development Commission, who are aware of the commercial as well as aesthetic value of an unspoiled landscape. In 1947, however, they were fought to a standstill by the high powered and lavishly financed campaign of the advertising interests—themselves well trained in the art of propaganda. Yet Vermont is one of the few states which has asserted sufficient independence of the lobby to write a restrictive law, and few doubt that over the years it will be tightened rather than relaxed.

A second campaign—to clean up Vermont's rivers and streams—has been launched by that ardent Vermonter and skillful propagandist, James P. Taylor, now secretary of the State Chamber of Commerce. Most cities and villages empty their sewers into the nearest river. Industrial plants—originally drawn to the streams by the need for power—now utilize them chiefly as a depository for waste. Yet one of Jim Taylor's most ardent converts is Edward P. Miller, President of the big Fellows Gear Shaper Company at Springfield, which now trucks away its industrial waste daily. By 1948 many cities were considering sewage disposal plants, and the 1949 General Assembly had before it a Taylor-inspired program for state action.

Most of what we have had to say thus far has concerned itself with summer vacations. And it is true that for a hundred years Vermont's recreation has been even more seasonal than its agriculture. But by the forties it began to look as though it might be ironed out on a year-round basis. Let's have a look at what goes on in the other half of the year. . . .

←*MOUNTAINS AND LAKES have ever been the core of Vermont's beauty and its chief attraction for tourists.*

"SNOWFLAKE" BENTLEY, a simple Vermont farmer, working with a homemade camera in sub-zero temperatures, laid the foundation for modern micro-photographic study of the white blanket of winter.

WINTER SPORTS

Along about April, when real Spring seems still far away, frozen and mud-sloshed Vermonters are often inclined to agree with the wits who sourly proclaim the state's two seasons: August—and Winter. But one Vermonter—Wilson A. Bentley—found in Vermont's abundant snow a new, undreamed of beauty, and from his microscopic examination of snow-flakes, became the world's foremost authority on this aspect of Nature's wonders. But the farmer took slight pleasure in the fact that the quantities of wood he cut to carry him through the winter warmed him twice. And the blanket of snow merely made his tasks more difficult, his isolation more absolute. Winter was an "off-season" for agriculture—and for the recreation industry as well. That is, until Vermont discovered winter sports.

WOODSTOCK, cradle of winter sports, in the old days, before skis.

SNOW BIRDS (above): Skiers pose between drifts and sky on Hogback mountain, site of the largest ski center in the Brattleboro area.

CROWD at Brattleboro's famous ski jump, scene of several national championships and a development of the Brattleboro Outing Club. →

ANNOUNCER'S STAND (above) overlooking the jump. Left foreground is Governor Gibson.

SKI HEIL! The winning Norwegian team at the 1948 Ski Jumping Meet. →

Of course, the private enjoyment of arctic diversions is as old as winter itself. But Woodstock claims the longest known record of continuous commercial promotion of winter sports, beginning with the opening of the mammoth Woodstock Inn in 1892. But then, and for many years afterward, it was confined to the age old sports of snowshoeing, skating, sleighing and tobogganing.

It was the bent boards known as "skis" which introduced a new era. An enthusiastic Brattleboro boy named Fred Harris built a ski jump in his back yard, and then in 1909 at Dartmouth organized the first "Outing Club." At the same time, the boys at Vermont Academy caught the bug, and soon were assisting the Dartmouth collegians to put on their first Winter Carnival, now a familiar school event nearly everywhere. Harris went on to build one of the first great ski jumps in Brattleboro in 1922. Commercial development began after the first "ski-tow" in the United States was set up in Woodstock in 1934. These early rope tows were improved upon as the great ski era opened in the forties. In 1940, on the slopes of Pico, near Rutland, was unveiled the first Alpine "T stick" lift in North America. In the following year, promoters spent a hundred thousand dollars to erect a chair lift—then the longest and highest in the world—more than half way up Mt. Mansfield, highest peak. Many of the same people invested more than twice that amount in a second chair lift at Fayston in 1948.

Even before World War II, serving the skier had become a major commercial proposition, requiring not only costly lifts, but lodges, slopes, trails, cleared highways and most of the conventional services demanded by the tourist, to boot. Major developments sprang up all over the State, and nearly every town in the "snow belt" (see map, pages 12 and 240) boasted some facilities. Manchester, for nearly a century a swank resort town, acquired "Snow Valley" and "Big Bromley"—and a new year-round life. The "snow train" appeared as a new feature of rail travel, and winter traffic was swelled by hordes of cars, skis strapped to their tops. The Vermont colleges adopted skiing as a major sport, and in 1947 and 1948 little Middlebury, trained on nearby Bread Loaf Mt., twice captured the national intercollegiate ski title.

The impact on the state's economy has been most significant. Recreation looks more like a year-round business now, and hotels and resorts which closed promptly with Labor Day now seek a new clientele in the "other" half of the year. In fact, the State now concentrates on promoting fall foliage tours to fill in between summer and winter. A whole new source of income has been added to one of the state's principal industries; the state Publicity Bureau estimates the value of the winter sports business now at $10,000,000.

Morever, washing off the harsh face of winter and bursting open its grim isolation, winter sports have done

AT PICO, Janet Mead emphasizes facilities for the very young as well as the college crowd. It was no coincidence therefore, that her 14 year old daughter Andrea (above) made the 1948 Women's Olympic Ski Team as its youngest member.

something for the morale of the average Vermonter as well. Many a farmer now runs a rope tow on his side-hill pasture, and some have even been known to venture forth on the "durned" contraptions known to youngsters—and oldsters—as skis.

BIG BROMLEY, one of Manchester's two major ski areas, boasts a J-bar ski lift with the country's largest capacity—over 4000 an hour.

GREEN MOUNTAIN NATIONAL FOREST promotes forest conservation and also serves as a summer and winter recreation area. Many of the state's major ski developments—Snow Valley, Big Bromley, Bread Loaf and Pico—are in it or on its fringes. (See over).→

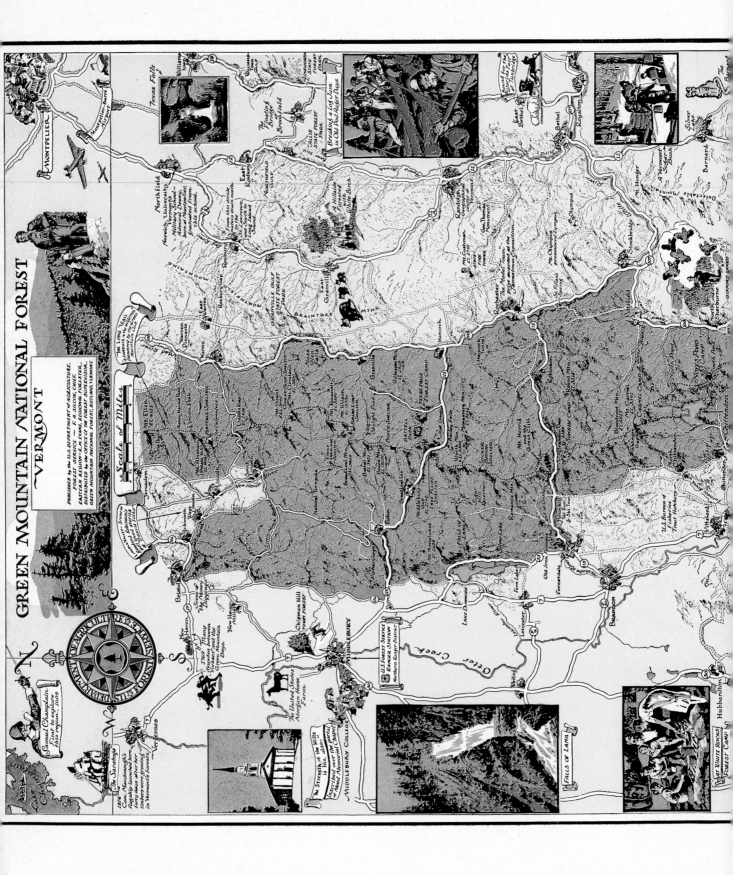

GREEN MOUNTAIN NATIONAL FOREST
VERMONT

PUBLISHED by the U.S DEPARTMENT of AGRICULTURE,
FOREST SERVICE — F. A. SILCOX, CHIEF.
EASTERN REGION—R. M. EVANS, REGIONAL FORESTER.
DISTRIBUTED by the OFFICE OF THE FOREST SUPERVISOR,
GREEN MOUNTAIN NATIONAL FOREST, RUTLAND VERMONT.

Scale of Miles

DEPARTMENT OF AGRICULTURE FOREST SERVICE

GIFFORD WOOD

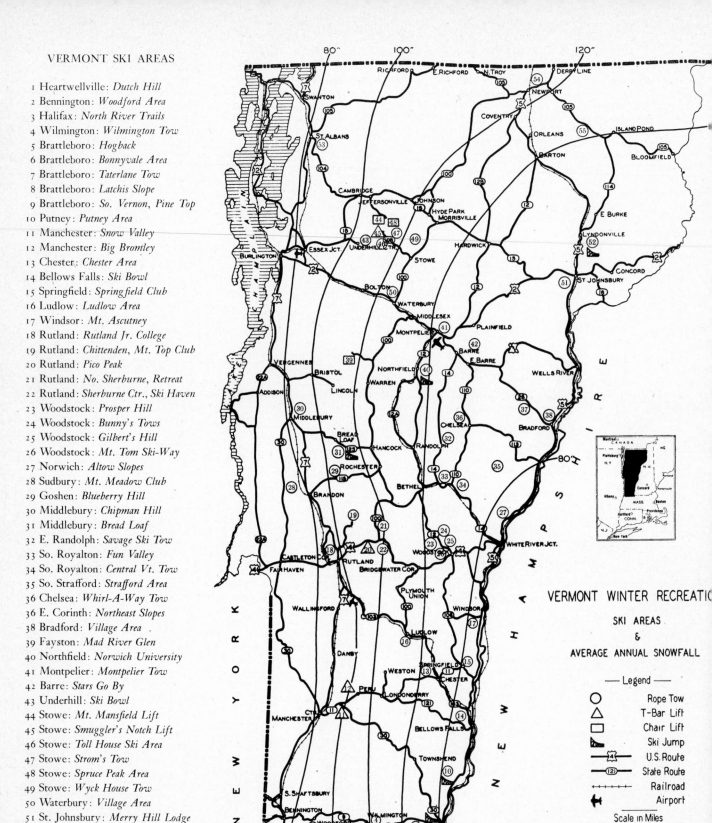

VERMONT SKI AREAS

1 Heartwellville: *Dutch Hill*
2 Bennington: *Woodford Area*
3 Halifax: *North River Trails*
4 Wilmington: *Wilmington Tow*
5 Brattleboro: *Hogback*
6 Brattleboro: *Bonnyvale Area*
7 Brattleboro: *Taterlane Tow*
8 Brattleboro: *Latchis Slope*
9 Brattleboro: *So. Vernon, Pine Top*
10 Putney: *Putney Area*
11 Manchester: *Snow Valley*
12 Manchester: *Big Bromley*
13 Chester: *Chester Area*
14 Bellows Falls: *Ski Bowl*
15 Springfield: *Springfield Club*
16 Ludlow: *Ludlow Area*
17 Windsor: *Mt. Ascutney*
18 Rutland: *Rutland Jr. College*
19 Rutland: *Chittenden, Mt. Top Club*
20 Rutland: *Pico Peak*
21 Rutland: *No. Sherburne, Retreat*
22 Rutland: *Sherburne Ctr., Ski Haven*
23 Woodstock: *Prosper Hill*
24 Woodstock: *Bunny's Tows*
25 Woodstock: *Gilbert's Hill*
26 Woodstock: *Mt. Tom Ski-Way*
27 Norwich: *Altow Slopes*
28 Sudbury: *Mt. Meadow Club*
29 Goshen: *Blueberry Hill*
30 Middlebury: *Chipman Hill*
31 Middlebury: *Bread Loaf*
32 E. Randolph: *Savage Ski Tow*
33 So. Royalton: *Fun Valley*
34 So. Royalton: *Central Vt. Tow*
35 So. Strafford: *Strafford Area*
36 Chelsea: *Whirl-A-Way Tow*
36 E. Corinth: *Northeast Slopes*
38 Bradford: *Village Area*
39 Fayston: *Mad River Glen*
40 Northfield: *Norwich University*
41 Montpelier: *Montpelier Tow*
42 Barre: *Stars Go By*
43 Underhill: *Ski Bowl*
44 Stowe: *Mt. Mansfield Lift*
45 Stowe: *Smuggler's Notch Lift*
46 Stowe: *Toll House Ski Area*
47 Stowe: *Strom's Tow*
48 Stowe: *Spruce Peak Area*
49 Stowe: *Wyck House Tow*
50 Waterbury: *Village Area*
51 St. Johnsbury: *Merry Hill Lodge*
52 Lyndonville: *Lyndon Club*
53 St. Albans: *Aldis Hill*
54 Newport: *Memphremagog Club*
55 Island Pond: *Brighton Club*

VERMONT WINTER RECREATION

SKI AREAS
&
AVERAGE ANNUAL SNOWFALL

— Legend —

○	Rope Tow
△	T-Bar Lift
□	Chair Lift
	Ski Jump
	U.S. Route
	State Route
	Railroad
	Airport

Scale in Miles

4 2 0 4 8 12

Vermont Development Commission
-1948-

Average Annual Snowfall in Inches

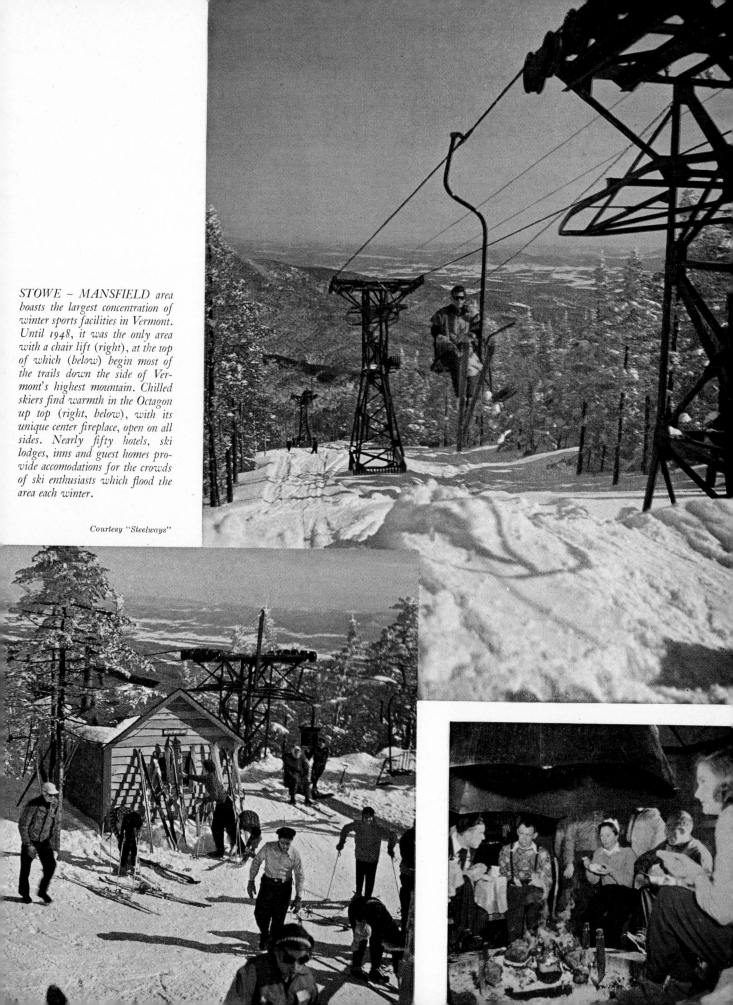

STOWE – MANSFIELD area boasts the largest concentration of winter sports facilities in Vermont. Until 1948, it was the only area with a chair lift (right), at the top of which (below) begin most of the trails down the side of Vermont's highest mountain. Chilled skiers find warmth in the Octagon up top (right, below), with its unique center fireplace, open on all sides. Nearly fifty hotels, ski lodges, inns and guest homes provide accomodations for the crowds of ski enthusiasts which flood the area each winter.

Courtesy "Steelways"

SUMMER HOMES

Having properly conceded that the Vermont winter offers surprising new possibilities, let us return to the summer, which has brought to the state from outside, not only new income but also new population. If the charm and loveliness of the countryside drew travelers, the serenity and security of living there drew new residents—both seasonal and permanent.

Visitors, charmed by Vermont's beauty, returned to purchase abandoned farms for summer homes. Metropolitan cliff dwellers perused the annual Publicity Service catalogs of farms and summer homes for sale with unconcealed longing. And many of those who restored old houses to a new life retired to them; others, unable to wait for old age, sought a livelihood in Vermont. It would be as unrealistic to ignore the spell which the word "Vermont" held over harried subway citizens, as it would be to deny the unreality of many of their flower-strewn dreams of cozy bungalows and a self-supporting farm among the Green Mountains. In the first place, living in Vermont involved much of the same struggle for existence to which man seems doomed everywhere. In fact, in providing the individual with a greater degree of independence, the Vermont "way of life" also delegated to him the basic responsibility for his own success or failure. Anxious immigrants found few ready-made jobs waiting, but the more enterprising used ingenuity—and often the magic of the word Vermont as well—to found successful small businesses.

Newcomers found the native Vermonters a different breed—and one often hard to understand. Some returned disillusioned to the bars and beauty shops of "civilization" after a brief flirtation with "country life." But others made a successful re-adjustment to a different way of life, and soon found its more leisurely pace and even its stubborn conservativism not unattractive.

Because the influx contained such a large proportion of artists and writers, the nation was soon treated to an intensive interpretation of the Vermont way of life on canvas and paper. The spate of books about an author's new home in the country, or his frustrations but eventual contentment in the restoration of an old house, finally brought the expected sour response in 1948, when someone wrote a volume entitled "Escape from Vermont."

But we may listen with reasonable attention to what Samuel R. Ogden has to say on the subject. Sam Ogden, with a hammer and trowel on the one hand, and an indefatigable and ingenious wife on the other, restored the deserted village of Landgrove to a new life, physical and social. For ten years he adroitly and tastefully built and remodeled houses, re-established schools, encouraged local crafts, and engaged in local politics—even to the extent of running unsuccessfully for Congress and successfully for the Vermont Legislature. Then he wrote a thoughtful and judicious volume called "This Country Life." No farmer, he drew a modest living from the land with a hoe, a bag of fertilizer, and that indispensable but often overlooked essential—daily labor. He then issued some printed advice on "How to Grow Food for Your Family."

No "booster," Sam Ogden served first as a member of the Vermont Development Commission, and in 1947 became its chairman. Yet he has no vast plans to lure great industries into the state, nor to promote a great wave of indiscriminate tourist travel. He represents the wise synthesis of the native and the new-comer in his desire to see the state develop along progressive lines without a sacrifice of its individuality and its more or less unique way of life. Thus it's worthwhile to quote him at some length, to help understand the problem of the newcomer face to face with the native.

"When a person makes the change from city living to country living, he becomes involved in situations and with conditions which could not possibly have been foreseen. As a result of these unforeseen contingencies, many of the experiments in rural living made in Vermont have ended in disaster and disillusionment. . . . Yet those who failed in country living failed because they were unwilling or unable to change their basic scale of values.

The Town of Waterford is typical of the many small communities which dot the Vermont countryside.

Life in the rural communities in Vermont offers the newcomer and his family opportunities for participation in the affairs of the community to an extent not possible elsewhere. In the cities interest in community affairs has practically disappeared. The growth of the large centers of population implacably absorbing surrounding towns and villages in their spread; the gathering together of rootless thousands, the impersonal and unnatural apartment house have all contrived to bring about the complete disappearance of community spirit in the cities. On the other hand this is not so in the country. Here the individual finds himself called upon to participate in the affairs of the community in which he lives. The newcomer to country living is quite apt to find himself regarded as an outsider at first, and if accepted at all, accepted under a special set of conditions reserved for "city folks." Some of these conditions are apt to be mildly annoying, to say the least, such as the one which stamps him as being one

with more money than sense, and as such fair game for anyone. Notwithstanding this initial handicap, it is perfectly possible for the "city feller" to become an integral and valued part of his community. Furthermore the fact that he comes from the outside gives him a freshness of viewpoint which leads to greater opportunities for community service than if he were a native. It has been the experience of many of those who have left the cities and come to Vermont to live, that from this direction have come the greatest satisfactions that living in the country has afforded.

So while at first there may be sound reasons for the newcomer to feel that his neighbors "tolerate" him at best, that they hold him off as an outsider and take advantage of him, still, humility and sincerity and patience will certainly eventually break down these barriers, and he will be called upon to accept his responsibilities as a citizen of the community.

The newcomer to country living will find many differences between country ways and city ways. The family larder will be handled on an entirely different scale, country hospitality is apt to make more demands on the store of provisions, and the possibility of being snowed in must always be counted on in winter. There will be less money spent casually; there will be more dependence on the mail order catalogs; prices and values will be scrutinized more carefully.

All I have said points up the matter I brought up at the very beginning. . . . The most difficult step to take in changing from city living to country living, is a shift in point of view and a change in values."

It is out of this continuing interchange between native and newcomer that we are learning more about the fundamental character of Vermont and Vermonters. As a native—whose ancestors were among the first settlers—Dorothy Canfield Fisher has this to say:

"Everybody in Vermont is still in a situation close enough to the primitive and natural [so that they] can by their own efforts to some extent make their environment and daily life more to their taste."

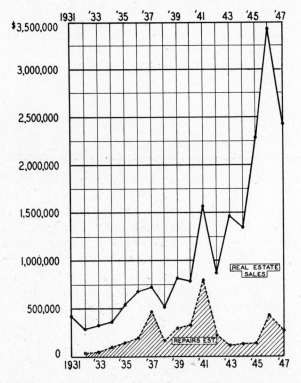

In any event, city folks went on buying summer homes, as the chart of real estate transfers shows. But only 6.7% of Vermont homes were seasonal in 1944 as compared with 10% in New Hampshire and Maine. Owner occupancy runs high—as much as 80% in Windsor and Windham counties. More and more of the newcomers were becoming permanent residents.

This much seems true, that there is actually something rather substantial behind the roseate dreams of returning to a "little farm in Vermont." Three elements—all of which we have mentioned before—loom large: beauty, serenity, and security. Vermont's beauty, as elsewhere, is bestowed by nature, but the state seems to have received an uncommonly large share, and succeeded rather better than her sister states in holding on to it. Her serenity stems from a predominantly rural way of life, from a conservative caste of mind, and from an exemption from the more feverish aspects of the industrial revolution. Security—a relative term anywhere in an interdependent world—has come from the pursuit of independent livelihoods, high home and farm ownership, and conservative financial policies, not to mention the practice of an ancient Puritan virtue—thrift. "Sound" finance, whether personal or public, has ever been the determined policy of the Green Mountain Yankee; in the face of an age of deficit financing, Vermont has hewed to the policy of "pay as you go." When the great flood of 1927 wiped a swath of destruction down through the state, Vermont launched its own bond issue for reconstruction, and paid it off within twenty years. But a bond issue for any purpose was a rarity. Vermont was the first state to vote a soldier's bonus in World War II, but every cent of it was paid out of current funds. The state's reluctance to make expenditures which could not be financed from current revenues has often kept her off the bandwagon of progressive social and economic advance, but has made her one of the best credit risks in the country. A small bond issue for capital construction was floated in 1947 at 1¼% interest rate.

Vermonters generally came through the depression years with less grief than the rootless proletariat and middle-class white-collar groups of the nation's more urbanized states. And in 1947 her income per capita was fourth among the New England states—not bad, really, for she was still the least industrialized. Among the Green Mountains—altered vastly by the twentieth century—self reliance still went hand in hand with independence.

ARTS AMONG THE NEWCOMERS

The movement out of the city into Vermont summer homes was led by a group especially talented in the cultural arts—perhaps because such people have greater freedom to indulge their personal preferences as to residence. Rudyard Kipling, Sinclair Lewis and his wife, commentator Dorothy Thompson, Alexander Woollcott (who bought an island in Lake Bomoseen), *The Saturday Evening Post's* William Hazlitt Upson, Vincent Sheean, world traveler and novelist, and other writers moved in; among the artists were Rockwell Kent, Norman Rockwell, Luigi Lucioni, Paul Sample, Mead Schaeffer, Herbert Meyer, Arthur K. D. Healy, John Koch, William Tefft Schwarz and a multitude of others, many of whom took

ROUTE 7 *by*
Arthur K. D. Healy

FREEDOM FROM
WANT *by*
Norman Rockwell

*Rockwell's "Four
Freedoms" were
among the most
widely circulated
paintings of World
War II. The artist
interpreted funda-
mental American
character as seen in
his Arlington neigh-
bors. "Freedom of
Speech" is repro-
duced on page 267.*
©*Sat. Evening Post*

up year-round residence. Barnard became a special retreat for the writers, and Dorset for the painters. The
latter town has as near to an art colony as Vermont can
boast. But most of these pilgrims are well scattered among
the hills.

What is commonplace to the native is often a subject of
special appreciation on the part of the newcomer. Vermont's authors and artists have endeavored to interpret
her to the country at large—often with varying success.
Norman Rockwell has affectionately interpreted the
Vermont character in the gentle caricature of his *Saturday
Evening Post* covers, while Luigi Lucioni has pictured
with infinite and loving detail its green and weathered
countryside. Most, in one way or another, have been
influenced by the locale.

At the same time, they have themselves brought a
new stimulus to the cultural life of the state and community. "Southern Vermont Artists," growing out of the
swarm of painters around Dorset and Manchester, now
holds an annual show, and has opened a more permanent
gallery in Manchester Center. "Mid-Vermont Artists"
and "Northern Vermont Artists" have also been organized
as active groups, though there is much over-lapping among
the three. Art exhibits now appear in the major fairs, and
regular changing exhibits are held at the Fleming Museum
in Burlington, the Wood Art Gallery in Montpelier, and
at Middlebury and Bennington.

CRACKER BARREL, *by Ruth Greene Mould*

JOSEPHINE, *by Hilda Belcher*

*LUIGI LUCIONI's landscapes mirror almost photo-
graphically the Green Montain land (see over).* →

VERMONT

Reproduced Through Courtesy of Life Magazine

in the paintings of LUIGI LUCIONI

VERMONT CLASSIC: *Shelburne, Vermont*
LAKE THROUGH LOCUSTS: *from Shelburne*

RED BUILDINGS IN THE SUNLIGHT: *Barre, Vermont (above)*   CLOUDS OVER EQUINOX: *Manchester, Vermont (below)*

VERMONT FORUMS presents an Indian and a British diplomat discussing the Far East (left). At right, Don Elberson leads a Neighborhood Club in a typical local discussion. Both are part of the renaissance in adult education.

Under the freshening influence of the new immigration, all aspects of Vermont life have taken on new vigor. Many have gone directly into small businesses and craft work, others have attempted to devise a way to encourage native craftsmen and market their goods. In 1933 Vermont-born Vrest Orton abandoned the big city and returned to Weston, where he organized the Vermont Guild of Old Time Crafts and Industries, bringing in a multitude of craftsmen to pursue various trades in connection with it. He himself operates the Vermont Country Store to market these and other Vermont products both directly and by mail. Soon there were a multitude of mail order "country stores," all trading on an increasing public interest in high grade Vermont products and handicrafts. Northampton and Amherst, Mass., each had a "Vermont Store," linked to a central one in Warren. And hundreds of producers began selling maple sugar, polished wood bowls, native woolens, and other like products by mail. In 1941 the state set up in the Department of Education, an Arts and Crafts Advisory Commission to help native Vermonters utilize their Yankee skills.

The state was also doing some notable things on the cultural level. A "Better Libraries Movement," led by the poet-professor Arthur W. Peach, resulted in the establishment of a Free Public Library Commission,

whose traveling "book-wagons" are now a familiar sight on country roads all over the state. The work of the Commission has also given new life to the many scattered and impoverished local libraries, and its regional system became a model for similar developments nationally.

Under industrialist Leon S. Gay's leadership, the Vermont Historical Society emerged from a cocoon of antiquarianism, helped establish the new state magazine *Vermont Life* in 1946, and supplemented its already reputable scholarly *Vermont Quarterly* with an educational program on the Vermont heritage. In 1947 it began a weekly series of dramatized sketches called "This is Vermont" over a state network of radio stations, and supplemented it with a regular newspaper column of the same name in 1948. In 1949 it began work on a feature length historical motion picture.

The Society also provided the stimulus in 1943 for the re-organization of the Public Records Commission to attempt reform in the care of official archives, both state and local. And in 1947 it proposed and obtained the establishment of a Historic Sites Commission. The latter body has embarked on a program of erecting historic markers along the state highways, and of caring for the historic sites at Hubbardton, Plymouth and elsewhere. It projects a series of "gateway museums" to help in telling the Vermont story to the traveler.

BOOKWAGON brings good reading to areas distant from libraries.

Vermont Historical Society, State Library and Supreme Court.

VERMONT STATE SYMPHONY ORCHESTRA

The Vermont State Symphony was the first in the country to organize on a state-wide basis. It recruits its volunteer players from all corners of the state bringing them by bus and car to the weekly rehearsals and the winter concert schedule. Summer concerts at the Green Mountain Festival are also a part of the schedule.

Supporting a symphony on such a basis has kept the orchestra in recurring but not unique financial difficulties. During 1947–1948 the Vermont Symphony Orchestra Association was organized, with chapters in the principal centers, to provide essential continuous support.

Musical Director of the orchestra during most of its existence has been Allen Carter, of Middlebury College. He has brought to the orchestra not only enthusiasm and musical competence, but also the physical stamina necessary for organizational work.

BURLINGTON MUSIC FESTIVAL

The Society also took the lead in establishing a War History Commission to prepare the story of Vermont's participation in World War II. Today the Director of the Vermont Historical Society serves as executive officer for all these other bodies as well, thereby furthering the coordination of their work with that of the parent body.

Forward steps in adult education have not been limited to official state agencies; indeed, the legislature has thus far refused repeated requests for the establishment of an adult education division in the Department of Education. But a state Adult Education Association was organized in 1947, and local communities—with and without its aid—have established programs of varying merit and success. Brattleboro's has been particularly outstanding. The extension work of the University has been influential, and Goddard College has steadily expanded a helpful program of adult education despite conservative suspicions of its alleged pinkish hue.

The most active state-wide programs, however, were those of the Farm Bureau and the newly organized Vermont Forums. The former, under the leadership of Arthur Packard and Don Elberson, established highly successful "Neighborhood Clubs" in rural areas for the discussion of local, national and international issues. And city folks got acquainted with a string of distinguished people as Vermont Forums, during 1947, 1948, and 1949, brought national issues under vigorous discussion on a circuit of seven Vermont cities—the entire program sponsored and financed by local memberships.

Drama and music saw a similar renaissance. Summer theatres in Weston, Brattleboro, Middlebury, Winooski, Dorset and elsewhere brought Broadway into the barnyard. Bennington College held festivals of the modern dance, and Goddard revivals of the old country dances.

Vermont's outstanding musical phenomenon is its State Symphony Orchestra, made up of volunteer players who pursue normal occupations as nurse, housewife, clerk, tradesman, or salesman in every corner of the state. Sunday nights they gather at Middlebury to rehearse, and, come Winter, give at least a half-dozen concerts, often with famous soloists. Because of its recurrent financial difficulties, friends of the orchestra organized in 1948 the Vermont Symphony Orchestra Association, with chapters in principal cities, each pledged not only to support an annual concert, but also to encourage musical activities of all kinds. The Washington County Chapter, for example, has its own Little Symphony and string quartet. Most of these cities were also on the New York sponsored Community Concerts series, which brought them great artists from the metropolitan musical centers.

In the summer of 1948 there was held a Festival of the Arts at Burlington, under the sponsorship of the University. Art, music (including the Vermont Symphony),

WESTON PLAYHOUSE, a summer theatre, occupies a restored church. Other groups have utilized barns and local auditoriums.

and literature joined hands in a vigorous three day program. The Burlington Lions Club sponsors also a Music Festival for school children, when bands, choral groups and youthful talented soloists gather annually in a great musical jubilee.

Nor should the cultural investigator overlook the local activities, such as theatre guilds or singing groups, of which one of the most distinguished is the Poultney Welsh Male Chorus (see page 211).

Most of this renaissance of cultural life is built upon native talent and abilities. Yet in many instances it has been stimulated, often led by enthusiastic "newcomers." All too often the latter saw with appreciation much that the native Vermonter took for granted. They brought the outside world to Vermont, and helped to speed the inevitable nationalization of its social, economic and cultural life. At the same time the unique qualities and values of the Green Mountain state found ardent exponents in these new immigrants, who interpreted Vermont to the nation through their work and vastly enriched its cultural heritage thereby. There are no more violent defenders of "unspoiled Vermont" than the late denizens of various Baghdads-on-the-subway.

251

XVI
"REPUBLICAN" GOVERNMENT

How Vermonters ran their common affairs in town meeting and state offices, and how a new liberalism crept into one party politics.

ALL over twentieth century America—despite the great growth of transportation and of industry—the biggest business was government. It was large, not only in terms of its working force, but especially so in terms of its expenditures. And its unprecedented growth had come in direct response to an insistent public demand.

The new tempo of the machine age had altered a simple, rural way of life—and complicated it. With a new feeling of helplessness in the face of the giants of the economic world, John Citizen called increasingly upon his government for protection against business abuses. Dependent no longer on himself alone for his livelihood, he increasingly leaned on government for those things he could no longer accomplish by himself. Thus there grew up the "Welfare State." But before we examine its structure, let's watch its evolution in party politics.

REFORMING ONE PARTY POLITICS

When the Republican Party was founded just before the Civil War, Vermonters embraced it with an enthusiasm which has varied little since. Though the Democrats have not disappeared—and have even occasionally given the dominant party a run for its money—the result has been one-party politics.

The Southern states have known one-party politics since the collapse of Reconstruction; and political scientists have generally agreed that its effect has been to retard social and economic change, to suppress progressive elements in politics, and to lodge control solidly in the hands of the most reactionary segment of the population.

Some of these same effects have been visible in Vermont, but not to the same degree. It is true that Vermont politics have had a heavily conservative slant—in startling contrast to the vociferous radicalism of early days. And blind resistance to change as well as a penny-pinching thrift has often kept Vermont's rank in many fields well down the nation's list.

But the exclusive emphasis on the traditional, stubborn conservativism of the Vermonter overlooks part of the story. Unlike the South, conservative one-party politics has not left government totally unresponsive to the need

for change. And it has furnished the nation with some outstanding leaders. In Congress were Matthew Lyon, Thaddeus Stevens, Stephen Douglas and a quartet of Vermont's own Senators: Jacob Collamer (whose statue the state selected to stand alongside Ethan Allen in the Hall of Fame), Justin Morrill, George F. Edmunds, and Redfield Proctor. All were prominent party leaders, and oft mentioned presidential possibilities. The state also furnished two presidents, Chester A. Arthur and Calvin Coolidge, and one Vice President, Levi P. Morton. Many other Vermonters migrated West, like Matthew Lyon and Stephen Douglas, and then went to Congress from their new homes.

Vermont's declining influence in national politics was signified by the progressive reduction of her representation in the House from five to one. But in the forties she regained prestige by sending three Senators who became nationally recognized as outstanding liberal Republicans in a party which many thought had gone to seed. Warren R. Austin, though conservative in domestic politics, led the liberal internationalist wing of the party and more than any one person made possible non-partisan unity in foreign policy during the critical war years. He was the logical choice to be the nation's first Representative to the new United Nations. George D. Aiken, after breathing new life into Vermont liberalism at home, trecked to Washington, where he became the acknowledged leader of the liberal Republicans and the farm bloc. After Austin's departure, Aiken was joined by businessman-philosopher Ralph E. Flanders, already recognized as one of the nation's leading liberal industrialists.

But the first revival of liberal elements in Vermont politics came forty years earlier, when the progressive movement swept the nation. Though relatively free from large-scale business abuses or industrial conflict, Vermonters responded to the revelations of the "muckrakers" and reformers.

"Reform" began in Vermont with a call to revise the methods of nominating candidates for public office—and everyone thought primarily of the governorship. As late as 1904 there were no laws governing the process of nomination—which in the Republican Party was tantamount to election. In effect, therefore, the people had nothing whatever to do except to rubber stamp the election of the party's hand picked candidate, who had been "nominated" in what was virtually a closed party "caucus." Men of wealth could and did control the party machine, and it was no coincidence that in non-industrial Vermont, a succession of businessman occupied the executive chair.

Of course, any move to control the party caucus met with bitter opposition from party politicians, and, indeed, for some time found few supporters in high office. But Governor Josiah Grout issued a call for caucus reform in 1898. It was completely ignored by his two successors, William W. Stickney and Edward C. Smith, despite a vigorous newspaper campaign in its behalf. But Governor John G. McCullough gave active support to the movement, and by 1904 a caucus act, establishing fair methods of conduct and voting, was on the books. Both of his successors, Charles J. Bell and Fletcher D. Proctor argued in favor of keeping it in force.

Real participation of the people in nominating their Republican governors, however, awaited establishment of a direct primary. The press campaign did not end with caucus reform, and by 1912 all parties pledged themselves to some system of direct nomination by the people. When the General Assembly of 1912 failed to act, other than to authorize a referendum on the subject, unfavorable comment was widespread. The popular verdict, despite skillful attempts to divide its proponents, was strongly in favor of a primary election, with the majority in favor of a direct primary. None the less, the Old Guard, led by ex-Governor Stickney, Percival Clement, railroad magnate, and Attorney General John Garibaldi Sargeant, decided to introduce a law at which the legislature would rebel—or failing that, pass one which could not work and which would therefore certainly be repealed. The original bill was advanced to third reading in the House 172–28, but was then amended so radically that the resulting bill was actually rejected. The press reacted immediately with a scathing attack, public opinion was aroused, and Governor Charles Gates sent in a special message urging the House to reconsider. Like frightened rabbits the legislators scurried for cover, and the bill shot through 147–25. The Senate OK'd it promptly. The whole incident was significant as a demonstration of the lack of fixed opinions among the solons, and their readiness to vote according to a momentary reaction to a word or a situation.

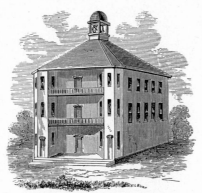

FIRST VERMONT STATE HOUSE
Built 1808; replaced 1833

---

1 For a further discussion, see page 263.

The new system provided for a direct vote of party members on their candidates for state office—though there was nothing to prevent Democrats from voting in Republican primaries if they chose. And they frequently did, since it was the only way of making their vote felt. In general, this participation usually served to strengthen the candidacy of non-"party men." As a result, recurrent attempts to close the primaries have been pressed by party stalwarts, but without success.

The new law did not eliminate all difficulties, of course. Wealth still gave a man a great advantage, though he no longer needed to use it to gain a hold on party machinery. Rather he utilized it to wage a vigorous campaign, with lots of campaign workers, printed matter and newspaper ads. Most elective officers were so miserably paid that no one but a man with independent means could afford to hold the office. It is significant that no small farmer ever became governor of rural Vermont, either before or after the direct primary.

SOCIAL LEGISLATION

The most significant legislation, however, was economic rather than strictly political.

The first movement to "regulate" the rising power of business, as elsewhere, was directed against the railroads. New England pioneered in the establishment of railroad commissions, and Vermont got hers in 1855. But it had no teeth, and the courts refused to support its decisions. Governor Proctor came to the aid of the Commissioners in 1906, and, with the aid of State Senator Ernest W. Gibson, obtained a new Commission with power to issue and enforce orders. The immediate success of the new agency strengthened the movement to bring public utilities under similar control. This was accomplished early in 1909 at the urging of newly elected Governor George Prouty. The new agency was designated as the Public Service Commission.[1]

A vigorous movement on behalf of labor gained impetus at about this time. Workers obtained their first state union in 1903, and the new Vermont State Federation of labor began to agitate immediately for the improvement of working conditions. In 1904 a law prohibiting the employment of children under twelve was passed, but was not enforced. Reinforced by the vigorous propaganda work of the Vermont Branch of the National Child Labor Committee, labor obtained in 1910, a second act, regulating both female and child labor. But it too was largely ineffective.

It was the active intervention of the Episcopal Church which turned the tide. A thorough investigation by the

Diocese showed particularly bad conditions in the textile mills. Shocked at some of the revelations, the legislature early in 1912 prescribed a 58 hour maximum work week, and provided for a Factory Inspector to make sure the laws were observed.[2] Industrialists fought the latter bitterly, but a tour of the Winooski mills of the American Woolen Company convinced the skeptical legislators.

The next step was a workman's compensation act, also violently opposed by industry, which protested that it would constitute a staggering burden for business. But the public demand was so strong as to force even the Republican Party to include it as a plank in their 1912 platform. The 1912 legislature, doubtful of the constitutionality of such an act, submitted a constitutional amendment to the citizens, who approved it in town meetings, March 1914. A legislative commission reported in favor of the projected law, and the legislature, unable to think of any further reason to delay, passed a comprehensive, but not perfect bill, in 1915. An Industrial Accident Board was appointed to administer it.

The wave of progressive sentiment which brought about the enactment of this sort of welfare legislation was in striking contrast to the normal conservative tenor of Vermont political life. In part, the liberal attitude taken by the Republican party reflected the new slant of public opinion. But, in 1912, at least, it also reflected a definite Progressive trend—the capital letter having been added to the word by ex-President Theodore Roosevelt. "Teddy," after an initial sneer at the "muck-rakers," had grafted into the national Republican program a considerable element of reform, if only as a result of his "trust-busting." Dissatisfied with the policy of his successor—though Taft pursued fully as progressive a program—TR decided to run with a third party in 1912. The Democrats offered a liberal candidate in Woodrow Wilson. In effect, the progressive tide having reached its crest, all parties were competing for the liberal label.

This was also true in Vermont, where all parties framed liberal platforms. Here also a new Progressive Party ran a close third in the 1912 gubernatorial elections. Combined Democratic and progressive votes exceeded the Republican by far.[3] Public opinion following the election was so strongly progressive as to prod a reluctant legislature into passing the bulk of the laws demanded by the Republican and Progressive platforms alike.

As in the nation, progressivism petered out in the war years, much as Vermont's early radicalism disappeared into the Civil War. The twenties found the state quietly enjoying the general national prosperity, and little concerned with special legislation on behalf of workers who had, it was assumed, a chicken in every pot. Vermont's own taciturn, unspectacular Calvin Coolidge symbolized the majority's conception of the role of the executive, national or state.

The impact of the Great Depression of the thirties effected a radical change in the public temperament. Nationally, Coolidge (and his successor, Herbert Hoover) were pilloried as narrow minded do-nothings. The people turned again to their government for protection—not now against the giants of industry, but against the operation of impersonal economic forces. Draw up a plan, they said to government, to get us out of this, and to keep us alive and kicking in the meantime. In the New Deal period Americans went most of the way toward the creation of a "welfare state," in which government provided more and more services—and handouts—for its citizens.

The Panic struck Vermont, of course. Banks closed, factories laid off men, and farmers found they could not sell their produce for what it cost to raise it. But on the whole, perhaps because Vermonters more than Americans generally could fall back upon the minimum security of the land, the state did not suffer as badly as the nation. It did not pass a quantity of social security and welfare acts, or labor legislation. It did agree to set up a Planning Board with federal funds, but after a couple of years of vigorous research, the Board gave up the attempt to draw up any master plan for Vermont.[4]

FARMER-PROGRESSIVE COALITION

But during this period a new element was drawn into Vermont politics. Farmers, always the largest element in the legislature, had only recently begun to think in terms of political action. The distress of depression years had acted as a catalytic agent, but it was the Vermont Farm Bureau, under the leadership of Arthur Packard, which guided his steps into effective political channels. Nominally a non-partisan organization, the Bureau has known the friends of the farmer, and has consistently aided them in an informal but effective fashion.

The first test of agriculture's new found political strength came in 1936, when a quiet, unassuming nurseryman was elected governor. George D. Aiken espoused many a liberal cause, and by 1941 was in ill repute with conservative elements generally. None the less, completing two terms as Governor, he determined to run for the United States Senate. At the death in 1940 of Senator Ernest W. Gibson—who had done yeoman service for the progressive cause in Vermont before leaving for Washington in 1934—his son Ernest Jr. was appointed to fill the

---

[2] Credit for establishment of factory inspection goes largely to newspapermen Arthur J. Cayo of Burlington, and his Workingman's Political League, which elected a labor representative to the General Assembly to press the cause. Governor Allen B. Fletcher gave valuable support to the movement. Cayo was also influential in getting a workman's compensation act.

[3] Vermont was one of only two states carried by Taft.

[4] As a matter of fact, the most comprehensive survey was conducted by the Vermont Commission on Country Life, a private committee manned by volunteer workers, whose report *Rural Vermont* (1933) is a classic of its kind.

unexpired term. The European and Pacific wars were closing in on the United States, and after several vigorous months as national Chairman of the Committee to Aid the Allies (succeeding the late William Allen White), he determined to join Vermont's 172nd Infantry in military service.

Aiken's opponent was Ralph E. Flanders, a self-made businessman of national reputation. Virtually every paper in the state supported Flanders, as did the "regulars." To the surprise of nearly everyone, Aiken won a resounding victory, and was returned again in 1946.

Aiken was succeeded in the governor's office by Governor William H. Wills, one of the state's most beloved chief executives. No flaming radical, he nevertheless set the Old Guard of the national party on its ear with his demands for fresh leadership. Wills' term was largely devoted to war-time problems, and he gave effective leadership to the state's civilian defense program.

After the conventional two terms, upon doctor's advice, Wills stepped down on behalf of Lt. Governor Mortimer R. Proctor, fourth of the prominent clan to seek the state's highest office.

Proctor was deliberate and slow moving, to the extent that his administration was unkindly characterized by an opposition paper as a "Study in Still Life." But he initiated a series of significant investigations of the various segments of governmental activity, the results of which did not emerge until the end of his term. Welfare and institutional problems were agitating politics, as well as the states' newspapers, and a new Welfare Board under Olin D. Gay, Cavendish industrialist, made a detailed investigation, many of whose recommendations were adopted by the 1947 General Assembly. A Commission on State Government and Finance made a series of requests, nearly all of which were implemented by the two succeeding legislatures.

In 1946 Ernest Gibson Jr. returned from the South Pacific with his commanding officer, Major General Leonard S. Wing, who was generally conceded the next governorship. But Wing barely outlived a series of jubilant celebrations, and anti-Proctor men turned to Gibson to take on his mantle.

Gibson had served as Secretary of the Vermont Senate before his term as U. S. Senator, and was well indoctrinated in state politics. But he had not proceeded up the ladder of service in House, Senate, and Lieutenant-Governorship, a well sanctified custom. Gibson centered his campaign in an attack on this "line of succession," and managed to convince the public that his opponent was far more conservative than he actually was.[5] This time the

5 Actually, the Proctor governors had allied themselves with important reform legislation: Fletcher with caucus reform and factory inspection, Redfield and Mortimer with governmental reorganization.

Major General Leonard F. Wing (above) assumed command of New England's 43rd Division in the field—the only National Guard officer to receive such a command in World War II. His 172nd Infantry regiment was composed largely of Vermonters, but most of them, as in World War I, were scattered all over the globe. 35,000 from the state served. Wing made a triumphant return in 1946, and was generally conceded the governorship in that year. Exhausted by four years of bitter jungle campaigning, he did not live to run for the office.

Colonel Ernest W. Gibson (right) served as Intelligence Officer on Wing's staff during the South Pacific campaigns. He stepped into Wing's shoes in 1946, running for Governor on a liberal platform. His victory over the old guard of the party brought the state a progressive revolution in politics.

255

papers divided about evenly, but Gibson staged a surprising upset. Without organization support,[6] poorly financed, and in opposition to the powerful Vermont Marble and other industrial interests, he denied a Proctor the governor's chair. As in Aiken's senatorial campaign, the support of the farm groups was clearly the dominating element in his success, though the candidate himself supplied an effective war record, a handsome youthfulness, and a forceful and effective personality—which are always valuable at the polls.

The 1947 Gibson victory was a vigorous shot in the arm to the liberal wing of the state Republican Party. Traditionally out of sympathy with party men, the progressives depended upon a friendly chief executive. The result was to restore, in effect, two-party politics *within* the Republican Party. Many Democrats, unable to get anywhere with or within[7] their party, crossed party lines to swell the liberal vote in the Republican primaries. As a result, a real contest of principles and program was restored to the one-party state, and new and healthy rejuvenation of political life begun. Its ultimate destiny—in 1949—still hinged on the personality of Ernest Gibson and his ability to hold together the liberal coalition. Most political seers agreed that the prospects of accomplishing the latter were slim without him.

Gibson's program, while anticipated in part by his predecessor, had a certain dramatic appeal. He did not hesitate to ask for more than Vermont governors even dared to request. To this he added drive and a determination to scotch the old idea of Vermont as a "poor" state, unable to "afford" progressive governmental services—particularly in the field of health.[8] His success —and in fact that of the new liberal program—was immensely aided by unprecedented farm prosperity. A dollar no longer looked so large to the farmer-representative, and he was more inclined than previously to overlook the pennies. Gibson's budget was unprecedented in size, but the legislature took it—along with most of his program.

The cost of bringing government up-to-date appalled more conservative politicians. Lt. Governor Lee Emerson decided to oppose Gibson in the 1948 primaries, and again, with newpaper support divided, the election seemed likely to go against the Governor. Again Gibson upset the prophets, and promptly presented the 1949 legislature

with the balance of his proposals. He got a large share of what he asked.

Gibson's recurrent victories at the polls—despite party rejections—and his success with the legislators, was significant of a new found determination in the state not to stand apart from current of change, as well as a new willingness to accept an expanded role of government in the daily life of the average man.

GOVERNMENTAL REORGANIZATION

One reform on which both conservatives and liberals could often be found in agreement was the streamlining of state government. Conservatives were appalled at the mounting costs of governmental operations; progressives wanted a more efficient administration of the new governmental services.

Unlike in Washington, the Republicans could not throw the responsibility for advanced costs onto their political opponents. Thus they showed greater enthusiasm for reorganization than for most other reforms which had been thrust upon them. In 1917 Governor Graham set forth a three point program: (1) a cabinet-like "Board of Control" (2) consolidation of overlapping agencies, and (3) a reorganization of the courts. The Governor got his Board of Control. The General Assembly consolidated a multitude of agricultural and conservation activities under a new Commissioner of Agriculture, and several agencies relating to factory inspection, workmen's compensation, and arbitration, under a Commissioner of Industries. But lawyers and judges lobbied the court reform out of existence.

In 1923, under the stimulus of Governor Redfield Proctor, the first wholesale reorganization of the executive division was undertaken. The general plan was in line with a growing national trend. Nearly all governmental activities were consolidated into seven major departments: finance, public service, public welfare, public health, highways, agriculture, and education. Each had a head directly responsible to the Governor. The first three were completely new, and brought together a group of related activities.

The Public Service Department took in most regulatory activities, including the Commissioner of Industries. Public Welfare consolidated charity and probation work with supervision of state institutions. And the Finance Department brought together the Commissioners of Taxes, Banking and Insurance, and the Purchasing Agent under a Commissioner of Finance—who was chief budget officer. But the State Treasurer and Auditor of Accounts, being constitutional, elective officers could not be included.

For this reason, as well as the reluctance of the various commissioners to submit to the Commissioner of Finance, the office gradually broke apart. Then in 1939 the industrial work was again removed from the Public Service

---

6 The organization has fought Gibson vigorously, and has thrown back his attempts to introduce new blood into party leadership. But Gibson continued to win popular verdicts.

7 The Democratic Party in Vermont is more firmly dominated by a small group of old time politicians than the Republican.

8 Greatly disturbed by Selective Service records of multiple rejections for poor health, Gibson proposed mobile health units, patterned after army models. The plan was defeated by the casting vote of Lt. Governor Lee E. Emerson, who ran against Gibson in 1948.

VERMONT HOUSE, in session above, Spring 1947, contains 246 representatives, one from each town.

Department and set up as the Department of Industrial Relations. In 1947 social welfare work and institutions were split apart again. Boards and commissions continued to multiply, until by 1949 state government was again a great amorphous mass of overlapping agencies, with little of the logical separations of 1923 left. Some attempts have been made piecemeal to introduce more logic into the division of governmental functions, and Mortimer Proctor's Commission on Finance and Government made some pertinent recommendations, some of which were carried into law. But a move to appoint a Reorganization Commission was beaten down by a narrow margin in the 1949 legislature—on the grounds that it constituted one more addition to the mass!

In part, the multiplication of Boards has resulted from an attempt to insulate departments from "politics" and to provide continuity of administration. Boards composed of citizens formulate policy; thus when the public expresses desire for a change in policy by replacing the governor, it is possible for him to alter the personnel of the boards without seriously disrupting the department and losing the valuable experience of its administrative head.[9] On the other hand, boards with members serving stated terms are not responsive to the chief executive, and it becomes nearly impossible for him to formulate and impose a congruent program on all divisions of the state government.

The problem of state organization eternally poses the problem of reconciling popular control with administrative

---

[9] Actually many "unprotected" departments, like Agriculture, have been the least subject to political shifts in late years. The Commissionership of Agriculture, though appointive by the Governor, is virtually a career job.

efficiency. The workings of "politics" often disrupt the efficient administration of state affairs. On the other hand, in a democracy, it is important to keep government responsive to the public will as expressed through elective officers, who should be able to impose resulting changes of policy on the administrative hierarchy. How, then, are we to organize government to minimize the unhappy effects of using public office as private reward, and at the same time reflect intelligently public opinion as to the proper activities of government?

Actually Vermont has not been as troubled by the difficulty as more populous states; her state offices are too poorly paid to classify as political plums. And whatever may be said against one party politics, it *has* reduced strictly partisan strife and minimized change-overs in office for purely party reasons. Continuity in office is the rule rather than the exception.

LAW-MAKING

The American constitution, it will be remembered, reserved to the states all powers not specifically assigned to the national government. Although the federal government's assigned powers have been broadened to include many fields of activity previously thought to be the exclusive province of the state, yet the state still stands closest to the life and labor of the citizen. What the state does in its field is determined by a legislature elected by the people. Laws passed by it govern the activity of the citizens of the state and control the work of executive departments set up to administer the functions the state has decided to take on, on behalf of its citizens.[10]

The legislature is, in essence, the people regulating their common affairs through representatives. The representative system evolved when it became clear that the pure democracy of the town meeting was adaptable only to small communities. Towns therefore each sent a representative to a General Assembly to act upon state affairs. It was, of course, a "unicameral"—one house—legislature.

Soon some towns grew and others declined. Still every town had one representative. As a consequence the many people of the big cities were overbalanced by the few people of the back country. Agitation for a more just plan of representation brought the compromise of a second house[11]—the Senate, with its county representatives apportioned by population.

Yet, for a bill—a law in the making—to pass, both

houses must agree. A small portion of the state's population can command a majority in the House and thus exert a veto over all legislation. Moreover, as a result of town representation, this small state has one of the nation's largest legislatures—a grievous burden.

Many proposals have been made to recast the legislative branch as well as the executive. The most comprehensive was offered by Auditor Benjamin Gates in 1935.[12] Gates proposed that county lines be abolished, and that Vermont's 246 towns be reduced to 50 or 60, related to population centers. Each town would then, he argued, send representatives to a unicameral legislature according to its population, and all parts of the state and segments of its population would be equally represented. But inasmuch as the constitutional amendment necessary to do this would need to pass a House dominated by the small towns due for abolishment, no such plan of consolidation has ever issued from the legislative branch.

INTERPRETATION OF THE LAW

Because all men do not read the same meanings into law, as well as because alleged violations of it must be proven, courts are established to interpret and apply the law. They must decide in some cases whether the law has been broken; in other cases juries of people do it. In either case the court exacts a penalty or makes an award within the limits of the Acts of the General Assembly or the common law of the land.

In Vermont petty civil cases and misdemeanors are tried in the fourteen municipal courts, located in population centers, or before Justices of the Peace in small towns. These judges are appointed by the governor. But most important cases originate in the county courts, presided over by two judges elected in the county plus one of the six Superior Judges, elected by the General Assembly, who also select the five justices of the Supreme Court, including the Chief Justice. The Supreme Court, as its name implies, is the court of last resort, and the bulk of its business relates to appeals from the decisions of the lower courts. It does have original jurisdiction in certain specified cases, however.

The Superior Judges sit as chancellors of Courts of Chancery to try cases in equity. There are also Probate Courts to handle estates and guardianships.

Although judges arrive at their positions by the political process—by election, the bench is classified as a career and does not suffer much—at least on the higher levels—from the inroads of partisan politics. Indeed, the custom of assigning the senior Supreme Court justice to replace a retiring Chief Justice, and of moving the senior superior judge up to the Supreme Court, is now well established. In obtaining election to the Superior Bench, candidates—usually legislators—put themselves on a fairly secure career ladder leading to the Supreme Court.

---

10 Two appointees of the legislature have evolved into executive officers: the ADJUTANT GENERAL heads the state's military department, and the SERGEANT-AT-ARMS is the chief house-keeper.

11 For a more detailed discussion of this change, see page 77.

12 Interestingly enough, Gates, an elective officer, also proposed a short ballot, eliminating the Treasurer and Auditor as elective offices. He proposed to consolidate them with other finance agencies in a single fiscal office, with an appointive Comptroller at its head.

THE "WELFARE STATE"

O'er forms of government let fools contest,
Whate'er is administered best, is best.

ALEXANDER POPE.

The significant thing about state government today is not its organization, but its functions—that is, the services it renders the citizens, who through taxes pay the bills for these services. The basic function of government is the protection of life and property, but in our modern world, where the industrial revolution has brought about a degree of inter-dependence among peoples, where each person is dependent on his neighbor for goods and services, citizens have consequently demanded that government undertake tasks which they could no longer handle by themselves. The industrial revolution also placed in the hands of "captains of industry" great economic power, which if abused, was as great a threat to the liberty and property of the individual as arbitrary political power. So the people also increasingly demanded laws to control the activity of dangerously powerful economic combinations and monopolies. The sum trend of laws to curb big business and laws to provide new services for citizens was a great increase in the size of government and the extent of its activities. Many saw this as necessary in an interdependent age—an inevitable outcome of economic concentration resulting from the industrial revolution. Others gloomily envisioned a dangerous trend toward socialism.

But Vermont, set somewhat apart from the industrial boom of the late nineteenth and twentieth century, saw little threat from her few industrialists, and only infrequently passed laws either regulating or penalizing big business. And because there was no mammoth concentration of industry there was no rootless proletariat. The rural Vermonter still found he could do most things for himself without the help of government. And what he did in common with others, he preferred to do through his town government, where he and his neighbors were the only public servants.

EDUCATIONAL AND CULTURAL FUNCTIONS

Nowhere more than in the field of education have local pride and jealousy manifested themselves—as we have already seen. Although the Constitution writers planned a state-controlled school system, their legislative successors turned it back to the towns, where it largely remained for a hundred years. By a gradual strengthening and extension of the role of the DEPARTMENT OF EDUCATION, and through a system of state aid to local schools, the state gradually gained control over education.

State aid for distribution to the towns was set up in 1935 on a complicated "equated pupil" basis. This granted more aid to the "poorer" towns—those with low "grand lists." But many towns purposely kept their grand list[1] low (and their tax rate consequently high) to obtain the maximum financial assistance from the state. Furthermore, there was a certain minimum for each school regardless of pupils, which promoted a multiplicity of small schools.

Educators deplored the artificial hot-house provided for these uneconomical and normally inefficient small units, and pressed for a change in the state aid formula. This was proposed to the 1949 General Assembly by a special commission established in 1947 to work out a more just basis of distribution, and one which would not discourage consolidation of wasteful small schools.

As the state has assumed a large share of the cost of education, its Department of Education has grown in size and functions. From a one man Commissioner it has expanded until today there are several divisions: Research, teacher certification, guidance, instruction, health, vocational education and rehabilitation.

Within the department there was also established in 1941 an Arts and Crafts Advisory Commission, for the purpose of encouraging native crafts, training artisans, and assisting in the marketing of these craft products.

As is indicated by the Arts and Crafts service, the educational services of the state have not been limited to the schools. As far back as 1894 a FREE PUBLIC LIBRARY COMMISSION was established to make books available to the isolated country regions. Within the last two decades it has blossomed out under the direction of librarian Dorothy Randolph, with regional libraries in five centers. These "bookwagons"—converted light trucks—travel the back roads with their choice assortments of volumes old and new.

Even older is the STATE LIBRARY, which began in 1825 —like most others—as a law library for courts, officials, and legislators. As the concern of government broadened, so also did the reference material shelved in the official library. Today its collections span the fields of human thought and research, though the more popular and ephemeral material is left to the FPLC, and local historical and genealogical material to the Vermont Historical Society, all in the same building with it. But it still maintains a special service to solons, in its Legislative Reference Bureau.

The VERMONT HISTORICAL SOCIETY, founded in 1838, is nearly as old. But initially it was a private membership organization. It soon was brought under the wing of the state, with quarters in the State Library. In 1917 space for the library and museum were provided in the new Library and Courts Building. Today the Society, retaining its dues-paying membership, acts as the historical agency of the state and receives, like other departments,

---

1 The total of evaluated property.

a regular legislative appropriation. Besides its role as a historical library and museum, the Society undertakes educational work in Vermont history, utilizing books, magazines, newspapers, radio, and motion pictures. It has sponsored other state agencies for special tasks, such as the WORLD WAR II HISTORY COMMISSION and the HISTORIC SITES COMMISSION, and its Director serves as executive officer of the first and chairman of the second. The latter has jurisdiction over the state's historic houses, sites, battlefields etc. and has supplemented the Historical Society's educational work by an extensive program of informational roadside historic markers.

The state government over its more than century and a half of operation accumulated a great store of records. In the beginning, the SECRETARY OF STATE, as recording secretary for a government then limited to the General Assembly and Governor, kept the records of official action. As executive departments multiplied, they created and kept their own records, until by 1943 a vast and ill-assorted conglomeration jammed offices and warehouses. At the impetus of the Vermont Historical Society, the inactive PUBLIC RECORDS COMMISSION (established in 1937) was recast[2] and given new powers to act to reduce the appalling mass. But in 1949 it still had no place to store records, and had taken custody of none, except the remnants of military records saved from the burning State Arsenal in 1945. But authority had been given to many state departments to destroy numerous useless accumulations. Most of its hopes for future action hung on its request to the 1949 legislature for added storage space on the rear of the Library Building. The Commission is a hybrid agency, concerned on the one hand with the preservation of historical records for the scholar, and on the other with the destruction of useless records to ease the burden of the contemporary administrator.[3]

It would be incorrect, however, to attribute all educational work to these specific agencies. Almost every department undertakes to educate the general public as to significance of its work. Certainly the publicity work of the Development Commission and its magazine *Vermont Life* has many educational aspects. And for a brief time, both the Highway and Welfare Departments had their own magazines. Both the Forestry and Fish and Game Services issue a quantity of conservation material; as does the Department of Agriculture and the Experiment Station in their field. The Motor Vehicle Department and the State Police vie with one another in safety campaigns, and even the Liquor Control Board makes occasional excursions into the field of temperance education. Like the national government, the state has become a great agency of adult education—or propaganda, depending on how you look at it. But the watchful arm of a jealous legislature soon draws back to earth any over-ambitious flights of printed rhetoric. The thoughtful, but to rural Vermonters grandiose plans of the State Planning Board of the thirties petered out in a multitude of miscellaneous special projects. It was eventually absorbed, with other development agencies, into the new Development Commission in 1945.

CONSERVATION AND DEVELOPMENT OF NATURAL RESOURCES

It was natural that rural Vermont's first official concern in the realm of conservation and development should come in the field of agriculture. Like education, action in this field early became involved in politics. In 1870 a Board of Agriculture, Manufactures and Mining was established, though the latter two were quickly forgotten. Football of agrarian politics, the agency changed its name and character several times, until a COMMISSIONER OF AGRICULTURE was established in 1908. The state was fortunate in its commissioners. Under Orlando Martin the dust of conflict settled. In 1912 Elbert S. Brigham began a twelve year program of improving marketing methods. Resigning to run for Congress in 1924, he was succeeded by Edward H. Jones, another successful dairyman, who continued Brigham's efforts to perfect milk marketing and brought to a successful conclusion the bitter and hardfought campaign to eliminate bovine tuberculosis.

Today the Department, one of the state's largest, is divided into seven sections: Plant Pest Control, Livestock, Creamery Inspection, Markets, Weights and Measures, Agriculture, and Office Services.

Of course, the products of the land include trees as well as grass and seed crops. In 1904 the Board of Agriculture was instructed to appoint one of its members Forestry Commissioner, and in 1908 the Board was authorized to hire a professionally trained State Forester —to manage state forest reserves and enforce forest laws. A separate FOREST SERVICE was established in 1923. In the years since its creation the State Forester has worked energetically to promote conservation of woodland resources and reforestation. The first state nursery was established in 1906, and since that date 31 million trees have been set out on waste acres. Beginning in 1909 woodland sectors of isolated hill areas were bought by the state and set aside as state forests for the development of good forest practices. Many more were given by private donors. Located in some of the loveliest, unspoiled parts of the state, they were gradually developed for recreational use, and some were designated as state parks.

Control of tree blights—like the malignant white pine

---

2 The President and Director of the Society, along with the State Librarian, Secretary of State, and one appointive member make up its present membership.

3 Printed public documents are housed and distributed by the State Library.

blister rust—and of forest fires, are other major functions of the State Forester. Lumber production, which had reached an all time low in 1930, began to rise again as the state initiated systematic restoration of its woodland resources.

A like attention to conservation of fish and game resources began even earlier (see page 222). Eventually the enforcement of fish and game laws was taken out of the hands of local wardens, and the FISH AND GAME SERVICE became a regulatory as well as a conservation activity. Because of the sportsman's interest in fishing and hunting, it engaged in extensive promotional activity as well.

Both Forestry and Fish and Game were absorbed into a new Department of Conservation and Development in 1935, along with the State Geologist and the Publicity Service, in an attempt to consolidate scattered conservation and development activities. After a change in name to Department of Natural Resources in 1943, the experiment was given up in 1947 when both the Forest Service and Fish and Game Service were turned loose again under the guiding eye of special supervisory boards. The Publicity Service and State Geologist were consolidated with the remnants of the old Planning Board into a new DEVELOPMENT COMMISSION in 1945. This was greatly expanded in 1947 by the creation within it of new divisions of research and of industrial development, though jurisdiction over flood control problems, inherited from the Planning Board, was shifted into a new, separate Water Resources Board. The Commission, preferences to the contrary notwithstanding, had devoted its first biennium almost exclusively to the problem of flood dams, to the neglect of other important work. Because of current political headaches involved in a burning issue, it released its jurisdiction with a sigh of relief.

The Commission now concerns itself chiefly with basic, but limited economic research, direct and indirect publicity to attract travelers and residents, and the encouragement of new small industry. Power and labor shortages have hobbled its efforts in that regard. Actually more effective work could usually be done by vigorous local action, as was demonstrated in Burlington, Brattleboro and St. Albans—all of which acquired one or more branch plants of larger companies.

Because of its scope, the Commission came the nearest to resembling an executive office of the Governor. Divested of the title "planning"—which sounded socialistic to extreme conservatives—its further expansion seemed likely.

There were other related activities outside these major departments. Principal one is the Industrial-Agricultural Products Commission, set up in 1939 to promote the development of new industrial and agricultural enterprises. Lacking staff or substantial funds, it has not been active, and its functions now parallel in large part the Development Commission's. Furthermore, while the independent Yankee farmer has been happy to accept the helping hand of the state, industry has preferred a hands-off policy, and there is no department doing for manufacturing what the Department of Agriculture does for farming.

HIGHWAYS AND PUBLIC WORKS

All departments extended their services in response to the twentieth century's new demands. But government saw its greatest expansion in one of its newest offices—the DEPARTMENT OF HIGHWAYS.

Mechanization invaded Vermont on the four wheels of the "horseless carriage." But automobiles run on roads, and these were the town's responsibility. The latter soon found it beyond their ability—and their purse—to construct and maintain through highways for commercial and tourist use. Increasingly the state found it necessary to come to their aid.

The first step was "state aid," begun in 1892. This was money furnished the towns for work on "permanent" roads. These funds were expended by the town road commissioner, but the restrictions on its use were steadily tightened, until full supervision was given the State Commissioner of Highways in 1912. In 1917 the state accepted federal aid for main through routes, and in 1931 all state aid highways which received federal aid also were designated "state highways." Over these the Highway Board had complete control, as well as full responsibility for construction and maintenance. As a result the state system is now divided among state, state-aid, and town roads.

As the state increasingly assumed the burden of building and maintaining modern high speed highways, the administrative organization of the Highway Department expanded. The first (1892) advisory Highway Board was replaced in 1898 by a State Highway Commissioner. The Board was restored in 1921 as the chief policy making body, with the Commissioner as its executive officer, and this remained the system through 1949. The tug and haul of local and state politics in the assignment of highway funds is thus worked out within the three-man Board, leaving the commissioner and chief engineer free for the technical problems of construction. Under direction of the Highway Board there are now eleven district highway commissioners, each acting as agent of the commissioner with respect to his territory.

Revenues to support the state's increasingly heavy burden come from two entirely new sources: registration of motor vehicles and the state gasoline tax.[4] At first small, income from these sources rose steadily with the multiplication of cars and their increasing use—as did the

---

4 Annual registration began in 1908. The first one cent gas tax was imposed in 1923; it now stands at five cents.

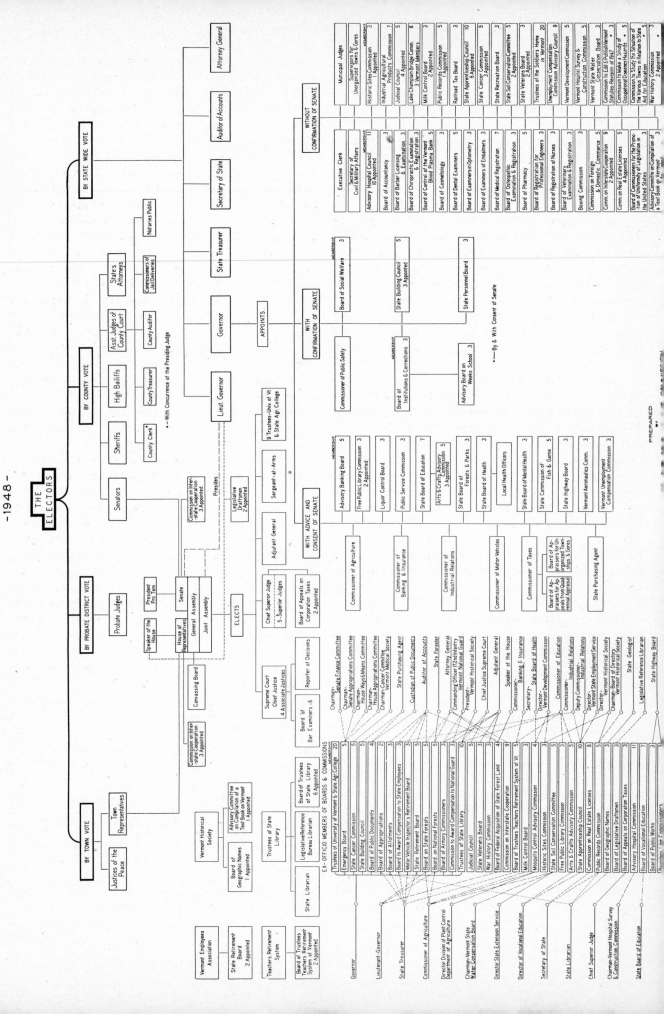

ORGANIZATION CHART OF STATE & COUNTY GOVERNMENT
-1948-

fees and the taxes. These two income sources now support almost all highway work.

Most public works other than highways are handled by the Highway Department, although there was a Public Works Commission, which was abolished in 1947. But the spate of building in state institutions and offices authorized by the 1947 legislature caused the creation of a State Building Council to supervise all work of this sort.

REGULATION OF BUSINESS

Industrialization proceeded more slowly in Vermont, thus minimizing industrial conflict and the growth of monopoly. But railroads came early, and as elsewhere, the people soon demanded regulation of the new collosus in the public interest. As financial abuses and juggling proceeded apace, aroused citizens insisted on stronger and stronger state control. Eventually, under its powers over inter-state commerce the federal government acquired substantially complete control over railroads for its Interstate Commerce Commission.

Vermont's intervention in the conduct of business "affected with the public interest" began with the appointment of a railroad commissioner, as early as 1855. His powers were, for the most part, limited to investigation of company finances. In 1886 a Board of Railroad Commissioners was established with substantially enlarged authority over freight and passenger traffic. Power to enforce its regulations was still lacking, however, until 1906, when the Board was empowered to issue judgments and orders having the force of law—powers hitherto reserved to the courts. This was the beginning of what came to be known as the "quasi-judicial" agency—an administrative body able to rule upon points of law and issue orders (all within the scope of the laws establishing it).[5]

The next General Assembly, in 1908, added similar powers over other utilities, communication and transportation facilities: gas and electricity, telephone and telegraph, express and sleeping car companies. At the same time the board received its present day title "PUBLIC SERVICE COMMISSION."

As the federal government increasingly took over regulation of transportation, the Public Service Commission concerned itself chiefly with public utilities, and especially electric companies. In cases where current was derived from water power, the Commission found itself involved also in the hot question of flooding valley farm lands behind the power and flood control dams.[6]

Control over manufacturing industries was chiefly exerted in the form of regulation and enforcement of workmen's compensation and industrial safety laws by the COMMISSIONER OF INDUSTRIAL RELATIONS, who began his work under the Public Service Commission. His office was established in 1917 to combine the duties of the Industrial Accident Board and the Factory Inspector. Only two years later he was given the right to suspend operating licenses as a result of non-compliance with his rule and regulations. This amounted to a life and death power over licensed businesses, as, for example, insurance companies.

Many of the laws under his jurisdiction were those covering the employment of minors and women, passed as far back as 1892.[7] In 1912 he was given the authority to investigate and assign the blame in industrial disputes, but he lacked any power other than public opinion to obtain a settlement. In 1939 parties submitting to arbitration were compelled to accept the verdict, but ten years afterward there was still no way of forcing arbitration of any dispute. As a result there was little attempted.

As an independent agency since 1939 the Department of Industrial Relations now exercises considerable though incomplete control over employment in manufacturing industries, but nothing comparable to the Public Service Commission's power to regulate rates and finances of public utilities and other agencies of transportation and communication.

The DEPARTMENT OF BANKING AND INSURANCE exerts limited regulatory powers over these two businesses, conducting regular examinations of their activities.

Although their chief functions may not be regulatory, several other departments exert special regulatory powers. The SECRETARY OF STATE, as chief recording officer, took on the duties of issuing and recording licenses and permits of various types. Through these he now regulates many activities indirectly, such as roadside advertising. For a while he issued automobile licenses and enforced regulations pertaining to their operation. As the job grew in magnitude there was established a separate MOTOR VEHICLE DEPARTMENT, incorporating a highway patrol. The latter was broken off in 1947 with the establishment of a State Police as part of a new DEPARTMENT OF PUBLIC

---

[5] The constitutionality of the quasi-judicial agency was established by the Vermont Supreme Court in *Sabre vs. Rutland RR Co.* (86 Vt. 350; 1913). In a surprisingly advanced decision, the Court declared that the Commission is "an administrative body clothed with functions of a judicial nature . . . [and is] authorized in the exercise of the police power to make rules and regulations required by the public safety and convenience, and to determine facts upon which existing laws shall operate. In a sense it has auxiliary, or subordinate legislative powers also; having made laws applicable to railroad corporations, the legislature could delegate the power to apply the general law to specific situations. This did not constitute, therefore, a violation of the separation of legislative, judicial and executive powers demanded by the state constitution. This case was extremely important in establishing broader powers for administrative agencies to act for the state, in the public interest.

[6] Both Governors Wills and Gibson acted vigorously to prevent further losses resulting from the construction or heightening of new or old dams.

[7] In 1931 the Commissioner was given the right to refuse a permit to work to an applicant under 16—a power previously exercised by the local superintendent of schools.

SAFETY, which had statewide powers of law enforcement similar to those of local police and county sheriffs.[8]

The FISH AND GAME SERVICE exercises similar powers in the issuance of fish and game licenses and the enforcement of fish and game laws through its force of wardens. The AGRICULTURE DEPARTMENT has extensive regulatory powers over livestock diseases and plant and pest control work. A major regulatory function is exercised by the MILK CONTROL BOARD (outside the Department but including many of its officials) which sets *minimum* prices to protect dairymen against sudden price collapses or arbitrary pressures by the distributors, and generally supervises the distribution and sale of milk.

The DEPARTMENT OF PUBLIC HEALTH has strong regulatory powers to enforce standards of sanitation, especially in businesses catering directly to the public, such as hotels, restaurants and tourist homes.

The BOARD OF AERONAUTICS exerts control similar to that exercised over automobiles by the Motor Vehicle Department. It issues flying licenses, enforces aeronautic laws, makes flying regulations, and approves airport locations.

The LIQUOR CONTROL BOARD issues regulations with regard to the retail sale of liquor in restaurants, and handles through state stores the entire distribution of bottled liquor.

There are also a multitude of licensing and examining boards for various professions and activities, from the Bar to barbers, embalmers to engineers, chiropodists to cosmetologists.

As the scope of modern economic activity grew, the state increasingly stepped in to see that only competent personnel were licensed to practice, that licensed automobile operators, fishermen, and hunters complied with state regulations, and that businesses "affected by the public interest" operated to the best interests of the public. If the state did not enter business, it at least proposed to protect its citizens against incidents and abuses of business operation.

HEALTH AND WELFARE

Vermont was early in the field—1886—with an official BOARD OF PUBLIC HEALTH, but it had little power other than to investigate sanitation and epidemics. But in 1892 it was authorized to appoint local health officers, whose powers to maintain healthful conditions were broadened. In 1902 the State Board was granted the power to make sanitary regulations for schoolhouses and other public buildings, as well as the authority to enforce quarantines. Its powers of enforcement were steadily strengthened,

and barbershops and slaughterhouses added to the scope of its jurisdiction. In 1904 inspection of food and drugs was authorized to prevent adulteration and fraud.

As in the regulation of public utilities, many of the Board's regulatory powers were brought into court, where they were sustained as a justifiable action of the state under its police powers to protect public health and safety.

Facilities for research and laboratory experiment were steadily improved, and with its headquarters located in Burlington, relationship with the UVM Medical College and the medical centers there were intimate and mutually profitable. In a complete reorganization in 1949, however, administrative headquarters were moved to Montpelier, although the laboratory remained in Burlington. Most medical men remained sceptical as to the workability of such a division of functions. At the same time the new department enfolded several previously independent commissions, and acquired jurisdiction over state institutions whose primary functions were in the field of public health or medicine: the State Hospital for the Insane at Waterbury, the Brandon State School and two TB sanatoriums.

Institutions grew one by one, quite independently of one another. The state's role began with correctional institutions. As public attitudes toward punishment changed, the State Prison at Windsor was erected in 1909. When the old reform school at Waterbury burned in 1874, it was moved to Vergennes and set up as the Vermont Industrial School, for the confinement and training of juvenile delinquents. Now known as the Weeks School, it has a population in excess of two hundred.

As a result of the new tendency to view insanity as a medical rather than criminal problem, the Brattleboro Retreat was founded with state aid in 1835. Today the Retreat still cares for nearly 400 state patients from the southern parts of Vermont. But in 1891 the Vermont State Hospital was opened in Waterbury, and today houses over 1000 insane. But the merely "mentally deficient" were not cared for until 1915, when the Brandon School was founded. It now houses over four hundred mental defectives.

The state moved into the field of physical hygiene when it took over the Vermont Sanatorium at Pittsford in 1921. This was founded in 1907 as a private institution for the isolation and care of tuberculosis patients. In 1931 the state also took control of the Washington County Sanatorium at Barre. Alone of state institutions, neither of these operate at full capacity—a testimonial to the effectiveness of preventive work in this field.

The constant expansion of institutions reflects the growing feeling of responsibility by the state for its mentally, psychologically and physically handicapped population. But it also reflects the increasing percentage

---

8 Prosecution for criminal offenses lies within the jurisdiction of the ATTORNEY GENERAL and the county states attorneys. The Attorney General's office was established in 1790, abolished in 1797, and revived in 1904.

of the population requiring institutional care. Mental deficiency has increased to the point where statisticians have gloomily calculated the date at which half the population of Vermont would need to be institutionalized and supported by the other half. Emigration has consistently drawn the best stock from isolated, exhausted, back country regions, leaving a series of "tobacco roads," where a pauperized, debilitated and often feeble-minded people multiply faster than the general population. Also multiplied are the financial burdens of the town overseer of the poor and the state welfare agencies.[9]

Public charity and care of the poor since the earliest days has been a function of the town, but one largely neglected because of the Vermonter's fierce independence and insistence on the individual's ability and obligation to care for himself. But neglect and inability of the towns to care for those needing public assistance caused the state to intervene, as in so many other fields. In 1917 a Board of Charities and Probation was established and given the responsibility of care for neglected, dependent or delinquent children, as well as powers of review over state institutions. The duties of town overseers of the poor were carefully specified, and they were required to report to the Board, which was granted supervision over town poorhouses. Two years later, despite bitter local opposition, an act was passed making the towns responsible for half the cost of maintaining children committed to state care.

The DEPARTMENT OF PUBLIC WELFARE was created in the extensive governmental reorganization of 1923, to consolidate all scattered boards and commissions acting in the field of social welfare or having charge of state institutions (other than educational). Under the new department expanded programs of social welfare work have been undertaken, often with federal aid. The national Social Security Act of 1936 stimulated the extension of services to children,[10] which are now administered from nine district centers. In addition to financial aid to the blind, administered through these district offices, the Department undertakes direct rehabilitation work and teaching to help rescue these unfortunates from complete dependence.

Probation and parole activities of the department are also administered through district offices. But despite decentralization from Montpelier of much of its most important activity, the trend toward increased state control of welfare activities has continued. As a result of

federal grants, old assistance is now available, though administered and partly supported by the state. Unemployment compensation, also supported by federal funds, is administered by a state UNEMPLOYMENT COMPENSATION COMMISSION. The Vermont State Employment Service is run as a division of this Commission.

In 1946, a comprehensive survey was made of state welfare activity, and in 1947, partly in response to this program and partly as a result of newspaper attacks on the administration of state institutions, a thoroughgoing shakeup of welfare activities was made. Social welfare work was consolidated with Old Age Assistance in a new SOCIAL WELFARE DEPARTMENT. Stripped of its other work the Department of Public Welfare was titled the DEPARTMENT OF INSTITUTIONS AND CORRECTIONS. In 1949, while consolidating public health activities, the legislature cut away institutions of a medical or public health nature, such as the State Hospital at Waterbury, the Brandon School and the two TB Sanatoriums. The result was a rump department having jurisdiction over little more than correctional institutions.

State institutions have unfortunately been one of the chief footballs of politics in Vermont, as elsewhere. During the period from 1946 to 1949 particularly, flamboyant newspaper charges revealed some abuses but obscured most of the fundamental problems of institutional care in an aging and not overly wealthy state.

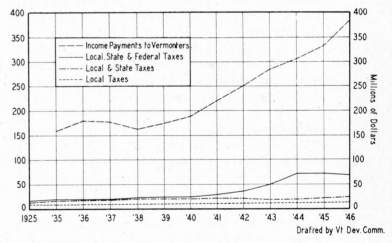

Drafted by Vt Dev. Comm.

FINANCES

In 1946 a special state Commission on State Government and Finance drew attention to certain provisions of the Vermont and Pennsylvania Constitutions, which read like this:

No public tax, custom or contribution shall be imposed upon or paid by the people of this state except by law for that purpose; and prior to any law being made to raise a tax, the purpose for which it is to be raised ought to appear evident to the legislature to be of more service to the community than the money would be if not collected.

---

[9] Some preventative work is attempted at Brandon and Waterbury, but inadequate funds have limited the department's psychiatric clinics to a single psychiatrist. The 1946 survey recommended three clinic "teams" of three persons each.

[10] In 1946 there were 1,637 receiving aid to dependent children, and 1,129 children committed to state care (759 were placed in foster homes). Kinstead Home in Montpelier acts as a temporary shelter home, but holds only about forty children.

Vermonters, advocates of extreme thrift in their private affairs, have traditionally been equally as insistent on conservative and thrifty administration of their public affairs. Thrift has often deteriorated into parsimony, and many things which badly needed doing were left undone as a farmer dominated legislature drew the purse strings too tight. But such a policy has also prevented wasteful expenditures of modest taxes and the creation of "paper factories" within the confines of state government.

As early as 1797 Vermonters established the office of AUDITOR OF ACCOUNTS to stand as watchdog over the STATE TREASURER and the Executive department in the disbursal of the state's monies. Like the Treasurer, Secretary of State, and Governor, the Auditor was elected by the people, and still is. But as government expanded and financial transactions multiplied, new offices were required, one being the familiar job of tax collector—more formally labelled COMMISSIONER OF TAXES. It became his function—at direction of the legislature—to raise enough money to cover the skyrocketing expenses of government.

In 1916 ex-Governor Edward C. Smith gave a horrified backward look over fifteen years of government expansion. Total expenditures of three quarters of a million dollars in 1901 had more than quadrupled by 1914. He found that legislative expenses had tripled, school costs had gone up *seven* times, and other administrative expenditures an equal amount. The parallel and inevitable increase in taxes tripled the burden on banks and insurance companies, quadrupled that on railroads and quintupled that on telephone and telegraph companies. Ex-Governor Smith, President of the Central Vermont Railroad, was naturally concerned about the effect on his company. Taxes, he pointed out, took 31% of its net revenue in 1901, but *108%* in 1914—resulting in an actual loss for the CV in that year!

Smith had no objection to the road and license taxes as being revenue drawn from specific sources to develop improved facilities for those sources. But the burden on corporations seemed to him crippling. State income taxes were then unknown; though by 1946 they were the third largest source of revenue.[11] The modern trend has been to leave property taxation to the towns, drawing state revenue from personal and corporate earnings. Strong opposition to any general sales tax exists both among the citizens and tax officials.

---

11 The income tax was instituted in 1931. In 1946,
Revenue from Income taxes:	$1,601,203.75
Revenue from Business taxes:	1,745,424.53
Revenue from Excise taxes (liquor):	2,377,897.63
Revenue from Excise taxes (cigarettes):	785,403.78
Revenue from Inheritance taxes:	666,801.85
Revenue from Old Age Assistance Tax:	371,740.60

Revenue from the gas tax and motor vehicle licenses, which exceed any of these general fund revenues are pledged to highway use.

MARCH MEETING

As the economic and social life of the people grew out of its local context, the state and federal governments took over more and more local functions and drew the political center of gravity away from the towns.

Yet it was the town which was the first and most important unit of government in Vermont—in some cases antedating the state government by a quarter of a century. In the days of little travel, of local self-sufficiency and a simpler life, men gathered together in town meeting to govern their mutual affairs and—inevitably—to lay modest taxes to pay for the merely minimum necessities of government. The town meeting—an ancient New England institution—was pure democracy in action. Even though a "representative" system has replaced it on the higher levels of government, the "warning" for March meeting is still posted all over Vermont—even in its largest cities with their mayors, councils and city managers—"to see whether the the town will vote to . . ."

Here is the simple, fundamental American democracy which inspired Norman Rockwell to turn to his own town meeting for the subject matter of his panel "Freedom of Speech" for his classic series THE FOUR FREEDOMS. It is the arena in which several score Calvin Coolidge's still run their affairs with careful thrift and tight lipped deliberation.

The simple, enduring values of a town meeting are like the precepts of a Vermonter like Calvin Coolidge—sound in essence, though sometimes inadequate in application. Yet, if Vermont proposes no panaceas for the aches and pains of an industrial age, she does have to offer a way of life with certain lasting values, expressed in the equalitarianism of a town meeting—or in the simple sincere tribute of a president to his native state. Calvin Coolidge is, to many, the apotheosis of Vermont.

FREEDOM OF SPEECH

Norman Rockwell's famous painting of an Arlington town meeting epitomizes the democratic grass roots character of Vermont local government.

VERMONT

FROM THE SPEECH OF

~ PRESIDENT COOLIDGE ~

AT BENNINGTON, SEPTEMBER 21, 1928

"Vermont is a state I love.

"I could not look upon the peaks of Ascutney, Killington, Mansfield and Equinox without being moved in a way that no other scene could move me.

"It was here that I first saw the light of day; here I received my bride; here my dead lie pillowed on the loving breast of our everlasting hills.

"I love Vermont because of her hills and valleys, her scenery and invigorating climate, but most of all, because of her indomitable people. They are a race of pioneers who have almost beggared themselves to serve others. If the spirit of liberty should vanish in other parts of the union and support of our institutions should languish, it could all be replenished from the generous store held by the people of this brave little state of Vermont."

To the Vermont Historical Society,

Calvin Coolidge

CARTOTTO PORTRAIT OF COOLIDGE, in the Vermont State House

POSTSCRIPT

*The truth of history is a sacred thing—
a thing of far greater importance than
its dignity. And the truth of history
should not be sacrificed to sentiment,
to patriotism or to filial piety.*

HENRY ADAMS.

THERE is a great dignity to the Vermont heritage. In seeking the true story behind the colorful epic of frontiersmen, Green Mountain Boys, pioneer inventors and industrialists—the whole vast pageant of the state's history—there is little opportunity for loss of dignity in the search for truth.

Yet this volume is not primarily a definite investigation into original sources. It is rather an attempt to arrange available knowledge, interpret it, and present it in a fashion which will both interest and inform the reader.

Let there be no mistake—one of the greatest needs of the present time is an authoritative, scholarly history, drawn from extended investigation of the massive quantity of manuscript material now being unearthed. The author, as Director and Editor of the Vermont Historical Society, is in daily contact with this material, and is now in the process of editing a documentary history of Vermont. Much of it has gone into this volume indirectly. But the job of preparing such a definitive history will require the undivided time of a scholar for at least five years. Thus, a historical society head almost automatically rules himself out of consideration, for his historical role is that of researcher, administrator, editor, museum curator, and educator—in short, the day-by-day job of unearthing and interpreting living history to the widest possible audience. As a result, this book has been written little by little, in moments snatched from a demanding schedule.

There has long been, it seemed to the Vermont Historical Society, as well as to me, an immediate need for a full and colorful history of the state. Previous historians have drawn up reins at the date 1791, when—they thought—the "romantic" period of Vermont history ended. At best, they added a few brief chapters on the War of 1812, the Civil War, and Admiral Dewey. The epic of industry and agriculture—in fact, for the most part, the whole social and economic history of the state—has been almost completely overlooked, except in excellent, but special studies of selected periods. These latter volumes are almost all to be found in the as yet incomplete ten volume history *Growth of Vermont*, edited by the author. Upon them I have drawn extensively, with deep appreciation to the authors.

There are many other debts due. But my principal debt is to the people of the Green Mountain State, who have provided narrative and drama for the "Vermont Story."

ACKNOWLEDGEMENTS

A writer's debts are frequently as much to living persons who have provided information which is not in print. I am greatly indebted to Elbridge C. Jacobs and Charles G. Doll for aid in the geological complications of chapter one, and to Stephen H. P. Pell and Eleanor Murray for help with illustrations for chapter two. Wallace Fay and E. R. Whitaker were indispensable to assembly of the marble and granite material, and Leon S. Gay and James F. and William E. Dewey the same as respects the woolen section. Vrest Orton, Clyde Smith, Harold Bailey and Philip Cummings were most helpful with the agricultural material.

Many have cooperated to make possible the great number of illustrations included. I am particularly indebted to Charles E. Crane, Assistant to the President of the National Life Insurance Company, for permission to utilize many of the drawings of Roy F. Heinrich and others, and also to Robert C. Lane, Harris W. Soule, and Walter R. Hard Jr. of the Vermont Development Commission, for assistance in the use of illustrative material developed by me as Editor of *Vermont Life*, and used previously therein. I am also indebted to numerous organizations such as the Bryant Chucking Grinder Co., Jones and Lamson Co., Fellows Gear Shaper Co., Fairbanks-Morse Co., Howe Scale Co., Gay Brothers, A. G. Dewey Co., the Barre Granite Association, the Vermont Marble Co., the Baltimore and Ohio R. R., the New Hampshire Historical Society, the New York Historical Society, the Vermont Historical Society, the Fort Ticonderoga Museum, the *Saturday Evening Post* and *Life* magazine, Watson-Guptill Co., the several universities, colleges, and schools, and a multitude of other people who have graciously aided me in the search for pictorial material.

Allan McDougall and Edward Sanborn have reduced the author's cartography to a neater and more pictorial form—how much so will be evident by one or two of the maps which did not get redrafted.

My heaviest debts are to people like John C. Huden, Mary G. Nye, Leon W. Dean, and especially Arthur Wallace Peach, who have read patiently these chapters and provided me with invaluable suggestions. And to others like Vrest Orton, Leon Gay, John Clement, Harold Rugg, William J. Wilgus, Clara Follette, Pliny Morse, Martha Parsons, Ben Lane, Proctor H. Page, Jr., and a score of others, I owe a great deal which would be difficult to specify. Finally, to my wife I owe thanks for help with the index and surcease from the back of my head at home.

I have no real way of adequately thanking Dorothy Canfield Fisher and Allan Nevins for their great courtesy in providing introductory material for the book and for their kind words about it. I sincerely hope that the general public will find the same values they see in it.   EN

Errata:

p. 47, col. 1, line 5: *for* Thomas Cockrane *read* Robert

p. 65, caption, right top: *for* Otter Creek *read* Wood Creek

p. 68, col. 2, line 24: *for* sands *read* lands.

p. 70, caption, right bottom: *for* expedition *read* Old First Church.

p. 244, col. 1, line 17: *for* a native *read* one. (Mrs. Fisher reports that her parents were temporarily outside the state at the time of her birth.)

BIBLIOGRAPHY

THIS BOOK is projected as the first of a series on the American States. State history has suffered for many years by being presented in a pedantic and unattractive fashion; even the school textbooks have hardly been such as to attract interest in the subject. Yet in the field of local and regional history there is a vast reservoir of unexploited material, which if authentically interpreted would necessitate the recasting of American historiography. For to date, the American heritage has been written and rewritten within a national-chronological framework. This consistently overlooks a great deal of the significant material which has determined American development and character, but which has not emerged sufficiently to the surface to be reflected in the textbooks of United States history.

The particular pages presented here are the outgrowth of the author's conviction that, since knowledge is daily acquired through the eye by visual images as well as textual print, information in book form should do likewise. This has long been recognized in the magazine field, but has been largely ignored as respects books. True, books *are* often illustrated; moreover, there are many picture books of distinction. But neither a book of words nor a book of pictures (nor for that matter a book of words with incidental and unrelated illustrations—often grouped in a "picture section") supplies the need for a joint textual-pictorial presentation. Where words will best convey the idea, they are used; where a picture or map will do it better, they have been used. And where both are needed, both have been used, and they have been placed, as nearly as possible, side by side.

This concept was the determining factor in designing the format of the volume. Despite a strong personal interest in typography, the latter was sometimes sacrificed to the needs of the material. And only by use of the large page—long since adopted for geographies—could maps and pictures be reproduced in a size suitable for proper visualization, or could pictures and text be grouped on the same or facing pages.

To provide the maximum number of pictures necessary to illustrate and supplement the text, we utilized all mediums: reproductions of old paintings and prints, portraits, old maps, old photographs, and where there were gaps, we utilized drawings and new photographs, which often the author had to go out and get himself. We also found it necessary to do the cartography for special maps to set forth important information which text could not make clear. And because of this concept of informational presentation, he also had to lay out the book from beginning to end to make sure that text and pictures came at the proper places.

The manufacturing process by which color and black and white forms were run off progressively over a period of two years made it impossible for the author to revise the entire text as a unit. The first chapters were printed before the last ones were written. Only by this process could production costs—which are extremely high for color work—be brought to the point where the book could be sold for less than a small fortune and thus to only a small audience. At that, it has been accomplished only by invaluable cooperation from the staff of Vermont Life and the Vermont Development Commission.

At times the requirements of our formula and of the format have circumscribed us in a way which we would have preferred not to be limited. The book would be handsomer *without* some of the illustrations which were included because they were needed. And many subjects needed expanding, which could not be done.

In fact, the limitations of space were the author's greatest "hair shirt." To condense and then condense again was a great trial. And it caused the elimination of much which ought to have gone in. Students of Vermont history will miss many of the good old stories of the pioneers and the Green Mountain Boys (all too many of them apocryphal). They may even find missing many of the familiar names, because the author does not believe in lists where adequate explanation cannot be given. Yet he was astounded by the ultimate number of entries in the name index, which may indicate that Vermonters as well as Vermont play a large role in this history of the people of the Green Mountain State.

BIBLIOGRAPHY

The general sources for Vermont history are scattered and mostly confined to the early period. Walter H. Crockett's *History of Vermont* (5 vol., N.Y. 1921) was intended to be a definitive history, but its material for the period following 1850 is largely of a routine political character. Social and economic history is passed over lightly throughout. Its usefulness as an authoritative history is diminished greatly by the lack of source footnotes. Arthur F. Stone's *Vermont of Today* (N.Y. 1929) is a series of essays on various conventional aspects of Vermont life and history, but is occasionally useful where other sources are totally lacking. In the process of assembly is a ten volume history of the state entitled *Growth of Vermont* (E. W. Newton, general editor, Vermont Historical Society, 1946–) which when complete will give an authoritative view into the Vermont past, functionally and chronologically. Only four volumes were out by 1949 and are noted below.

For the early period of Vermont history the student has first Dr. Samuel Williams' *History of Vermont* (1794 and 1809), a first hand narrative by a friend and contemporary of many of the leading men of the time. It comes close to being primary rather than secondary source material, and displays a surprising concern for social and economic topics. Ira Allen's *History of Vermont* (London, 1798) is a personal narrative and defense of the activity of the Allens. No student should overlook Zadock Thompson's pioneering *History of Vermont* (Burlington 1842), still indispensable for some material.

A half century later, building upon the indefatigable activity of Henry Stevens in the collection of source material, two histories of early Vermont appeared. The first was written by a Yorker, Benjamin Homer Hall, whose interest was primarily in the *History af Eastern Vermont.* (N.Y. 1858). His conclusions were not sufficiently favorable to the partisans of the Westside to please Vermont historians, and in 1868 Governor Hiland Hall published his *History of Early Vermont* to present the case for the Allens and their friends. He then joined hands with G. G. Benedict and E. P. Walton to extend this work through the Vermont Historical Society. Like the subjects of their writing, they found it necessary to defend themselves against the onslaughts of the Yorkers (now historians rather than "land-grabbers"), and the result was the first two volumes of the *Collections of the Vermont Historical Society*, in which documents were coupled with argument on behalf of the founders of the state. Walton shortly afterward began the compilation of the invaluable series *Records of the Governor and Council*, (Montpelier 1873–1880) in which he continued the work begun by Stevens in the assembly of the basic source materials of early Vermont history. In part, these too were an offset to the source collections published somewhat earlier by the State of New York, entitled *Documentary History of New York* (Albany 1849), the fourth volume of which included an equally useful selection of documents on events in the eastern New York counties now Vermont.

The sesquicentennial year 1941 brought forth two new survey histories of the early days, both drawn entirely from secondary material, but both well written. Charles Miner Thompson's *Independent Vermont* (Boston, 1942) was a thoughtful interpretation based largely on the original researches of Matt Jones and Henry S. Wardner, and not very favorable to the Green Mountain Boys and their leaders. On the other hand, Frederic F. Van de Water's spritely *Reluctant Republic* (N.Y., 1941)—probably the most readable volume on the state ever issued—takes a more conventional tact, following closely in the footsteps of Governor Hall.

The most important manuscript collections are the Stevens-Allen papers in the New York State Library, most of which (after the bulk had been destroyed in the Capitol fire of 1911) were photostated by James B. Wilbur and are now the core of the manuscript collections of the Wilbur Library at the University of Vermont. The Washington Papers, the Papers of the Continental Congress and a group of Vermont Miscellany at the Library of Congress are invaluable and largely unused; microfilmed by the author, they are now also available at the Vermont Historical Society. The Society's own collections are very miscellaneous, but nonetheless valuable. In the vaults of the Secretary of State are a multitude of manuscript State Papers from the earliest days of the state government, most of them carefully indexed by the indefatigable Mary G. Nye, who has also edited some into the printed *State Papers* (published irregularly by the Secretary of State). An extension of this series is in progress to provide a documentary history of Vermont to 1800, incorporating manuscript material from the state

archives with additional material gathered by the editors, Mrs. Nye and the author.

The student should not overlook also the personal narratives of the principal actors, such as Ethan Allen's flamboyant *Narrative of Col. Allen's Captivity*, (Phila., 1779) as well as some of the pamphlet literature issued by the Green Mountain Boys and described in the text earlier.

In drawing upon existent material, the author has utilized all of the above, but also certain more special material with respect to each of the several chapters.

For chapter one, the reader must go to the Reports of the State Geologist to supplement the old but useful Hitchcock and Hager *Geology of Vermont* (Claremont, 1861).

For Chapter II, turn first to the Journal of Samuel Champlain, available in several editions. Morris Bishop's excellent biography of the explorer appeared too late to be of use to the author, but should be to his readers. No one should fail to re-read the classic volumes of Francis Parkman covering this period and area. More specifically, the single most significant study is Guy O. Coolidge's "French Occupation of the Champlain Valley" (*Proceedings VHS*, vi, no. 3, 1936). The *Bulletins* of the Fort Ticonderoga Museum are filled with helpful material. And the reader looking for a lively narrative will again turn to Frederic Van de Water's *Lake Champlain and Lake George*, in the "American Lakes Series" (Indianapolis, 1946).

For Chapter III the basic and authoritative text is Matt Jones' scholarly but sometimes labored *Vermont in the Making* (Cambridge, 1939). It should be read with John Clement's cautions in mind (see the *VHS Proceedings*, n.s. vii, 178–184). B. H. Hall's *History of Eastern Vermont* (N.Y., 1858) is also useful.

Chapter IV covers the romantic era of the Green Mountain Boys, who have left a multiplicity of legend and history in their train. Here again Matt Jones is the most authoritative volume, but many will want to turn back to Governor Hiland Hall as an offset. L. S. Mayo's biography of *John Wentworth* (Cambridge, 1921) is well done, but includes all too little on his relationship to the Grants. Edward P. Alexander's exhaustive study *James Duane* (N.Y., 1939) is essential to an understanding of the Yorker position, and Dixon Ryan Fox expands on the antipathy of *Yankees and Yorkers* (N.Y. 1940). For the colorful career of Ethan Allen turn first to John Pell's scholarly biography (Boston 1929), and then to Stewart Holbrook's more spritely and more imaginative one (N.Y. 1940). The early

chapters of Henry S. Wardner's *Birthplace of Vermont* (N.Y. 1927) are well documented.

Chapter V on the Revolution must be approached—as far as modern material goes—mostly through the general histories like Crockett and Thompson. L. F. Chittenden's *Capture of Ticonderoga* (Rutland 1872) should be supplemented with Allen French's more recent *Taking of Ticonderoga* (Cambridge 1928). Here again the Fort Ti *Bulletins* are valuable. John Spargo, who probably knows more about the Battle of Bennington than anyone else, tells some of the story in his Presidential Address (Bennington Battle Monument Assoc, 1925). But we have nothing at all in print from John Clement, the expert on the Battle of Hubbardton. The Burgoyne campaign is treated in Hoffman Nickerson's *Turning Point of the Revolution* (Boston 1928).

For Chapter VI, the reader will want to supplement Pell, Hiland Hall, Wardner, and the *Governor and Council* volumes with James B. Wilbur's biography of *Ira Allen* (Boston, 1928), which is the result of an exhaustive search for documentary material, but which overreaches itself in an attempt to prove its subject to be the principal instigator of everything. Wilbur is also somewhat careless in the use and interpretation of his documents. Frederick Chase's *History of Dartmouth College* (vol. 1, Cambridge, 1891) contains a great deal about the activities of the "valley men," but we lack really extensive material on the various factions on the East-side during this period. One of the most influential men, Jacob Bayley, can be found only in Frederick Wells' *History of Newbury*, (St. Johnsbury 1902) and in a brief biographical sketch by Edwin A. Bayley in *The Upper Connecticut* (2 vol. *VHS, Collections*, vol. 3, 55–92), along with documentary material on Col. Thomas Johnson and other figures in this region. The most extensive treatment of the Haldimand Negotiations will be found in Chilton Williamson's *Vermont in Quandary* (*Growth of Vermont*, vol. IV, Montpelier, 1949), but excellent brief opinions on this highly controversial topic can be found in Henry S. Wardner's essay in VHS *Proceedings*, n.s. vol. 2, no. 1) and in Clarence Rife's "Ethan Allen; an Interpretation" (*New England Quarterly*, vol 2, 561–584, Oct. 1929). Rife has been working for 25 years on an authoritative study on the subject. There is no biography of Vermont's first governor except Daniel Chipman's brief *Memoir of Thomas Chittenden* (Middlebury 1849). The same author also issued a *Memoir of Seth Warner* (Middlebury 1848); there is little else. Isaac Tichenor is most fully treated in Williamson's volume, but there is no biography. Charles Phelps and the Yorkers of Windham County receive no treatment except B. H. Hall's and that in the rare *Family Memoirs* by John Phelps (Brattleboro, 1886).

Sources for Chapter VII are hopelessly scattered, and must be dredged out of the extremely variable and often unreliable town histories, particularly the monumental five volume Hemenway *Gazetteer*, (v.p., v.d.). Ernest L. Bogart's Peacham: *the Story of a Vermont Hill Town* (Montpelier, 1948) is a model for local history and is one of the few to include thorough economic and social material.

Chapter VIII's cultural material is also well salted away in town histories. In addition to *Peacham*, and *Newbury*, H. H. Vail's *Pomfret*, E. T. Fairbanks' *St. Johnsbury*, Henry S. Dana's *Woodstock*, and Isaac Jennings' *Bennington* are among the best of the poor. The only complete volume on Vermont architecture is Herbert Wheaton Congdon's *Old Vermont Houses* (N.Y. 1946), though there are articles in the White Pine Series as well as a series by Mabel W. Mayforth in the newspaper clipping files of the Vermont Historical Society. For religious history, turn to J. M. Comstock's *Congregational Churches of Vermont* (St. Johnsbury, 1942), Crocker's *History of the Baptists in Vermont*, (Bellows Falls, 1913), *The Documentary History of the Protestant Episcopal Church in Vermont* (Claremont, 1870) and Rev. George R. Brush's *St. James Episcopal Church, Arlington* (n.p., 1941). F. S. Child's *Colonial Parsons of New England* (N.Y., 1896) is interesting though very general. VHS clippings on various churches are particularly helpful. For education there are two volumes: Mason Stone's *History of Education in Vermont* (Montpelier 1934) and John C. Huden's *Development of State School Administration* (Montpelier, 1943). See also W. E. Ranger's articles in the *Vermonter* (viii, 383–406; ix, 7(15) as well as J. E. Goodrich's Educational History of Vermont in *The New England States* (vol III, 432, Boston, n.d.). General material can be found in Clifton Johnson's *Old Time Schools* . . . (N.Y. 1904) and Walter H. Small's *Early New England Schools* (N.Y. 1914). For the printed word, turn to M. D. Gilman's monumental *Bibliography of Vermont* (Burlington 1897) and E. F. Cooley's *Vermont Imprints* . . . (Montpelier, 1937). The best interpretative study is Harold G. Rugg's *The Dresden Press* (n.p., n.d.). Henry S. Wardner has a brief essay on Alden Spooner in the *Vermonter* (36:15–22).

Walter Coates writes sketchily on Samuel Williams in the same magazine (36:82–83). George P. Anderson writes learnedly of Thomas Young—and Ethan Allen—in the *New England Quarterly* (X:685–696) and the *Dictionary of American Biography*.

Writers in the field of early 19th century social history (Chapter IX) are inevitably principally indebted to David M. Ludlum's thorough *Social Ferment in Vermont* (*Growth of Vermont* VI, Montpelier, 1948). There is little else except in the pamphlet literature of the period. Educational history can be found in Stone and Huden; civil war material in Crockett and G. G. Benedict's bulky *Vermont in the Civil War* (Burlington, 1886).

The economic history of the same period (Chapter X) is similarly treated in an exhaustive fashion in Lewis D. Stilwell's *Migration from Vermont* (*Growth of Vermont*, V, Montpelier, 1948). This can be supplemented by Lyman Hayes' essay on "Navigation of the Connecticut River" (*Collections VHS*, V, 201–238), Thomas Davenport and Samuel Morey are treated in biographies by Walter R. Davenport (Montpelier, 1927) and G. C. Carter (Concord, N. H., 1945), respectively.

The Vermont Railroads (Chapter XI) are comprehensively viewed against the general economic development of the state in William J. Wilgus' *Role of Transportation in the Development of Vermont* (Montpelier, 1945). A more detailed information on the rail systems can be found in George P. Baker's *Formation of the New England Railroad Systems* (Cambridge, 1937).

There are no single sources for the industrial history of Vermont (Chapter XII), though there are some miscellaneous sketches of various firms in Stone's *Vermont of Today*. For granite, and marble there is some material in the pamphlets of the Barre Granite Association and the Vermont Marble Co. E. S. Leland's article on Barre in *Vermont Life*, (Fall, 1947, 24–29;47) is valuable. For the woolen industry we have only Janet Mabie's *Neither Wealth nor Poverty*, a Gay Bros. 75th anniversary volume (Montpelier, 1944). The A. G. Dewey Co. have also produced a brief volume on their company (Brattleboro, n.d.). Several manuscript speeches of Leon S. Gay on the industry have provided the basic material for this section. The machine tool industry has been more thoroughly investigated through Guy Hubbard's "Leadership of Early Windsor Industries in the Mechanic Arts" (*VHS Collections*, VI, 239–263) and Muriel Follett's "Vermont's Machine Tools . . ." in *Vermont Life* (Fall, 1946, 32–37; Winter 1946, 20–27;42).

The scale industry is represented only by some brief material on Fairbanks in the Fairbanks-Morse elaborate volume *Pioneers of Industry* (Chicago, 1945).

Chapter XIII is based largely on the thorough researches of Harold Fisher Wilson's *Hill Country of Northern New England* (*Growth of Vermont*, X, Montpelier, 1948) and the reports of the Vermont Commission on Country Life, as embodied in *Rural Vermont* (Burlington, 1933). Edwin C. Rozwenc's *Agricultural Policies in Vermont* was completed after the printing of this book, and was not available, though projected for issuance by the Vermont Historical Society in early 1950.

In Chapter XIV turn to Stone and Huden for the educational material. For the press, see T. D. S. Bassett's "First Vermont Dailies" (*Vermont Quarterly*, XIV, 155–167) and Lorraine Spaulding's "Free Press" (*Vermont Life*, Spring 1948, 20–21;52). Most of the rest—including material on writers and artists—must be pieced together from scattered scraps.

For a picture of "Unspoiled Vermont" (Chapter XV) you'll enjoy Charles E. Crane's lively *Let Me Show You Vermont* (N.Y. 1937) and *Winter in Vermont* (N.Y. 1941); don't overlook the excellent American Guide Series *Vermont*, edited by Dana Doten (Boston, 1939). But, again, there is no single source even for parts of this material.

The principal sources for material on government (Chapter XVI) are the reports of the various state departments and the *Legislative Directory*, published biennially by the Secretary of State. The state constitution is published in a separate pamphlet available from the State Library. There are two good studies: D. B. Carroll's *Unicameral Legislature in Vermont* (Montpelier 1932) and Winston A. Flint's *Progressive Movement in Vermont* (Washington, 1941).

Since so much information must be obtained from miscellaneous sources, the student can use. to advantage the *Index to the VHS Proceedings* and to the *VHS Collections*, by E. W. Newton, (Montpelier, 1943 and 1946). The files of the *Vermonter* are inadequately indexed through volume 17, and more completely so (at least by author and title) from 18–44. Abbe Maria Hemenway's colossal *Gazetteer* of town histories in five thick volumes is indexed (principally names, but a few subject entries) in an equally thick volume published by the State Library. And the very detailed card catalog of the Vermont Historical Society, plus their clipping files from 1942 on, are indispensable to one who can go there.

ALPHABETICAL INDEX

2/12/52